ISBN 978-1-330-53526-4
PIBN 10075175

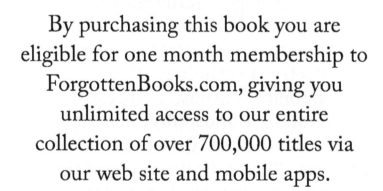

English
Français
Deutsche
Italiano
Español
Português

www.forgottenbooks.com

Mythology Photography **Fiction**
Fishing Christianity **Art** Cooking
Essays Buddhism Freemasonry
Medicine **Biology** Music **Ancient
Egypt** Evolution Carpentry Physics
Dance Geology **Mathematics** Fitness
Shakespeare **Folklore** Yoga Marketing
Confidence Immortality Biographies
Poetry **Psychology** Witchcraft
Electronics Chemistry History **Law**
Accounting **Philosophy** Anthropology
Alchemy Drama Quantum Mechanics
Atheism Sexual Health **Ancient History**
Entrepreneurship Languages Sport
Paleontology Needlework Islam
Metaphysics Investment Archaeology
Parenting Statistics Criminology
Motivational

HISTORICAL

Biography of the United States,

CLASSIFIED.

CONTAINING ALL THE HISTORICAL, NOTED EVENTS, AND INTERESTING
INCIDENTS CONNECTED WITH THE SETTLEMENT OF THE
UNITED STATES SINCE ITS FIRST DISCOVERY,
UP TO THE PRESENT TIME.

CLASSIFIED AND ARRANGED UNDER APPROPRIATE HEADINGS.

PUBLISHED BY

J. RIPPEY & CO., 177 W. BALTIMORE ST.
BALTIMORE, MD.

TABLE OF CONTENTS.

INDEX TO ADVERTISEMENTS.

INDEX TO TOWNS AND CITIES.

AMERICA DISCOVERED, INCIDENTS, &C.

(SEE ALSO, EARLY CONQUESTS, &C.; ALSO, EXPEDITIONS, &C.)

Columbus Discovers America, October 12, 1492.—At 2 o'clock Friday morning land was discovered. It was one of Bahamas, called by the natives Guanahani, but named by Colnmbus San Salvador, who took possession of it in the name of Ferdinand and Isabella.

Cuba was discovered Oct. 28, 1492. It was here that Columbus first saw the natives smoking tobacco, and here also that maize (afterward called Indian corn by the Pilgrims) was first discovered.

Columbus' Second Voyage.—On Sept. 25, 1493, with 3 ships, 14 caravels and 1,500 adventurers, he sailed from Cadiz for the New World. Horses and domestic animals were taken upon this expedition. Fonseca, afterward Bishop, and for a long time at the head of Indian affairs, became the enemy of Columbus upon this voyage.

at this colony and found affairs in a disheartening condition. He determined to give them active employment, and sent 400 men to St. Thomas with instructions to make thorough explorations.

Spanish Oppression of the Haytiens.—Mar. 27, 1495, Columbus set out to subdue the island. Having done which he levied a tribute of gold dust and cotton, payable monthly or quarterly. The rapacity of their conquerers was such that it required the unremitting toil of the miserable natives to satisfy it. Then their lands were gradually divided among the Spaniards and the Indians were enslaved to cultivate them. They perished so rapidly under this oppression that within fifty years the race was almost annihilated.

First Colony.—Nov. 27, 1493, the fleet arrived at La Navidad, Hayti, where Columbus had left 39 men on his first expedition. He found that they had disregarded his injunctions and had quarrelled with the natives, who had slain them and demolished their fort. He founded another colony on the same island, which he called Isabella. He discovered that cotton grew wild and that the natives used it for clothing and fishing nets.

Fort St. Thomas, Mar. 12, 1494, Columbus, with 400 men, explored the interior of Hayti. He selected a defensible position, built Fort St. Thomas, and leaving a garrison of 56 men, returned to Isabella.

Sickness and Discontent at Isabella.—Mar. 29, 1494, Columbus arrived

Cuba Explored by Columbus.—April 24, 1494, he sailed along the south coast of the island with 3 caravels and landed at different points. The trip consumed several months. When near the west end he concluded to return. The unanimous conclusion of the explorers was that they had discovered a continent.

Columbus' Third Voyage, May 30, 1498.—He sailed from San Lucar de Barrameda with 6 vessels. Fonseca's treasurer, Ximeno Breviesca, had harrassed him in all his preparations, and at the moment of sailing the patience of the Admiral gave way and he knocked the treasurer down and kicked him. This unfortunate act somewhat estranged Ferdinand and Isabella.

North America was discovered June 24, 1497, by John and Sebastian Cabot, who sailed under a patent from Henry VII., of England, in the "Matthew," in search of a passage to India. They discovered Labrador. The coast of North America was carefully explored from North Carolina to Nova Scotia in 1524 by John Verrazzano, a Florentine in the service of Francis I., of France. He gave a detailed and accurate description of it, and upon this was based the French claim to North America. In 1768 Jonathan Carver arrived in Boston. For several years he had been (or professed to have been) exploring the interior of North America, and had reached the Minnesota river. He made numerous charts and journals. The British government rewarded him.

Newfoundland Discovered in May, 1498.—Sebastian Cabot, with 2 ships and 300 men, sailed on a second voyage to the New World. He coasted from Labrador to the Chesapeake bay—perhaps to Florida. He named "Newfound-

which all reference to Columbus was carefully omitted, and thus by craft and the dullness of the times, his name was bestowed upon the new continent instead of that of the true discoverer. The only credit to which he is entitled is that he recognized the fact that instead of the India already known, another continent had been discovered.

Columbus at Jamaica, June 24, 1503.—He was compelled to beach his worm eaten and worn-out vessels upon this island. He was obliged to remain there one year. Mutiny among his men, and hostility from the natives environed him with difficulties. The latter refused to supply him with food, and knowing that an eclipse of the moon would occur, Columbus sent word to them that the Great Spirit would show his displeasure by darkening the moon. After this provisions were forthcoming.

land," and reported at home that codfish were so abundant as to impede the progress of his ships, which originated the great fisheries on its banks. Sir Humphrey Gilbert sailed in 1583 with 5 vessels and 260 men. Landing on New Foundland he erected royal arms and proclaimed government. Unsuccessful in searching for gold they resolved to return to England. The vessel in which Gilbert took passage foundered during a gale and he was lost.

Americus Vespucius, a Florentine merchant, accompanied Alonzo de Ojeda in a voyage of discovery in 1499 as navigator and geographer. They followed the charts of Columbus and reached the Gulf of Paria. Finding an Indian town built on piles over the water they named it Venezuela or Little Venice. Vespucius gave to Europe the first published account of the Western World, in

Atahuallpa, Inca of Peru, was made captive by the Spaniards under Pizarro, November 16, 1532. He offered to fill the room in which he was confined, 22 feet by 17 feet, 9 feet high with gold, and another room twice full of silver as a ransom. The offer was accepted, but before they were quite filled the soldiers clamored for a division. After deducting the royal fifth the gold melted down produced $15,500,000, beside the silver. Then the Spaniards executed Atahuallpa upon the pretext that he was secretly instigating a rebellion.

Jacques Cartier, a noted French sailor, sailed from St. Malo, France, April 20, 1534, with two 60 ton vessels and 122 men for a voyage of exploration to the New World, and after wintering on the St. Lawrence, and losing 25 men by scurvy, he sailed again for France March

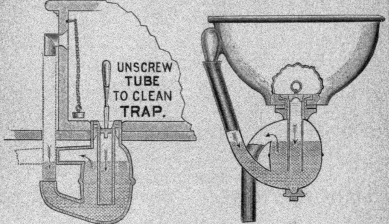

6, 1536, taking with him 10 Indian chiefs as captives.

Montreal.—Cartier having sailed through the Gulf and River St. Lawrence arrived at the Indian village of Hochelaga, Oct. 2, 1535. He climbed a mountain back of the village and called it Mount Royale, which afterward was corrupted into the present name of Montreal, and is applied not only to the island but also to the great city.

Santa Fe de Bogota, in the U. S. of Columbia, S. A., was founded in 1538 by Gonzalo Ximenes de Quesada, who erected 12 houses in honor of the 12 apostles.

Sable Island, off Nova Scotia, was colonized in 1598 by 40 criminals brought from France by Marquis de la Roche. He was driven off in a gale and they were not visited for five years. Only 12 survived.

EXPEDITIONS AND DISCOVERIES.
(ALPHABETICALLY ARRANGED.)

Amazon River was navigated in 1616 by two monks in a canoe, who had fled from their missions in Peru because of Indian persecutions. They finally reached Para.

American Voyage round the world was first completed in 1790 by Captain Gray, of Boston, in the "Columbia." She left Sept. 30, 1787, for China, via the Pacific coast, and returned via Cape of Good Hope.

Block Island was named by Adreain Block, who in 1614 explored Long Island Sound, Naragansett Bay, sailing through Hellgate, a rocky channel in the East River. His trip was made in the "Unrest," a vessel 42½ feet long, 11½ feet wide and 16 tons burden, built at Manhattan.

Brazil was visited in 1502 by Americus Vespucius. He discovered the Bay of All Saints and returned to Spain with a cargo of Brazil wood.

Canada Explored by Champlain in 1603. De Chastes, Governor of Dieppe, France, under a patent for colonizing Canada, sent two vessels of 12 and 15 tons, under Champlain, for preliminary explorations. They reached and ascended the St. Lawrence to Montreal, then returned to France.

Cape St. Augustine was discovered Jan. 28, 1500, by Vincent Yanez Pinzon.

He also discovered the Amazon River and was the first to cross the Equator in the Western Atlantic.

Cape Cod and Martha's Vineyard were discovered in 1602 by Bartholomew Gosnold. He built a fort upon Cuttyhunk, one of the Elizabeth islands, and then returned to England.

Cape Horn was discovered by Garcia Jofre de Loaya, a Spanish commander, in 1525.

Columbia River discovered May 8, 1792, by Captain Robert Gray, in the Boston vessel "Columbia Redivivia." Lewis and Clark broke up their winter camp upon the Missouri River April 7, 1805, and started up the river and crossed the mountain ridge on horseback, amid great obstacles. They reached the mouth of the Columbia River Nov. 15, 1805, and began their return trip up the Columbia River March 23, 1806. They arrived at St. Louis September 23, 1807, having been gone on their great exploring trip 28 months.

Florida was discovered by De Leon April 2, 1512, and was so named because of the luxuriant vegetation. He found neither gold nor fountains, and returned to Porti Rico. The Gulf stream was first noticed by Alaminos, a pilot on this expedition.

Fremont, John C. commenced an

exploration of the Rocky Mountains on May 2, 1842, by order of the U. S. government. He planted the American flag on the summit of a peak 13,570 feet high, which has since been known as Fremont's peak. Fremont's second expedition to the Rocky Mountains started in May, 1843. His party explored the Great Salt Lake in Utah, thence north to the Columbia River, following it to its mouth. They returned over the Sierra Nevadas into the Sacramento Valley, through deep snows, and reached Kansas in July, 1844. Col. Fremont's exploring party suffered terribly in the Rocky Mountains in 1854. They fed on mule meat for 45 days, and would have perished but for relief from another party.

Hayti was discovered December 6, 1492, and named by Columbus "Hispaniola," or Little Spain.

the United States. Col. Clark put Capt. Helm in command. In August, 1778, the Virginia Assembly, by an act, named the whole region "Illinois County."

Japan.—U. S. expedition to Japan, under Commodore Perry, son of the hero of Lake Erie, sailed in 1852. He arrived at Japan July 14, 1853, and delivered the letter from the President of the United States to the care of the Imperial Commissioners.

Lake Champlain was discovered July, 1609, by Champlain, who had accompanied a war party against the Iroquois, who dwelt in Central New York.

Louisiana was the name given to the entire region on the banks of the Mississippi by La Salle, who arrived at the Gulf of Mexico April 9, 1682, and took formal possession of the mouth of the river in the name of Louis XIV., King of France.

Hudson River was discovered Sept. 12, 1609, by Sir Henry Hudson, who sailed in the "Half-Moon" to where Albany now stands. He called it the Great North River. He was in Dutch service, whose claims in North America were based on his discoveries.

Illinois River.—The exploration of the Illinois river was made by a party from Fort Crevecœur, in February, 1680.

Illinois, Indiana and Kentucky. In 1779 Col. Geo. Rogers Clark marched with a force against the French settlements in Illinois, his object being to extend the authority of Virginia over the scattered settlements of Illinois, Indiana and Kentucky. He occupied Kaskaskia without bloodshed. He became so popular there that the French priest influenced the inhabitants of Vincennes, in the absence of the British governor at Detroit, to change their allegiance to

Lower California was explored by two expeditions sent out in 1532-3 by Cortez.

Maine—Martin Pring's Explorations in 1603. The "Speedwell" and "Discoverer" were sent by Bristol merchants to follow up Gosnold's discoveries. Under Pring's command they explored the coast of Maine and Massachusetts—searching for sassafras root—as far as Martha's Vineyard, and then returned to England. The coast of Maine was again explored in 1604 by Champlain. He named Mt. Desert, visited the Penobscot and returned to St. Croix.

Mississippi River.—This great river was discovered by De Soto in May, 1541. Allouez and Dablon left Green Bay, Wisconsin, in 1670, to visit some Indian towns on Lake Winnebago. They were told much about the great Mississippi. During 1763 Jacques Marquette, a Jesuit missionary, and Louis Joliet, a Quebec trader, having heard of a "Great Western River," set out from the Straits of Mackinaw, in birch bark canoes, to find it. They were guided by Indians to the Wisconsin river, where their guides left them. Descending the Wisconsin they entered the Mississippi on the 17th of June, down which they floated past the Des Moines, Illinois, Missouri and Ohio rivers to the mouth of the Arkansas on July 17th, whence they decided to return lest falling into the hands of Spaniards they should lose the fruits of their discoveries. They reached Green Bay in September, and Joliet went at once to Quebec to report. La Salle set out Aug. 10, 1680, with 25 men, to explore the Mississippi, and to relieve Tonti and his companions, who were waiting at Crevecœur for their leader. Most of the garrison had deserted and gone to Michilli-

this company set out for Lake Erie. Their course from there is not certainly known, but it is claimed that they discovered the Ohio and Mississippi before Marquette reached the last river.

Pacific Ocean Discovered.—Balboa started Sept. 1, 1513, with 190 men and Indian guides, to search for the great sea, said to lie at the South. After a difficult march through the wilderness he discovered the Pacific ocean September 26, 1513, from the summit of a mountain. Proceeding to the coast he waded into the water with a royal standard and took possession of it in the name of Spain. He called it the South Sea. During the expedition he learned of the rich kingdom of Peru at the South. The name Pacific Ocean was given November 28, 1520, by Magellan, who had just completed the boisterous passage through the straits which bear his name.

mackinac, committing depredations on their route. He arrived at the ruins of the fort in December, but found no traces of Tonti and his few faithful companions, who had gone to Green Bay to avoid the hardships they were subjected to in consequence of a war having broken out between the Illinois and Iroquois Indians. La Salle and his company then started for the Mississippi, Dec. 21, 1681, by way of the Chicago river, and reached the Mississippi Feb. 2, 1682, and amid floating ice started down its stream.

New Mexico. — In 1581 Augustin Ruyz, with two other priests and eight soldiers, started to explore the seven cities of Cibola. One priest was killed by Indians and the soldiers returned, leaving the two priests, whose fate is unknown.

Ohio and Mississippi Rivers— Expedition of La Salle. July 6, 1669,

Pearl Islands.—Margarita and Cubagua, noted for pearl fisheries, were discovered by Columbus in 1498. He obtained a quantity to be sent to Spain.

Salt Springs in Illinois were known to the French and Indians in 1720.

South America discovered August 1, 1498, by Columbus, while cruising along the southern shore of Trinidad. He entered the Gulf of Paria and landed upon what he supposed to be another island, but which was the continent. He procured large strings of pearls from the natives. Ill health and scarcity of provisions compelled his return to Hayti.

Wheeler Surveys, from Pueblo, Colorado, July 15, 1874, of unexplored territory west of one hundredth meridian, by 9 parties, including eminent scientists. Thorough explorations were made.

Wilkes' Exploring Expedition to the South Sea sailed April, 1838.

EARLY CONQUESTS, INVASIONS AND SETTLEMENTS,
(SEE ALSO, EXPEDITIONS.)

Acadia.—Expeditions of De Monts and Pontgrave sailed in April, 1604, from Havre-de-Grace to Nova Scotia. De Monts entered the Bay of Fundy and discovered Annapolis Harbor, which Poutrincourt begged for himself and named it Port Royal. Pontgrave, after sailing to the St. Lawrence to trade returned to France. De Monts proceeded around the Bay of Fundy and out into Passamaquoddy Bay. An island was selected for the colony and named St. Croix, upon which 79 mén were left. The severity of the winter and scurvy killed 35. In 1604 De Monts undertook to colonize this region, under a grant embracing the territory now between Philadelphia and Lake St. Peter, in the St. Lawrence river. Champlain and Baron de Poutrincourt

Boston.—Its present site was settled upon in 1623 by William Blackstone, who sold out and removed to Rhode Island upon the coming of the Puritans. He was said to be a slaveholder. The first house was built in Boston in July, and the town was organized Sept. 17, 1630.

Castine, Maine, was settled by the English in 1760.

Canada.—The expeditions against Montreal and Quebec in 1690 by land under Winthrop resulted in a most miserable failure. Phipps had no better success, although his equipment consisted of 32 vessels and 2,000 men. He found Quebec prepared, and after a slight demonstration returned to Boston. Canada was again invaded Aug. 10, 1711, by

accompanied the expedition, which included both Catholics and Hugenots. On July 27, 1606, Poutrincourt returned to Annapolis harbor with supplies. He found but 2 Frenchmen, the others having built boats and gone in search of game and fruits. They were found and brought back. Poutrincourt and Champlain explored the southern coast for a good site for a colony, but made no selection. The succeeding winter was mild, and only 4 men died of scurvy.

Alabama.—In 1702 the first settlement was made on Mobile river by the transfer of a French fleet from Biloxi.

Astorio, Oregon, was founded in 1811 by the Pacific Fur Company. It was named after John Jacob Astor, and was the depot for the fur trade west of the Rocky Mountains.

Bethlehem, Pa., was settled in 1741 by the Moravians or "United Brethren."

a fleet of 15 ships and 40 transports with 7,000 men, which sailed from Boston to capture Quebec. Admiral Hovenden Walker's obstinacy in sailing up the St. Lawrence on a dark and stormy night caused the loss of 8 ships and 1,000 men. Discouraged, he abandoned the enterprise and sailed for England. An army of 4,000 men that had been assembled at Albany for an attack on Montreal, turned back upon receiving news of the failure of the naval expedition.

Carolina was invaded by French and Spaniards in 1706, who were defeated.

Charlestown, Mass., was founded July 4, 1629, by a company of Puritans from Salem.

Charleston, S. C., was abandoned in 1680, and the present city was founded, which became the capital of the province.

Chicago.—In the records of a great

council of French and Indians, held in 1671, at the foot of Lake Superior, this name first appeared in 1671. Chicago appeared as "Chicagon" upon a map published in Quebec, Canada, in 1683. Fort Dearborn was built by the U. S. upon the present site of Chicago in 1804. Chicago was laid out and building lots sold in 1829.

Cincinnati, O., was settled Dec. 24, 1788, by emigrants from Springfield, N. J. Mathias Denman bought the site at 5 shillings per acre, continental currency.

Delaware and Pennsylvania were settled by Swedes and Fins in 1627. William Penn landed at New Castle, on the Delaware, Oct. 27, 1682.

Detroit was founded July 24, 1701, by De la Motte Cadilliac, who named the post Fort Ponchartrain.

Dismal Swamp was surveyed in 1728 by Col. William Byrd. It lies partly in

head of Appalachee Bay, where they remained for the winter. De Soto's expedition pushed forward in 1540 in the country northwest of the present limits of Florida. They were resisted by the Indians and lost 18 men and all their baggage. They camped for the winter in Northern Mississippi.

Florida Colonization.—In 1558 an expedition of 1,500 soldiers sailed from Vera Cruz, Mexico, under Tristan de Luna to explore and colonize Florida. A great storm broke up their ships after they landed. For lack of supplies the colony dwindled away and the survivors were taken home in a year or two by a vessel sent from Mexico.

Hugenots Settle in Florida.—Two vessels left Havre Feb. 18, 1562, under command of Jean Ribaut with a company of emigrants. They landed at St. John's River May 1, 1562. Called it the

Virginia and partly in North Carolina.

Exeter, N. H., was founded in 1683 by Rev. Mr. Wheelwright, who was banished from Massachusetts for his sympathy with the religious views of Mrs. Hutchinson, his sister-in-law, upon land bought by the Indians at the falls of Swamscot.

Florida.—In 1528 Pamphilo de Narvaez landed with 300 men, 80 of them horsemen, with the intention of conquest. They wandered 800 miles and reached the Bay of Pensacola. They made boats, embarked, and were lost. Four only of the expedition survived to reach Mexico in 1536.

Hernando de Soto, former governor of Cuba, made an expedition to Florida, and reached Tampa Bay May 30, 1539, with 9 vessels, 600 men, a herd of swine and ample supplies. They toiled westward across the country and reached the

river of May, erected a stone pillar bearing the arms of France, then sailed northward.

French Colony, in three vessels, settled on the River of May in 1564 and began a fort which they named "Caroline." Scarcity of food led some of them to turn pirates. Pedro Menendez de Aviles, a Spaniard, fitted out an expedition to destroy the French colony, arrived on the coast of Florida Sept. 8, 1565.

Fort Caroline received ample supplies and reinforcements of 300 men Aug. 24, 1565, by Jean Ribaut.

Massacre at Fort Caroline, Sept. 20, 1565.—Menendez marched across from St. Augustine and fell upon the French at Fort Caroline and murdered them. Ribaut had, meantime, sailed to attack St. Augustine, but was shipwrecked on the coast. Menendez murdered the most of them in cold blood.

Georgia.—New Inverness, Ga., was settled in 1736 by a colony of Scotch Highlanders.

Hartford, Conn.—In 1633 the Dutch established a trading post near this site. They also reoccupied Fort Nassau on the Delaware. Hartford was founded in June, 1636, by Hooker & Stone, who emigrated from Newtown. They journeyed across the country with their families and 160 head of cattle (carrying Mrs. Hooker, who was an invalid, on a litter), in two weeks.

Indian Territory not open to white settlers April 26, 1879. President Hayes issued a proclamation forbidding the trespass of whites upon Indian reservations.

Immigration from Germany.—Under the patronage of Queen Anne, of England, several thousand emigrants from the Palatinate settled in New York, Pennsylvania, Virginia and Carolina in 1710.

Jamestown, Va., founded May 13, 1607, by 105 persons sent out by the London company. The river and town were named in honor of the King, and Capes Charles and Henry for his two sons. Captain John Smith, chosen President of the Jamestown Council, Sept., 1608, by vigorous efforts, promoted *real labor*, and the colony was benefitted. 70 persons arrived, including 2 women—the first who came to Jamestown. Smith declared that 30 workingmen were preferable to 1,000 such colonists as had come.

Starvation at Jamestown, May 24, 1610.—Three Commissioners of Lord Delaware arrived and found the colony reduced from 500 to 60 persons through their own improvidence. It was decided to return to England, and on June 8th they sailed down the river, intending to reach Newfoundland and get passage with English fishermen from thence.

Jamestown Resettled, June 9, 1610. The deserting colonists met Lord Delaware with supplies at the mouth of James River, who persuaded them to return to their homes, which they reoccupied on the 10th. The governor's commission was read, Church of England service was held, and hopefulness cheered the colonists. All colonists were to attend church twice each Sunday "upon pain for the first fault to lose their provision and allowance for the whole week following; for the second, also to be whipped; and for the third, to suffer death."

Private Property in Jamestwn. In Aug., 1611, Sir Thomas Gates brought supplies and additional colonists to Jamestown. He superceded Dale, and for the first time each man was granted a few acres for private cultivation. Cows and other domestic animals were brought over by Gates. The colony now numbered 700.

Kennebec, Maine, was colonized Aug. 16, 1607, by 49 persons sent by the Plymouth Company. George Popham commanded the colony. They passed through an exceedingly severe winter.

Kennebec Colony Abandoned.—Feb. 5, 1608, Geo. Popham, the governor, died. His successor, Raleigh Gilbert, returned to England, having fallen heir to his brother's estate. Sir John Popham, a chief supporter of the colony, also died. The discouraged settlers, therefore, returned to England. They had built the first vessel built by Englishmen in the New World—a 30 ton pinnace named the "Virginia," which crossed the Atlantic.

Kaskaskia.—Indian mission at Kaskaskia, Oct. 25, 1674. Father Marquet started to found a mission at this point. Feeble health detained him near the mouth of the Chicago until March, 1675, when he again undertook the trip, but his strength failing he decided to return.

Kentucky was first explored by John Finley and others in 1767. First house in Kentucky was built in 1769 by Daniel Boone and brother, who explored and hunted that beautiful "Middle Ground." The Indians killed one of his five companions, two returned, and the Boones remained through the winter and built a hut. State of Kentucky organized May 23, 1775, by 17 settlers in convention at Boonesborough.

Louisburg Besieged, on Cape Breton Island, June 17, 1745.—This place 18th of June the fortress capitulated. By this surrender the English acquired the whole of Cape Breton.

Long Island was settled by the Dutch in 1626.

Manhattan Island and Albany were settled by Protestant refugees of French descent, known as Walloon settlers. They were sent out by the Dutch West India Company in 1623 and formed the first real colonies at those points. They also settled Fort Nassau, on the Delaware, but abandoned it within a year to reinforce the Manhattan colony. First tavern on Manhattan Island was built in 1642 at the head of Cowenties slip.

Marietta, Ohio, was founded April 7, 1788, by 60 New Englanders under Gen. Rufus Putnam. Improvements were vigorously begun and provisions made for churches and schools.

Maryland.—March 27, 1634, Leon-

had been fortified at vast expense by the French. Its location enabled it to command the principal entrance to the gulf and river St. Lawrence, and it was regarded as a key to the Canadian provinces. It was also a standing menace to Newfoundland and Nova Scotia. Gov. Shirley, of Massachusetts, resolved upon its capture and invited the aid of the other colonies, which was granted, and an army of over 4,000 troops was raised. William Pepperell, of Maine, was appointed commander. Commodore Warren, commanding the English fleet in the West Indies, was instructed to assist. The first knowledge the French had of the expedition was the sight of the fleet in the offing on the 30th of April. A landing was immediately made and the siege commenced. On the 18th of May a 64 gun French ship with stores for the garrison was captured by Warren. On the ard Calvert arrived with a colony sent out by Lord Baltimore. He purchased of the Indians the site and founded St. Mary's. Good relations were established with the Indians; religious toleration was declared. Lord Baltimore's charter guaranteed representative government and exempted the colony from any power to tax or superintend it.

Irish Emigrants, numbering some 6,000, arrived in 1729 and settled principally in Maryland and Virginia.

Rebellion in Maryland in 1645, instigated by William Clayborne and Capt. Ingle, on which account Governor Calvert retired to Virginia. Governor Calvert returned from Virginia in 1646 with a large force, expelled Clayborne and Ingle, and resumed his authority.

Massachustts Settlements in 1630. The towns of Dorchester, Roxbury, Newtown (now Cambridge), Saugus (now

Lynn), Watertown and Boston were founded by Winthrop and the 1,000 emigrants who accompanied him. He selected Boston. Each town constituted a little Republic almost complete within itself.

Mount Washington.—In 1819 Abel Crawford and his son, Ethan, cut a footpath to, and built a hut on the summit for visitors.

Natchez was located in 1700 by De Tonty. It was called Rosalie, and was soon abandoned and not again settled for 16 years, when it was settled by the French in 1716.

New Amsterdam.—May 4, 1626, Peter Minuit, the newly-appointed governor, landed on Manhattan Island. He bought the island—containing 22,000 acres—from the Indians for 60 guilders, or $24, and named it New Amsterdam,

but alarmed by the religious agitations there, they preferred to establish a separate community and bought of the Indians a tract, 10 miles by 13, north of Quinapiack Bay upon which they settled.

New Netherlands.—In 1633 Wouter Van Twiller, who succeeded Peter Minuit as governor, arrived at New Amsterdam. Adam Roelandsen, the first school master, came with him. Rev. Everadus Bogardus succeeded Rev. Jonas Michaelis as minister of the Reformed Dutch Church. He had the first church building on what is now Broad street. He married the widow, Annetje Jansen, whose farm now forms the Trinity Church property. The first brewery in the province was built here.

New Orleans was located in 1718 at the mouth of the Mississippi by the French. It was part of John Law's scheme.

and it speedily became an important trading point.

New England was so named in Mar., 1614, by Capt. John Smith, who explored the coast from Nova Scotia to Cape Cod and made a map of it, which he sent to Prince Charles. Hugenot settlers arrived in New England in 1686.

New Hampshire was first settled in 1623 at the fishing villages of Dover and Portsmouth. The boundary line between New Hampshire and New York was decided in 1764 by the English crown, upon appeal, to be the Connecticut River. The disputed territory was the land now embraced by Vermont.

New Haven Colony was founded April 15, 1638, by John Davenport, a nonconformist minister, and Theopolis Eaton and Edward Hopkins, merchants from London. Advantageous offers of settlement were made them by Massachusetts,

Newport, R. I., was founded in 1636 by William Coddington and his associates, who separated from the colony of Mrs. Hutchinson.

New Rochelle, N. Y., was settled by a colony of Hugenots in 1689.

New York was first settled by the Dutch in 1613 both on Manhattan Island and at Albany. New York city was incorporated June 12, 1665, by Governor Nicholls, under a mayor, five aldermen and a sheriff. Thomas Willett was the first mayor.

North Carolina.—In 1650 a colony from Virginia settled on the Chowan river in North Carolina. Clarendon county colony, North Carolina, was settled May 29, 1664, by Sir John Yeamans with a colony from Barbadoes, including negro slaves, settled on Cape Fear river. William Drummond was elected governor.

Ohio Land Company was organized in 1749 by Thomas Lee and Lawrence and Augustine Washington and other citizens of Maryland and Virginia. Half a million acres were granted to the company south of the Ohio and between the Kanawha and Monongehela rivers upon condition of building a fort and settling 100 families thereon. The French claimed all the territory from the Alleghanies westward before the company could comply with these conditions.

"Oklahoma."—In Dec., 1880, a Capt. Payne with a band of raiders attempted to settle upon lands in the Indian territory owned by the Indians. The U. S. troops foiled their plans. This movement was thought to be backed by railroad companies which wished to secure right of way through the nation.

Oldest House in U. S. stands in Guilford, Conn. It was built in 1639 for on Plymouth Rock. Mary Chilton, a young woman, was the first whose feet touched the rock. Buildings were hastily constructed. Town meetings were held from the first. Half their number died the first year from hardship and exposure.

Plymouth Land.—In 1624 one acre was set apart for each colonist to own as his private property. In 1627 it was increased to 25 acres each, and 25 acres water front.

Port Royal, S. C., was the name given to their settlement by the Hugenots, May 27, 1562. The Colonists becoming sick of their location, built a brigatine in 1563 and sailed for France. They were captured by an English vessel and carried to England.

Providence, R. I., was founded July 4, 1636, by Roger Williams. The settlers agreed "to submit themselves in active

the minister, Rev. Henry Whitfield.

Pensacola, Florida.—In 1696 the Spaniards built a fort here.

Penobscott Bay was the seat of the first permanent settlement in Eastern Maine, by Gov. Pownall, in 1755.

Peoria, Ill.—Fort Crevecœur was built by La Salle in January, 1680, upon the present site of Peoria, Ills. It was the first settlement of whites in the State.

Philadelphia was located and surveyed for a town to be the capital of Pennsylvania in May, 1682.

Point Comfort was so named because of deep water and good anchorage. Captain John Smith and Bartholomew Gosnold were of the Colonists who passed through severe sufferings and lost 50 lives, including Gosnold, during the summer.

Pilgrim's Landing, Dec. 21, 1620, and passive obedience to all such orders and agreements as should be made for the public good of the body in an orderly way, by major consent of the present inhabitants, masters of families, incorporated together into a township, and such others whom they shall admit into the same, only in civil things."

Quebec founded July 13, 1608, by Champlain whom De Monts had sent out, he having obtained a renewal of his grant.

Raleigh, Virginia.—April 26, 1587, a colony of 115 persons under Governor White was sent out by Sir Walter Raleigh. They located on Roanoke Island. The City of Raleigh was destroyed in 1590. Gov. White arrived at Roanoke with supplies for this colony, but could get no trace of it. Its loss has always been a mystery.

Rhode Island Colony was founded

in March, 1638, by Mrs. Anne Hutchinson and 18 others, on the island of Aquiday, which they bought of the Narragansetts. They signed a covenant to "incorporate themselves into a body politic" and to "submit to our Lord Jesus Christ."

Roanoke Colony.—April 9, 1585, Raleigh sent Sir Richard Grenville with 7 vessels and 108 colonists to settle Virginia. They arrived and settled Roanoke Island in June. The same month in 1586, the second Roanoke Colony was organized by Sir Richard Grenville, who left 15 men to hold the island. They were killed by Indians, and the remaining colonists returned to England with Sir Francis Drake, who touched at Roanoke Island on his way home, and the entire colony took passage with him.

Rugby, Tenn., an English industrial colony, founded by Mr. Thomas Hughes,

cattle, goats, tools and supplies, arrived for this colony June 29, 1629. A brick kiln was set up.

Saratoga Springs was visited in 1767 by Sir William Johnson, the first white man. He was carried on a litter to a spring known to the Indians, that he might test its efficacy as a remedy. It was the "Round Rock Spring." The first hut was erected on this site by Derick Scowton in 1773. General Philip Schuyler erected the first frame house at Saratoga Springs in 1784.

Savannah, Georgia.—Feb. 1, 1733, Oglethorpe and 120 emigrants laid the foundations of the oldest English town south of the Savannah. The colony was composed of honest and moral poor debtors from English prisons.

Saybrook, Conn., was founded Nov. 1635, at the mouth of the Connecticut river, named in honor of Lord Say-and-

was formerly opened with appropriate ceremonies and an address by Mr. Hughes Oct. 5, 1880.

St. Augustine, Florida, the oldest city in the U. S., was founded Sept. 8, 1565, by Menendez. Expedition against Spaniards under Gov. Moore, of South Carolina, in 1702, blockaded St. Augustine unsuccessfully.

St. Louis, Mo.—In 1763 the settlement of St. Louis was first made by two brothers named August and Pierre Chouteau, as a port for trade with the Indians.

Salem, Mass., the first Puritan colony in America, consisting of 70 persons under John Endicott, settled on the present site of Salem, Mass., Sept. 14, 1628. They differed from the Pilgrims of Plymouth in clinging to and desiring to reform the Church of England, while the Pilgrims renounced all obedience thereto. A large number of emigrants, with

Seal and Lord Brooke, who had obtained a grant of the territory in 1631.

South Carolina.—In 1525 Lucas Vasques de Ayllon attempted to colonize this territory, but the Indians, remembering that he had kidnapped a large number of them a few years before, fell upon them at a friendly feast and killed all but the leader and a few others, who effected their escape. A colony of French refugees settled in Carolina in 1690. In 1670 William Sayle and Joseph Wert landed a colony at Port Royal, S. C., and proceeded to what is now Charleston harbor, and settled above the mouth of the Ashley river, naming it Charleston. In 1695 Rev. Joseph Lord and his congregation went from Dorchester, Mass., and settled on the Ashley river, 20 miles above Charleston, S. C. It was a permanent and influential colony.

Texas.—La Salle's colony at Matagorda Bay, Texas, which he temporarily established while searching for the mouth of the Mississippi, on his second expedition, was nearly destroyed by Indians in 1689.

Trenton, N. J., was founded in 1724 by Sir William Trent.

Vineland, N. J., was founded in 1858 by Charles K. Landis. Intoxicating liquors cannot be sold without vitiating titles to the lots, hence taxes are light and a police department is almost unnecessary. Although the soil is poor poverty is unknown and it is a prosperous city.

Vincennes, Indiana, was settled in 1702 by French soldiers from Canada.

Virginia City, Nevada, over the Comstock silver mine, had 20,000 inhabitants in 1865. It was 4 years old.

Virginia.—Raleigh sent out two vessels under Philip Amidas and Arthur Barlow, April 27, 1582. They reached Carolina July 13, 1582, of which they took possession and named it in honor of the virgin Queen. They explored Albemarle sound and Roanoke island and returned. The population of Virginia in 1649 was 15,000 whites and 300 negroes. They owned 20,000 cattle, 200 horses, 50 asses, 3,000 sheep, 5,000 goats, besides swine and all kinds of fowl. There were six brewhouses, 4 windmills, 5 watermills for grinding corn, and 20 churches.

Windsor, Conn.—Sept. 16, 1633, the first frame house was set up near this site by William Holmes, of Plymouth.

Williamsburg, Va., was made the seat of government in 1698. The streets were laid out in the form of a W in honor of King William.

MEDICAL.

Proprietary Medicine of great value. Is a certain, safe and sure cure for

CANCEROUS DISEASES.

A never failing Remedy WITHOUT THE USE OF KNIFE, loss of blood or pain. No Money exacted UNTIL A CURE is effected, other than the cost of Medicine. Also a

FEMALE REGULATING PILL.

Safe, sure and efficient.   Apply to

R. R. RUSSELL,

134 North 7th St., Philadelphia, Pa.

POLITICAL ACTION OF THE COLONIES.

Colonial Assembly.—The first in America met at Jamestown, July 30, 1619. It consisted of the Governor, the council and 22 representatives from the eleven burroughs into which the colony was divided.

Mayflower arrived in Cape Cod Harbor Nov. 21, 1620. Before landing a compact of civil liberty was drawn up and signed in the ship's cabin by the 41 male members of the company. Under this compact John Carver was chosen Governor for one year and Miles Standish was chosen military captain.

Written Constitution for Jamestown was prepared in 1621 providing for a legislative bod·· and trial by Jury.

Self-Government.—In Aug. 1629 a plan was formed for a large migration of the company, with its charter, to the Massachusetts Bay Colony. New officers were chosen from those who proposed to emigrate, John Winthrop being made governor. The effect of this arrangement was to make a total change in the political condition of the colony, which, from being subject to a distant corporation, now became self-governed, with power to elect their own general court.

General Court.—The first was held in Massachusetts at Boston, October 19, 1630.

Elective Franchise.—The second general court of Massachusetts voted, in 1631, that nobody could thereafter become a citizen and voter unless he were a church member. The same court, in 1632, ordered the election of two deputies from each town—16 in all—to confer with the magistrates about taxation. This was the germ of a second house in the general court.

Penalties for Refusing Office.— In 1632 Plymouth Colony passed an act imposing a fine of £20 upon any person who should refuse the office of governor, and £10 for refusing that of councilor or magistrate.

Representative Government in Massachusetts, May 19, 1634. Twenty-four delegates from the towns of the colony appeared before the governor and magistrates at their annual meeting and claimed seats in the general court. They were admitted. The freeman's oath was established at this time, requiring every freeman to pledge his allegiance to Massachusetts instead of to King Charles.

Voting by Ballot was first used at the general election in Massachusetts Bay in May, 1635.

Representative Assembly was held in Maryland in 1636. Lord Baltimore nor and assistants, and to send them sealed up by the hand of their deputies.

Connecticut, in a convention of the towns, Jan. 14, 1639, adopted a written constitution based on that of Massachusetts, except that residents of acceptable character might be admitted freemen though not church members. Legislative power was vested in a governor and assistants, with a house of deputies, who were to sit by themselves, chosen by the towns, constituting a general court.

New Haven Colony held an assembly in Mr. Robert Newman's barn June 4, 1639, to complete their political organization.

Maryland Statutes were enacted and a "House of Assembly" established at a third general assembly held in Feb. 1639, Lord Baltimore having yielded the disputed point of the initiative. Deputies were to be elected by the people. A

declared the laws enacted void, claiming the right to himself initiate legislation. Two years later he withdrew this claim.

Massachusetts' Town Governments were made legal and their powers defined by an act passed March 3, 1636, by the general court of the province.

Right to Tax.—In 1636 the Plymouth colony declared that no taxes should be levied but by the consent of the freemen of the colony in public assembly.

Code of Laws.—Oct. 4, 1636, Plymouth colony chose a committee to codify its statutes, of which there were about 60.

Local Elections in Massachusetts.—In 1637 a law was passed by the general court dispensing with the attendance of all the freemen at the Court of Elections, and allowing them to give their votes in their own towns for gover- water mill was provided for at public expense, and for every acre of tobacco planters were required to plant two acres of corn.

"Body of Liberties," a curious code prepared chiefly by Rev. Nathaniel Ward, of Ipswich, Mass., was adopted as its constitution by the colony of Massachusetts in Dec. 1641. There were 100 enactments, some of which may now be found embodied in the U. S. constitution. It forbade husbands to whip their wives, cruelty to animals, decreed capital punishment for idolatry, witchcraft and blasphemy, prohibited slavery except upon certain conditions, and provided that there should be no monopolies but of new inventions. and that for a short time only.

Colonial League was formed May 19, 1643, by Massachusetts Bay, Plymouth, New Haven and Connecticut

colonies, under the name of "The United Colonies of New England," for mutual protection against the Dutch and Indians. Runaway slaves and criminals were to be surrendered, an assembly composed of two commissioners from each colony was to be held.

Two Legislative Branches of the General Court were instituted in Massachusetts in 1644. Stray swine had occasioned lawsuits and difficulties of several years standing, which finally culminated in this important political change, which was made in order that each branch might possess a negative vote on the other.

Religious Tolerance.—In May, 1647, the Providence Colony was organized under its charter. The government was declared to be "democratical." Freedom of faith and worship was assured to all—the first formal and legal establishment of religious liberty ever made.

Property Qualification for Voters was established in Connecticut in 1683. Each voter must possess an estate worth £20, beside certain personal property.

"Charter of Liberties" was adopted by a representative assembly called in 1663 by the Governor of New York. It gave the right of suffrage and of trial by jury, but the king annulled it.

New Haven and Connecticut were united into one colony in 1665.

Naturalization Act. — Maryland passed the first act in 1666 for the naturalization of aliens, the first of the kind in the colonies.

Revolution in New York.—In June, 1689, a militia captain, Jacob Leisler, took advantage of the situation, proclaimed the new king, and, by aid of the troops, seized the government of the city, which he held for 18 months. The city being weakly garrisoned was taken by the Dutch July 30, 1673.

American Congress. —The first ever called was by Gov. Leisler at New York in May, 1690, to unite in a defence of the colonies. It was determined to attempt the conquest of Canada and Acadia.

CONTINENTAL CONGRESS.

First Continental Congress assembled Sept. 5, 1774, in Carpenter's Hall, Philadelphia. . There were 53 delegates from all the colonies except Georgia. Peyton Randolph, of Virginia, was elected President, and Charles Thompson, of Philadelphia, Secretary. Patrick Henry made the opening speech.

Second Continental Congress met at Philadelphia May 10, 1775, and voted to raise 20,000 men. The formation of a federal union was initiated, also steps taken to organize an army and navy. A petition to the king was prepared.

Massachusetts Provincial Congress was first organized Oct. 5, 1774, by members of the General Court, which Gov. Gage had convened, and then dissolved for fear of its patriotic action.

political connection between them and the state of Great Britain is and ought to be totally dissolved; that it is expedient forthwith to take the most effectual measures for forming foreign alliances; that a plan of confederation be prepared and transmitted to the respective colonies for their consideration and approbation." They were seconded by John Adams, of Massachusetts.

Richard Henry Lee's Resolutions were passed in Congress July 2, 1776, by the vote of 12 colonies, New York delegates not voting.

Declaration of Independence adopted by Congress July 4, 1776. Thos. Jefferson was its author and John Adams its champion. Its passage was welcomed by ringing the State house bell and the enthusiastic joy of the citizens.

A Declaration of Rights was passed by Congress Oct. 14, 1774.

Declaration of Independence by Rhode Island. May 4, 1776, the Assembly passed an act declaring the province free from the crown of Great Britain.

The First Congress Adjourned October 26, 1774, to meet May 10, 1775. It had adopted an "Address to the people of Great Britain," a "Petition to the King," besides other papers.

George Washington Elected Commander-in-Chief of the American forces by Continental Congress June 15, 1775.

Famous Resolutions of Richard Henry Lee, of Virginia, were read in Congress June 7, 1776. They were "That these united colonies are, and of right ought to be, free and independent states; that they are absolved from all allegiance to the British crown, and that all

Homestead Act.—Sept. 16, 1776, Congress promised grants of land to those who remained in the army until the end of the war.

Congress Adjourned to Baltimore December 12, 1776, because of the approach of the two armies across New Jersey.

Reorganization of the Army was entrusted to Washington December 27, 1776, by Congress. The funds being nearly exhausted Robert Morris, of Philadelphia, sent 410 Spanish dollars to Washington.

Declaration of Independence by Vermont was made in convention Jan. 15, 1777. The authority of New York and of any other power or government was denied.

Stars and Stripes.—June 14, 1777, Congress resolved "That the flag of the 13 United States be 13 stripes, alternate red and white; that the Union be 13 stars, white on a blue field, representing a new constellation." The stars formed a circle at first, but the great increase of states compelled a change. Paul Jones first unfurled this flag on the "Ranger."

Congress Adjourned to Lancaster and thence to York, Pa., Sep. 30, 1777, after Howe entered Philadelphia. Continued to meet at York till Howe left Phila.

Continental Congress in 1777 returned from Baltimore to Philadelphia.

Congress Created a Board of War October, 1777, making Gen. Gates President. He was popular because of Burgoyne's surrender Washington wrote to Patrick Henry: "If the cause be advanced, it is indifferent to me when or in what quarter it happens."

Articles of Confederation for a closer union between the colonies were adopted by Congress on November 15,

1777. A national union was a necessity, but the jealousies of the different states made them cautious in entrusting power to a central government. These "articles" merely established a league of states, without essential power. Congress could not raise taxes, and the national credit immediately declined. The provincial assemblies ratified the articles, some of them after much delay.

England Attempts to Treat for Peace, June 4, 1778. Lord North's 3 Peace Commissioners arrived in Philadelphia. Having no authority to recognize the independence of the United States, or to order the removal of the army from America, Congress refused to hold any intercourse with them till these things were agreed upon.

Continental Congress Elected John Jay, LL. D., President, Dec. 10, 1778, vice Henry Laurens, resigned.

UNITED STATES GOVERNMENT.

Federal Union Consummated on March 1, 1781, by the ratification of the articles of confederation by Maryland. Up to this time Congress had governed through its committees.

Project to Make Washington King, by the aid of the army, was crushed by his peremptory refusal, May, 1782.

Great Seal of the United States Adopted June 20, 1782. It was designed by Sir John Prestwitch, an English antiquary, and consists of "a spread eagle bearing on its breast our national shield, in its beak a scroll with the words E. Pluribus Unum; in its right talon an olive branch, a symbol of peace; in its left a bundle of 13 arrows, a symbol of the United States and of war; the crest, a glory breaking through a cloud

and surrounding a cluster of stars, forming a constellation."

Congress Elected Thomas Mifflin of Pennsylvania, President, to succeed Elias Boudinot, Nov. 3, 1783.

Congress Elected as its President Richard Henry Lee, of Virginia, November 30, 1784, to succeed Thomas Mifflin.

Algiers Declared War with the U. S., 1785.—Congress advised building five 40-gun war vessels, but had no power, hence the depredations continued.

Congress Elected as its President June 6, 1786, Nathaniel Gorham, of Massachusetts, in place of John Hancock, who had been elected to succeed Richard Henry Lee, but was prevented by illness from serving. Daniel

Ramsey, of S. C., was elected pro tem. *Annapolis Convention,* held Sept. 1786. Delegates from New York, New Jersey, Pennsylvania, Delaware and Virginia assembled to devise plans for uniformity in the commercial relations of the states. They voted to advise Congress to call a convenrion to revise the Articles of Confederation.

Constitutional Convention met at Independence Hall, Philadelphia, May 14, 1787, to revise the "Articles of Confederation." All the states but Rhode Island were represented. Geo. Washington was president and William Jackson, secretary.

Congress Elected Arthur St. Clair as its president February 2, 1787, to succeed Nathaniel Gorham.

Congress called a convention Feb. 12, 1787, to revise the "Articles of Confederation."

1788; Connecticut, January 9, 1788; Massachusetts, Feb. 7, 1788. Maryland, April 28, 1788; South Carolina, May 23, 1788; New Hampshire, June 21, 1788; Virginia, June 26, 1788; New York, July 26, 1788; North Carolina, Nov. 21, 1789; Rhode Island, May 29, 1790.

Congress Elected Cyrus Griffin, of Virginia, its president, to succeed Arthur St. Clair, June 22, 1788.

Congress Decided, July 14, 1788, to carry the new government into effect over those states that had not ratified the constitution. The new Congress was to open its session March 4, 1789, in New York. The choice of electors was to be made the first Wednesday in January, and the electors were to vote for President and Vice-President on the first Wednesday in February, 1789.

Presidential Electors were first chosen Jan., 1789, by state legislatures.

Constitutional convention placed all plans for revising the "Articles of Confederation" in the hands of a committee composed of Madison, Hamilton, King; Johnson and Gov. Morris, Sept. 10, 1787.

Constitution of the United States framed by the committee was adopted and signed by all but 16 members Sept. 17, 1787. It was agreed, in estimating the basis of representation, to count 500 slaves equal to 300 whites, which is the famous "three-fifths." The convention voted that Congress should have power to abolish slavery 20 years after the adoption of the constitution.

New Constitution was sent out by Congress to the states for ratification Sept. 28, 1787, which was done by them in the following order: Delaware, Dec. 7, 1787; Pennsylvania, Dec. 12, 1787; New Jersey, Dec. 18, 1787; Georgia, January 2,

The First Electoral College met and voted for President and Vice-President February, 1789. Each elector voted for two persons, and the one receiving the highest vote of all was pronounced President, and the one receiving the next highest vote Vice-President. Sixty-nine votes were cast for Washington, he being the unanimous choice for the highest office. John Adams received 34 votes and was elected Vice-President, the remaining 35 votes having been cast for Jay, Hancock and others.

Presidential Cabinet.—The first was formed in 1789, composed of Alexander Hamilton, of New York, Secretary of the Treasury; General Henry Knox, of Massachusetts, Secretary of War—both Federalists—and Thomas Jefferson, of Virginia, Secretary of State—a Democrat-Republican.

The New Congress did not open

until April 6, 1789, no quorum of members having before arrived. Frederick A. Muhlenburg, of New York, was elected Speaker.

Inauguration of George Washington, April 30, 1789, as President of the United States, in Federal Hall, New York. The oath of office was administered by Robert R. Livingston. Inauguration day was one of great jubilee.

State Department was organized July 27, 1789, with Thomas Jefferson as Secretary, under the name of Department of Foreign Affairs.

War Department was established August 7, 1789, with General Henry Knox, of Massachusetts, as secretary. It covered Army, Navy and Indian Affairs.

Treasury Department was established September 2, 1789, with Alexander Hamilton as Secretary.

Amendments to the Constitution of U. S.—Congress declared ten amendments, which had been proposed the previous year, in force December 15, 1791. North Carolina and Rhode Island had refused to ratify as the constitution stood.

Kentucky was the fifteenth accession to the United States, June 1, 1792.

Fugitives and Criminals, in whatever state found, were required to be surrendered by act of Congress February 12, 1793. This was applied to fugitive slaves, although there was trouble in executing it.

Stars and Stripes.—In 1794 Congress voted that the United States flag should consist of 15 stripes, alternate red and white, and 15 white stars on a blue field. A star and stripe were to be added for each new state.

Embargo on American Ports was

Judiciary of the U. S. was established by Congress September 24, 1789. John Jay was appointed Chief Justice and Edmund Randolph Attorney General.

Capital of the U. S.—July 10, 1790, Congress passed a bill making Philadelphia the capital until 1800. After that date the President was authorized to select some place on the Potomac.

Naturalization Law passed March 24, 1790.

Patent Right Law.—The first in the United States passed April 15, 1790.

Vermont was the fourteenth state to take its place in the Union, March 4th, 1791.

Internal Revenue.—Congress taxed domestic distilled spirits in 1791. It aroused immediate opposition in certain quarters, and was the origin of the "Whisky War" in Pennsylvania in 1794.

voted March 26, 1794, for 60 days, in order to prevent the British in the West Indies from securing provisions. This was in retaliation for their "Order in Council," authorizing the seizure of vessels laden with supplies for French colonies.

Tennessee was admitted to the Union June 1, 1796, being the sixteenth state.

"X. Y. Z." Mission.—Oct., 1797, C. C. Pinckney, John Marshal and Elbridge Berry were sent to France to negotiate peace. It was fruitless, as the French government demanded large sums of money as a condition of reception. The letters containing suggestions concerning these bribes were signed "X. Y. Z.," hence the name was applied to the mission. To them Pinckney replied "Millions for defence, but not one cent for tribute."

Eleventh Amendment to the U. S.

Constitution was declared in force January 8, 1798. It makes it impossible for a suit to be brought against a state in the United States court, which enables states to repudiate debts.

Alien and Sedition Laws passed by Congress July, 1798. The first empowered the President to arrest and send any foreigner out of the country, and the latter imposed fines and imprisonment upon any who should aid or abet resistance to the United States government. These laws were unpopular and led to the final overthrow of the Federalists.

Congressional Library.—An appropriation of $5,000 was made for it April 24, 1800.

Sedition Law expired by limitation and the Alien law was modified in 1801.

Presidential Message from President Jefferson to Congress in Dec., 1801, was the first written message, his prede-

Louisiana was the eighteenth state admitted into the Union April 30, 1812.

Indiana was the nineteenth state to be received into the Union, December 11, 1816.

Stars and Stripes.—April 4, 1818, Congress enacted that the stripes on the United States flag should be permanently reduced to 13, and that a new star should be added to the field whenever a state was admitted to the Union.

Illinois was the twenty-first state admitted to the Union December 3, 1818.

Alabama was the twenty-second state admitted into the Union December 14, 1819.

Maine was the twenty-third state admitted to the American Union March 15, 1820.

Roger Brook Taney, of Maryland, was confirmed as Chief Justice of the United States by Congress, March, 1836.

cessors having delivered theirs in person.

Twelfth Constitutional Amendment declared in force September 25, 1804. By it the votes are cast for President and Vice-President respectively.

English Vessels of war were ordered, July 2, 1807, by proclamation of the President, to leave all waters and ports of the United States until satisfaction was given for the outrage on the Chesapeake.

Embargo Bill passed Congress on Dec'r 27, 1807. It detained all vessels, American and foreign, in our ports, and ordered American vessels home immediately that the seaman might be trained for war.

Embargo Repealed March 4, 1809, except as to France and England, with the latter of whom no intercourse was to be permitted until her obnoxious decrees were repealed.

Arkansas was the twenty-fifth state admitted into the Union June 15, 1836.

Patent Right Commissioner was created under a law of Congress passed July, 1836.

Michigan was the twenty-sixth state admitted to the Union January 26, 1837.

Department of Agriculture.—In 1839 Congress appropriated $1,000 for the collation of agricultural statistics. It was led to this by the large importation of breadstuffs into the United States. Yearly and increasing appropriations followed until the above department was organized in 1862 and $60,000 was appropriated.

Sub-Treasury of U. S. instituted by law. July 4, 1840. By this act an independent treasury was established for public funds, thus keeping them out of banks.

Right of Petition.—In 1842 a fierce contest occurred in the United States

House of Representatives over the presentation of petitions by John Quincy Adams. For several years petitions relating to slavery had been excluded. "The Old Man Eloquent" contended, in the face of a hostile House, almost single-handed, for the right to petition, for eleven days, and finally conquered.

Texas was the twenty-eighth state admitted to the Union, December 29, 1845. It added 247,356 square miles of territory and $7,500,000 of debt to the United States.

Iowa was the twenty-ninth state admitted to the Union December 28, 1846.

Wisconsin was the thirtieth state admitted to the Union May 29, 1848.

Interior Department was organized March 3, 1849, by Congress. Thos. Ewing, of Ohio, was appointed Secretary. Indian affairs were transferred to this from the War Department.

ing the Lecompton pro-slavery constitution by a vote of the people.

Minnesota was the thirty-second state admitted to the Union, May 11, 1858.

Oregon, the thirty-third state, was admitted to the Union February 14, 1859.

Kansas was admitted to the Union January 29, 1861, as the thirty-fourth state.

Senators Expelled.—United States Senate expelled ten of its members July 11, 1861, and on the 13th the House expelled John B. Clark, of Missouri.

Iron Clad Oath.—In July, 1862, Congress adopted the oath to be taken by all officers of the United States government.

West Virginia was admitted into Union June 20th, 1863, as the thirty-fifth state.

Fugitive Slave Law was enacted by Congress September, 1850. This was the most obnoxious feature to the northern states in Henry Clay's "Omnibus bill." It also provided for the abolition of slavery in the District of Columbia, the admission of California as a free state, the future formation of four new states out of Texas, with or without slavery, and the organization of New Mexico and Utah into territories.

California was admitted to the Union as the thirty-first state September 9, 1850.

House of Representatives expelled four of its members February 19, 1857, for corupt conduct. They were from New York and Connecticut.

Kansas.—Congress by vote April 30, 1858, offered to admit Kansas to the Union and donate to it valuable public lands, upon the condition of its adopt-

Important Acts of Congress.—At the session ending July 2, 1864, the Fugitive Slave Law was repealed, an income tax of 5% on incomes over $600 enacted, also an internal revenue law and a national bank law.

The Thirteenth Amendment to the constitution passed Congress January 31, 1865. It forbade slavery on any soil of the United States. This amendment being ratified by three-fourths of the states was officially declared by Secretary Stewart to be part of the Constitution of the United States December 18, 1865.

Civil Rights Bill was passed by Congress April 9, 1866, over President Johnson's veto. It made freedmen citizens of the United States and gave them powers of legal resort if their rights were infringed.

Fourteenth Amendment, incorporating the Civil Rights Bill into the Constitution of the United States was passed by Congress June 13th, 1866, in opposition to the President. It was ratified by the necessary number of states and became part of the Constitution July 28th, 1868.

Nebraska was admitted as the 37th state into the Union March 1, 1867.

The "Military Government" and "Tenure-of-Office" bills were passed by Congress over President Johnson's vetos, March 2, 1867.

National Obligations to be paid in coin, in accordance with an act of Congress passed March, 1869.

United States Weather Bureau in the signal service was established by Congress, February 9, 1870. General Albert J. Myer, popularly known as "Old Probabilities," was made its chief.

Fifteenth Amendment passed by Congress February 26, 1869, was ratified by three-fourths of the states and declared part of the Constitution of the U. S. March 30, 1870. It guaranteed right of suffrage to all citizens of the United States regardless of race, color, or previous condition of servitude. This amendment was officially declared to have been ratified March 30, 1870.

Department of Justice, with the United States Attorney General at the head, who also became a member of the President's cabinet, was established by Congress June 22, 1870.

Income Tax was repealed by Congress January 26, 1871.

Ku-Klux Bill.—A bill for the enforcement of the Sixteenth Amendment was passed April 20, 1871, by Congress, which was popularly known by this title.

Weather Bureau of U. S. was authorized by act of Congress June 10, 1872, to increase its stations and publish reports for the special benefit of the commercial and agricultural interests of the country.

Bankrupt Law was repealed by the United States House of Representatives December 16, 1873.

Pensions.—An appropriation of $29,533,500 was made by Congress January 14, 1876.

Colorado was, on August 1, 1876, admitted as the thirty-eighth state into the Union.

Resumption of Specie Payment by the United States upon first January, 1879, was provided for by Senator Sherman's bill passed by Congress and signed by the President in December, 1874.

BRITISH OPPRESSION OF THE COLONIES.

Jamestown Ruled by Martial Law, May 10, 1611. Sir Thomas Dale arrived with supplies, assuming charge of the colony, administering both church and state by his severe rule.

Exports of Tobacco and other colonial productions to any foreign port, "until they were first landed in England and the customs paid," were forbidden by decree of the English government in 1621.

Parliament in 1650 declared Virginia and the West India colonies, which refused to acknowledge the Commonwealth, in rebellion, prohibited trade with them and sent an armed force against them.

Thankfulness for Ignorance.— In 1670 Governor Sir William Berkeley, of Virginia, in his report to the commissioners of the colony, wrote: "I thank

emnize marriage, that the episcopacy should be established, and that no printing press should be used.

William of Orange having landed in England in 1689, the colonists seized and imprisoned Andros and in July sent him a prisoner to England.

Francis Nicholson was appointed Governor of Virginia in 1690.

Governorship of New York.— William III. having, in 1691, appointed Colonel Henry Sloughter to this position, there was a conflict of authority between him and the incumbent Leisler. Leisler and his son-in-law Milborne were arrested, tried and executed for treason. Governor Sloughter was drunk when he signed their death warrant.

"Mast Trees."—The new charter of New England of 1692 imposed a fine of

God there are no free schools nor printing, and I hope we shall not have these hundred years, for learning has brought disobedience into the world, and printing has divulged them and libels against the best governments. God keep us from both."

Tax Collectors.—In 1679 Edward Randolph was made collector and surveyor of all New England by the King, with power to appoint deputies. They were persistently opposed, Randolph being at one time imprisoned by the colonies, and finally ceased to comply strictly with the laws, which gradually fell into disuse, until after the French and Indian wars, when their revival caused the revolution.

Andros Arrived at Boston Dec. 19, 1686, and created immediate trouble by taxation, by ordering that only a Church of England minister should sol-

£100 for cutting pine trees in the forests which were more than two feet in diameter at a foot above ground, they being reserved for masts for the royal navy. A "Surveyor General of the King's Woods" was appointed to stamp a broad arrow upon them. It enraged the lumbermen, who had built up a trade in spars with the French and Spanish islands, to find the "broad arrow" stamped on their best trees, and shook their belief in the justice of the King's prerogative.

Board of Trade was established in England in 1696. It was to have a general oversight of colonial affairs and to enforce the laws of trade and the Navigation acts. This Board's acts helped to bring on the revolution.

The Independent Spirit of the Colonies was made the subject of a memorial to the English government in 1703

by Quarry, who recommended that it be "checked in time."

Lord Cornbury was Governor of New York from 1702 to 1708. He was a profligate, and sometimes appeared in public dressed as a woman.

Singular Subject for a Sermon.— In 1719 Dr. Coleman preached a sermon upon the "reasons for a market in Boston." The press was under censorship, and a license was required for every pamphlet issued. Therefore the pulpit was the only place left for the free expression of views on public matters.

Forest Tree Strife still continued in New England in 1722. Government had for thirty years confiscated the best trees, for which the colonists vainly demanded compensation. They were forbidden to sell timber to Spain and Portugal. Royal authority was losing its power in New England.

Freedom of the Press Vindicated in New York November 17, 1734, by the acquittal of John Peter Zenger, publisher of the "New York Weekly Journal," after a long trial and imprisonment for defending popular rights against the crown, caused great rejoicing and inspired the colonists with a fresh spirit of opposition to parliamentary restrictions.

Impressment in Boston.—In Nov. 1747, Commodore Knowles, commander of the English squadron in the harbor, seized several men for his fleet. A mob of several thousands demanded redress from the Governor. The excitement increased for two or three days, when, fearing the consequences, the men were released.

American Iron Manufactories, such as rolling mills, plating forges and furnaces, were declared ",com-

American Competition with English manufactures was the subject of a report of the Board of Trade to the House of Commons in 1731. In it mention was made of the Massachusetts paper mill, which it was "feared would interfere with the profit made by British merchants on foreign paper sent thither." They were also alarmed by the shoemakers who went from house to house making foot-wear for families.

Exportation of hats from the American Colonies was forbidden by act of parliament in 1732. Neither could they be carried from one province to another.

"Molasses Act."—In 1734, in order to compel the colonists to purchase their sugar, molasses and rum in the British West Indies, instead of from the British and Dutch West Indies, Parliament imposed a duty that was virtually prohibitory.

mon nuisances," and a fine of $1,000 was imposed upon every one built in excess of those already in occupation, by an act of the British Parliament in 1750.

Pennsylvania Protests against British restrictions.—In February, 1757, Benjamin Franklin was appointed to "represent in England the unhappy state of that province," consequent upon the persistent efforts of the English government to restrict popular rights.

British House of Commons, in 1757, by formal resolution, denied the rights of the colonists to raise and appropriate money by their own acts alone.

Writs of Assistance, or warrants, to search when and where they pleased for smuggled goods, were issued by the English government in 1761, in order to a more strict enforcement of the acts of trade. They were so unpopular as to be seldom used. Massachusetts first resisted the enforcement of these acts, in a stirring speech delivered by James Otis. Writs of Assistance were warrants issued by the Supreme Court, authorizing deputy collectors to search any place or building for the discovery of smuggled goods. It was conceded that the government had the right to issue a writ for the searching of a special building named in the writ, but it was denied that writs could be lawfully issued to enable an officer of the law to search wherever he pleased. Writs were finally issued, but seldom, if ever, used. This was one of the first kicks of the colonies against British tyranny.

Tampering with the Judiciary.—On December 9, 1761, the colonial governors were forbid to issue judicial commissions, except at the pleasure of the ment and signed by the King June 29th, 1767. This measure greatly excited the colonists, who had been quieted by the repeal of the stamp act.

British Troops were ordered to Boston June 8th, 1768. The Boston patriots were deeply excited. The Governor had dissolved the Legislature and refused to call another.

The Ship of War Romney seized the sloop Liberty, owned by John Hancock, on the 10th of June, 1768, for an alleged violation of the revenue law. A great mass meeting was held at Fanieul Hall, and then at the Old South Church, where James Otis and others made eloquent speeches. The agitation was intensified by the impressment of men for sailors and the bringing of soldiers to Boston by the officers of the Romney.

British War Vessels on the American coast were, in 1770, ordered to ren-

King. This was considered an attempt to make judges subservient to the will of the King.

Stamp Act.—The famous stamp act was signed by the King March 22, 1765. It required all legal documents to be written on stamped paper, to be bought only of the tax collectors—(the stamps cost from 3 cents to £6)—that every newspaper and pamphlet must bear a stamp costing one-half penny to four pence, and that each advertisement should pay two shillings duty.

Stamp Act Repealed.—In 1766 the stamp act was repealed, but Parliament claimed the right to exercise unlimited power over the colonies. In order to quarter troops in American cities the mutiny act was applied to America.

A Duty on glass, paper, painter's colors and tea imported into America was imposed by a bill passed by Parlia- dezvous in Boston harbor. Castle William was ordered strengthened, greatly exciting the people.

Liberty Pole Cut Down by British soldiers in New York, January 17, 1770. Great indignation meeting of citizens, who affirmed the rights of the people in speeches and resolutions. Another liberty pole was speedily erected in another place.

British Soldiers murdered a young man named Snider, in a quarrel with citizens in Boston, February 22, 1770.

Gray's Rope Walk, Boston, was the scene of a fight between a soldier and a workman. The soldier and his fellows were beaten off by citizens, Mar. 2, 1770.

Boston Massacre, March 5th, 1770, a quarrel arose between soldiers and citizens near the old State House. The guard being called out to quiet the disturbance fired, killing three and wounding eight. Crispur Attucks, a mulatto, was the first man killed. Captain Preston and several soldiers were imprisoned, tried, and all acquitted but 2, who were convicted of manslaughter. .

Funeral Obsequies of four victims of Boston massacre held with great parade, March 8, 1770, amid tolling of bells and suspension of business.

Tax on Tea of 3 per cent. was adhered to, all other taxes on imports to the colonies being repealed by Parliament April 12, 1770.

Leaden Statue of George III. set up in Bowling Green, New York, Aug., 1770. It had been ordered four years before, in honor of the repeal of the stamp act A marble statue of William Pitt was also set up in New York.

Tea, Amounting to 17,000.000 pounds, was shut up in the East India

obeyed. In New York a similar meeting was held with like results. In Charleston, S. C., tea was landed, but rotted in the cellars where it had been stored.

Postmaster General Benjamin Franklin was deposed from his office, which he had held since 1753, by the English government Jan. 30, 1774.

The Quebec Act, which was designed to prevent that province from joining with the other colonies, guaranteed to the Roman Catholic Church the possession of its ample property and the free exercise of its religion, approved by the King in 1774.

Boston Port Bill passed March 7, 1774, ordering the port of Boston to be closed against all commercial transactions whatever, and the removal of custom house, courts of justice and other public offices to Salem.

Company's warehouses because the Americans would not buy. The British government decreed that it might be shipped to America without paying an export duty. They hoped that the low price at which it could now be sold would induce the colonists to pay the *import duty*, thus surrendering the principles for which they contended. During the summer of 1773 several cargoes were shipped.

Boston Tea Party.—December 16, 1773, after a mass-meeting in Fanieul Hall, about 50 men disguised as Indians boarded three tea vessels in the harbor, broke open the hatches and dumped 342 chests of tea into the water. Perfect order was maintained. The actors have never to a certainty been known.

A Tea Ship at Philadelphia was ordered to depart by a mass-meeting held December 26, 1773. The order was

Charter of Massachusetts violated by act of Parliament March 28, 1774. This bill gave to the crown the appointment of counselors and judges of the Supreme Court. The appointment of all other officers, military, executive and judicial, was bestowed on the Governor independently of any approval by the council. Jurors could be selected only by sheriffs. Town meetings were prohibited.

Gen. Gage Appointed Governor, vice Hutchinson, removed, landed at Boston May 17, 1774. Troops were ordered to follow him. He was instructed to arrest and send principal patriots to England.

"The Murder Act" received the King's signature May 20, 1774. It provided for the trial in England of all persons charged with murders committed in support of the government.

Boston Port Bill went into effect June 1, 1774. The day was observed by a solemn fast.

Independence of the U. S.—British Parliament passed a bill July, 1782, enabling the King to acknowledge the independence of the United State.

American Seamen Impressed by a British squadron off Cuba in 1798. Great and prolonged agitation resulted, which culminated in the war of 1812. .

English Hostility to America was shown in 1793 by preventing the Western Indians concluding a treaty with U. S. Commissioners, by impressing seamen, by refusal to surrender western ports and to pay for slaves captured in the revolution.

American Commerce crippled by England June 8, 1793, by an order that all vessels loaded with corn for France should be compelled to go to English ports.

England Seized and condemned several American merchantmen and cargoes in 1805, alleging violations of neutrality.

English Insults induced the United States to retaliate April 18, 1806, by prohibiting the importation of British manufactures after Nov. 15, 1806.

Insolence of the British Minister was such that in 1810 Congress voted that he be no longer recognized by the President.

British Government finally, in 1811, disavowed the act of the Leopard in firing upon the Chesapeake in 1807.

Right of Search was the subject of correspondence between England and the United States in 1859, British cruisers having searched American merchantmen on suspicion of being slavers. Congress ordered men-of-war to the gulf, and England disavowed the acts of her officers and abandoned the right of search.

British Authorities at Kingston, Jamaica, seized the American steamer "Edgar Stuart," as a Cuban privateer, April 15, 1872.

The Canadian Authorities seized the American fishing schooner "Enola C.," May 29, 1872, for violating fishery laws.

Canadian Cutter "Stella Marie" seized the American fishing schooner "James Bliss," June 18, 1872, for violating the fishery laws, and insulted the American flag by turning it upside down under the Dominion flag.

Fishery Damages to the amount of $103,000 were demanded of England by America, Aug. 19, 1879, because of illegal interference at Fortune bay.

ACTS OF THE COLONIES RESISTING OPPRESSION.

Massachusetts retained control of the funds raised by herself for the war in 1758, to the dissatisfaction of the royalists.

Massachusetts, in May, 1765, sent out a circular proposing a Colonial Congress to meet in New York in October.

Patrick Henry Offered his five famous resolutions on May 29th, 1765, in the Virginia Assembly, upon the announcement by the Speaker of the passage of the stamp act. They declared that the American colonists ought to possess all the characteristics of English freedom, chief among which was the right to levy taxes by no body save that which represented the tax-payers. The movement was sudden and surprising and produced intense excitement. Mr. Henry defended his resolutions with fiery eloquence, and at one point exclaimed:

dent, and Robert Ogden, of New Jersey, refused to sign the papers. The Massachusetts Assembly reprimanded the former, and the New Jersey Assembly deposed the latter from his position as Speaker.

Non-Importation agreements were made October 31st, 1765, by New York merchants. Philadelphia and Boston merchants followed their example.

The Stamp Act became a law Nov. 1, 1765. It was a day of intense feeling and general gloom, and all business was suspended. Soon domestic manufacturers began everywhere to manufacture articles which before had been imported. The "Daughters of Liberty" organized in Boston for spinning, knitting and weaving. Maple sugar and molasses began to be manufactured in New England. In New York a society agreed to

"Cæsar had his Brutus, Charles the First his Cromwell, and George the Third—" "Treason! Treason!" shouted Mr. Speaker Robinson, and the cry was re-echoed from all parts of the House. Mr. Henry, undismayed, took advantage of a hush to add, "May profit by their example. If that be treason make the most of it!" The resolutions were adopted. The last one was, however, reconsidered and rejected in Mr. Henry's absence the next day. They were, however, published as originally offered, and their effect was potential in uniting the colonies.

An American Congress of twenty-seven delegates from nine of the thirteen colonies, met at New York, Oct'r 7th, 1765. A Declaration of Rights, a Petition to the King, and a Memorial to Parliament was drawn up. Timothy Ruggles, of Massachusetts, the Presi-

wear no imported clothes and to encourage home manufactures.

The Governor of New York, in June, 1768, requested the Assembly to vote supplies for troops then on their way to that city, which was refused.

A Massachusetts Convention, at which 96 towns were represented, met September 22d, 1768, and held a six days session. It defined provincial rights more clearly. Local self-government was the basis of the patriot cause, and the right of Parliament to make any laws for the colonies began to be denied. A Union sentiment was growing. The British government was more exasperated, and Lord North said: "Whatever prudence or policy might hereafter induce us to repeal the late paper and glass act, I hope we shall never think of it until we see America prostrate at our feet."

James Otis was chosen moderator of a mass meeting held in Fanieul Hall, September, 1768. It was resolved that "The inhabitants of Boston will, at the utmost peril of their lives and fortunes, maintain and defend their rights, liberties, privileges and immunities."

Seven Hundred British Soldiers commanded by Colonel Dalrymple, were brought from Castle William, Boston Harbor, and encamped on the common, Oct. 1, 1768. Others were also lodged in the city during the two months following. The town refused to furnish quarters, and the officers were compelled to prepare them at government expense. Efforts to obtaid the removal of these troops culminated in the Boston massacre two years later.

North Carolina Regulators was the name assumed, in 1771, by people who had banded together in that state sisting British oppression, was elected first in March, 1773, by the Virginia Assembly.

Tea Meetings, Oct'r 15, 1773.— In New York a meeting was held to consider the question and patriotic resolutions adopted. At a similar meeting in Philadelphia, held October 16, 1773, resolutions were passed declaring the sending of tea to be an attack on the liberties of America. A meeting was held under the Liberty tree, Boston, November 3, 1773, and a ccmmittee appointed to request the consignees not to sell the tea when it arrived. The request was denied. Frequent other meetings were held and constant pressure was brought to bear on the authorities to procure the rejection of the tea.

Virginia Provincial Assembly was originated in Raleigh Tavern, Williamsburg, Va., May 25, 1774, by mem-

---

---

to resist the extortions of the provincial tax collectors.

The Battle at Alamance Creek was fought May 16, 1771, between the "North Carolina Regulators" and a militia force under Governor Tryon. A number on both sides were killed. Many "Regulators" were made prisoners, of whom six were hung by Tryon.

"Boys of Plymouth" was a juvenile military organization in a school kept by Alex. Scammel and Peleg Wadsworth, in 1771, both afterwards distinguished army officers. Elkanah Watson, in his "Men and Times of the Revolution," says: "We were taught military evolution by either Scammel or Wadsworth, and marched over hills, through swamps, often in the rain, in performance of these embryo military duties."

Committee of Correspondence, to induce co-operation of provinces in re-bers of the House of Burgesses, which Governor Dunmore dissolved on account of their positive action. They voted in favor of a general Congress, according to the recommendation of New York.

Last Colonial Assembly of Massachusetts met at Salem June 7, 1774. The time and place for a Continental Congress were determined, delegates elected and patriotic resolutions passed. Gov. Gage undertook to dissolve them, but the doors were locked against his secretary until business was done.

Aid for Boston, June, 1774. The following were among the gifts that came pouring in: From South Carolina, 200 barrels of rice; Windham, Conn., 250 sheep; Schoharie, N. Y., 550 bushels of wheat; Georgia, 63 barrels of rice and $720 in specie.

"Powder Alarm" was caused by the seizure, September 1, 1774, of 250

half-barrels of powder at Charleston and two field pieces at Cambridge, belonging to the province, and the fortification of Boston Neck by General Gage, who was alarmed at the spirit of the colonists. Great excitement ensued in Boston, and the report spread through New England that war had actually begun, which caused thirty thousand patriots to pour toward Boston to take part in the conflict.

Tea Ship Burnt.—On October 15, 1774, at Annapolis, Maryland, the tea boat "Peggy Stewart" was burnt by its owner to allay the excitement of the populace, who would not permit her cargo to land.

"Minute Men."—November, 1774, Massachusstts' Provincial Assembly ordered the organization of 12,000 minute men; also made provision for military stores and ammunition.

Munitions of War having been forbidden by the King to be exported to America, in Dec., 1774, the citizens of Providence, R. I., seized 40 cannon from a fort near Newport. One hundred barrels of powder, some small arms and cannon were seized from a fort in the harbor of Plymouth, N. H., which was dismantled.

Harrisburg, Pa.—*Hotels and Restaurants Continued.*

DINING HALL,
Basement of U. S. Hotel, Opp. the P. & R. Depot.
HARRISBURG, PA.
Meals served at all Hours — Regular Meals 35 Cents.
W. J. ADORE, Proprietor.

Donmoyer House,
Cor. Third and Mulberry S's., Harrisburg, Pa.
J. W. DONMOYER, Proprietor.
Choice lot of Wines, Liquors and Cigars constantly on hand. Lodging by Night or Week.

EAGLE HOUSE,
625 RACE St., HARRISBURG, PA.
THEODORE DUFFNER. - - Proprietor,
Good Boarding at reasonable rates. The best Wines and Liquors constantly on hand.

EUROPEAN HOTEL,
P. RUSS, Proprietor.
Centrally located. Good accommodations
Market St. & Penna. R. R., Harrisburg, Pa.

Russ, N., Proprietor Gross House, 233 Walnut St.

WM. T. SOLLERS,
Hotel De Paris and Restaurant.
Meals at all hours. Game in Season. Domestic Wines a Specialty.
11 and 13 N. Market Square, HARRISBURG, PA.

JONES HOUSE,
ED. A. TINKER, ... Proprietor.
A. E. MILLER, with Jones House.
Cor. Market and Market Square, Harrisburg, Pa.

KAPPHAN'S HOTEL,
CHAS. L. KAPPHAN, Proprietor.
Centrally Located. Good Accommodations Charges Reasonable.
324 BROAD St., HARRISBURG, PA.

Lancaster House, Mrs. B. Meyer, Proprietress, 21 Sixth St.
McDonell House, S. L. McDonell, Proprietor, 501 East State St.
Mitchell House, James Mitchell, Proprietor, 629 East State St.

National Capitol and District of Columbia.

Maryland.—On December 22, 1788, Maryland ceded the county of Washington, containing 64 square miles, to the United States, to become part of the national capitol.

Virginia, December 3d, 1789, ceded the county of Alexandria, containing 36 square miles, to the United States to form a part of the capitol.

Congress, on July 16, 1790, accepted the territory ceded to the United States for a capitol.

President Washington, March 30, 1791, by proclamation, ordered the lines of the new capitol upon the Potomac to be run.

The First Corner Stone of the District of Columbia was set at Jones' Point April 15th, 1791, by Hon. David Carroll and Dr. David Stewart, with masonic ceremonies.

Locating U. S. Capitol.—On Sept. 9, 1791, the commissioners appointed to locate the new capitol of the United States, directed Major L' Enfaut, who was designing maps for it, to call the city Washington and the whole district the Territory of Columbia. The corner stone for the Capitol was laid with masonic ceremony, September 18, 1793.

The White House at Washington, D. C., was designed by James Hohan, after the country house of the Duke of Leinster, England. The corner stone was laid October 13, 1792.

Washington, D. C., was officially occupied by the United States government in June, 1800. One sloop conveyed sufficient furniture for all the departments from Philadelphia to Washington.

District of Columbia.—On July 9, 1846, the United States re-ceded to Virginia that portion of the District of Columbia originally acquired by her.

REVOLUTIONARY WAR.

The First Blood—February 26, 1775, Gen. Gage decided to disarm the colonists, and despatched a party of British soldiers from Boston, under Leslie, to Salem and Danvers, Mass., to seize provincial supplies. Finding none at Salem they started for Danvers, but found the draw of the North Bridge raised, which the citizens refused to lower. Attempting to seize two large gondolas a scuffle took place, in which a boatman received a bayonet thrust. Rev. Thos. Barnard proposed a compromise, which was accepted. The draw was lowered, the soldiers marched across into Danvers about 30 rods, turned about and started for Boston.

ALPHABETICALLY ARRANGED.

Battle of the Kegs.—In January, to Vermont to capture supplies), and the Americans under Gen. John Stark. On the eve of battle Stark exclaimed: "We beat the red coats to-day or Mollie Stark is a widow." He did beat them and captured 700 prisoners. One old man had five sons in the battle. When it was over he was told that one had been unfortunate. "Was he a coward or a traitor?" he eagerly inquired. "Oh, no; he fought bravely, but was killed." "Ah! then I am satisfied," said the father.

Bunker Hill.—The battle of Bunker Hill was fought June 17, 1775. Col. Wm. Prescott, of Pepperell, Mass., with 1,000 Americans, began entrenching Breed's Hill, which commanded Boston and the harbor, on the night of June 16. By daylight a strong redoubt eight rods square,

---

1778, David Bushnell, of Saybrook, Connecticut, invented a contrivance designed to destroy the British fleet at Philadelphia. Kegs of powder, having attachments for exploding them when they struck, were floated down the Delaware. The vessels had been removed and were not injured, but great alarm was created in the city by their explosion. Judge Francis Hopkinson wrote a comic ballad entitled "The Battle of the Kegs."

Bemis Heights.—On September 19, 1777, Burgoyne attacked the Americans under General Gates, who, with proper energy, could have destroyed the British army. The bravery of Arnold and Morgan carried the day. American loss 300; British loss 600.

Bennington.—This battle took place Aug. 16, 1777, between a large force of Germans and British regulars, under Lt. Col. Baume (whom Burgoyne had sent together with an earthwork running to a swamp, was completed. The English fleet began bombarding it and landed 2,000 regulars, under General Howe. At half-past two they advanced, firing as they went. The Americans silently permitted the British to approach within eight rods. They then delivered so effective a volley that almost the whole front rank of officers and men fell dead. The balance fled precipitately to the foot of the hill. The fleet now threw shells into Charleston and set it on fire, hoping to smoke the Americans out, but the breeze bore it in another direction. A second advance was made to within six rods of the redoubt, when another murderous volley caused the British again to retreat. A third assault was made, and the front rank fell as before, but the Americans had now exhausted their ammunition. The British pushed into the redoubt with fixed bayonets and nearly surrounded the patriots, who retreated slowly to Bunker Hill, holding back the foe with clubbed muskets and stones. The British did not pursue far, having lost over one thousand officers and men. The American loss was less than five hundred.

Brandywine.—This battle occurred September 11, 1777. Gen. Washington attempted to stay the progress of Lord Howe, who, with a large force, was marching along the Delaware toward Philadelphia. The Americans were defeated with 1,000 loss. The British loss was 500.

Camden, S. C.—A battle was fought here August 16, 1780, between Generals Cornwallis and Gates. Gates had about 3,000 raw recruits, many of whom were sick, and he was totally defeated. He retired from the battlefield almost alone,

1777, Washington attacked the British camp at Germantown, with partial success—enough to strengthen the cause of the patriot army.

Great Bridge, near Norfolk, Va., was the scene of a fight on December 9, 1775, between some tories under Gov. Dunmore and a patriotic force. The tories were defeated with some loss.

Guilford Court-House, N. C.—At this place a battle was fought March 15, 1781, between Cornwallis and Greene. It was disastrous to both parties, but British influence was destroyed in North Carolina and Cornwallis was forced to retreat to Virginia. The Americans lost 419 and the British 570.

Hanging Rock, S. C., Aug. 6, 1780. A huge rock, 30 feet in diameter, overhangs a precipice 100 feet high, which makes one side of the hill. General Sumpter charged and nearly destroyed

and so rapidly as to make 200 miles in three and one-half days.

Cowpens, S. C.—January 17th, 1781, Gen. Morgan, with an inferior force, defeated Tarleton, capturing 500 prisoners, 800 muskets, 2 standards, also cannon and horses. American loss only 72 killed and wounded.

Eutaw Springs, S. C.—A battle was fought here September 8, 1781, between Greene and the British under Col. Stewart. Greene was at first victorious, but was finally driven back. The British retreated to Charleston the next day.

Fort Mercer Attacked, October 22, 1777, by Count Donop, with 1200 Hessians and artillery. It was on the Delaware river, and was held by Col. Greene, of Rhode Island, with 400 men. The attempt failed, and Count Donop, and 400 Hessians, were killed.

Germantown, Pa.—On October 4,

the Prince of Wales' regiment on the summit of this hill.

Harlem Plains.—An engagement occurred here Sept. 16th, 1776, between the British advance guard under General Leslie and two companies of Americans commanded by Col. Knowlton and Maj. Leitch. The Americans were victorious, but lost about 600, including both their commanders.

Jamestown Ford.—Cornwallis and Wayne fought at Jamestown Ford July 4, 1781. Wayne was entrapped by strategy, but made a bold charge and escaped being aided by Lafayette.

King's Mountain, S. C., October 7, 1780.—Gen. Ferguson, commanding a British and tory army, was defeated and slain by a patriot force of 900 backwoodsmen. The British lost 1,108 killed and prisoners and 1,500 stand of arms. The Americans lost 88. They hanged 10 tories. This battle turned the tide in favor of the Colonists in the Carolinas, and Cornwallis had to retreat.

Lexington.—A battle occurred here Apr. 19, 1775. Gen. Gage sent 800 British troops to destroy military stores at Concord. At Lexington they encountered about 70 militia under Captain Isaac Parker. Major Pitcairn, the British commander, rode forward shouting, "Disperse, ye rebels!" and fired his pistol, which was followed by a volley from his troops, killing 8 and wounding 10 Americans. The British pushed on to Concord and destroyed the stores. The "Minute Men" gathered and harassed the invaders by a constant fire from behind stone walls, buildings, &c., so that they lost 280 men during their retreat of 16 miles. The American loss was 95.

Long Island.—An engagement occurred here August 27, 1776. The Brit-

quently dismissed for treachery. The British continued their march to New York, but one thousand deserted on the way.

Newport, R. I.—Near this place occurred a battle August 29th, 1778. The Americans under General Sullivan were attacked by the British. Gen. Greene, commanding Sullivan's right, defeated his opponents with a loss of 260, his own loss being 200. At other points the Americans suffered defeat.

Rahway River.—Repulse of General Knyphausen, on Rahway river, near Springfield, N. J., June 23, 1780. With 5,000 troops he had started for a raid into New Jersey. General Greene drove him back with severe losses. The wadding giving out Rev. James Caldwell supplied the Americans with hymn-books from the Presbyterian church. Said he, "Now, boys, put Watts into them."

ish under Gen. Clinton, landed and advanced before daylight upon the patriot army, who were defeated, losing 2,000, half of whom were prisoners, including Gens. Sullivan and Stirling. The British loss was about 400.

Monk's Corners, S. C.—Gen. Huger was defeated here April 14, 1780, by Tarleton's British cavalry. Two regiments were cut to pieces.

Monmouth. — Washington pursued and overtook the British army at Monmouth, and fought a battle, June 28th, 1778. It was Sunday and the thermometer stood 96° in the shade. Gen. Charles Lee began the attack, but was repulsed. Gen. Washington stopped the flight and continued the battle until dark. The American loss was 362; the British 355. Gen. Lee was court-martialed for cowardice and insolence to Washington. He was suspended for one year, and subse-

Stillwater, October 7, 1777.—Gen'l Arnold fought this battle in disobedience to Gen. Gates, who sent a messenger to recall him as he entered the field, but Arnold contrived to elude him until the battle was won. The British fought desperately, but were driven at all points. Major J. A. Ackland, one of Burgoyne's officers, was wounded and made a prisoner. His wife was permitted to attend him. They subsequently returned to England impressed with respect for the American cause. He was killed afterward by Lieut. Lloyd, in a duel. Lloyd aspersed the American character, which Ackland hotly defended.

Stone Ferry, S. C.—An engagement occurred here June 20, 1779, between a British guard to the ferry and General Lincoln's force. The loss was about 300 on each side.

Strategy of Washington.—On Jan.

3, 1777, Cornwallis attempted retaliation for the British loss at Trenton. With a fine army 7,000 strong he penned the American force between the Delaware river and Assanpink creek. The mud was so deep that flight seemed impossible. Early in the night a freezing wind made it solid. Leaving pickets to build fires, Washington silently marched to Princeton, where he encountered three British regiments, fought and defeated them, inflicting a loss of about 300. The sound of his cannon was the first intimation Cornwallis had that he was outgeneralled. These exploits added to Washington's fame. Frederick the Great declared them unexcelled. The Americans took fresh courage and organized armed bands, who constantly harrassed the invaders.

Trenton.—The battle of Trenton was fought Dec. 26, 1776, Washington had assisted by a crowd of citizens, led by Isaac Sears. The English war vessel "Asia" sent some sailors ashore to resist the removal and fired upon the battery. One sailor was killed and others wounded. The cannon were wanted for the defence of the Hudson.

RAIDS, INVASIONS, ETC., DURING THE REVOLUTION.

Gen. Gage ordered the Queen's Guard, of 100 men, under Capt. Balfour, to Marshfield, Mass., Jan. 23, 1775, to protect a "Loyal Association" against the patriots. The "Guard" was there until April 18. Capt. Belfour visited Plymouth intending its future occupation, but public feeling was so great he concluded not to risk it.

Raid on Islands in Boston Harbor, May 27, 1775. An all-day fight occurred on Hog and Noddle islands. 70

---

retreated across the Delaware with all the boats he could find. On a cold stormy night he recrossed and surprised the enemy. After a short, sharp fight he captured 1,000 Hessians, 1,200 small arms, 6 cannon and all the standards. James Monroe, afterward President of the U. S. was slightly injured in this attack, and two soldiers received slight wounds.

Waxhau Creek, S. C.—May 29, 1780, Col. Buford's Virginia regiment was mercilessly cut to pieces by Tarleton's British Cavalry. Andrew Jackson, then 13 years old, was made prisoner.

White Plains, Oct. 28, 1776, an attempt of the British to surround the American camp, brought on a battle in which they lost 229 and the Americans 100.

Cannon at the Battery, in New York was successfully removed in 1775, by a military company under Capt. Lamb,

British were killed and wounded, and 4 Americans slightly wounded. The Americans captured 12 swivels, 4 four-pound cannon, some sheep and other supplies.

Benedict Arnold's Expedition against Canada, across the wilderness of Maine, began Sept. 13, 1775. The force consisted of 1,100 men. On Oct. 3 they left the last white settlements at Norridgewock, and were six weeks in reaching the St. Lawrence; and, after terrible privations, Arnold's fierce determination carried it through. Arnold returned with his troops and crossed the St. Lawrence Nov. 13, 1775. Climbing to the plains of Abraham, he demanded the surrender of Quebec unsuccessfully.

Montgomery and Arnold joined forces near Quebec Dec. 3, 1775. The two armies numbered less than 1,000. With this combined force they assaulted Quebec Dec. 31, 1775. The troops were equally divided, and were to approach from opposite directions, and together assault the town. Montgomery was killed and Arnold wounded at the outset. Morgan took command, but after several hours hard fighting surrendered with 400 men. This virtually ended the attempted conquest of Canada.

Norfolk Burned by British troops under Governor Dunmore January 1, 1776. Its population was 6,000. The loss was $1,500,000.

Gen. Howe Arrived at Sandy Hook, New York, July 1, 1776, where he was joined by Admiral Howe, from England. Their united force was 32,000 men in over 400 vessels.

Stony Point Stormed.—July 16, 1776, General Anthony Wayne, with an American detachment, surprised and captured this fort at midnight. Five hundred and forty-three prisoners were

one hundred and the British three hundred men.

Sagg Harbor Raided by Col. R. J. Meigs, with 170 men, May 23, 1777. He crossed from Guilford, Conn., and in 25 hours burned the British shipping and supplies, and captured 90 tories without losing a man.

Burgoyne's Invasion of New York.—June 20, 1777, a splendid British army of 8,000 men with 40 pieces of artillery, left Canada to unite with Howe's army on the Hudson river.

Gen. Prescott Made Prisoner July 20, 1777. He commanded the British in Rhode Island. Lieut. Col. William Barton of Providence, with a few men, captured him at his headquarters. A strong negro butt in his bed-room door with his head. Prescott was afterward exchanged for Gen. Charles Lee. Barton received a sword, a colonel's commission and a

---

---

taken. The Americans lost 15 killed and 83 wounded. The cannon and stores were removed and the post abandoned.

Capture of Gen. Charles Lee, Dec. 13, 1776, at Baskingridge, by a small British party. Lee was repeatedly ordered by Washington to bring up his troops, but he lingered in the rear. Thereafter he ceased to aid the patriots efficiently.

Winter Quarters were selected by both armies Jan. 6, 1777, Washington at Morristown, N. J., and Cornwallis at Brunswick.

Connecticut Raided by Ex-Gov. Tryon of New York, April 25, 1777, at the head of 2,000 British and tories, destroyed 1,600 tents and a large quantity of stores at Danbury. They were bravely resisted by the Americans under Sullivan, Arnold and Wooster. Wooster was killed and Arnold wounded. The Americans lost

grant of land in Vermont from Congress.

Cornwallis Sailed from New York for the South with 18,000 men July 23, 1777. Destination unknown, but it proved to be Philadelphia via Delaware river.

Paoli Massacre.—Sept. 20, 1777, Gen. Wayne attempted to surprise Gen. Howe, but being betrayed by tories, was himself surpised and lost 300 men, the British losing only 7.

Howe's Strategy.—Dec. 4, 1777, he left Philadelphia in an attempt to draw Washington into battle, but he was forewarned by Lydia Darrah, at whose house the Howe arranged his plan, and the scheme failed.

Valley Forge.—Dec. 11, 1777, Washington's army went into Winter quarters here. Many soldiers were barefooted, and but little straw could be obtained for their huts. Their sufferings were extreme. Howe luxuriated in Philadelphia, and Franklin said, "Howe did not take Philadelphia, so much as Philadelphia took Howe."

Wyoming Valley Massacre.—July 3, 1778, Col. John Butler, with 1,000 tories and Indians cruelly murdered the defenceless inhabitants of this Pennsylvania valley, the able-bodied men being in the patriot army.

Suffolk Co., Virginia was raided May 9, 1779, by 2,500 British troops. They captured 3,000 hogsheads of tobacco, burned over 100 vessels, and devastated the region. The damage caused amounted to over $2,000,000.

Tryon Again Raided Connecticut July 5, 1779. He destroyed New Haven, East Haven, Fairfield and Norwalk.

Major Henry Lee, Aug. 19, 1779, with an American force, got into the fort

service, and was made a Major General of the American army.

Col. Williams of Ninety-Six, routed a British Garrison of 500 men at Musgrove's Mills, S. C., Aug. 18, 1780. .

Gen. Marion Surprised the British guard at Nelson's ferry, on the Santee River, Aug. 20, 1780, and recaptured 150 prisoners taken at Camden.

Virginia Raided.—Benedict Arnold and Cornwallis, with a British force, raided Virginia Jan. 2, 1781, destroying $15,000,000 in property and carrying off 30,000 slaves.

New London, Conn., Burned, on Sept 6, 1781, by Benedict Arnold, with a British force. He also captured Fort Griswold and massacred the garrison in cold blood, after its surrender.

Last blood shed in the Revolution, Sept. 1782, at Somes Ferry, where Capt. Wilmot was killed.

---

at Paulus Hook, (now Jersey City) N. J., through mistake of the sentinel, and captured 159 of the garrison.

Wyoming and Cherry Valley Avenged Aug. 29, 1779. Generals Sullivan and Clinton fought the Indians of Western New York at Chemung, now Elmira. They whipped 800 tories and Indians, and burned numerous villages and stores, scattering their inhabitants. The Indians received a terrible retribution.

Washington at Morristown, N. J. in Winter quarters in 1779. The winter was one of the coldest of the century, and the troops suffered more than at Valley Forge.

Baron John DeKalb was mortally wounded at the Battle of Camden, Aug. 16, 1780. He was born in Alsace, June 29, 1721. He had been in the French

NAVAL ENGAGEMENTS, ETC., OF THE REVOLUTION.

The "Gaspee" burnt June 10, 1772.—She was an 8 gun British Schooner, under Lieut. Wm. Duddingston, sent into Narragansett Bay to prevent smuggling. Sixty-four Providence men boarded and burned her at night. Lieut. Duddingston was wounded by the only shot fired. The plot originated with John Brown, a Providence merchant. The British government offered £1,000 for the leader, but could obtain no evidence against him, although the actors were well known in Providence. In 1775, Sir James Wallace. blockaded Narragansett Bay and wrote to the then known leader as follows : "You, Abraham Whipple, on the 10th of June, 1772, burned his Majesty's vessel, the Gaspee, and I will hang you at the yard arm. James Wallace." To which was replied, "Sir, always catch a man before you hang him. Abraham Whipple."

First Naval Victory for Americans was won in May, 1775. A bold company from New Bedford and Dartmouth, Mass. sailed in a small vessel and retook a vessel from the British sloop Falcon ; also 15 prisoners.

Schooner "Margaretta" was captured June 11, 1775, by some young Maine lumbermen headed by Jeremiah O'Brien. Loss of 20 killed and wounded.

Naval Commission.—The first one was issued by Washington to Nicholas Br ghton, of Marblehead, Mass., Sept. 1775, with orders to cruise upon the high seas in the Schooner "Hannah."

United States Navy.—Congress on Oct. 13, 1775, voted to fit out two vessels, one with 10, another with 14 guns, to capture British supply vessels. Within the month two more were authorized, and a

over 200 killed and wounded. The Americans lost 10 killed and 29 wounded.

Naval Battle on Lake Champlain, between Benedict Arnold and Gen. Carleton of Canada, Oct. 11, 1776. This was a desperately contested fight, in which Arnold lost all his vessels and part of his crew. By running his own vessel ashore he escaped with most of his force.

Capture of the Hancock.—A 32 gun vessel under Capt. Manley, was captured June 1, 1777, by the British 44 gun frigate Rainbow· The Boston, of 24 guns, commanded by Capt. Hector McNeil, was in company of the Hancock, but before the action she sailed off. Both were subsequently courtmartialed. Manley was acquitted and McNeill dismissed the service.

Disastrous Naval Engagement, occurred March 7, 1778, between the

"Marine Committee" was appointed to execute the orders.

Capt. Manley, commanding a 4 gun vessel commissioned by Washington, captured a British supply ship in Nov. 1775. There were 2,000 muskets, 100,000 flints, 30,000 round shot, 30 tons musket balls, 11 mortar beds, a 13-inch brass mortar, and other stores, all of which were sent to the American forces besieging Boston.

Esek Hopkins, of Rhode Island, was made commander-in-chief of the Navy Dec. 22, 1775.

Battle in Charleston, S. C., Harbor, June 28, 1776. The fort, now Fort Moultrie, on Sullivan's Island, garrisoned by 400 men under Col. Moultrie, was attacked by the combined fleets of Sir Henry Clinton and Admiral Sir Peter Parker. It was so gallantly defended that the shattered fleet departed, after losing

"Randolph," an American, and the "Yarmouth," an English vessel. The "Randolph's" magazine exploded, killing all her crew of 315 men but 4.

Paul Jones' Great Naval Victory, Sept. 23, 1779, over the Serapis and Scarborough, two English men-of-war in charge of a fleet of merchantmen. Commodore Jones had 5 vessels, one of which, the Bon Homme Richard, of 42 guns, he commanded in person, and fought the Serapis, of 50 guns, at close quarters, lashed side by side. During the dreadful conflict Com. Pearson cried out to Jones, "Has your ship struck," who replied, "I hav'nt begun to fight yet." At last Pearson surrendered. During the fight one of Jones' own vessels, the Alliance, Capt. Landais, fired a broadside into the stern of the Bon Homme Richard. The Scarborough surrendered to the Pallas, Capt. Cottineau. Com. Pearson was knighted for his bravery. Com. Jones remarked, "Well, he deserved it, and if I meet him again I will make a lord of him."

SURRENDERS, CAPTURES, ETC., DURING THE REVOLUTION — ALPHABETICALLY ARRANGED.

Ethan Allen, with a small force, was captured near Montreal October, 1775. He was sent to England in chains and closely confined for three years. Was finally exchanged.

Augusta, Ga., taken June 5, 1781, by Americans under Lee and Pickens.

Boston Besieged, April 20, 1775, by the "Minute Men," who poured in and immediately invested the city. The news of the battle of Lexington swept through New England like wild fire and twenty thousand men were soon in the intrenchments. Israel Putnam, of Con-

goyne surrendered to Gates 5,791 troops, 1,856 prisoners, 42 brass cannon, 4,600 muskets and other supples. The British were to leave the country and not again engage in war against the Americans. Burgoyne was humorously known as "Elbow Room." When entering Boston harbor in 1775, a packet was met coming out. Burgoyne inquired the news. Being told that Boston was surrounded by 10,000 country people, and there were 5,000 regulars in the city, he exclaimed: "What! 10,000 peasants keep 5,000 King's troops shut up! Let us get in and we'll soon find elbow room!" After his surrender he was conveyed to Boston. As he stepped off the Charleston ferry boat an old lady perched upon a shed above the crowd called out in a shrill voice: "Make way! Make way! Give the General *elbow room!"*

Camden Evacuated by the Brit-

---

necticut, left his plow in the field and rode one hundred miles in eighteen hours. John Stark, of New Hampshire, shut down his saw mill and started for Boston in his shirt sleeves.

Baylor's American Light-horse were surprised asleep in barns in New Jersey, the night of August 30, 1778, and were bayoneted without mercy by British troops under General Grey.

Boston Evacuated, March 17, 1776. General Howe, with the whole British army, accompanied by 1,100 loyalists, sailed for Halifax. Several vessels were captured by American privateers. Gen. Washington made a triumphant entry into Boston the day of the evacuation. Congress voted him thanks and a gold medal—the first one in America.

Burgoyne's Surrender.—October 17, 1777, finding it equally impossible to join Howe and to safely retreat, Bur-

ish, May 10, 1781. Nelson's Ferry, Fort Motte and Orangeburg surrendered to the Americans immediately afterward.

Charleston, S. C., was surrendered May 12, 1780, by General Lincoln to a British land and naval force under Gens. Clinton and Cornwallis, after a forty days siege. The city was given up to plunder. The British evacuated Charleston December 14, 1782.

Cherry Valley, N. Y., Massacre. A band of Tories under Walter N. Butler, and Indians under Brant, devastated the valley with fire and scalping-knife on November 10, 1778.

Forty Fort, in Wyoming Valley, was taken July 4, 1778, by the British under Col. John Butler. The entire region was burned and desolated.

Fort Galpin, Ga., surrendered to Americans, May 21, 1781.

Fort Lee evacuated by Gen. Greene,

Nov. 20, 1776, because the British began to cross the Hudson. Then began the famous retreat through New Jersey, in which the British were constantly on the heels of the Americans.

Fort Washington, Harlem Heights, was captured by the British November 16, 1776. They lost 1,000 men. The Americans 100 killed and wounded and 2,500 prisoners, many of whom were confined in loathsome prison ships. The British were aided in taking Fort Washington by a letter from Wm. Demont, a traitor in the American army.

Fort Watson, at Wright's Bluff, S. C., was captured from the British April 26, 1781, by Gens. Marion and Lee.

Long Island Evacuated.—August 29, 1776, Long Island was evacuated by General Washington and his troops at midnight under cover of a heavy fog.

Montreal was Taken November who fled July 19, 1781, on the approach of Lord Rawdon, but turned and offered battle, which Rawdon refused. Greene captured 48 British dragoons.

Pensacola, Florida, captured May 9, 1781, from the British by the Spaniards.

Philadelphia Occupied by the British under General Howe September 26, 1777, and was evacuated by the British June 18, 1778. Under orders from England the entire army, 14,000 strong, started across New Jersey.

Siege of Quebec Raised May 1, 1776, on account of the approach of a British fleet. Upon their retreat the Americans attempted to take Three Rivers, but lost 225 of their little army. They reached Crown Point in June with a British force at their heels.

Rhode Island Evacuated by Gen. Sullivan Aug. 30, 1778. The British then

13, 1775, by General Richard Montgomery, and Colonel Robert Prescott and the garrison, with a large quantity of supplies, were captured.

New Jersey Evacuated, June 30, 1777. General Howe failing to entrap Washington, evacuated New Jersey and crossed to Staten Island with his army.

New York Occupied by the British September 15, 1776. While the British army was crossing to New York at Kip's bay, the Americans under Putnam hurriedly retired along the North river to Harlem Heights. Gen. Howe stopped to lunch with Mrs. Murray, on Murray Hill, who entertained him so delightfully that he failed to observe the Americans marching by within a short distance.—New York was evacuated by the British November 25, 1783. It was their last foothold in the United States.

Ninety-Six was besieged by Greene, ravaged the coast, including Martha's Vineyard, New Bedford and Fair Haven.

Savannah, Georgia, captured Dec. 29, 1778, by British under Lieut. Colonel Campbell, who lost 24 men. The Americans lost half their troops, baggage and guns.

Savannah, Ga., Surrendered, on October 9, 1779, to the Americans under General Lincoln, and the French fleet under Count d'Estaing. It had withstood a siege of several weeks, but succumbed to a bloody assault in which the Americans lost 400 and the French 600. Count Pulaski was also killed.

Savannah, Georgia, evacuated by the British, July 11, 1782.

St. John's, Canada, commanded by Maj. Preston, Nov. 2, 1775, surrendered to 1,000 Americans under Gen. Richard Montgomery. Valuable military stores and 600 prisoners were taken.

Ticonderoga Captured on May 10, 1775, by Ethan Allen and Benedict Arnold, with 83 men. Allen demanded the surrender of the fort "in the name of the Great Jehovah and the Continental Congress." Over 100 cannon were taken, some of which were hauled on ox-sleds to aid in the siege of Boston.

Vincennes, Indiana, was surrendered and recaptured December, 1778. The British Governor at Detroit, with a force of 500 whites and Indians, marched against Vincennes. Approaching the fort they were halted by Captain Helm, who stood in the open gate prepared to discharge a loaded cannon. Governor Hamilton demanded the surrender of the garrison. Captain Helm replied: "No man shall enter here until I know the terms." Hamilton granted the honors of war and drew up his army to receive the garrison. They were astonished the news caused people to weep with delight, and the doorkeeper of Congress actually died from joy. In England Lord North was greatly agitated, and wildly exclaimed: "Oh, God, it is all over!" The House of Commons voted that "whoever advised a continuance of the war was a public enemy." The war was virtually ended.

INCIDENTS OF THE REVOLUTION.

Liberty Bell was imported in 1752 from England. It was cracked shortly after its arrival and was recast in Philadelphia, and the inscription "Proclaim liberty throughout all the land, unto all the inhabitants thereof. Lev. xxv, 10," was then cast thereon. When Henry Clay visited Philadelphia it was again cracked by violent ringing.

Declaration of Independence.— This important document was foreshad-

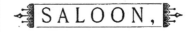
to see Captain Helm and one private march out of the fort, they being the only troops in the place. Colonel Clark now being separated from the East took immediate steps to recapture Vincennes before the British could reinforce it in the spring. Raising a force, on February 5 he began his march across the country, which was flooded, and his men were in frequent danger of drowning. He finally reached and besieged the fort, which surrendered in a few days. Col. Clark thereby saved the Western country to the United States, which would have been lost but for his remarkable energy.

Yorktown, Va., Besieged.—The siege began Sept. 30, 1781, by the combined French and American forces.

Yorktown, Va.—Cornwallis surrendered Yorktown, October 19, 1781, with 12,000 prisoners, 8,000 muskets, 235 cannon and 28 standards. At Philadelphia owed in 1773, at a convention held at Mendon, Worcester county, Mass. Resolutions were passed including statements "that all men have an equal right to life, liberty and property; that all just and lawful government must originate in the free consent of the people; that a right to liberty and property, which are natural means of self-preservation, is absolutely inalienable, and can never lawfully be given up by ourselves, or taken from us by others."

Dr. Adams, a tory, of Arlington, N. Y., who gave offense to the patriots in 1774, was tied and exposed upon "Landlord Fay's sign-post, upon which was fixed a dead catamount."

Patriotic Carpenters, who were employed on soldiers' barracks by Governor Gage, quit work on September 26, 1774, and no other carpenters in Boston would build them. After a long time he got some from New York. Merchants refused the trade of soldiers.

"Yankee Doodle" was introduced or composed in America in 1775. Its origin is obscure. The verses were composed in derision of the Americans. The tune was used in England in the reign of Charles I.

The Mecklenburg Declaration of Independence was issued May 31, 1775, by a convention at Charlotte of the inhabitants of Mecklenburg county, N. C., chiefly Presbyterians of Scotch-Irish descent, in which they asserted that their loyalty to the King was ended.

General Gage, in an insolent proclamation, June 12, 1775, offered pardon to all rebels who would lay down their arms, except Samuel Adams and John Hancock.

Continental Currency amounting

army at Cambridge by Washington, on Jan. 2, 1776.

British Theatre in Boston was supported by the officers and troops during their occupation. On the evening of January 8, 1776, the "Blockade of Boston" was being performed. Washington was caricatured by an actor with a large wig and a long, rusty sword, and was attended by a rustic with a rusty gun. Suddenly a sergeant cried out: "The Yankees are attacking our works on Bunker Hill." It was a false alarm, but Gen. Howe ordered his officers to their duty, and the audience was thoroughly frightened.

Hessian Troops sailed from England to America April, 1776. England had vainly applied to Holland, Russia and Prussia for aid, but finally succeeded in purchasing seventeen thousand Hessians of some of the small German prov-

to $2,000,000, was voted by Congress on June 22, 1775. Paul Revere, of Boston, engraved the notes on copper.

Falmouth, now Portland, Maine, was burned October 16, 1775. Thomas Coulson, a tory, imported sails and rigging in defiance of a law of the "Merchants' Association." It was ordered reshipped. Coulson refused and procured the aid of a British force under Captain Mowatt, which burned the town.

First Traitor.—Dr. Benj. Church, a supposed patriot and a member of the "Provincial Congress," was tried Oct'r 27, 1775, and expelled and imprisoned for communicating with the enemy. Released on parole in May following, he sailed for the West Indies and was never afterward heard from.

First Union Flag, composed of 13 stripes, with the British "union" in the corner, was unfurled over the American

inces at $36 per head. They became notorious for cruelty in America.

Leaden Statue of George III., in Bowling Green, N. Y., pulled down by excited citizens July 9, 1776. It was sent to the family of Gen. Wolcott, at Litchfield, Conn., whose daughters and friends moulded it into 42,000 bullets.

Declaration of Independence was signed August 2, 1776, by 54 delegates. President John Hancock wrote his name first and said to the others: "We must be unanimous; we must all hang together!" "Yes," rejoined Franklin, "or we shall all hang separately."

Capt. Nathan Hale executed as a spy, September 22, 1776. Disguised as a farmer he entered the British camp, but was recognized by a tory. He died bravely, exclaiming: "I only regret I have but one life to give for my country."

Margaret Corbin.—During the capture of Fort Washington, Nov. 16, 1776, the husband of this woman was killed while she was aiding him to serve a gun. She immediately took his place without a murmur and continued with extra exertions.

General Howe issued a proclamation of pardon, November 30, 1776, to all who would lay down their arms. A large number took the oath of allegiance to Great Britain.

Robert Morris spent New Year's Day of 1777 in borrowing funds upon his own credit from his Quaker friends to aid the revolutionary cause. He raised and sent $50,000 to Washington. Without his aid the cause must have failed.

French Aid amounting to 2,000,000 livres was granted by the French government to America in January, 1777. Permission to purchase supplies was also

Lafayette Arrived July 31, 1777, and tendered his services to Gen. Washington without pay. His sympathy for American liberty had been aroused by the Declaration of Independence. He left France in a vessel purchased by himself, and accompanied by Baron De Kalb and other officers, entered the American army. Congress commissioned him a Major-General.

Jane McCrea murdered on July 27, 1777, by two Indians, who were escorting her to her lover, a British officer.

Depreciation of Federal Money, January 1, 1778, was so great that one dollar in gold was equal to seven or eight in paper.

Baron Steuben, of Russia, arrived at Valley Forge in February, 1778. He had served seven years under Frederick the Great. He was appointed Inspector

given. American independence was not, however, recognized.

Spanish Aid.—1,000,000 livres was secretly granted by Spain in 1777.

Bounty Jumpers.—In Feb., 1777, Washington issued an order sentencing to death those who, having enlisted in one regiment and received the bounty allowed by Congress, should be convicted of desertion and enlistment into others, recovering new bounties therefor.

Exchange of Prisoners.—In April, 1777, a correspondence occurred between Washington and General Howe. Early in this year Howe had sent 3,000 into the American lines who were so disabled by confinement and maltreatment in prisonships and crowded buildings that many died on their way home. Washington claimed that it was unjust to return an equal number of able-bodied men, and refused to do it.

General of the army and brought it to a state of great efficiency.

British Revelry at Philadelphia.— May 18, 1778, on the eve of Gen. Howe's departure for England a great peagent was given in his honor under the direction of Major Andre. It was called "The Meschianza," and consisted of a regatta, a tournament, a ball and a banquet.

Gen'l Joseph Reed, in June, 1778, was offered £10,000 by the British peace commissioners if he would use his influence for reconciliation His famous reply was: "I am not worth purchasing, but such as I am the King of England is not rich enough to buy me!"

Mollie Pitcher assisted her husband in loading a cannon at the battle of Monmouth, June 28, 1778, until he was killed. Washington granted her a sergeant's commission and half pay for life.

Gen. Putnam's remarkable escape,

April 26, 1779. Ex-Governor Tryon was raiding Connecticut with 1,500 British and Hessians. A small force of Americans had gathered at Greenwich to resist them, but fled on their approach. The dragoons chased Putnam toward Stamford meeting-house, which stood on the brow of a steep hill. He dashed recklessly down a number of stone steps, which faced the declivity, and escaped. Tryon destroyed some property and returned to Kingbridge, followed by Putnam and his men, who recovered some of the plunder and captured thirty-eight prisoners.

Stratagem of Col. White, near Savannah, Ga., Oct. 1, 1779. During the siege Capt. French, with some regulars, had charge of five British vessels on the Ogeechee, about 25 miles from Savannah. White, with 4 men, kindled numerous fires in the surrounding woods, and

daughter, employed over 2,200 sewing women to work for the American troops in 1780.

Robert Morris, of Philadelphia, in June, 1780, sent 3,000,000 rations to the American army, which was so destitute as to nearly break up its organization.

Major Andre was condemned and executed as a spy October 7, 1780. Great efforts were made for his release, and Washington was at first censured in England for the sentence, but was afterward held justified by the laws of war.

Gen. Marion was gaining frequent victories over the British, and in November, 1780, he invited a British officer, who had come to negotiate an exchange of prisoners, to a dinner of sweet potatoes. "Is this your ordinary fare?" exclaimed the astonished Briton. "Yes," said Marion, "and we are fortunate in having more than usual to-day." Upon

rode about giving orders to an imaginary army. He then demanded and obtained the surrender of the British, who thought they were surrendering to a large force. White started the prisoners off with a guard of 3 men, and raising a force of militia overtook the captives before they had gone far.

Paper Money depreciated in 1780 to $40 for $1 of specie. This was a bill for goods January, 1781: 1 pair boots, $600; 6 yards chintz, @ $150 per yard, $900; 1 skein thread, $10.

Nancy Hart, of Georgia, in 1780, captured 6 tories who had ordered her to set dinner for them. When they were eating she seized one of their stacked guns and threatened to shoot the first one that stirred. Her little son ran for help and all were captured.

Mrs. Sarah Bache, Dr. Franklin's

his return the officer resigned his commission, saying that "Such a people cannot and ought not to be subdued."

Pine Log Cannon.—Col. Washington in 1781, with a few light horse and a cannon made of a pine log, captured Col. Rudgeley and 112 tories in a barn.

Revolt of Penna. Troops. January 1, 1781, at Morristown, N. J. Thirteen hundred unpaid and suffering troops marched to Princeton, accompanied by General Wayne, who had vainly tried to prevent them, and demanded redress of Congress.

Emily Geiger, a messenger from Greene to Marion, was arrested July 19, 1781, by tories, but swallowing Greene's letter, nothing was found on her, and she was released.

Col. Isaac Hayne was hung without trial by Lord Rawdon, Aug. 4, 1781. He had taken the oath of allegiance to

England, conditioned upon the assurance that he would not be required to fight against his countrymen. Being ordered to do so he considered himself absolved from his oath, and raised a patriot force and was captured and executed without mercy.

Manning, one of "Light Horse Harry" Lee's troopers, at the Eutaw Springs fight, September 8, 1781, dashed recklessly after the retreating British and found himself alone amid the enemy. Snatching the sword of an officer and seizing him by the collar, he retreated, keeping the officer between himself and the foe. The frightened Briton began to enumerate his title. "I am Sir Henry Barry, Deputy Adjutant General, Captain in the 52d Regiment, and—" "Enough," said Manning, "You are just the man I was looking for."

French Fleet of 25 vessels, under Count de Grasse, arrived in Chesapeake Bay September 5, 1781, and drove off the English fleet.

French Aid.—In 1781 Colonel John Laurens was sent by Congress to France and negotiated a loan, obtaining also a subsidy of $1,200,000.

Robert Morris helped the army through its summer campaign in 1781 by giving his notes for $1,400,000.

A Tory Parson was ducked at York, Pa., in 1776, by his indignant townsmen because he persisted in praying for George III.

Nathan Coffin was offered, by the commissioners from England to conciliate a peace, in 1778, a position in the royal navy. He said: "Hang me, if you will, to the yard-arm of your ship, but do not ask me to become a traitor to my country."

Citizen Genet, Minister from France, arrived in the United States April 8th, 1793, and began to fit out privateers to prey upon English commerce, and attempted to raise men and supplies for France. His conduct created great excitement, and at the request of the United States France recalled him.

Bunker Hill Monument.—In December 2, 1794, it was a plain wooden pillar 28 feet high on a brick pedestal, erected on the spot where Warren fell. In 1825 it was presented to the "Bunker Hill Monument Association."

Prison-Ship Victims.—In 1808 the remains of 10,000 soldiers, who had perished on British prison-ships in New York harbor during the revolution, were dug out of the sand on the shore and placed in a vault in Brooklyn, N. Y.

Major Andre's Remains were removed from the United States in 1821 and interred in Westminster Abbey.

PEACE MEASURES OF THE REVOLUTION.

Independence of the United States announced by George III. in a speech to the House of Commons, Dec. 5, 1782.

Washington Resigned his commission to Congress December 23, 1783, and refused any compensation save for actual expenses.

Washington's Farewell to his officers December 4, 1783, at Fraunces tavern, corner Broadway and Pearl streets, New York, was a touching scene. His farewell orders to the army were issued November 2d, 1783.

Army Disbanded Nov. 3, 1783.

The entire number of troops furnished by the states was 231,791. The war cost $130,000,000, exclusive of state and private losses.

Independence of the United States acknowledged by Holland, April 9, 1782; by Russia, July, 1783; by Sweden, Feb. 5, 1783; by Denmark, Feb. 25, 1783; and by Spain, March 24, 1783.

Soldiers Discharged by Congress October 18, 1783.

Cessation of Hostilities proclaimed by Washington to the army April 19th, 1783, on the eighth anniversary of Lexington and Concord.

THE TEXAS REVOLUTION.

Revolution in Texas against Mexico was organized in 1832. The following year a Constitutional Convention was held to make laws for the government of the Republic.

Battle of Gonzales, Texas, was fought October 2, 1835, between 600 Texans and 1,000 Mexicans under Santa Anna. The latter was defeated.

A Provisional Government was organized in Texas November 12, 1835, and Henry Smith was selected as Governor.

Independence of Mexico was declared by Texas March 21, 1836.

Fort Alamo Massacre was committed March 6, 1836. Santa Anna, with 4,000 Mexicans, captured Fort Alamo, and massacred the garrison of 172 persons, except one man, a woman and a child. Sixteen hundred Mexicans were slain by the heroic defenders.

Constitution of Texas was adopted March 17, 1836. Slavery was established, and David G. Burnett was chosen first President of the Republic.

Colonel Farmin and 357 Texans, who had surrendered to Santa Anna, were cruelly murdered by his order, on March 27, 1836.

Battle of San Jacinto was fought April 21, 1836, by Texan volunteers under Gen'l Sam Houston and 1,600 regular troops under Santa Anna. The Mexicans were routed in a single charge, losing 630 killed, beside prisoners. The war cry of the Texans was "Remember the Alamo!"

Independence of Texas was secured by treaty with Santa Anna Apr. 26, 1836, who was captured in disguise by General Houston.

General Sam Houston inaugurated President of the Republic of Texas Oct. 22, 1836.

Republic of Texas applied for admission to the United States in 1837. It was not granted.

Santa Fe Expedition. — In 1842 Texas sent a force of 300 poorly equipped men under Gen. McLeod to capture Santa Fe from Mexico, but the Mexicans captured them, marched them 2,000 miles barefoot to the City of Mexico. Thirty-five died, four were shot, and the survivors were imprisoned, but Santa Anna finally liberated them upon his birth-day.

Austin Jones, in 1844, served as the last President of the Republic of Texas.

INDIAN WARS, INCIDENTS, ETC.

Pope Paul III. issued a decree in 1537 declaring native American Indians to be rational beings and entitled to the privileges of Christians.

Juan Ortiz, one of Narvæz's men, met De Soto shortly after he left Tampa Bay. He had been captured by the Indians and lived with them until now—1539. He proved valuable as a guide and interpreter to the expedition. When first captured chief Ucita, condemned him to be burnt at the stake, but his life was saved by the daughter of the chief, who represented to her father that it would be a great honor to the tribe to possess a white captive.

Lord Roanoke was an Indian chief named Manteo, who was baptized Aug. 13, 1587, by an English minister, and created a peer with the above title. This

April 1, 1621. It remained unbroken over 50 years.

Indian Massacre in Virginia.— March 22, 1622, the Indians suddenly fell upon the white settlements near Jamestown and killed 347 persons. A converted Indian gave warning in time to save Jamestown and a few neighboring plantations. The University estate was abandoned, the glass and iron works destroyed, and the colony had no settled peace for 14 years.

Pequod War in 1636-7 resulted in the extermination of the tribe by the Connecticut colony.

Massacre of Indians near New Amsterdam was instigated in 1643 by Governor William Kieft. It caused great trouble to the Dutch colonists afterward. Mrs. Hutchinson, who had re-

is the solitary English peerage created in America.

Pochahontas and Captain John Smith.—In December, 1607, the latter was captured by Indians and condemned to die. His life was spared by the chieftain Powhattan at the solicitation of his favorite daughter, Pochahontas. This circumstance has been discredited of late years, but the evidence is in favor of its truth.

"Welcome Englishmen!" was the salutation of the Indian Samoset, who entered the little settlement at Plymouth March 16, 1621. This was the first Indian the settlers had seen. Samoset had been acquainted with English fishermen on the coast of Maine, and he gave them valuable information.

Indian Fidelity.—A league was formed between the Plymouth colonists and Massasoit, chief of the Wampanoags,

moved into New Netherland, was killed in one of the Indian attacks.

Massacre of Indians by the Dutch near Greenwich, Conn., occurred in February, 1644. 500 perished. The Dutch had 15 wounded.

Second Indian Massacre in Virginia, April 18, 1644. The Indians, instigated by Opechancanaugh, attempted the extermination of the colonists and killed 500 whites, but after a short war were entirely defeated and the aged chief captured and shot by a vindictive guard.

King Philip began war in New England June 24, 1675, by killing some of the citizens of Swansea, who were returning from a meeting. This bloody war ended only with King Phillip's death in 1676.

Penn's Treaty with the Indians was made Nov., 1682, under the old treaty tree at Shakamaxon. A monument has been erected upon the spot.

Indian War broke out in Eastern Maine in 1689.

Major Waldron, who made slaves of 300 Indians in 1676 was hewn in pieces in 1689 by Indians, who captured him at Dover, N. H., by strategy.

Schenectady N. Y., was burned on February 8, 1690, and the inhabitants massacred by the French and Indians during a violent snow storm.

Salmon Falls, N. H., was burned by Indians March 27, 1690.

Haverill, Mass., was, attacked by Indians in March, 1697, and 40 persons were butchered. Mrs. Hannah Dustan, her nurse and a lad were taken captives. The week old babe of Mrs. Dustan was dashed against a tree. Their captors, 12 in number, took them to an island in the Merrimac, and while asleep at night the 3 prisoners arose and with tomahawks quietly dispatched 10 of the

captured their fort and 800 prisoners, who were given to the allies and sold by them into slavery. The remainder of the tribe left their country and went north and were admitted into the confederacy of the Five Nations, thus forming the sixth nation.

Indian League in South Carolina. In 1715 the Yemassees, Catawbas, Cherokees and Creeks, being enraged by gross provocations from persons trading with them, united in hostilities against the whites. After massacreing over 400 persons they were defeated and driven into Florida by the energy of Governor Charles Craven. The damages inflicted by this war amounted to £100,000, besides a debt incurred in bills of credit for nearly an equal sum.

Brunswick, Maine, was burned by the Abenaki Indians in 1722. Thus be-

12, two escaping by flight. Mrs. Dustan carried home a bag containing the scalps of her neighbors. The government of Massachusetts paid them £50.

An Expedition Against Indians friendly to Spain, in 1703, was made by the Governor of South Carolina, who burned villages and took 800 prisoners.

Indian Settlements of East Maine were burned in 1704, and many prisoners taken by Col. Benjamin Church, with a force of 500 men, in retaliation for depredations on the whites.

Massacre in North Carolina in Oct'r, 1711. The Tuscaroras attempted the extermination of the whites and butchered 137 in one night. They were driven off after three days outrages.

"Six Nations."—In 1713 the Tuscaroras renewed the war upon the whites in Carolina. Moore, of South Carolina, with 40 militia and 800 friendly Indians,

gun the third Indian war in New England.

Fryeburg, Maine, was the scene of a severe fight May 8, 1725, between a company of whites under Captain John Lovewell and the Pequawkett Indians under Sachem Paugus. Both leaders were slain and the Indians went further north to live.

Natchez Indians Massacred the French on the present site of Natchez in 1729.

Natchez Indians were exterminated in 1730 by the French in retaliation for the massacre of the Rosalie colonists.

Great Pedestrian Feat.—In 1737 a dispute arose between the Pennsylvania and Delaware Indians. It was to be settled by as much land as could be determined by the walk of a day and a half. Three men were selected for the walk. In consequence of over-exertion one died, another permanently injured his health, but the third, Edward Marshall, walked 86 miles within the time, and lived to be 90 years old.

Queen of the Creek Indians.—In 1749, Mary Musgrove, a half-breed, who claimed to be Queen of the Creeks, attempted to secure for herself the province of Georgia. She had a large number of Indian followers, and intended to use force in accomplishing her design. She was foiled by the vigilance of the whites.

Missionaries Slain.—Nov. 24, 1755, 12 Moravians fell in an Indian attack upon Mahoney, Penn.

Cherokee Indians, with whom the whites had always been at peace, in 1759 became involved in a quarrel, which became a war through the arrogance of Governor Littleton, of South Carolina.

Detroit was occupied Nov. 29, 1760,

soldiers and hunters were under arms, and his plot discovered. Pontiac therefore retired.

Fort at Detroit besieged May 9th, 1763, by Pontiac, he having failed to massacre the garrison on the 7th.

Fort at Sandusky, on Lake Erie, under Ensign Paul, was captured by the Indians May 16th, 1763.

English Garrison massacred at the mouth of the St. Joseph river, May 25th, 1763.

Michillimackinac was taken by massacre, June 2d, 1763, at a signal given during an Indian game of ball.

Presque Isle, now Erie, Pa., under Ensign Christie, was taken by the Indians June 22d, 1763; also Forts Le Boeuf and Venango.

Bloody Bridge, near Detroit, where Pontiac had camped, was attacked, but being betrayed and ambushed the party

by a party of rangers. Pontiac then began a plot for exterminating the whites.

Cherokee War.—In 1760, Col. Montgomery, with 1,200 Scotch Highlanders and some provincial levies, invaded and ravaged the Cherokee country. The Indians gathered in large force, and after a severe battle Montgomery retired to Charleston.

Pontiac's War.—In March, 1763, Ensign Holmes discovered that Pontiac was plotting with the Western Indians to exterminate the English, and a Great Indian Council was held by Pontiac on April 27, 1763, at which it was agreed to begin war by an attack on Detroit.

Indian Plot Revealed.—May 6th, 1763, Major Gladwyn, commanding at Detroit, learned that the Indians intended to attack him the following day, and when Pontiac, with 300 warriors, entered the fort at Detroit, he found that the

was almost wholly destroyed, July 31st, 1763.

Peace was sued for by most of the Indians, who submitted to English authority, October 12th, 1763.

The Ottawas also sued for peace, October 30th, 1763, but the siege of Detroit was continued until the following summer.

Pontiac, Having Failed in his desperate efforts to rouse the Western tribes, gave in his formal submission to Sir William Johnson in 1766.

Bushy Run.—August 5th, 1763, an English force under Boquet, for the relief of Fort Pitt, encountered and defeated the savages at Bushy Run. This victory destroyed the Indian power in the Ohio Valley, and discouraged all the Western tribes, who found that they could not depend on France for aid.

£100 reward was offered for killing Pontiac by General Amherst.

Conestoga, Penna., Massacre.—
A few Indians living at Conestoga, Pa., were massacred by a party of whites from Paxton, near the Susquehanna, on December 14, 1763, and on the 27th of December, some who had escaped the previous massacre were murdered by the Paxton men in the jail where they had been lodged for safety.

Paxton Men at Philadelphia.—
On February 4, 1764, these men undertook an expedition to Philadelphia to seize the remnant of converted Moravian Indians, who had been sent there for safety at the time of the Conestoga massacre. The Indians were sent first to New York and afterward to New Jersey, but refuge in both provinces was denied them. They were returned to Philadelphia, and when the "Paxton Boys" ap-

Gen. Anthony Wayne was appointed commander of the army against the Western Indians, April, 1792.

"Mad Anthony Wayne" won a victory over "Little Turtle" on the Maumee river, O., August 20, 1794. General Wayne, with 2,000 men, so completely routed the Indians that they never rallied from their defeat. Their loss was unknown. Wayne's loss was 139. The fight occurred near a British fort, and the savages were aided by Canadians.

Jacksonville, Ala.—Creek Indians were defeated, Nov. 3, 1813, near Jacksonville, Ala., by the Americans under General Coffee.

Talladega, Ala.—General Jackson defeated the Creeks at Talladega, Ala., November 8, 1813.

Lowndes County, Alabama.—General Claiborne. with one thousand men, defeated the Indians in Lowndes

peared they found that preparations had been made to give them a warm reception, which influenced them to abandon their enterprise.

Indian War in the Carolinas.—
In September, 1776, instigated by British agents, an Indian war raged in the Carolinas for a short time, but was speedily ended by the activity of the patriots.

Chillicothe, O.—An Indian fight occurred near this place October 17, 1790. General Harmer, with a poorly equipped, undisciplined force was defeated. They, however, crippled the enemy by burning their villages.

Defeat of Gen. St. Clair, November 4, 1791. He had succeeded Harmer, and with a force of 2,500 was encamped near the Wabash. He was surprised and routed by "Little Turtle" with a large force of Indians. He lost half his army.

county, Alabama, on the 23d of Nov., 1813.

Tallapoosa River.—General John Floyd, with 900 men, defeated the Indians November 29, 1813, at Antossi, on the Tallapoosa river, upon the spot the savages deemed "holy ground," upon which no white man could live.

Horse-Shoe Bend.—The battle of Horse-Shoe Bend occurred March 27, 1814, between General Jackson and the Creeks, who had assembled in a fortified camp on the Tallapoosa river. Until 600 of their warriors were slain they refused to surrender, then their chief, Weathersford, suddenly appeared in Jackson's tent and exclaimed: "I am in your power; do with me what you please. I have done the white people all the harm I could. My warriors are all gone now, and I can do no more. When there was a chance for success I never asked for peace. There is none now, and I ask it for the remnant of my nation." He was spared and humanely treated by Jackson. This was the death blow to the Creeks.

Tippecanoe.—General Harrison was attacked early in the morning of Nov. 7, 1811, at Tippecanoe, by the Indians led by the Prophet. A severe battle lasting until dawn resulted in the repulse of the savages. who were driven off by successive bayonet charges.

Massacre at Fort Mimms, Ala., August 30, 1813, by Creek Indians under Chief Weatherford. The British had offered $5 for each scalp. 300 persons were slain.

Seminole War.—In 1817, the Creeks and Seminoles, with bad negroes, made frequent raids upon United States Government property, then, after completing their destruction, hid in the Florida

were surprised at dinner, murdered and scalped by Osceola, and a band of warriors. The war thus begun lasted four years.

Creek Indians were subdued in 1836 by Gen. Winfield Scott, and many of them removed beyond the Mississippi.

Battle between the Seminoles and 500 Georgians under Gen. Call, Nov. 25, 1836, was severe but not decisive, and resulted in continued warfare during the whole winter.

Colonel Zachary Taylor, with 600 troops, defeated a large force of indians at Macaco Lake, Dec. 25, 1837.

Cherokee Indians were removed from Georgia to West of the Mississippi in 1838, by Gen. Scott. They felt greatly agrieved at being violently torn from their homes.

Seminole War Ended in 1842 by the complete capture, death and removal

Swamps. Gen. Gaines commanding a post on Flint river, made several unsuccessful efforts to stop them. Gen. Jackson, in the following year, with 1,000 riflemen from Western Tennessee, overran the hostile Indian country and captured St. Marks and Pensacola. He sent the Spanish authorities to Havana, and hung Arbuthnot and Ambrister, two Englishmen, for inciting the savages to depredations.

Second War with the Seminoles. The United States government attempted to remove this tribe, West of the Mississippi, in 1835, which they resisted. Gen. Clinch commanded a post in Florida which was threatened by the Indians. Major Dade, with 117 men, was sent to his relief, but on the way his command was ambushed, and all but one man massacred by the Indians. The same day, Dec. 28, Gen. Thompson and five friends

of the tribe. It had lasted seven years. One thousand five hundred whites had been slain and ten millions of dollars expended.

Massacre of Capt. Gunnison and his party was committed Oct. 26, 1853, by the Utah indians. His was one of 4 expeditions to explore routes for a railway to the Pacific.

Sioux War.—In the fall of 1862 bands of Sioux Indians commanded by Little Crow, being incited by Confederate emissaries, committed horrible massacres upon the whites of Minnesota and Dakota, murdering over 700 of them. Gen. H. H. Sibley routed Little Crow at Wood Lake and took 500 prisoners, of whom 300 were sentenced to death by courtmartial. President Lincoln pardoned all but 39 who were hung at Mankato, Minn., February 28, 1863.

Fort Kearney Massacre.—The Indians massacred one hundred United States troops at Fort Kearney December 21, 1866.

Indian Outrages.—In 1871 the Apache's murdered about 200 whites and destroyed much property.

Indians Massacred by the Settlers.—April 30, 1871, at Camp Grant, Arizona, 100 Apaches, captives, were murdered by settlers who had suffered from their atrocities.

Red Cloud and a delegation of Sioux Indians had a reception June 7, 1872, at Cooper Institute, N. Y.

Lee Family Murdered.—June 9th, 1872, Comanche Indians murdered the Lee family consisting of 7 persons, near Fort Griffin, Texas.

Modoc Massacre.—April 11, 1873, the attempt of the United States government to remove the Modoc indians of Oregon to their reservation culminated

Lieut. james H. Bradley were killed. Gen. Gibbons, Capt. Williams and Lieut. Coolridge, English and Woodruff were wounded.

Chief Joseph and his band of Nez Perces Indians surrendered to General Miles on Snake Creek in the Northwest of the United States, Oct. 5, 1877.

Sitting Bull and his Sioux warriors were offered full pardon for past offenses by a United States Commission under Gen. Terry, Oct. 8, 1877, at Fort Walsh, Canada, upon condition of returning to their reservation and future good behavior. The overtures were scornfully rejected. The British government promised to locate them on Red Deer river in a fine game country, and they remained subjects of Queen Victoria.

Indian Chief Gall, and 150 of Sitting Bull's warriors surrendered to United States troops May 7, 1878.

in the murder of Gen. Canby and Rev. Dr. Thomas, and the almost killing of the Peace Commissioner Col. A. B. Meachem, among the Lava beds, to the strongholds of which they had retreated. A peace council had been arranged with the Indian leader Capt. Jack when the treacherous murders took place. The Indians were finally hunted down and Capt. Jack and others were hung Oct. 3, 1873, at Fort Klamath.

Custer Massacre.—Gen. Custer and 300 soldiers were massacred June 25, 1876, by Sitting Bull and his Sioux warriors on the Little Big Horn river, near Montana territory, in an attempt to capture a large Indian village. They were ambushed by an overwhelming force.

Indians of the Northwest were beaten in a severe battle July 12, 1877, at the mouth of the Cottonwood by a force under Gen. O. O. Howard.

Nez Perces Indians and General Gibbons' Command fought August 9, 1877, on the Big Hole river, M. T. The result was indecisive and loss heavy on both sides. Capt. William Logan and

Cheyenne Indians were beaten in a fight with United States troops Sept. 27, 1878, 250 miles south of Denver, Colorado, but shortly afterward they raided Northwest Kansas, committing depredations and horrid murders.

Sitting Bull returned to United States territory from the British possessions June 7, 1879, with 800 lodges.

Ute Outbreak.—Sept. 29, 1879, a United States Cavalry escort of a wagon train was attacked by the Utes near Milk river. Major Thornburg, commanding, and 11 men were killed, the balance were afterward rescued by Gen. Merritt. The indians also butchered Mr. Meeker, the Indian Agent at White river and carried his wife and daughter into captivity, whence they were restored after suffering horrible outrages.

The Apaches Butchered twenty-one whites at Silver City, New Mexico, Oct. 19, 1879.

Sioux Indians Surrendered Aug. 19 and 20, 1880, to United States troops at Fort Keogh, Montana. They numbered 800.

FRENCH AND INDIAN WARS, INCIDENTS, ETC

Maj. Schuyler, of Albany, N. Y., defeated a French force of 800 men, with an English force and 300 Mohawks in 1691.

Deerfield, Mass. was surprised Mar. 1, 1704, by French and indians who murdered 47 and carried 147 captives to Canada.

Haverhill, Mass. was burned by French and indians Aug. 29, 1708.

Kittanning, an Indian village in Western Pennsylvania, was destroyed by 300 whites Oct. 7, 1756, in revenge for depredations committed.

Expedition Against Louisburg, under the Earl of London, sailed June 20, 1757, from New York. He had a fine army of 10,000 men, but learning at Halifax that the French had a few more vessels than he had, he returned to New York.

defeated by the French, who killed and captured nearly all.

Fort Pitt, so named in honor of Wm. Pitt, was erected by Washington upon the site of Fort Du Quesne, which the French destroyed and evacuated Nov. 25, 1758, upon his approach with a detachment from Gen. Forbes' army. The city of Pittsburg is now located there.

Quebec Captured, Sept. 13, 1759. The English troops under Gen. James Wolfe had besieged the city for two months. Wolfe and part of the army climbed the heights during the night and defeated the French under Gen. Montcalm. Wolfe and Montcalm were both mortally wounded.

Conquest of Canada, by the English, was consummated in 1760 by the surrender of Montreal and all other

British Army, under Abercrombie, in 1758 had twenty-two thousand Regular and twenty-eight thousand Provincial troops, or more than the entire male population of new France.

Lord Howe was killed July 6, 1758, in a skirmish with the French during the advance by Abercrombie on Fort Ticonderoga.

Fort Ticonderoga was assaulted July 8, 1758, by 1,600 English troops under Abercombie. He was defeated with a loss of 2,000, and was retired for Gen. Amherst.

Louisburg Captured July 27, 1758, from the French. The English commanders were Gen. Amherst and Admiral Boscawen. By this victory England gained control of all the country on the Gulf of St. Laurence.

Battle Near Fort Du Quesne.— Sept. 14, 1758, a British detachment was

French ports, to Amherst's army by the Governor.

George Washington, 21 years old, was sent Oct. 31, 1753, across the Alleghanies to the French posts, by Gov. Dinwiddie of Virginia, to demand the release of English traders captured by them, and an explanation of their warlike preparations. He reached the Venango post— distant 400 miles—in 41 days. He had but four or five attendants and had to traverse dense forests through heavy snows. Ioncaire, the commander sent a sealed message to Dinwiddie, but the French officers made no secret of their intention to permanently occupy all that country. On their return, Washington nearly lost his life in crossing the Alleghany upon a raft mid floating ice, and they were shot at by indians, but reached Williamsburg safely.

Washington's Report, Jan. 16, 1754,

induced the Assembly to vote £10,000 toward the defense of the frontiers. A small party was sent to build a fort on the present site of Pittsburg, Penn., and a regiment of 600 men followed, under command of Col. Frye and Lieut Colonel George Washington.

Fort Du Quesne.—April 17, 1754, the French drove off the party who were building the fort, finished it, and named it after the Governor General of Canada.

Washington, with a detachment surprised and defeated a French party under Jummouville (who was killed) at Redstone, May 28, 1754. Frye also died, and Washington in command pushed forward to Great Meadows, and constructed a stockade which they called Fort Necessity.

Fort Necessity capitulates July 4, 1754, to a superior force of French and Indians after nine hours severe fighting.

Gen. Braddock, commissioned Commander-in-Chief, arrived from England with two regiments. At a convention of Colonial Governors at Alexandria, Va., held April 14, 1755, four expeditions were planned—one against Fort Du Quesue, a second against Forts Niagara and Frontenac, a third against Crown Point, and a fourth against Nova Scotia.

Braddock's Campaign.—The expedition against Fort Du Quesne started from Foit Cumberland on Wills Creek June 7, 1755. It consisted of 2,200 men, Washington, by Braddock's invitation, acting as Aid-de-Camp.

Braddock's Defeat.—July 9, 1755, after traversing the rough ridges of the Alleghanies for a few miles, Braddock impatiently pushed forward with 1,300 picked men. When within five miles of Fort Du Quesne he fell into an ambush of 200 French and 600 indians, who poured in a deadly and continuous fire, creating a panic among his British regulars, who were unaccustomed to indian warfare. Braddock had five horses shot under him and was finally killed ; 60 of his officers were killed or disabled, and the entire loss was 700. A flight ensued, which was partially covered by Washington at the head of some provincials. This defeat was the result of Braddock's contempt for the warnings given by Washington and others of the character of indian warfare. Gates, Gage, Morgan and Mercer, all afterward Generals in the Revolution, were engaged in this conflict.

Hendrick, a famous Mohawk Chieftain, in 1755, and Gen. Wm. Johnson, Superintendent of Indian Affairs, were good friends. Seeing some fine clothing which Johnson had received from England, he greatly desired a fine suit. Shortly after, the Chief told Johnson that he had dreamed that he had been presented him with it, which the General accordingly did. Soon after, Johnson told Hendrick that he had dreamed that the Chief had presented him with 500 acres of the finest land in the Mohawk Valley. Hendrick gave the land, but concluded not to dream any more with the Englishman. Hendrick and his warriors were influenced by Johnson to aid the English in the French and indian war. He was slain in the battle of Lake George.

THE WAR OF 1812

War Policy inaugurated in 1811, in the Democratic-Republican party, under the leadership of William H. Crawford, of Georgia, and John C. Calhoun, of South Carolina. Until now this party had been a peace party, but over 900 American vessels having been seized by France and England since 1803, induced a change of sentiment.

"Henry Documents" were bought in March, 1812, of John Henry, for $50,-000, by President Madison, out of the secret service fund of the United States. Henry claimed to have been an agent of the British government, to induce leading New Englanders to renounce the United States government and join the Eastern States to Canada. Great public indignation prevailed and increased the war feeling.

killed. Col. Brooks assumed command. A severe battle followed in which the British received a check. Meantime the fleet bombarded Fort McHenry for 25 hours, which was gallantly defended by Major Armisted. The British re-embarked on the 14th and sailed away on the 15th of September, having undertaken more than they could accomplish. They lost nearly 700 in these engagements.

Bladensburg.—Battle of Bladensburg, 4 miles from Washington, D. C., occurred August 24, 1814, resulted in the defeat of the American militia.

British Expedition to Destroy Scituate, Massachusetts, in 1812, was frightened away by two girls—Rebecca Bates and Sarah Winsor, who, with drum and fife, marched behind a head-

War Declared.—On June 4, 1812, the House of Representatives passed a bill declaring war against England. It passed the Senate June 17th, and two days afterward the President proclaimed war. Henry Dearborn, of Massachusetts, was made the commander-in-chief. Congress voted to raise 25,000 regulars and 50,000 volunteers, and the states were requested to call out 100,000 militia.

ALPHABETICALLY ARRANGED.

Baltimore.—The British attempted to capture Baltimore, on September 12, 1814, with an army and fleet, which was defended by General Samuel Smith and ten thousand militia. The British army, under General Ross, landed at the mouth of the Patapsco, but when about half way to the city encountered the Americans under General Stricker. A skirmish ensued and General Ross was

land. The soldiers, ceasing their work of destruction, hurried to their boats and pulled for the ship, believing an army was after them.

Battle of Chrysler's Field, fought near Williamsburg, Canada, November 11, 1813. It grew out of an attempt to capture Montreal. Neither party was victorious, but the British had the advantage, and the Americans lost 300.

Chippewa.—Battle of Chippewa, fought July 5, 1814, between the American Generals Scott and Ripley, and the British General Riall. The latter were driven to their entrenchments with a loss of over 500. The Americans lost 338 men.

Fort Bowyer (now Morgan), at the entrance of Mobile bay, successfully repulsed a British attack, September 15, 1814.

Frenchtown, near Detroit, Jan'y 22,

1813, was the scene of a battle between a British and Indian force under Gen. Proctor, and the Americans under Gen. Winchester. After a severe fight the Americans capitulated under Proctor's pledge of protection, but he shamefully gave the wounded to the scalping-knife of the savages, and dragged the other prisoners to Detroit, where they were ransomed at an enormous price.

Fort Stephenson, at Lower Sandusky, was bravely defended August 1, 1813, by Major George Crogan, a stripling 21 years old, and 160 men, with one gun, against Proctor with his British and Indian force. Proctor accompanied his demand for surrender with the threat of massacre. Crogan replied that when taken nobody would be left alive to massacre. Proctor was repulsed with a loss of 120, the Americans losing one man.

Lundy's Lane, the hardest of the

American loss was *only 8 killed and 13 wounded.* This was the final land battle of the "War of 1812."

Ogdensburg, N. Y.—A small force of Americans was overpowed here by 800 British, who crossed the St. Lawrence on the ice, Feb. 22, 1813.

Oswego, N. Y., defended by three hundred Americans and a small flotilla, was attacked May 5, 1814, by a British squadron and three thousand men. It was held two days and then yielded to the superior force of the British, after inflicting a loss of 235 against 69. The object of the British was to destroy a large quantity of stores at Oswego Falls, but this fight caused them to abandon the attempt.

Pensecola, Florida, having permitted the British to use its forts and harbor, was stormed by General Jackson, November 7, 1814, who drove out

war, was fought July 25, 1814. It began at sunset and lasted until midnight. The British force was 5,000 strong and the American 4,000. The advantage was with the latter. Generals Brown and Scott were wounded, also the British General Drummond, and Gen. Riall and his staff were captured. The British lost 878 and the Americans 858.

New Orleans.—The Battle of New Orleans was fought on January 8, 1815, between 12,000 British under General Packenham and 6,000 militia under Gen. Jackson. The latter were protected by earth-works, sand-bags and cotton-bales. The British advanced at daylight and were received with heavy cannonading and successive deadly volleys from the American riflemen. Before 9 o'clock the British were defeated, Packenham and 700 of his troops being slain, 1,400 wounded, and 500 taken prisoners. The

he British and compelled the Spanish authorities to surrender the town and sue for mercy.

Plattsburg, N. Y.—On September 11, 1814, a battle was fought here. Gen. Prevost, with 14,000 British, attacked General Macomb's small army, which was posted on the south side of the Saranac, and for 4 days successfully resisted every effort of the enemy to cross. Prevost retreated at night, abandoning his wounded and a large quantity of military stores. His loss was 2,500 men and $2,500,000 in property.

Queenstown Heights.—This battle occurred October 13, 1812. Col. Van Ransselaer, with a force of Americans, crossed the Niagara river at Lewistown, and although he was wounded the British batteries were carried. The British under General Brock attempted their recapture, but were repulsed and General

Brock was killed. They were reinforced, however, from Fort George, and the American militia, refusing to cross the river to aid their comrades, Colonel Van Rensselaer was obliged to surrender after losing 1,100 men altogether.

Sackett's Harbor attacked May 28, 1813, by the British, who were repulsed.

Stonington, Conn. — Sir Thomas Hardy, with a British squadron, bombarded Stonington, Conn., from the 9th to the 12th of August, 1814. It was successfully defended and the fleet driven away.

Thames. — Battle of the Thames, near Detroit, was fought between the American Gen. Harrison and the British commanded by Proctor, October 5, 1813. The latter being a coward fled early in the conflict. Harrison was aided by Col. Richard M. Johnson and the British by Tecumseh and 1,500 Indians. The

ing small, and ignorant of the war, was surprised.

Major Van Horn, having been sent from Detroit by Hull to meet a supply party, was ambushed August 5, 1812, by a British and Indian force. Col. Miller, also sent out August 8, 1812, to relieve the supply party, met and defeated the British and Indians, and was recalled by Hull.

Fort Dearborn, situated on the present site of Chicago, waa evacuated August 16, 1812, and the garrison massacred by a body of treacherous Indians.

Gen. Wm. Henry Harrison was appointed to command the Northwestern army, September 24, 1812.

The Americans captured a British force at St. Regis, Oct. 22, 1812.

Detroit Surrendered, August 16, 1812, by General Hull, to the British under Brock, without a contest, to the

Americans were victors and Tecumseh was slain. This battle ended the Western campaign.

Washington, D. C., captured and burnt, August 24, 1814, by General Ross. The capitol being defenceless, President Madison and his cabinet fled. Mrs. Madison saved a portrait of Washington and the Declaration of Independence. Ross, acting under orders from his superiors, burned the White House and all the public buildings, except the Patent Office, together with many residences. The national loss was about $2,184,282.

SURRENDERS, CAPTURES, ETC., OF THE WAR OF 1812.

Embargo for 90 Days was laid on all British shipping in the United States by Congress, from April 4, 1812.

Mackinaw Surrendered to the British July 17, 1812. The garrison be-

amazement of both friend and foe. The whole country was humiliated at this cowardly surrender. The United States government exchanged 30 prisoners for Hull and then court-martialed him upon charges of treason and cowardice. He was convicted of the last and sentenced to be shot, but was saved by the clemency of President Madison.

Russia offered to act as mediator between the United States and Great Britain in 1813. The former accepted, but the latter refused the offer.

York, now Toronto, Canada, was captured by the Americans under Gen'l Zebulon M. Pike, April 17, 1813. The British were driven out of their fort, but exploded the magazine with a slow match, just as the Americans entered, causing great loss among them. Gen. Pike was mortally wounded, but lived long enough to request that he might die with the captured flag under his head.

Fort Meigs Besieged, May 1, 1813, by British and Indians under Proctor and Tecumseh. Gen'l Harrison, commanding, withstood the siege successfully. He was reinforced by 1,200 Kentuckians under Gen. Clay, who attacked the enemy, but lost a detachment by imprudent pursuit. The siege was renewed, but the desertion of his Indian allies compelled Proctor to withdraw to Malden.

Invasion of Norfolk, Va., was attempted by the British, June 22, 1813. They were successfully repulsed.

Beaver Dam was surrendered by the Americans June 24, 1813. A woman walked 19 miles and informed the British commander of the intended capture of this post by 600 Americans. Securing the aid of the Indians he turned the tables against the Americans, and compelled them to surrender the post.

Newark, Canada, burned Dec. 10, 1813, by Americans. This cost Northern New York dearly. The British captured Fort Niagara, and burned Youngstown, Lewistown, Manchester, Black Rock and Buffalo.

Fort Erie, Canada, surrendered to Generals Scott and Ripley, who crossed the Niagara river at night, July 3, 1814.

Fort Erie was Besieged by the British August 4, 1814. On the 15th the British attempted to carry the works by assault, but failed, losing 962 men. The British again besieged the fort on Sept. 17, 1814, but they were defeated and retired to Fort George. On November of the same year the Americans destroyed and abandoned the fort.

Peace Negotiations began in Aug., 1814, but were fruitless.

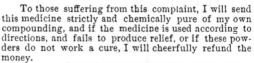
NAVAL ENGAGEMENTS AND EXPLOITS,

From 1800 to 1815.

Guadaloupe.—A naval conflict occurred near Guadaloupe, W. I., between the American frigate Constellation, Com. Truxton, and the French frigate La Vengeance, with 54 guns and 500 men. After fighting five hours the former was victorious, but owing to the fall of her main mast his enemy escaped. The Americans lost 39 men and the French frigate 150.

Naval Engagement between the United States schooner Experiment and a Tripolitan cruiser, August 6, 1801. The latter was captured after 3 hours hard fighting, with a loss of 50 killed and wounded. The Americans lost none.

Com. Preble was sent, in 1803, to humble the Algerine pirates. After bringing the Emperor of Morocco to terms he sailed to Tripoli. In the harbor one of his squadron, the Philadelphia, struck on a rock, and was captured with her crew by the Tripolitans. On the evening of February 15, 1804, Lieut. Decatur, with only 75 men, boarded, recaptured and burnt the frigate Philadelphia in the harbor of Tripoli without losing a man.

Tripoli was bombarded by Com. Preble repeatedly during August, 1804, with great effect.

Fire Ship, laden with powder and iron, sent into Tripoli at night, Sept. 2, 1804, exploded prematurely, annihilating two boats' crews in charge of it. Congress erected a monument to their memory west of the capitol in Washington, D. C.

British Ship Leopard. Capt. Humphries, attacked the United States frigate Chesapeake, Com. Barron, June 22, 1807. The Leopard fired several broadsides into the Chesapeake, killing and wounding 20 of her crew. The Chesapeake, being unprepared for action, fired but one gun. The cause was an attempt to search for alleged deserters, of whom 4 were afterward taken by the Leopard. Com. Barron was tried and suspended for 5 years without pay.

Naval Action between the United States frigate President and the British sloop Little Belt, off the coast of Virginia, May 16, 1811. The latter was preying upon American merchantmen. Being hailed by the President she replied with a cannon shot, and received a broadside in return, killing and wounding 32 of the crew of the Little Belt. She then made answer and sailed for Halifax.

lenges to American vessels to come out and fight. After manœvering awhile the Constitution closed with her antagonist, and at half pistol shot poured in a terrible broadside, killing and wounding 68 of the Guerriere's crew. The American loss was 14 killed and wounded. Dacres surrendered, and the Guerriere, being unmanageble, was blown up.

Fight at Night among the Thousand Islands, occurred July 31, 1812, between two British vessels and two American boats. The latter were successful in taking 6 British schooners at Ogdensburg, to be converted into American vessels of war.

U. S. Brig Nautilus was captured by a British squadron July, 1812.

British Fleet repulsed from Sackett's harbor, on Lake Ontario, July 29, 1812, by the Oneida and an old thirty-two pounder stationed on shore.

Depredations by British Vessels were carried on along the New England coast in June, 1814. Towns and property were destroyed.

Hampton, Va., overpowered by Admiral Cockburn, June 25, 1813, who made his name infamous by permitting atrocities upon the defenceless inhabitants.

Alexandria, Va., being threatened by a British fleet, August 27, 1814, was saved from destruction by a ransom of 21 ships, 16,000 barrels of flour and 1,000 hogsheads of tobacco.

U. S. Frigate Constitution, Captain Isaac Hull, escaped from a British squadron, July 19, 1812, after a 60 hours chase. Captain Hull, commanding the same frigate, captured the British frigate Guerriere, Capt. Dacres, Aug. 19, 1812, off the coast of Massachusetts. Dacres had been boasting and sending chal-

U. S. Frigate Essex captured the British brig Alert, August 13, 1812, off the Banks of Newfoundland, in an eight minutes fight.

Lieut. Elliott surprised and captured two British vessels on Lake Erie, Oct'r 8, 1812, by rowing across the Lake in small boats from Black Rock, near Buffalo.

American Sloop of War Wasp, 18 guns, on 18th October, 1812, captured the British brig Frolic, off the coast of North Carolina, after a severe engagement in which only 4 out of 84 of the Frolic's crew remained unhurt. The same day the Wasp and its prize was captured by the British seventy-four gun ship Poictiers.

U. S. Frigate United States, Com. Decatur, captured the British frigate Macedonia, October 25, 1812, after two hours fighting, in which the British loss was over one hundred and the American loss twelve.

Com. Bainbridge, commanding the United States frigate Constitution, captured the British frigate Java, December 29, 1812, off San Salvador, Brazil, after two hours hard fighting. Every mast was torn from the British ship, and she was reduced to a wreck before she struck, when she was burned at sea by her captors.

Captain Chauncey, on November 8, 1812, with 6 armed schooners, blockaded Kingston harbor on Lake Ontario, disabled the British flagship and captured several merchantmen.

U. S. Sloop Hornet, Captain Lawrence, sunk the British brig Peacock, in a 15 minutes fight at the mouth of the Demarara river, Feb. 24, 1813.

"Don't Give Up the Ship," was the famous utterance of Captain Law-

sels carrying 63 guns. Perry had never been in a naval battle. Barclay was a veteran. Perry, on the ship Lawrence, led the attack on Barclay's flagship Detroit. They fought for 2 hours, when the Lawrence, being disabled, Perry transferred his flag in an open boat to the Niagara. In 15 minutes after he won the victory and returned to the Lawrence to receive the surrender. He then sent his famous despatch to Gen'l Harrison: We have met the enemy and they are ours—2 ships—2 brigs—1 schooner and one sloop."

Lake Ontario.—The American fleet on Lake Ontario, under Com. Chauncey, fought the British fleet commanded by Sir James Leo, September 18, 1813, and forced them to retreat to Kingston.

Com. Rogers, commanding the United States frigate President, captured the British brig Highflyer, by stratagem,

---

T. A. McELWAIN,

281 CHESTNUT STREET, MEADVILLE, PA.

— AGENT FOR —

THE NEW HIGH ARM HOWE SEWING MACHINE for Crawford Co. Pa.

All kinds of Sewing Machines repaired and warranted. Furnishing of parts for old Machines made a specialty

S. J. AFFANTRANGER,

LIVERY AND SALE STABLES.

First-class Carriages and Buggies constantly on hand. Funerals promptly attended to.

1010 WATER STREET, Next door to Budd House,

MEADVILLE, PA.

---

rence, commander of the United States frigate Chesapeake, who was mortally wounded in an engagement with the British ship Shannon, June 1, 1813, off Boston harbor. The Chesapeake was captured after a furious conflict, in which she lost 146 killed and wounded, the Shannon losing 99.

U. S. Brig Argus captured by the British brig Pelican, Aug. 14, 1813, after she had taken 20 merchantmen.

British Brig Boxer, Capt. Blythe, surrendered to United States brig Enterprise, Lieut. Burrows, after a 40 minutes fight, in Portland harbor, Maine, on September 5, 1813. Both commanders were slain and buried side by side at Portland.

Perry's Great Victory over Com. Barclay, on Lake Erie, Sept. 10, 1813. The American fleet was composed of 9 vessels with 54 guns, the British 6 ves-

on September 23, 1813. In her cruise the President had captured eleven merchantmen and three hundred prisoners.

U. S. Frigate Constitution, Capt. Stewart, captured the British brig Picton off the coast of Surinam, February 14, 1814.

"Old Ironsides," otherwise the U. S. frigate Constitution, Com. Stewart, captured two British brigs, the Cyane, of 36 guns, and the Levant, of 18, on Feb. 20, 1814, off cape St. Vincent.

U. S. Frigate Essex, commanded by Captain Porter, was captured in neutral harbor of Valparaiso, Chili, Mar. 28, 1814, by British frigate Phœbe and sloop of war Cherub. After fighting until he lost 154 men Capt. Porter surrendered.

U. S. Vessel Peacock, Capt. Warrington, commander, captured the British ship Epervier and $118,000 in specie April 29, 1814.

U. S. Vessel Wasp captured and burnt British sloop Reindeer on June 28, 1814. The Wasp also captured the Avon, September 1, 1814, but was compelled to relinquish her prize by the Avon's convoy.

McDonough's Victory on Lake Champlain, over Downie's British fleet, September 11, 1814, was complete and glorious. The engagement lasted two hours and forty minutes. Com. Downie and 193 men were killed. American loss 116.

U. S. Vessel Hornet, Capt. Biddle, captured the British ship Penguin, off Brazil, March 23, 1815.

Algiers.—Com. Decatur, commanding an American squadron, sent by the United States against the North African powers, captured two Algerine war vessels and 600 prisoners in the straits of Gibraltar, June 17, 1815. Within a few days he dictated a treaty to the Dey of Algiers, who was compelled to release all his prisoners without ransom, and pledge no more aggressions on American merchantmen. Decatur next proceeded to Tripoli and Algiers, from whom he exacted similar treaties and large sums for past outrages.

Last Naval Engagement with England occurred June 30, 1815. The British vessel Nautilus was captured by the United States vessel Peacock, in the straits of Sunda. Hearing of peace the prize was relinquished the following day. The Americans had captured one thousand six hundred British merchantmen in three years.

The War of 1812 cost the United States $180,000,000.

RELIGIOUS SECTS, INTOLERANCE, ETC.

Inquisition was established in America in 1570 by Philip II.

Mass was First Celebrated in Canada in May, 1615, by four Franciscan friars who came from France to Convert New France, at the solicitation of Champlain.

Pilgrims, were a company who came to America, not to enrich themselves, but for "freedom to worship God" in their own way. They had been driven from England to Holland by persecution, but did not feel at home there. They obtained a grant from the London Company to settle in their territory of Virginia. A portion of John Robinson's congregation in Leyden, Holland, sailed from Delft Haven in 1620, in the Mayflower and Speedwell. The latter being leaky, returned.

Religious Difficulties.—In 1624, John Lyford came from London as a minister for the Colonies. Claiming the right to administer the sacraments by virtue of his Episcopal ordination, he, with his adherents, John Oldham and Conant were expelled, and established themselves at Nantasket.

Reformed Dutch Church.—In 1628, Rev. Jonas Michaelis—the first minister of this church in America—came to New Amsterdam.

Congregationalism was established in Salem, Mass., Aug. 6, 1629, by the organization of a church with the counsel and fellowship of delegates from Plymouth. Samuel Skelton was appointed Pastor, and Mr. Higginson teacher. Two brothers—John and Samuel Browne—malcontents—instituted a Church of England service in opposition, and were accordingly shipped back to England.

Boston.—In 1632 the first church was erected near the present corner of State and Devonshire streets. It had mud walls and a thatched roof.

Ecclesiastical Jurisdiction over all the British Colonies was conferred upon the Bishop of London in 1634.

Roman Catholic Mission among the Indians of Maryland was established by Andrew White in 1634.

Roger Williams was banished from the Colony of Massachusetts Bay in Oct. 1635, because of his persistent opposition to church and magistrates.

Ecclesiastical Synod convened at Newtown, Massachusetts, August 30th, 1637, before which was laid a list of eighty-two "false and heretical opinions," nine "unwholesome expressions" and "divers perversions of Scripture."

Mrs. Anne Hutchinson was banished from Massachusetts Colony and excommunicated from the church in 1637,

Baptists were Banished from Massachusetts, by law, Nov. 13, 1644.

Indian Missionary.—In 1646 Thomas Mayhew, Jr. began preaching with great success to the Indians of Martha's Vineyard.

Petition to the General Court of Massachusetts, in 1646, that other English subjects, besides church members, might have civil rights, was adjudged a contempt, and the petitioners were fined from £10 to £250 each.

Maryland passed an "Act of Toleration" in 1649, giving the rights of liberty to all Christian sects.

Religious Intolerance in Virginia.—In 1649 a Puritan Congregational Church of 118 members was obliged to leave the Colony, and most of them located in Maryland, not far from the present site of Annapolis.

Jesuits.—In 1649 Massachusetts passed

for holding and disseminating hetrodox opinions.

First Baptist Church in America was founded at Providence, R. I., in 1639, by Roger Williams.

Religious Intolerance.—In March, 1643, the Virginia Assembly ordered nonconformists with the Church of England "to depart the Colony with all conveniency." This broke up the labors of the three ministers from Massachusetts Bay, for whom 70 Puritan settler, in Virginia, had sent for in 1642.

For Heretical Opinions, the settlement of Samuel Gorton, at what is now Warwick, R. I., was broken up by military force, sent by Massachusetts magistrates, in 1643.

Second Baptist Church in America was founded in 1644, at Newport, R. I.

a law against them. Death was the penalty for them to return to the State the second time.

Seventh Day Baptist Church was established at Newport, R. I. in 1651.

Baptist Persecutions in Massachusetts.—In 1651 John Clarke, Obadiah Holmes and Mr. Crandall were arrested for disseminating Baptist doctrines. Being tried and fined, Clarke and Crandall's fines were paid, but Holmes, refusing to have his paid, received 30 lashes. Two other sympathizers were fined and imprisoned.

Massachusetts passed a law in 1654 requiring each town to support a minister.

Religious Troubles in Maryland. A battle was fought in Maryland Mar. 25, 1655, between the Catholics and Protestants, for the possession of the government. The former were defeated with heavy loss and the Protestants remained in power.

Quakers Persecuted and Imprisoned in Boston.—In July, 1656, Anne Austin and Mary Fisher, two Quakers from Barbadoes, and eight more from England were tried, imprisoned and shipped back from whence they came. In 1657, two more Quakers named Mary Dyer and Anne Burden arrived in Boston and were imprisoned. The first was sent back to England, the other was taken to Rhode Island by her husband. Mary Clarke, another Quaker went to Boston and was whipped.

Quaker's Again.—In July, 1657, two Quakers arrived in Salem, Mass., and began efforts for the extension of their faith. Others arrived and located in different Colonies. They were arrested, imprisoned, whipped and banished. They were dreaded as the authors of re-cuted. They were repeatedly whipped afterward, and their persecutions never ceased until royal commands forbade it. While the harsh treatment of this sect is inexcusable, yet their repeated interruptions of Divine Service, and the marching of young Quaker women through the streets of Salem, naked, as a testimony against its sinfulness, was an outrage upon strict Puritan feelings.

Religious Intolerance in Virginia.—In 1661 the Church of England was re-established, and non-conformists were subjected to a penalty. Quakers were not tolerated.

Political Privileges in Massachusetts.—In 1662 Charles II demanded the repeal of the law which restricted the privilege of voting and tenure of office to church members; he also demanded the complete toleration of the Church of England.

ligious contention and ruin to all the Colonies.

Death to Quakers was threatened in Massachusetts in Oct. 1658, as a penalty for their return after being once banished.

Two Quakers were Hung in Boston Oct. 27, 1659, named William Robinson and Marmaduke Stephenson, and in March, 1660, Mary Dyer suffered the same fate.

First Indian Church in America was established in 1659 on Martha's Vineyard, by Mr. Mayhew.

Second Indian Church in America was founded in 1660 at Natick, Mass., by John Eliot. This zealous man was instrumental in the conversion of 1,100 who were known as "Praying Indians."

Quaker Execution.—William Leddra, a Quaker, was hung on Boston Common in 1661. He was the last one exe-*Baptist Church in Boston.*—May 28, 1664, Thomas Gouland and eight associates secretly organized the first Baptist Church in Boston. The leaders were fined and banished by the authorities.

Quakers were Outlawed in Rhode Island in 1665 for refusing to bear arms.

Old South Church was organized in Boston in May, 1669, by the separation of a minority from the Boston Church, because of the "Halfway Covenant" by which those who were not church members were admitted as a means of grace. In 1729 the building known as the Old South Church was erected.

New England Synod was held in 1679. The subjects of its deliberations were "public calamities," and how to "promote reformation of manners" in the Colonies.

Roman Catholics were disfranchised in Maryland in 1681.

Oldest Church in New England. In 1681, a church styled the "Old Ship" was built and is still used by the Unitarians of Hingham, Mass., as a place of worship.

Catholics Tolerated.—The General Assembly of Pennsylvania met Dec. 4, 1682. It was called by Penn, and held at Chester. Laws were passed and Roman Catholics tolerated.

Friends First "Yearly Meeting" was held in Philadelphia in July, 1683.

Presbyterian Church.—The first founded in America was at Snow Hill, Md., in 1690, by Francis Mackenzie.

Catholics Disfranchised. — Lord Baltimore, in 1691, was deprived of the administration of Maryland because he was a Papist. The Church of England was established by law and Catholics were disfranchised.

Hugenots were Enfranchised,

Church of England was established by law in Carolina in 1703.

First Presbytery in America was organized at Philadelphia in 1705 by seven Presbyterians.

Saybrook Platform.—In 1708 the churches of Connecticut held a convention at Saybrook and adopted the Westminster and Savoy Confessions, and the 39 articles as a basis of belief.

Presbyterian Church.—The first in New England was built at Derry, N. H. in 1718, by Irishmen. They also manufactured linen by the foot spinning wheel.

"New Born" was the name adopted by a sect of Perfectionists, founded at Oley, Berks Co., Penna., in 1719, by a German named Mathias Bourman.

Dunkers.—This sect came from Germany in 1719 and located at Germantown, Penn. They called themselves "Breth-

and Catholics disfranchised in South Carolina in 1691.

Episcopalians, Baptists and Quakers in Massachusetts were no longer compelled to contribute to the support of the Congregational Church after 1692.

Church of England Ministers were settled in New York in 1693 through the influence of Goveror Fletcher. The act of settlement embraced the counties of Westchester, Queens and Richmond.

Papist Priests were not permitted to enter the Province of New York under penalty of being hung, by a law passed in 1700.

Jesuits and Popish Priests were declared incendiaries and subject to perpetual imprisonment by acts passed by New York and Massachusetts in 1701.

Episcopal Church was first established in New Jersey and Rhode Island in 1702.

ren," and part of their religious ceremony consists in the practice of washing of feet, the kiss of charity, threefold immersion, and annointing the sick with oil. They number about 50,000.

Danish Missionaries to the West Indies.—In 1732 Dober and Nitschman went from Denmark to St. Thomas to impart religious instruction to the negroes. Their joint capital consisted of twelve dollars, yet they established a successful mission.

Jews Emigrate to Georgia.--Forty Jews came to Georgia in 1733 and erected a Synagogue. The prejudice against them was so strong that they would have been driven out but for Oglethorpe. They proved to be good citizens.

Schwenckfelders.—A sect defying the efficacy of the Scriptures settled in Pennsylvania in 1734.

German Lutherans from Salzburg,

Austria, fled from persecution and in 1734 founded Ebenezer, Georgia.

Moravian Colony in Georgia.—In 1735 a settlement of these pious people was made upon the Ogeechee.

John and Charles Wesley came to Georgia Feb. 1736.—In the same ship was a company of Moravians, who, in a dreadful storm on Sunday calmly continued their worship, while the other passengers were in great terror. When the storm ended John Wesley asked one of them, "were you not afraid?" "I thank God, no." "Were not your women and children afraid?" "Our women and children are not afraid to die," was the response.

Moravians, of Georgia, emigrated to Pennsylvania in 1738, to avoid bearing arms against the Spaniards.

Religious Revival.—In 1740 a great revival of religion began in New Eng-

Embury was the first Methodist preacher in America. He was formerly a local preacher in Ireland. In 1766, at the solicitation of a woman named Barbara Heck, he preached to a company of six Irish Methodists in his own house in New York. Later, he was aided by Captain Thomas Webb, who had been ordained by Wesley as a local preacher, and in 1767 they worshipped in a rigging loft in William street.

Shakers.—Nine in number, led by "Mother Ann," arrived from England, August 6, 1774, and settled at Watervleit, near Albany, N. Y.

Free Baptist Church, the first in the world, was organized in 1780 at New Durham, N. H., by Rev. Benjamin Randall.

Universalist Church, the first in America, was organized in 1780, at Gloucester, Mass., by Rev. John Murray.

land under the powerful preaching of George Whitefield.

Universalism was first preached in America by Dr. George de Benneville, in 1741.

Moravians Expelled from New York in 1746, settled in Nazareth and Bethlehem, Penn. David Zeisberger here began his missionary work among the Indians, which he continued for sixty-two years. He composed an Onandaga grammar and dictionary.

United Brethren in Christ was a sect established in Lancaster county, Pa., by Otterbein, in 1760.

Sandemanjans.—In 1764 Rev. Robert Sandeman, established a religious colony at Danbury, Conn. They had separated from the Scotch Presbyterian church in Dundee, Scotland, under the name of Glassites.

Methodist Congregation. —Philip

First American Episcopal Bishop was Rev. Samuel Seabury, D. D., of Connecticut, who was ordained at Aberdeen, Scotland, Nov. 14, 1784.

Methodist Episcopal Church was first organized at Baltimore, Md., Dec'r 24, 1784. Rev. Thomas Cooke, L. L. D., who had been ordained by Wesley, and Frances Asbury, were elected Bishops.

First Universalist Convention in the United States was held in 1785.

Roman Catholic Heirarchy was first established in the United States by the appointment of John Carroll as Vicar General, in 1786.

Sunday School was first organized in Hanover county, Va., in 1786, by Bishop Frances Asbury, of the M. E. Church.

"*The Society for Propagating* the Gospel among the Indians and others in North America," was founded in Boston in 1787.

First Roman Catholic Bishop in the United States, Vicar General John Carroll, was appointed Bishop of Baltimore in 1789.

Swedenborgian Churches were organized in 1794 by Rev. William Hill, from England.

"Disciples," — otherwise known as "Christians," "Church of Christ," and "Campbellites." They were organized in 1809 by Thomas and his son Alexander Campbell, who were originally Presbyterians, but adopted "immersion" as the only baptism. They claimed that the Bible was their only creed.

Sunday Schools.—In 1809, changes were made by which volunteers were substituted for paid teachers, and instead of instructions being confined to the low and ignorant, it began to embrace all classes for continued Bible study. At a

the Mormons settled in Kirtland, O. in Jan. 1831, where they lived seven years.

Brigham Young joined the Mormons in 1832.

Mormons having been expelled from Missouri, settled at Nauvoo, Ills. in 1839, and here Joseph Smith announced his pretended revelation instituting polygamy.

Utah Settled by Mormons.—Brigham Young, with 16,000 Mormons entered Deseret, now Utah, in Jan. 1847, and founded Salt Lake City. They were two years crossing the plains.

Oneida Community was founded in 1847, near Syracuse, N. Y., by John H. Noyes.

Young Men's Christian Association.—The first in America was organized at Montreal in 1851.

Roman Catholic Church held its first plenary council in the United States

later day similar changes were made in England.

Bible Society.—The first in America was organized at Philadelphia in 1808.

Orangemen.—In 1829, "The Loyal Orange Institution" of Protestant Irishmen was introduced into British America.

Mormonism.—April 6, 1830, Joseph Smith organized the first Mormon church at Manchester, N. Y. He claimed to have found the Book of Mormon, an appendix to the New Testament, and the Urim and Thummim by which he could translate the unknown tongue in which it was written into English. It has since been proven to be an unpublished manuscript written by Solomon Spaulding, containing a pretended history of America from the dispersion of the nations at the tower of Babel. Under Joe Smith,

at Baltimore, Md., in May, 1852. Archbishop F. P. Kenrick presided.

Great Revival of 1857-8.—Sept. 23, 1857, a noon-prayer meeting for business men was established in the old Fulton St. Church, New York, by J. C. Lanphier, the City Missionary of the church. After praying alone for half-an-hour five persons came in. A week afterward twenty were present. In two weeks forty came. A daily noon-meeting was then appointed, which has never been discontinued. About the same time a similar meeting was established in Plymouth Church, Brooklyn, and shortly they were held in numerous churches. A powerful revival spread all over the land, resulting in the conversion of thousands.

Catholics held immense meetings Jan. 6, 1871, in Boston, Mass. and Cleve-

and, Ohio, to protest against the Italian occupation of Rome.

Mormons.—Chief Justice McKean of Utah decided against Mormons serving as grand jurors in federal Courts Sept. 27, 1871.

Brigham Young was arrested Oct. 2, 1871, by the United States Marshal for Mormon proclivities. He secured his release and fled from the authorities. He returned to Salt Lake City Jan. 2, 1872, and surrendered to the officers of the law under an indictment for the murder of Richard Yates.

Mayor Daniel H. Wells, of Salt Lake City, a Mormon Bishop, was arrested Oct. 3, 1871, for Mormon proclivities.

"Tools of the Devil."—The Mormons held a special conference Oct. 5, 1871, in their Tabernacle at Salt Lake

organized under Bishop George D. Cummings in 1873.

Archbishop McCloskey was made a Cardinal at Rome March 15, 1874.

Execution of John D. Lee, Mormon bishop, Mar. 23, 1877, convicted of being the leader in the Mountain Meadows massacre in 1857. This massacre was one of the most attrocious fanatical religious murders of the last thousand years. One hundred and fifty men, women and children were assaulted, and all, save seventeen infant children, were murdered. Lee was shot to death by a file of United States soldiers, on the same spot where the massacre was committed. Lee's allies were Mormons and Indians. It is generally believed that Brigham Young was the instigator of this bloody deed.

Anti-Mormonism—In 1879 the pub-

City, and denounced the Federal Authorities as "tools of the devil."

Mormons Charged with Murder. Oct. 28, 1871, Mayor D. H. Wells, Ex-Attorney-General Hoza Stout and William Kimball were arrested on a charge of murder in Salt Lake City.

Archbishop Bailey was installed as primate of the Roman Catholic Church in the United States, at Baltimore, Oct. 13, 1872.

Mennonites.—Aug. 16, 1873, a band of 100 Mennonites from Russia arrived in New York. They are Baptist-Quakers, and were compelled by the Government to choose between giving up their religion or their homes. They chose the latter and became settlers in the Western States of America.

Reformed Episcopal Church was

lic sentiment against Polygamy began to be strongly manifested. President Hayes issued a message against it, and Elder John Taylor instructed the Mormons to obey "God's law," no matter what the United States Government might do about it.

Salvation Army.—March 10, 1880, an advance guard of 8 members arrived in New York. The army was organized by a minister in London in 1865, who held open-air meetings for the purpose of converting those who attended no place of public worship.

Mormon Delegate to Congress was denied a certificate of election Jan. 8, 1881, by Gov. Murray, because he had never been naturalized and was living in polygamy. A. G. Campbell, the Gentile nominee received the certificate, although he had the fewest votes.

TERRITORIAL ACQUISITION AND GOVERNMENT.

Massachusetts purchased the Province of Maine from the heirs of Gorges, in 1677 for £1,250. This defeated the King's plan to buy it himself in order to get it out of the jurisdiction of Massachusetts.

New Hampshire was made a royal province in 1679, and John Cutts appointed Governor.

New York and New Jersey were annexed to New England in 1688, with Sir Edmund Andross Governor of the whole territory. The present boundary line between New York and Connecticut was now located.

Carolina was Sold to the English Government in 1729 by the proprietors of the province, for £8,000. North and South Carolina were made separate provinces.

Georgia became a Royal Province in the Miami region, because the United States Courts had not yet been set up under the ordinance for governing the Northwest Territory. They were superceded in August by the United States Courts.

"Maxwell Code" was the title given to a body of laws adopted in 1795 by the Governor and judges of the Northwest Territory, for its government, because they were printed at Cincinnati, Ohio, by William Maxwell.

General Assembly of the Northwest Territory first met at Cincinnati, O. Feb. 4, 1799. W. H. Harrison was elected to Congress. A law was passed forbidding the sale of whiskey to Indians.

Louisiana Purchased by United States from Napoleon I. for $15,000,000, April 30, 1803. It extended from the Mississippi river to the Rocky Mountains,

1752. The restrictions upon rum and slaves were removed.

Paris Treaty of Peace.—This treaty was made February 10th, 1763, by which England received certain West India islands, Florida, and Louisiana as far as the Mississippi River, except the island of New Orleans, Acadia and Canada. France retained two small fishing islands on the banks of Newfoundland, and got Guadaloupe and Martinique in the West Indies. Spain received New Orleans, all of Louisiana West of the Mississippi, and Havana, Cuba.

First Governor of "Northwest Ter.Territory."—Arthur St. Clair was elected to this post by Congress, Oct. 5, 1787. He was instructed to treat with the Indians and adjust the relations between them and the Government.

Irregular Courts were Organized in May, 1788, by the Emigrants in and from the British possessions to the Gulf of Mexico. It contained 899,579 square miles and more than doubled the area of the United States. Napoleon exclaimed, "that this accession of territory to America strengthens forever the power of the United States. I have just given England a maritime rival that will, sooner or later, humble her pride."

Florida and adjacent islands were ceded by Spain to United States Feb. 22, 1819, for $5,000,000, and the relinquishment of Texas.

Texas was annexed to the United States March 1, 1845, and the Legislature of Texas ratified its annexation to the United States July 4, 1845.

New Mexico was annexed to the U. S. Aug. 22, 1846.

Gen. John C. Fremont was appointed Governor of California by Com. Stockton, in January, 1847.

Gen. Kearney proclaimed himself Governor of California, March 1, 1847. Col. Fremont refused obedience and was courtmartialed for it at Washington.

Gadsden Purchase. — A dispute arose about the boundary line between New Mexico and Chihuahua in 1853 The difficulty was adjusted by the purchase from Mexico of the disputed territory, which finally became the territory of Arizona.

Vancouver's Island was taken possession of July 9, 1859, by Gen. Harney, in behalf of the United States.

Alaska.—The treaty for the purchase of this territory from Russia was ratified by the United States Senate May 20, 1867. It contains 500,000 square miles and 60,000 inhabitants. The price paid was $7,200,000.

Black Hills were ceded to the United States by the Indian owners Sept. 20th, 1876.

COLONIAL GRANTS AND CHARTERS.

Sir Walter Raleigh obtained a patent from Queen Elizabeth for territory in America in March, 1582. On the 7th of March, 1589, he ceded part of his rights, under his Virginia patent, to a company of London merchants.

London and Plymouth Companies were chartered by King James I. of England in 1606. The first was authorized to colonize between the 31st and 38th degrees North latitude, and the latter between the 40th and 45th, extending Westward to the Pacific. No colony had the right to self-government granted, and the Church of England was the only form of religion tolerated.

Port Royal Abandoned.--DeMonts patent having been annulled, the Colonists all returned to France, in 1607.

New Charter for Jamestown.—In May, 1609, the London Company obtained a new charter for this Colony. The local council, which was appointed by the King, was abolished, and power was given to the stockholders to elect their own. Lord Delaware was appointed Governor for life, with almost absolute power. Nine vessels and 500 Colonists were sent out. Sheep and swine were also sent.

Third Charter for Virginia was granted March 12, 1612. It empowered the stockholders to manage the affairs of the Colonist instead of the council, and the limits of the Colony were extended 300 leagues from the main land to include the Bermudas.

Jesuits, in 1612, obtained from the French King a grant of all North America, from the St. Laurence to Florida.

Charles Calvert, a Roman Catholic and afterward Lord Baltimore, obtained a grant from King James of Avalon, on the S. E. Coast of Newfoundland where, in 1621, he began a little Colony called Ferryland.

Maryland.—June 20, 1622, Lord Baltimore received a grant of lands West of the Delaware river which he named Maryland in honor Queen Henrietta Maria.

Patroons.—In 1629, the Dutch West India Company issued a decree called the "Charter of Liberties" authorizing any one to purchase large tracts of land in New Netherland, and upon forming a Colony of 50 persons within the same, to govern it. This was the foundation of the feudal tenure which existed so long in New York.

"Providence Plantations."—Under this title Roger Williams received a royal charter March 14, 1644. The Pro-

vidence and Rhode Island Colonies were separate before, were now united by this charter. The government was a pure Democracy.

Virginia was assigned, in 1673, by Charles II. to Lords Culpepper and Arlington for 31 years. The citizens were troubled by this injustice.

Pennsylvania granted to William Penn, Mar. 4, 1681, by Charles II. in satisfaction of a debt of £16,000 due him as heir of his father Sir William Penn, from the English Government. Penn appointed Capt. William Markham Governor.

East Jersey. — William Penn was one of twelve persons who, in 1682, bought East Jersey, which was sold to pay the debts of Sir George Cartaret, deceased. Penn thus became one of the owners of the whole province of New Jersey.

Delaware was deeded by the Duke of York to William Penn in 1682, who requested it that Pennsylvania might have access to the Atlantic ocean.

Virginia again became a royal province in 1684, by the King's revocation of the grants made to Lords Arlington and Culpepper.

Massachusetts' charter was revoked by the King in 1684.

New England Charters were all annulled in 1686 by the King, who appointed Sir Edmond Andross governor of the entire territory.

"Charter of Liberties" was the title of a new constitution adopted for Pennsylvania in 1701. The qualification for a voter was 50 acres unincumbered land, or personal property worth £50. A new charter was also given to Philadelphia.

Georgia. — The thirteenth colony was founded by James Edward Oglethorpe and other philanthropists. They obtained a charter June 9, 1732, for the territory between the Savannah and Altamaha rivers for 21 years, to be held in trust for the poor. Compensation or land for themselves was forbidden.

GOLD, SILVER, PETROLEUM, Etc —When Discovered.

Gold was Discovered Jan'y, 1494. Alonzo de Ojida, with an exploring company sent out by Columbus, returned from the interior of the country with specimens of gold ore and dust. Gold was discovered in the coast range of Venezula, S. A., in 1540.

Copper was mined in Cuba in 1515.

Mexican Silver Mines of Zacatecas were discovered in 1532.

Silver. — The Potosi Silver Mines in Bolivia were discovered accidentally in 1545 by an Indian named Hualpa, who, in chasing wild goats, pulled a bush up by the roots and uncovered the ore. The mountain containing the mines rises, cone-like, 16,000 feet above the sea. Five thousand mines have been opened in this cone, and in two hundred and forty-two years after discovery $1,000,000,000 was taken out.

Quicksilver Mines of Huancavelica, Peru, were discovered in 1564. They yielded largely up to the end of the last century. The mines at Santa Barbara, Peru, began to be worked in 1566 by Spaniards. Native Peruvians had worked them before the Spaniards came.

Gold was discovered in Brazil in 1699.

Dubuque Lead Mines were discovered in 1700 by Le Sueur, but were not worked until 1788, and then by Julien Dubuque.

Diamonds were discovered in Brazil in 1710.

Lead Mines in Missouri were discovered and worked by Renault and La Motte in 1720.

The Braganza Diamond, weighing 1680 carats, was found in Brazil in 1741. It is now owned by Portugal.

Anthracite Coal was first used in 1768 by two Pennsylvania blacksmiths named Gore. Because it was difficult to kindle it was only used in forges.

Lead Mining in Iowa was begun in 1788 by Julien Dubuque, a French Canadian, who settled upon the site of the present town of Dubuque.

Anthracite Coal was discovered in Carbon county, Pennsylvania, by Philip Ginter, while hunting, in 1791. The same coal was sold in 1812 in Philadelphia. The purchaser, a manufacturer, tried for half a day to make it burn. In disgust he shut the furnace door and went to dinner. Returning he was amazed to find the furnace door red hot and the

Anthracite Coal was first burned in iron furnaces, with the hot air blast applied, by Dr. Geessenheimer, in New York, in 1833.

Copper Fever.—In 1845 the extent of the Lake Superior copper mines became known. A great excitement ensued. Land was sold at enormous prices, fictious companies were organized, and for two years speculation was rampant. The bubble burst in 1847.

"Kerosene" was the name given in 1846 to Oil, which was made from coal, by Abraham Gesner.

Quicksilver Mines were worked in Santa Clara County, Cal., in 1846, by the Mexicans.

California Gold Fever.—Feb. 9th, 1848, a little daughter of a man named Marshall, overseer of John A. Sutter's mill, on the Sacramento river, picked up a piece of gold in the race. This created

coal burning finely. This revealed the secret.

Mining in Missouri.—Moses Austin, of Virginia, sunk the first shaft and built a furnace and shot tower in Missouri in 1798.

Stone Coal was first used for fuel in a fire place in 1808 by Judge Fell, of Wilkesbarre, and Obadiah Gore, of Wyoming, Valley, Pa.

Petroleum was discovered in Ohio in 1820, and it was struck on the Alleghany river, above Pittsburg, in 1845. In both instances the parties were boring for salt. It had before been gathered in limited quantities from the surface of streams, and used by the Indians for medicinal purposes, under the name of "Seneca Oil."

Tin was First Discovered in America in 1829, at Goshen, Conn., by Prof. Hitchcock, of Amherst College.

an excitement which caused an immense emigration to California, and the permanent prosperity of that country.

Valuable Diamond weighing 23.7 carats was found in 1856, at Manchester, Virginia.

Gold Discovered in Western Kansas in 1858, caused great emigration to that country. Washington and Oregon territories also had their gold excitements this year.

Pike's Peak was discovered to be rich in gold deposits May 6, 1859. Great excitement and emigration followed.

Comstock Lode.—This great Nevada Silver mine was discovered in 1859 by James Fennimore and Henry Comstock. So little did they know the value of their "find," that Fennimore sold his interest to Comstock for a mule and a pinch of gold dust. Comstock afterward sold the whole for a moderate sum. By 1866,

$70,000,000 had been taken from this lode.

Oil Fever.—Col. Drake, of New Haven, Conn., bored the first oil well near Titusville, Penn., in 1859. It produced 160 barrels per day·from a depth of 71 feet.. Other wells were bored, some of which flowed from 1,000 to 3,000 barrels per day. In 1865–7 immense fortunes were made and lost. Refineries were built—Railroad tank cars constructed—pipe lines laid, and the business soon grew to enormous proportions.

Phosphate Mining Company was organized in 1867, upon the discovery of extensive beds of bone by Professor S. F. Holmes, in South Carolina.

Black Hills Gold Excitement.—In August, 1875, an immense immigration began to this section. As the Indians owned the country, United States troops were sent to drive out the gold hunters. The Indians finally ceded their rights to the United States, since which the mineral resources have been developed.

PRINTING PRESSES, PUBLICATIONS, ETC.

Printing in Mexico.—In 1545 the first book book printed in America was a school manual entitled "The Spiritual Ladder," published under the direction of the Viceroy. Ninety-three other books were printed in Mexico during this century, and seven in Peru.

"Sin and Danger of Self-Love," was the title of the first American sermon ever printed. It was preached in Plymouth December 12, 1621.

Printing Press at Cambridge, Mass., was set up by Stephen Daye, in March, 1639, who received 300 acres of land from Massachusetts because he was the first printer in the North American Colonies.

The Bay Psalm Book was prepared by Eliot and others, and published at Cambridge, Mass., in 1640. In 1876 a copy of it sold for $1,025.

Concordance of the Bible.— In 1658 Rev. Saml. Newman, of Rehoboth, Mass., published a massive concordance of the Bible.

Indian New Testament.—In 1661 John Eliot published his translation of the New Testament into the Indian language. Saviour is written on its title page "Nuppoquohwussuaeneumun."

Licensers of the Press were appointed by the Legislature of Massachusetts in 1662.

Eliot's Indian Bible.—In 1663 John Eliot published his translation of the Old Testament into the Indian tongue, at Cambridge, Mass. This, with the New Testament published in 1661, completed his Bible.

Printing Presses in Virginia were forbidden by the English government in 1681, and no printing was done in the province till 1789.

In Pennsylvania a printing press was set up in 1686, at Shakamaxon, by William Bradford, whose first publication was an Almanac.

"News Placard" issued in Boston in 1689. It was the pioneer of newspapers.

Newspaper.—In 1690 Benjamin Harris published the first number of a newspaper called "Public Occurrences, both Foreign and Domestic," in Boston, Massachusetts.

In New York the first printing-house was established by William Bradford, of Philadelphia, in 1693 He was allowed £40 a year by the government for undertaking the enterprise.

Emigration Pamphlet was issued in Boston in 1699, setting forth inducements for New Englanders to settle in Panama.

" *Boston News Letter* " was established April 24, 1704. It was in existence forty years before it had 300 subscribers.

Printing in Louisiana was introduced by the French in 1704.

In Connecticut Thomas Short set up the first printing press at New London in 1709.

The American Weekly Mercury was issued at Philadelphia December 22, 1719, by Andrew Bradford and John Capson.

" *The Boston Gazette* " was the second newspaper in the Colonies. It was published December 21, 1719, by James Franklin, a brother of Benjamin.

The New England Courant was established in Boston in 1721 by James

The Virginia Gazette was issued at Williamsburg, Virginia, in 1736.

Benjamin Franklin, in 1741, published the first literary magazine in America. It was the "General Magazine and Historical Chronicle," and lasted only 6 months.

Luther's German Bible was reprinted in 1743 by Christopher Sower, the type-founder, at Germantown, Penna.

" *Directions How to Dress any Common Dish* " was the title of the first American Cook Book, published in Boston in 1747.

City Directory.—The first in America was published in Baltimore in 1752.

Bible.—In 1752 Kneeland and Green of Boston, published the first in English in America.

German Printing Press was set up at Philadelphia in 1755 by the London Society of Religious Knowledge.

Franklin. He was imprisoned because of the free criticism permitted in its columns, It lasted about six years. Benjamin Franklin set type and wrote some articles for it.

The New York Gazette was established by William Bradford in New York in 1725.

First Newspaper in Maryland was issued at Annapolis by William Parks in 1728.

The Barbadoes Gazette was issued at Barbadoes in 1731 by Samuel Keimer.

The South Carolina Gazette was issued at Charleston 1732.

The Rhode Island Gazette was issued in Rhode Island in 1732 by James Franklin.

" *Poor Richard's Almanac* " was issued in 1732 by Benjamin Franklin. Its wise sayings became very popular.

Printing in Texas, in 1760, was begun by the Spaniards.

The Connecticut Courant is the oldest newspaper of continuous publication in the country. Thomas Green established it at Hartford, Conn., in 1764.

First Daily Paper in America was established in Philadelphia in 1784. It was called "Poulson's Daily General Advertiser."

First Printing Press west of the Alleghanies was set up in Kentucky in 1786.

The Federalist was a serious of papers published in 1788 by Hamilton, Jay and Madison, over the signature of *Publius*, for the purpose of explaining and defending the new Constitution.

" *The Centinel of the Northwest Territory* " was the title of a newspaper issued at Cincinnati, Ohio, by William Maxwell, Nov. 9, 1793.

Medical Journal.—The first in the United States was issued in New York in 1797.

"The Gazette" was the title of a paper issued by the students of Dartmouth College, N. H., in 1800.

In St. Louis, in 1808, Jacob Hinkle set up the first printing press ever used beyond the Mississippi river.

In Mississippi.—The first printing press was set up in 1809.

Printing Press was first introduced in Michigan in 1810.

The American Farmer, an agricultural newspaper, was first established in 1818, by John S. Skinner at Baltimore, Md.

Anti-Slavery Periodical, issued by Benjamin Lundy, in 1821. He called it the "Genius of Universal Emancipation," and was one of the pioneers in publishing anti-slavery periodicals and lecturing against slavery.

Printing Press.—Richard M. Hoe made the first cylinder press in America in 1830.

William Lloyd Garrison began to publish the "Liberator," an Abolition paper, in Boston, in 1831.

"The Sun," the first penny newspaper in America, was issued in New York Sept. 3, 1833. It was sold by newsboys, and soon had a circulation of 60,000.

Merchants' Magazine was established July, 1839, by Freeman Hunt. It became an important and influential journal.

New York Tribune founded April 10, 1841, by Horace Greeley. It started with 500 subscribers.

Bloomerism.—January 1, 1849, Mrs. Amelia Bloomer, of Seneca Falls, N. Y., established the "Lilly," a newspaper advocating women's rights and the adoption of a peculiar female costume devised and worn by Gerritt Smith's daughter, afterward known as the "Bloomer" dress.

"Illustrated News," published by P. T. Barnum and Beach Bros., January 1, 1853. It had a sale of 150,000 copies the first issue.

Associated Press organized in New York in 1855 by the daily papers, for gathering and distributing news more expeditiously.

The Graphic Company was organized in New York in 1873, issuing a daily paper illustrated by the process of photo-lithography, by which engravings can be reproduced upon stone in half an hour.

TREATIES WITH FOREIGN POWERS AND INDIANS.

Oglethorpe and the Indians.—By Oglethorpe's invitation a conference was held in Georgia May 29, 1733, with the chiefs of the neighboring tribes. Mutual presents were made and friendly relations established. The fame of Oglethorpe's humanity spread far and wide among the Red men.

Peace with the Indian tribes dwelling between the Ohio and the great lakes was made in 1758.

France acknowledged the independence of the United States in a treaty of alliance and commerce, which was concluded between the two nations Feb. 6, 1778.

Commissioners of Peace.—Sept., 1782, Congress appointed John Adams, John Jay, Dr. Franklin, and Henry Laurens to treat with Mr. Oswald, who had full power from the British government to negotiate for peace.

Holland.—Treaty of amity and commerce was concluded between the United States and Holland October 7, 1782.

England. — Preliminary treaty of peace between England and the United States signed at Paris Nov. 30, 1782.

Treaty of Peace of a definite character was signed between United States and Great Britain Sept'r 3, 1783, with Canada and Nova Scotia as Northern and Eastern, and the Mississippi river as Western boundaries.

First Minister to England.—John Adams was sent, Feb., 1785, to try to adjust the standing difficulties in connection with the fulfillment of the treaty of 1783.

Jay's Treaty with Great Britain, Nov. 19, 1794. This was a treaty of commerce and navigation, rendered necessary by alleged violations of the treaty of 1783. It caused great indignation, as

ries between Florida and the United States, and opened the navigation of the Mississippi to both powers.

Treaty with France was temporarily made September 30, 1800.

Tripoli. — A treaty of peace with Tripoli was concluded June 3, 1805, by which prisoners were exchanged and $60,000 paid to the Dey for an excess of 200 held by him. It provided that no further ransom should ever be exacted by the Dey.

Treaty with Great Britain was rejected by President Jefferson, Dec., 1806, because it conceded to her the right of search and seizure.

Great Britain.—A treaty of peace between Great Britain and the United States was signed at Ghent, Belgium, December 24, 1814. None of the distinctive issues of the war of 1812 were settled or named. The principal arti-

it contained no provision for stopping impressments. Washington was threatened by the anti-Federalists if he signed it, but he did it notwithstanding, and the result justified his wisdom.

Wayne's Indian Treaty was concluded at Greenville, O., August 3, 1795. A council with 1,130 Indians was held, who agreed to refuse British influence, and to make peace. This ended the Indian war and opened up the great Northwest to white immigration.

Algiers.—Treaty with Algiers was concluded September 5, 1795. The United States was compelled to pay $800,-000 for captives then living, give the Dey a frigate worth $100,000, and submit to an annual tribute of $23,000 to secure future peace.

Spain.—A treaty between Spain and the United States was concluded Oct'r 20, 1795, which determined the bounda-

cles related to a few unimportant boundaries. The chief feature of the treaty was that Great Britain and the United States agreed to be at peace.

Russia.—A treaty between Russia and the United States was made in 1824, by which the latter relinquished all claim to territory south of latitude $54° 40''$, leaving England and the United States to settle their own boundaries.

Naples.—A treaty with Naples was concluded in 1831, by which that government agreed to pay the United States one million seven hundred and twenty thousand dollars for sequestration of American property under King Joachim Murat.

France.—A treaty with France was made in 1831, by which 25,000,000 francs were to be paid the United States for depredations on American commerce by Napoleon I.

Belgium paid the United States, in 1839, for damages to American property during the siege of Antwerp.

Holland paid the United States for spoliations on American commerce during the war of 1812, $62,692 in 1839.

Treaty Between Sardinia and the United States was made in 1839. It was the first treaty with any country ever made by that government.

Webster-Ashburton Treaty between the United States and England, defining the boundaries between the United States and British America, for suppressing the slave trade, and surrendering fugitive criminals, was signed in August, 1842.

Embassy to China.—In 1843 Con-

fornia were ceded to the United States; the Rio Grande river was made the western boundary of Texas, for which the United States was to pay Mexico $15,000,000 and to assume debts of Mexico to American citizens not to exceed three million five hundred thousand dollars. This was the result of the Mexican war, which cost the United States $160,000,000 and 25,000 lives.

Treaty Between Japan and the United States was concluded March 23, 1854.

Reciprocity Treaty between Canada and the United States was signed June 5, 1854. By this treaty agricultural products were made articles of free trade between the States and Canada.

Japanese Embassy to the United

gress appropriated $40,000 to send a special envoy to China to adjust our trade relations with that Empire. In 1844 Caleb Cushing negotiated a treaty between the United States and China.

Mexico.—President Polk asked Congress for an appropriation of $3,000,000 August 8, 1846, for the purpose of negotiating a treaty with Mexico.

Oregon Boundary Controversy between Great Britain and the United States was definitely settled by treaty June 15, 1846. The forty-ninth parallel was established as the international boundary. Every point in the controversy was yielded to England.

Treaty Between United States and Mexico, Feb'y 2, 1848, at Guadaloupe, Hidalgo. New Mexico and Cali-

States arrived at San Francisco March 28, 1860. It was composed of Nobles of the Empire, and was the first ever sent by that nation to any power. Its errand was to ratify the treaty between the two nations. President Buchanan gave them a reception at the White House in May.

San Juan Boundary.—In the controversy between Great Britain and the United States, October 21, 1872, the German Emperor decided in favor of the claim of the United States to several islands between Washington and Van Couver islands, including San Juan.

Chinese Treaty made at Shanghai November 18, 1880. It conceded to the United States the right to control Chinese immigration, but not to prohibit it altogether. Opium could not be carried into either country.

MONETARY AND FINANCIAL EVENTS.

Mint in Mexico.—The first mint on the continent was established in Mexico for coining silver in 1535.

At Lima, Peru, a mint was established in 1565. It is still in operation.

Musket Bullets were made legal tender in Massachusetts in 1635, in lieu of farthings, in order to keep them in the country in view of anticipated trouble over the charter of the colony.

Odd Financial Crisis.—In 1641 Indian money, consisting of sea shells strung together and known as "Wampum" or "Seawant," was the chief currency of New Netherland. The New Amsterdam City Council complained "That a great deal of bad Seawant, nasty rough things imported from other places, was in circulation, while the good, splendid Manhattan Seawant was out of sight

signed by the officials, was issued in 1685 by the Intendant of Quebec. Others issued it also, until in 1714 it amounted to 2,000,000 livres and ruined trade.

Bills of Credit to the amount of £40,000 were issued in 1690 by Massachusetts. This was the first paper money ever seen in the English colonies.

Paper Money to the amount of $26,000, was issued by South Carolina in 1702.

Pennsylvania issued paper money to the amount of £45,000 in 1722.

Legal Tender in Maryland.—Corn at 20 pence per bushel and tobacco at one penny per pound was legal tender in 1732.

Maryland issued paper money in 1733 to her great injury.

The Bank of Pennsylvania was

or exported, which must cause the ruin of the country."

"*Wampum*" became valueless as currency in 1651 in Massachusetts, in consequence of an order that it should no longer be received in payment of taxes. It continued current in New Netherland for a long time after.

Mint at Boston.—June 10, 1652, the general court of Massachusetts established the first mint in the English colonies, under charge of John Hull, goldsmith. Silver pieces were coined of the value of 3 pence, 6 pence and 12 pence. The largest became known as the "pine tree shilling," from the pine tree stamped upon it. It operated for 30 years.

Mint in Maryland was established by the Legislature of that colony in 1662.

Cards for Currency, made of common playing cards cut in 4 pieces, stamped with the French royal stamp and

chartered March 1, 1780. It was the first in the United States.

The Bank of North America was chartered December 31, 1781. Capital $400,000. Its bills were payable on demand, and were legal tender for all taxes and dues to the United States. Robert Morris was its founder. It began business in Philadelphia January 7, 1782, and aided the government greatly in paying the army.

Second Bank in the United States was organized in Massachusetts July 5, 1784. Capital $300,000.

Decimal Coinage was adopted by Congress, August, 1786.

United States Bank.—Upon the recommendation of Alexander Hamilton, Secretary of the Treasury, Congress in February, 1791, incorporated a United States Bank with a capital of $10,000,000, of which one-fifth was to be subscribed by the United States and four-fifths by individuals. Its charter was for twenty years. In July, 1791, stock books opened for subscription to this bank, and in less than one day all was taken. Branches in other cities were soon established.

National Bank of the United States.—Its charter having expired in 1811 it was not renewed, being defeated by one vote in the House and the casting vote of the Vice-President in the Senate.

Financial Panic.—In 1814 Treasury notes were 17 per cent. below par. Peace men in New England induced Boston banks to exact specie from Southern banks in redemption of their notes. They also arranged with Canadian, bankers to buy up American specie.

Crisis of 1821.—A great financial distress prevailed west of the Alleghanies in 1821. Banks failed, business suspended, and farmers were unable to pay their debts. Under the land laws of 1800 large tracts of government land had been sold, and the purchasers were unable to pay for them. The debt due the United States at the Western land offices was twenty-two millions of dollars. Relief was afforded by Congress permitting portions of the land to be returned and the money paid to be applied on the remainder. Land was reduced to one dollar and twenty-five cents per acre, and lots of eighty acres were offered for sale.

National Debt of the United States was entirely liquidated in 1835, and the surplus in the treasury, some

United States Bank.—A second one was chartered April, 1816, for twenty-five years. Capital thirty-five millions of dollars, of which the government was to take seven millions.

Philadelphia Saving's Fund Society, organized November, 1816, was the first savings bank in America.

The Provident Institution, for savings, was incorporated in Boston on December 13, 1816.

Great Financial Crisis in 1819 resulted from extravagant speculations, fraud, unlimited credits and excess of imports over exports. Currency declined 59 per cent., cotton and breadstuffs 50 per cent., and the Bank of the United States barely escaped bankruptcy.

forty millions of dollars, was distributed among the States.

Specie Circular.—By direction of President Jackson, the Secretary of the Treasury issued an order in 1836, directing United States land agents to receive nothing but coin for lands, as the country was flooded with the bills of unsound banks. This action precipitated the panic of 1837.

Panic of '37.—In March and April, 1837, failures in New York and New Orleans amounted to one hundred and fifty millions of dollars. On the 10th of May New York banks suspended, and the business of the country was prostrated. Credit was nearly annihilated, and finally the United States could not pay the President's salary when due. At the solicitation of business men an extra session of Congress was called. The cause of this panic was over-speculation and heavy importations consequent upon the low tariff.

Banks Resumed specie payments in 1839.

Bank of Pennsylvania, with a capital of $35,000,000. failed in 1841. This was the successor of the old United States Bank. The failure was caused by the directors having speculated with the bank's funds.

California.—A financial panic occurred in California in February, 1855.

Panic of 1857.—August 24th the land and railway speculation culminated in the failure of the Ohio Life and Trust Company, which was the beginning of a

Jay Gould and James Fisk, Jr., created a disastrous panic by cornering the gold market and forcing the price up to 160. Their aim was to reach 200, but United States Secretary of Treasury Boutwell spoiled their game by throwing forty millions of dollars in Government gold on the market. As it was they ruined multitudes, gave a staggering blow to the commercial prosperity of the nation and pocketed eleven millions of dollars.

Bowles Brothers, American Bankers in Paris, suspended November 9th, 1872.

Panic of '73 was inaugurated by the failure of Jay Cooke & Co., a great banking house of Philadelphia, September 19th. Confidence was at once destroyed and business paralyzed. It was

disastrous panic which swept over the country.

Philadelphia Banks all suspended payment on the 25th and 26th days of September, 1857, followed by country banks throughout the region.

New York Banks were compelled to suspend payment Oct. 13 and 14, 1857. The Massachusetts banks followed on the 14th.

Greenbacks were first issued by the United States in 1862.

Credit Mobilier of America, with a capital of two million five hundred thousand dollars, was organized in May, 1863, for banking.

Black Friday, September 24, 1869,

4 years before the country recovered from the effects of this panic.

Freedman's Bank Busted in 1874. Cause, reckless management and loans upon unsafe security. The poor depositors realized but little.

Duncan, Sherman & Co., an old New York banking house, failed July 27, 1875.

Bank of California suspended on the 26th of August, 1875, in consequence of a run made upon it. William C. Ralston, its President, resigned and was drowned the same day. The shock to the business community was great, but on the 2d of October it resumed business.

Savings Bank Panic prevailed in

April, 1878, throughout the country. In Massachusetts the trouble was greatest, but in a short time the excitement wore away.

Gold Sold at Par in New York on Dec. 17, 1878, for the first time since January, 1862.

Archbishop Purcell's Failure.— In December, 1878, "Father" Purcell, of Cincinnati, Ohio, who had received a large amount of money on deposit from the people of his diocese, became bankrupt. He owed three millions dollars to eleven thousand depositors. He had used it for church purposes, but the church has thus far failed to respond to the demands of the creditors. March 5, 1879, Archbishop Purcell and his brother, Father Edward Purcell, of Cincinnati, transferred all their property to J. B. Mannix for the benefit of their creditors. An appeal for sympathy was made by the Archbishop to the church, to assist the father in his financial troubles, but no benefit ever resulted from it, and the poor depositors are still with little or no return from their savings.

Bank Suspension in New Orleans. On March 20, 1879, thirteen banks suspended payments, except by certified checks. Aid came from New York banks and in 10 days they resumed payment. The suspension of the New Orleans banks was to avoid a panic threatened by the failure of two banks.

Resumption of Specie Payments January 1, 1879.—Specie payment was suspended in December, 1861. July 11, 1864, gold reached 2.85 premium. The following table gives the highest and lowest points reached by gold for each year. It also gives the value in gold of $100 in currency:—

Year.	Highest.	Lowest.	Average.	Worth of Paper.
1862	134.0	101.12	113.3	88.3
1863	172.5	122.12	145.2	68.9
1864	285.0	151.5	203.3	49.2
1865	234.37	128.12	157.3	63.6
1866	167.75	125.12	140.9	71.0
1867	146.37	132.12	138.2	72.4
1868	150.0	132.0	130.7	71.6
1869	102.5	119.5	133.0	75.2
1870	123.25	110.0	114.9	87.0
1871	115.37	108 37	111.7	89.5
1872	115.62	108.5	112.4	89.0
1873	119.12	106.12	113.8	87.9
1874	114.37	109.0	111.2	89.9
1875	117.62	111.75	115.1	86.9
1876	115.0	107 0	111.5	89.6
1877	107.87	102.5	104.7	95.5
1878	102.87	100.0	101.43	98.5

Reading Railroad Co. Failed May 21, 1880, its liabilities being $104,-000,000. The failure was caused by the attempt to monopolize immense coal and iron interests.

Great Financial Excitement was caused Feb. 25, 1881, by the prospect of the 3 per cent. funding bill becoming a law. This was a Democratic measure, and a stringency in the money market was the immediate result, but the crisis was passed by the action of the Senate in promptly repealing the tax on bank deposits, and the calling in of $10,000,000 of United States bonds by Secretary Sherman.

SCHOOLS AND COLLEGES.

Henrico College.—In 1620 the London Company set apart one thousand acres of land on the James river to endow a college for settlers and Indians.

Harvard College.—In 1636 £400 was voted by the General Court of Massachusetts Bay for a school or college, which finally became known as Harvard college. It was so named after Rev. John Harvard, who willed to it £800 and all his library in 1638, and the General Court of Massachusetts changed the name of Newtown to Cambridge, in lies a grammar school capable of "fitting youths for the university." Similar laws were afterward passed by Connecticut, Plymouth and New Haven.

College Lands were set apart in New Haven Colony in 1654.

Legacy for Education.—In March, 1657, ex-Governor Hopkins, of Connecticut, died and left £1,000 for grammar schools in Hartford and New Haven, and £500 for a college, which was given to Harvard.

Compulsory Support of Minis-

honor of Cambridge, England. Henry Dunster, an eminent Hebrew scholar, was its first President.

First Commencement at Harvard College took place on October 9, 1642, and nine candidates took the degree of A. B.

Contributions for Harvard College.—In 1645 the Commissioners of the Colonial League recommended that every family contribute a peck of corn or a shilling to the support of Harvard College. A general compliance afforded timely aid to this institution.

Free and Grammar Schools.—Massachusetts, in 1649, enacted a law that every township should maintain a free school, and every town of 100 families ters and Grammar Schools was made legal by the General Court of Plymouth Colony in 1657.

William and Mary College.—In 1661 Virginia appropriated funds to establish a college which afterward was known by this name. It was founded at Williamsburg, Va., in 1693.

Free Schools were supported by every town in New England in 1665.

School in Pennsylvania.—In 1683 Enoch Flower taught "reading, writing and casting accounts" for 8 shillings a year.

Public Schools were established by the Quakers of Philadelphia in 1689.

Schools and Libraries in Maryland.—In 1694 it was agreed that each county should have a school and each parish a library. King William's school was opened at Annapolis, where there was a library of 1,100 volumes.

Yale College originated in 1700. Ten Connecticut ministers met and each deposited several books upon a table, saying, "I give these books for the founding of a college in Connecticut." This resulted in the establisment of "Yale." It was chartered in 1701, and £120 per annum granted by the Connecticut Assembly. It was located at Saybrook. The college was removed to New Haven in 1717. Its name was taken from Elihu Yale, who donated £500 to its aid.

The Log College was founded in 1728 at Neshaming Penna., by William

the revolution was at New York in the year 1767.

Brown University, under the auspices of the Baptists, was chartered in 1764. It was located at Warren, and afterward removed to Providence, Rhode Island.

Dartmouth College, Hanover, N. H., was chartered in 1769. Eleazar Wheelock, D. D., was its founder and first President.

Homespun Clothes were worn by the graduating class at Harvard College in 1770.

Rutger's College (formerly Queen's), was founded by the Reformed Dutch Church at New Brunswick, N. J., in 1770.

"Phi Beta Kappa," the great col-

Tennent, from Ireland, for the education of Presbyterian ministers.

Princeton College, New Jersey, was founded in 1738.

Moravian High School for Girls was established at Bethlehem, Penna., in 1749.

University of Philadelphia, for the instruction of youth, was founded through Dr. Franklin's influence in 1749.

Columbia College, N. Y., was founded as "King's College" in 1754. Seventeen thousand dollars was raised by lottery in its aid.

Medical School of Philadelphia was organized in 1764 by Drs. Shippen and Morgan. It was the first founded in the colonies; the only other founded before

lege society of the United States, was founded at William and Mary College, Virginia, in 1775.

The American Academy of Arts and Sciences was founded May 4, 1780.

Washington and Lee University at Lexington, Virginia, was chartered in 1782. It took Washington's name in 1796. It took General Robert E. Lee's name in 1870. Lee was President from 1865 to 1870.

Law School.—The first in America was established at Litchfield, Conn., by Hon. Tapping Reeve, in 1784.

First Roman Catholic College was founded at Georgetown, D. C., in 1789.

The University of Vermont was

established at Burlington in 1791. Ira, the brother of Ethan Allen, made generous gifts to this institution.

Williams College was founded in 1793 at Williamstown, Mass.

Bowdoin College, named after Gov. James Bowdoin, was chartered at Brunswick, Maine, in 1794.

Union College was founded at Schenectady, N. Y., in 1795.

Common School Fund.—Upon the recommendation of Governor Clinton, in 1795, the legislature of the state of New York appropriated $50,000 for the estabishment of common schools.

"*The Agricultural* and Mechanical College of the University of North Carolina," for instruction in mining,

Teachers' Seminary was opened at Concord, Vermont, in 1823, by Rev. S. R. Hill. It was the first in the United States.

Race Prejudice was exhibited at a mass meeting in New Haven, Connecticut, September 8, 1831, held at the call of the Mayor, to denounce the establishment of schools for negroes.

Normal School at Lexington, Massachusetts, was opened July 3, 1839.

Roman Catholics first claimed a share of the Public School funds of New York in 1840.

"*Comer's Commercial College,*" the first one in America, was established in Boston in 1840.

York, Pa.—*Continued.*

Kraber, M. C., Mrs., Millinery and Fancy Goods, 432 West Market St.

Lafayette House,
No. 114 S. George Street, York, Pa.
EDWARD C. PEELING, - - - PROPRIETOR.
FIRST-CLASS ACCOMMODATIONS.
Good Stabling Connected with Hotel. Sale and Exchange Stables.

Laumaster, William D., Commercial Book and Job Printer, 19 S. Duke St.

Leathery, Eli G., Tinner, Plumber, Gas and Steam Fitter, 403 W. Market St.

LITCHENBERGER & SHEARER,
Dealers in Stoves, Ranges, Heaters, Cutlery, House Furnishing Goods, Tin Roofing, Spouting and Jobbing a Specialty.
No. 489 East Market Street, York, Pa.

WILLIAM MACK,
STEAM BOTTLING HOUSE,
Imported Lager, Ale and Porter,
EAST DUKE STREET, YORK, PA.

Menough & Yessler, Sash, Doors, Blinds, Frames, 440 & 442 W. Philadelphia St.

Michael, T. N., Merchant Tailor, Ladies' Coats a Specialty, 24 S. George St.

Musser, Henry, Coal, Wood, Grain, Flour, N. Hartley St., Cor. Main.

CHAS. H. NEFF & SON,
[ESTABLISHED 1810.]
Manufacturers of all kinds Light and Heavy Platform and Carriage Works,
10 AND 12 W. PHILADELPHIA ST., YORK, PA.

Neiman, E. H., Dentist, 14 W. Market St.

---

civil engineering, etc., was opened in 1795.

Frederick College, Frederick, Md., was founded in 1797.

Middleburg College, Middleburg, Vermont, was founded 1797.

Teachers' Association.—The first in America was formed in 1799, at Middletown, Conn., and was called "The Middlesex County Association for the Improvement of Common Schools."

University of North Carolina was founded in 1799 at Chapel Hill, N. C.

Theological Seminary.—The first in America was founded by the Associate Reformed Church in 1804.

Troy Female Institute was established in 1821 by Mrs. Emma Willard.

"*Woman's Medical College*" of Pennsylvania was founded in 1849.

Vassar College for young women was founded in 1861, at Poughkeepsie, N. Y., by Mathew Vassar.

Agricultural Colleges.—President Lincoln, July 3, 1862, signed a bill for establishing such colleges in the several States. The bill appropriated 30,000 acres of land for each representative, the proceeds to be given to found these institutions.

Free Public Schools in Texas were first opened in Austin in 1871.

Gray Nun's Act of 1875 was repealed by the New York Legislature on April 18, 1876. Under it the Superintendent of Public Instruction issued certificates of qualification as teachers to any graduate of Catholic seminaries who had received a diploma from the Gray nuns.

Catholic Schools.—On January 3, 1880, Bishop McCloskey, of Louisville,

Ky., ordered Roman Catholic schools to be established throughout his diocese, and bade Catholic parents to send their children under nine years old under penalty for refusal of being denied the sacraments.

Party Organizations, Sectional and Political Strife.

Federalists and Democrat-Republicans were the names of two great political parties that arose in 1787 out of the ratification of the Constitution of the United States.

Tammany Society of New York was organized on May 12, 1789. An Irishman named William Mooney was its founder. Its name was taken from a deceased Delaware chief, who was made its patron saint. The titles of Sachems, Sagamores and Warriors are applied to its officers and members. It was organized in imitation of the Jacobin clubs of Paris, but for *charitable purposes only.* It has since become a political engine of great power in the Democratic party.

Democratic Clubs were first organized in the United States in 1793, modeled from the French Jacobin clubs.— They were violently hostile to the Government. Washington denounced them publicly as instigators of the whiskey insurrection of 1794.

Nullification in Kentucky.—On November 14, 1799, the Legislature declared "that a state may nullify and declare void any act of Congress which it thinks unconstitutional."

Removal From Office.—The first removal from office for political reasons was made by President Jefferson in 1801. Elizur Goodrich, Federalist, was removed from the collectorship of the port of New Haven, Conn. Samuel Bishop, Democrat-Republican, was appointed in his place.

Party Strife in 1806 reached such a pitch that in Boston a Democrat-Republican named Austin attempted to chastise a Federalist named Selfridge, who shot him.

Doughfaces was an opprobious epithet applied by Randolph, of Virginia, in 1820, to the supporters of the Missouri compromise. It has since been applied to Northern men with Southern principles.

Monroe Doctrine.—In December, 1823, President Monroe sent a vigorous message to Congress, in which he declared that for the future the American continents were not to be considered as subjects for colonization by any European power.

Anti-Masonry. — In 1826 William Morgan published a book revealing the secrets of Masonry, at Batavia, N. Y. He was abducted and believed to have been drowned in the Niagara river by Colonel King and four other Knights Templars. The Anti-Mason party arose from this incident. It controlled 30,000 votes in New York State, and carried Vermont in 1832.

Political Discriminations. — Removal from office for political reasons was first extensively practiced by President Jackson, who, in 1829, removed five hundred postmasters.

Jackson's " Kitchen Cabinet." — In 1831 General Jackson's cabinet was frequently disrupted through dissensions

tary power if necessary. He also instructed the collector of the port of Charleston to use the revenue cutters to enforce the tariff.

Removal of Government Funds. In October, 1833, President Jackson ordered the Government funds (about $10,-000,000), deposited in the Bank of the United States, to be distributed among certain designated State banks. His action was denounced by the opposition, of which Webster, Clay and Calhoun were the leaders, as "unwarranted, arbitrary and dangerous." The Whig party arose from this incident. The Bank's charter expired in 1835 and was not renewed.

President Jackson was censured

York, Pa.—*Continued.*

Shetter, George J., Sign Writer, 421 W. Market St.

SAMUEL A. SHROFF,

Real Estate and General Insurance

AND PATENT AGENCY,

245 West Market Street, York, Pa.

Sipes, Alexander, Groceries and Notions, 400 Queen St.

Sonneman, A., Pure Havana and Domestic Cigars, 103 S. George St.

Spahn, George, Marble and Granite Works, Nos. 402 and 404 S. Duke St.

ALEX. SPANGLER,

CARRIAGE and SLEIGH BUILDER,

Rear No. 15 South Duke Street,

YORK, PA.

ALL WORK WARRANTED.

BUGGIES & PHAETONS.

D. F, STAUFFER,
STEAM

CRACKER, CAKE AND BISCUIT WORKS,

No. 128 S. George St., York, Pa.

Strack, Charles A., Cabinet Maker and Undertaker, 130 S. George St.

Strayer, John, Saddle and Harness Maker, 21½ N. George St.

---

among the families of its members, and on account of these domestic troubles it was given the name of "Kitchen Cabinet."

Nullification in South Carolina. In November, 1832, at a State Convention held in South Carolina, it was declared that the tariffs of 1828 and 1832 were null and void. The State Legislature afterward passed an ordinance of Nullification, to take effect February 1, 1833, which declared that force would be used to resist the collection of duties in the port of Charleston.

Nullification Crushed. —December 16, 1832, General Jackson issued a proclamation, declaring that he would enforce the United States laws by mili-

by a resolution of the United States Senate, March 28, 1834, for removing the funds of the Government from the United States Bank.

Censure of Jackson Removed.— United States Senate's resolution of censure upon President Jackson, passed in 1834, was expunged from the records on the 16th of January 1837, chiefly through the efforts of Thomas H. Benton, of Missouri.

Free-Soil Party. — This party was organized August 9, 1847, at a convention of barn-burners, and the Liberty party, held at Buffalo, New York. The motto adopted was "a free soil for a free people." Martin Van Buren, of New York, was nominated for President, and

Charles Francis Adams, of Massachusetts, for Vice President.

Squatter Sovereignty.—In 1849 the pro slavery members of Congress advocated the right of territories to decide for themselves whether they would come into the Union as slave or free States.

Ostend Manifesto.— Pierre Soule, John Y. Mason and James Buchanan held a conference at Ostend, Belgium, in 1854, and published a paper drawn up by Buchanan, declaring that there could be no peace until the United States had acquired Cuba, either by purchase or force.

Republican Party Organized.— This party held its first meeting on February 29, 1854, in the Congregational Church at Ripon, Wisconsin. It was

that was destined to change and control the policy of the National Government for twenty-four years.

Kansas-Nebraska Bill.—January, 1854, Senator Stephen A. Douglas, of Illinois, introduced a bill into Congress for the organization of the two above territories, with the power to decide for themselves whether they should be free or slave-holding. This was virtually a repeal of the Missouri compromise. After a bitter sectional debate until May it became a law.

"Bleeding Kansas." — Upon the passage of the Kansas-Nebraska bill emigration began to pour into Kansas from the North and the South, each section determined to out-vote the other on

composed of men opposed to the passage of the Kansas-Nebraska bill, and had been called by Major Alvan E. Bovay. It was presided over by Deacon William Dunham, and it was proposed to organize a new party based upon the non-extension of slavery. After the bill had passed the Senate a second meeting was held under a call signed by fifty-four citizens, which dissolved the Whig and Free-Soil town committees and chose a new committee of five, three of whom were Whigs, one Democrat and one Free-Soiler. Major Bovay suggested the name of "Republican" for the new party, which was adopted. In June the name was adopted by the Michigan State Convention. Thus was a party inaugurated

the slavery issue. At an election held in November, 1854, a pro-slavery delegate was elected to Congress, chiefly by bands of "border ruffians" from Missouri. The general territorial election was held next year and carried by the same party, and the Legislature thus chosen, assembled at Lecompton, organized a government permitting slavery. The Free-Soil party met at Topeka in convention, declared the election illegal on account of fraudulent voting, and organized a government excluding slavery. Civil war followed. Congress recognized the Lecompton government, and President Pierce issued a proclamation to that effect. The struggle continued four years, and until Kansas was admitted to the Union as a free state.

N. P. Banks, Jr., was elected Speaker of the House of Representatives on February 2, 1856, after a contest of nine weeks, by a plurality of three votes.

"Know - Nothing" Convention, held February 22, 1856. This secret organization, pledged to oppose foreigners and "put none but Americans on guard" as office-holders, nominated Millard Fillmore, of New York, for President and Andrew J. Donelson, of Tennessee, for Vice-President.

Kansas Troubles.—In Jan'y, 1857, the United States troops broke up a meeting of the free State Legislature.

giving the right of suffrage to negroes in the District of Columbia.

"Ku-Klux-Klan" was organized in the South in January, 1868. By May it numbered half a million. General N. B. Forrest was at its head, and his title was "Grand Wizard of the Empire." Its alleged object was to redeem the South "by preventing the negro from voting and being educated, deterring Northern emigration, and securing the domination of the Southern whites." It inaugurated a "reign of terror," and thousands of negroes and poor whites were killed and driven from their homes on account of their political opinions.

President Johnson and Congress in Conflict.—February 21, 1868, the

Governor Geary resigned, and Robert J. Walker of Mississippi, was his successor. The House of Representatives denounced the acts of the Pro-Slavery Legislature as "cruel, oppressive, illegal and void."

The Lecompton Constitution Rejected, August 3, 1858, by the people of Kansas by a heavy majority.

Republican Victory.—February 1, 1860, a bitter contest of eight weeks, in the House of Representatives, ended in the election of William Pennington, of New Jersey, as Speaker.

The Impeachment of President Johnson was proposed on January 26, 1867, in the House of Representatives, upon the occasion of his veto of the bill

President attempted to remove Secretary of War Stanton and appoint Gen. Lorenzo Thomas in his place. Mr. Stanton refused to surrender the office, and was sustained by the United States Senate.

The Impeachment of President Johnson was voted upon by the House of Representatives February 24, 1868, for violating the Tenure-of-Office Act and his bitter denunciation of Congress. The Court of Impeachment was organized by the United States Senate, March 5, 1868, Chief Justice Chase presiding. The trial continued until May 16th. The result was 35 for conviction and 19 for acquittal, which was short of the necessary two-thirds majority.

Female Suffrage.—On January 20, 1871, a motion to strike out the word "male" in the XIVth amendment to the United States Constitution was defeated in the House of Representatives by 117 to 55.

Armed Bands in South Carolina were ordered, March 4, 1871, by proclamation of President Grant, to disperse within 24 hours.

Newspaper Destroyed.—The Ku-Klux-Klan destroyed a Radical newspaper office in Rutherford, N. C., April 30, 1871.

Writ of Habeas Corpus was suspended in nine counties in South Carolina by President Grant, October 7, 1871.

Ku-Klux-Klan in South Carolina

1874, McEnery's partizans, claiming that he was the Governor of the State, overthrew the Kellogg government. In the affray 8 police and 8 White Leaguers were killed and 32 wounded.

Proclamation From President Grant ordered the "White Leaguers" to disperse, and troops were ordered to New Orleans.

Kellogg's Government was reinstated September 19, 1874.

Louisiana Legislature.—January 4, 1875, United States troops entered the Legislature and forcibly expelled some of the members who had not received certificates from the Returning Board. Owing to frauds it was difficult to determine the legal government of the State.

---

were ordered to disband October 12, 1871, by the proclamation of President Grant.

Ku-Klux Investigations by Congress, in 1872, revealed the fact that horrible atrocities had been committed by this "Klan" throughout the South for political ends.

Ejected From Office. — Governor Baxter, of Arkansas, was forcibly ejected and the executive office usurped by Governor(?) Brooks. A fight between their respective adherents at Pine Tree, April 30, 1874, resulted in the killing of 11 and wounding of 27 men. Baxter was recognized as the lawful Governor by President Grant.

Louisiana Embroglio.—Sept'r 14,

Wheeler Compromise, passed by the United States Congress, was adopted by the Louisiana politicians in April, 1875. By it Kellogg was recognized as Governor, and the representatives that had been expelled by the United States troops were re-seated.

Rifle Clubs in South Carolina were ordered to disband in 3 days by President Grant's proclamation, October 17, 1876. Troops were ordered to Columbia, South Carolina, to enforce the proclamation.

Dennis Kearney was assaulted and severely beaten March 20, 1879, at Santa Anna, California, for abusive language, which he used in a lecture at that place.

Communists' Parade occurred in

Chicago on Sunday, April 20, 1879. They numbered four hundred and were armed with rifles. This was a demonstration against a bill in the Legislature forbidding the drill of armed bodies not enrolled according to law.

United States Troops were withdrawn from the State House at Columbia, South Carolina, April 10, 1877, by order of President Hayes. This caused Chamberlain to resign his claims to the governorship, and left Wade Hampton in possession of the office.

United States Troops withdrawn from Louisiana Apr 24, 1877. The Packard government being unable to maintain its position without them, abandoned the field to the Nichols faction.

23, 1879, Rev. I. S. Kalloch was wounded by Charles De Young, editor of the *Chronicle*. The former was a candidate for Mayor, and the *Chronicle* had published some reflections upon his former life, which Kalloch had denied with gross vituperation from his pulpit. This led to the affray. The controversy finally ended in the killing of Charles DeYoung, editor of the *Chronicle*, by the son of Rev. Mayor Kalloch, April 23, 1880.

The Maine Election Troubles.— On the 15th day of December, 1879, Governor Gracelon and his council, who were the legal canvassers of election returns, deliberately counted out eight Republican Senators and twenty-nine Republican Representatives, who had

Chisholm Tragedy at De Kalb, Mississippi. — April 29, 1877, Judge Chisholm, a Republican, was confined in jail, with his family, upon a pretext of having instigated the murder of John W. Gully, a Democrat. A mob attacked the jail, killing the Judge, his daughter and little boy, and Mr. Gilmer, his friend. No attempt was made to punish the murderers.

Yazoo County, Miss., Outrages. On August 20, 1879, Henry M. Dixon, independent Democratic candidate for Sheriff, was killed by James H. Barkesdale, for running against the regular nominee. The murderer was released upon $15,000 bail.

Kalloch Controversy.—On August

been elected on September 8th, in order to give the Fusionists, or Democrats and Greenbackers, a majority of the Legislature. This would enable them to elect a Governor on January 7th, 1880, neither of the candidates having received a majority over all, as required by law, at the popular election. Before the close of the year public opinion run so high that Governor Gracelon was forced to submit the issues between himself and the Republicans to the Supreme Court of the State, which rendered a decision against him on the 16th of January, 1880. The Legislature thereupon elected D. T. Davis, Governor, and on the 31st the State seal and other property was surrendered by the Fusionists.

THE MEXICAN WAR.

Mexican Minister.—Gen. Almonte ceased diplomatic relations with the United States, and left Washington on March 6, 1845, on account of the annexation of Texas.

General Taylor, under orders from Washington, marched to Corpus Christi, at the mouth of the Neuces, upon the territory in dispute between Texas and Mexico, in August, 1845, and formed a camp of four or five thousand troops.

Commencement of Hostilities.—General Taylor was ordered to advance to the Rio Grande, which he reached in March, 1846. He hastily constructed fort Brown, opposite Matamoras. Gen.

under General Arista, and 2,000 Americans under General Taylor. After five hours severe fighting the Mexicans were driven from the field. American loss in killed and wounded 53. The Mexicans lost about 600.

Battle of Resaca de la Palma, fought May 9, 1846. The Mexicans rallied and posted themselves advantageously. Their artillery was well served and galled the Americans severely, until Captain May's regiment of dragoons charged the battery, sabered the gunners and captured General La Vegas. The Mexicans fled in a general rout across the Rio Grande. American loss in killed and

Ampudia, the Mexican commander, ordered him to retire within twenty-four hours. Colonel Cross, an American officer, riding alone beyond the lines, was murdered by Mexican cavalrymen, who beat out his brains.

Fort Brown, on the Rio Grande River, was attacked by the Mexicans on May 3d, 1846. The fort was defended by three hundred men under command of Major Brown. After suffering a bombardment of 160 hours the garrison received reinforcements, and the Mexicans trembled for the safety of Matamoras. Major Brown, in whose honor the fort was named, was mortally wounded.

Battle of Palo Alto was fought on May 8, 1846, between 6,000 Mexicans

wounded 110; Mexican loss at least 1,000.

War was Declared May 11, 1846, by the United States against Mexico.

Volunteers.—May 13, 1846, Congress authorized the President to accept the services of 50,000 volunteers, and $10,000,000 was placed at his disposal. Three hundred thousand men offered.

Matamoras was Captured by General Taylor on May 18, 1846, and the American flag waved upon Mexican soil.

Mexico Declared War upon the United States May 23, 1846.

Monterey, on the California coast, was taken possession of on July 7, 1846, in the name of the United States, by Com. John D. Sloat, of the navy, who announced himself governor of the territory.

San Francisco was occupied July 9, 1846, by Com. Montgomery, of the United States navy.

Santa Fe, New Mexico, was taken in August, 1846, by General Stephen W. Kearney, who, with sixteen hundred men, had marched nine hundred miles. A force of 4,000 Mexicans fled at his approach, while 6,000 citizens quietly submitted to his authority.

Los Angelos, Cal., Captured.— Commodore R. F. Stockton, of the navy, and Fremont, combined in a successful movement against Los Angelos, Cal., on August 15, 1846.

*Monterey.—*On September 21, 1846,

Antonio, at Montclova, 70 miles from Monterey, with 3,000 volunteers.

Tabasco, on the Mexican coast, was bombarded and the shipping in the harbor destroyed by Com. Perry, October, 1846.

Tampico, upon the coast of Mexico, was captured by Com. Conner, November 14, 1846.

Satillo, seventy miles southwest from Monterey, the capital of Coahuila, was captured November 15, 1846, by the American advance under General Worth.

*San Pasqual.—*Gen. Kearney deated the Mexicans at this place, Dec. 6, 1846.

Battle of Braceti, December 25, 1846. Colonel Doniphan, in command

Gen. Worth carried the fortified heights in the rear of the city, cutting off its supplies. General Taylor, now in command of 6,000 men, commenced the siege of Monterey. The city was defended by General Ampudia and 9,000 troops. The conflict lasted four days, a part of the time within the streets of the city, where the carnage was fearful. Ampudia surrendered. American loss in killed, wounded and missing, five hundred and sixty-one. The number lost by the Mexicans was never ascertained, but it was supposed to be more than one thousand.

General John E. Wool, Inspector-General of the United States army, arrived, on October 30, 1846, from San

of 1,000 Missouri volunteers, while on his march to Chihuahua to join General Wool, met a large force of Mexicans at Braceti, in the valley of the Rio del Norte, under General Ponce de Leon. He sent a black flag to Doniphan with the message : "We will neither ask nor give quarters. The Mexicans then advanced and fired three rounds. The Missourians fell upon their faces, and the enemy, supposing them to be all dead, rushed forward for the purpose of plunder. The Americans suddenly rose, and delivering a deadly fire from their rifles, killed about two hundred Mexicans and dispersed the remainder in confusion.

Colonel John C. Fremont captured Sonoma Pass, Cal., and a Mexican garrison, in 1846.

Rio San Gabriel, Cal., January 8, 1847. Com. Stockton defeated the Mexicans under General Flores.

Plains of Mesa, Cal., January 9, 1847, Com. Stockton again defeated the Mexicans and drove them. from the country.

General Winfield Scott arrived in Mexico in January, 1847, and assumed command of all the American forces. He ordered a large part of Gen. Taylor's army to join him at Vera Cruz.

Satillo, February 23, 1847. Captain Webster defeated 800 Mexicans here.

Buena Vista.—February 23rd, 1847, General Taylor posted his army of 4800 men and awaited the Mexicans, 20,000

and entered Chihuahua. The Mexicans lost 600.

Ceralvo.—May 7, 1847, Major Giddings defeated a Mexican force here.

Vera Cruz Surrendered on March 29, 1847, to the combined army and naval attack under General Scott and Commodore Conner, after a week's siege. The Mexicans lost one thousand, the Americans eighty. The trophies were 5,000 troops, 500 cannon and military stores.

Colonel Stevenson's California volunteer regiment from New York was sent to occupy Monterey and Santa Barbara. It reached San Francisco in March 1847.

Cerro Gordo.—Marching to Jalapa, April 18, 1847, the American army found Santa Anna with 15,000 troops in an ap-

strong, under Santa Anna. The Mexican General, assuring General Taylor he was surrounded, ordered him to surrender within an hour. Taylor refused, and both armies prepared for battle. It was a desperate and bloody fight, commencing at sunrise and lasting until sunset, but finally the Mexicans fled in confusion, leaving their dead and wounded behind, and the Americans were left masters of the field. The Americans lost 267 killed, 456 wounded, and 23 missing. The Mexicans lost almost 2,000. They left 500 of their comrades dead on the field.

Battle of Sacramento.—February 28, 1847, Colonel Doniphin defeated four thousand Mexicans, losing only 18 men,

parently impregnable position upon the heights and commanding the pass of Cerro Gordo. General Scott's army numbered 8,500. The heights could only be taken by assault, which was made, and the position captured with a loss of only 431, while the enemy lost 1,000 in killed and wounded and 3,000 prisoners. Santa Anna escaped with his life by fleeing upon a mule taken from his carriage, abandoning his private papers and his wooden leg.

Battle of Churubusco.—On Aug. 21, 1847, Gen Scott advanced on Churubusco, where Santa Anna was in command of the main body of the Mexican army. The enemy were defeated, and Santa Anna abandoned the field and fled to the City of Mexico. This defeat of the Mexicans was the final destruction of an army 30,000 strong by another about one-third its strength in number. Full 4,000 of the Mexicans were killed or wounded, 3,000 made prisoners, and 30 pieces of cannon taken. The Americans lost in killed and wounded 1,100.

Perote, a Strong Castle and town, surrendered, April 22, 1847, to General Worth, with a park of artillery and a vast amount of military stores.

Pueblo, the sacred city of the angels, with 80,000 inhabitants, surrendered without resistance May 15, 1847. Here the army rested and opened negotiations for peace, but the stubborn and foolhardy Mexicans haughtily rejected the overtures.

suffered dreadfully. The Mexicans lost about 1,000 dead on the field and the Americans about 800.

Chapultepec, which was on the site of the Hall of the Montezumas, was carried by storm, September 13, 1847. The Americans under General Scott routed the enemy with great slaughter, and unfurled the Stars and Stripes over the shattered castle of Chapultepec. The Mexicans fled to the city, pursued by General Quitman to its very gates. That night Santa Anna and his army, with the officers of government, fled the doomed city.

City of Mexico.—September 14th, 1847, General Scott took formal possession and the American flag floated over the Halls of the Montezumas.

Contreras was attacked at sunrise on August 19, 1847, by General Persifer F. Smith and 4,000 troops, and in seventeen minutes 6,000 Mexicans under Gen. Valencia were utterly routed. Eighty officers and 2,000 private soldiers were made prisoners, and 33 pieces of artillery were captured.

Molina del Ray and Casa de Mata, the western defences of Chapultepec, were held by 14,000 Mexicans. General Worth, with 4,000 Americans, stormed and carried these positions, September 8, 1847. The Americans were first repulsed with great slaughter, but, returning to the attack. they fought desperately for an hour, and drove the Mexicans from their position. Both armies

Hospitals at Pueblo, October 9, 1847, containing 1,800 sick men, in charge of Colonel Childs, were besieged forty days by Santa Anna. General Lane, on his March to Mexico, relieved them and scattered the Mexicans.

Atlixco.—October 18, 1847, General Lane defeated a Mexican force at this place.

Guaymas, a port in the Gulf of Mexico, was taken, October 20, 1847, by an American squadron.

General Scott issued a proclamation against Mexican guerillas, Dec. 12, 1847

American Army from Mexico arrived at New Orleans in June, 1848.

Peace between the United States and Mexico was declared July 4, 1848.

SLAVERY AND ANTI-SLAVERY.

Indian Slaves.—In 1494 Columbus sent four ships to Spain with gold, metals, fruits and 500 captives, to be sold into slavery. Queen Isabella ordered them returned immediately, and sent commands that the islanders be treated mercifully.

Labrador Natives were kidnapped and sold into slavery by Gaspar Cortereal, a Portugese navigator, in 1500. It is thought that the name "Labrador," meaning laborer, was applied as a result of this expedition.

Spanish Oppression in Hayti.—From 1500 to 1550, two millions of Indians had been worked to death as slaves by the Spaniards.

dians was warranted by the laws of God and man, and that only so could they be converted to the Christian faith."

England Slave Trade was inaugurated by Sir John Hawkins, who, in 1562, enticed some and captured other Guinea negroes on the coast of Africa, three hundred in all, and sold them in Hayti. He had obtained Queen Elizabeth's sanction to his voyage, upon condition that he would take none from their homes save with their own consent. Hawkins made another voyage to Guinea for negroes in 1567. Queen Elizabeth was interested in this expedition. Five hundred negroes were se-

Slavery Sanctioned.—In 1501 an ordinance was passed permitting Spanish emigrants to the New World to take with them negro slaves who had been born among Christians.

Negro Slavery increased so rapidly that in 1503 Ovando, Governor of Hayti, wrote to the Spanish government praying that the importation might cease.

Slavery Forbidden.—In 1506 slaves were, by royal degree, forbidden to be exported to the New World, except from Seville, and then only on condition that they had been taught Christianity.

Indian Slavery in the New World was opposed by the Dominican priests, thereupon, in 1513, the Privy Council of Spain decreed that the "bondage of In-

cured and were sold in Cartagena, the result of this voyage.

Slaves Brought to Jamestown.—Aug., 1620, a Dutch Captain brought 20 negroes to Jamestown and sold them for servants for life.

Slavery began in Netherland in 1626.

New England.—Slaves were introduced into New England in 1638 by a vessel trading between Guinea and the West Indies.

Boston.—In 1645 two negroes were brought to Boston who had been kidnapped on the coast of Guinea. The magistrates, upon complaint of Richard Saltonstall, ordered them sent back as "having been procured not honestly by purchase but unlawfully by kidnapping."

Man-Stealing was made a capital crime in Massachusetts in 1646. Similar laws were passed by the other New England colonies shortly after.

Connecticut.—Slavery in Connecticut was made lawful under certain restrictions in 1650.

Rhode Island.—Slavery was prohibited in Rhode Island, May 13, 1652.—Slave selling and life servitude was forbidden under penalty of £40 for each offense, but the trade was so lucrative that it continued to exist for many years, and Newport grew rich by its prosecution.

New York.—In 1652 the New Netherland Company granted permission for the importation of African slaves.

King Phillip's and other Indians at Dover, N. H., and sold them into slavery. In 1680 an Indian war broke out in Carolina, and a bounty was offered for each captured Indian, many of whom were sold for slaves to the West Indies. The proprietors stopped this as soon as they learned of it.

Slave Trade.—From 1680 to 1786 2,130,000 negroes had been imported into the English colonies, exclusive of thousands that had died on the way.

Slavery Denounced.—Slavery was first publicly denounced in 1688 by the German Friends, who, at their meeting in Germantown, Penna., on February 18, adopted a paper setting forth the unlawfulness of "traffic in men body."

Virginia.—Children were made free or slave in Virginia, in 1662, according to the condition of their mother. It was defined by law in this state in 1670 for the first time.

Maryalnd.—Slavery was first defined by law in Maryland in 1663. It was provided that the condition of the child should follow its father, because English women married negro slaves.

Abolitionism of Slavery was urged upon by the "Friends," of Barbadoes, by George Fox, in 1671.

Runaway Slaves.—A decree of the Virginia Assembly made it lawful to kill them in 1672.

Indians Enslaved.—In 1676 Major Waldron captured three hundred of

Quakers Oppose Slavery.—In 1696, at their yearly meeting, the Quakers resolved to "discourage the buying of more negroes, and to provide for the moral well being of such as were owned as slaves."

Legislation Against Slavery.—In 1701 Boston instructed its representatives to "put a period to negroes being slaves."

Slave Market was opened in New York City in 1711.

Petition to Abolish Slavery.—In 1712 a petition to abolish slavery was received by the Pennsylvania Assembly, from William Southby, a Roman Catholic of Maryland.

Maryland Passed a Law in 1715

making a child follow the condition of its mother. A law had existed from 1663 to 1683, that children should follow their father's condition.

Massachusetts.—In 1716 there were 2,000 slaves in this State.

Mississippi Valley. — In 1719 the French introduced a large number of slaves there.

South Carolina. — In 1727 bitter complaints were made by this State of the excessive importations of slaves. It was not defined by law in this State until 1740, although Sir John Yeamans introduced negro slaves into the province in 1670.

Georgia.—Slavery was excluded from Georgia by act of the Trustees in 1733,

cans, as it has existed among us, is a gross violation of the righteousness and benevolence which are so much inculcated in the gospel, and therefore we will not tolerate it in this church."

Slave Property Prohibited.—The right to hold slaves in Massachusetts was denied by the Superior Court in the case of James vs. Lechmere in 1770, but slaves were held until the constitution of 1780 was adopted.

Colonial Opposition to Slavery. "The American Association" was the title of a series of articles adopted by Congress, October 20, 1774, for the maintainance of the rights of the colonies.— Its second article declared "that we will neither import nor purchase any slave

and was defined by law, for the first time, in 1770.

Duty Upon Slaves.—In 1761 the States of Virginia and South Carolina, by an act of Assembly, voted a prohibitory duty upon importing slaves into those States.

Anthony Benezet, a Quaker, of Philadelphia, in 1762 published a book in opposition to slavery.

Church and Slavery.—Slave-holding church members were first disciplined in 1769, by the Congregational Church at Newport, R. I. Dr. Samuel Hopkins, its pastor, so fearlessly denounced the traffic that the church voted the following: "*Resolved,* That the slave trade and the slavery of the Afri-

imported after the first day of December next, after which time we will wholly discontiue the slave trade, and will neither be concerned in it ourselves, nor will we hire our vessels nor sell our commodities or manufactures to those who are engaged in it." Similar articles had been adopted in Virginia, North Carolina and other colonies. Jefferson said before the Virginia Convention: "The abolition of domestic slavery is the greatest object of desire in these colonies, where it was unhappily fixed in their infant state." The above articles were generally adopted both in the Southern and Northern colonies. Subsequently most of the States took measures to abolish the slave trade, which was however renewed by South Carolina in 1803. Laws existed at this time in some of the colonies for the gradual abolition of slave-holding itself.

Quakers Refuse Fellowship with slaveholders. In 1774, at their yearly meeting in Philadelphia, the Friends withdrew fellowship from all members who continued to buy negroes. In later yearly meetings William Burling, of Long Island, Ralph Sandiford, of Philadelphia, Benjamin Lay, John Woolman and Anthony Benezet were active in their efforts to secure its cessation.— Benjamin Lay was especially zealous. He once seated himself in a meeting of slave-holding Friends with a bladder of blood hidden under his cloak. In the

bored steadfastly to abolish slavery.— President, Benjamin Franklin; Secretary, Benjamin Rush.

Vermont.—Slavery was abolished in Vermont by a convention held January 15, 1777. This was the first "Abolition State."

Pennsylvania.—Gradual emancipation of slaves was provided for March 1, 1780, by an act of the Pennsylvania Assembly.

Horrors of the Slave Trade.— In 1781 Captain Collingwood, commanding the Zong, threw a large number of sick negroes overboard, and afterward tried to collect their value from the insurers, but the English courts decided against him.

hushed stillness of their worship he arose and pierced the bladder, spilling blood on the floor and seats and garments of those nearest to him, and solemnly exclaimed: "Thus shall the Lord spill the blood of those that traffic in the blood of their fellow men." Some fainted, some shrieked, and the meeting broke up in disorder. In 1776 the Society of "Friends" decided that slaveholders should no longer remain members of their body.

Abolition of Slavery.—"The Pennsylvania Society for the Abolition of Slavery," organized April 14, 1775, in the Sun Tavern, on Second street, Philadelphia. The war prevented regular meetings until 1787. Thereafter it la-

An Anti-Slavery Barbacue took place at Woodbridge, N. J., in 1783, Dr. Bloomfield presiding.

New Hampshire. — In 1783 this State excluded slavery by the adoption of a constitution containing a declaration of rights, to take effect June, 1784.

Connecticut, by an act in 1784, gradually abolished slavery.

Rhode Island, in March, 1784, declared all persons born thereafter in the State free. The slave trade was strictly prohibited in the State October, 1787.

Anti-Slavery Society was organized in New York on January 25, 1785. John Jay was its first and Alexander Hamilton its second President.

Northwest Territory.—By the ordinance of 1787, passed July 11, for the government of the Northwest territory, "Slavery, or involuntary servitude, except for crime," was forbidden, and tracts of land were ceded for schools.

Prohibition of Slave Trade.— Three negroes having been kidnapped in Boston and sold in the West Indies, Massachusetts passed a law against slave-trading in 1788. Pennsylvania and Connecticut passed similar acts.

Congress Petitioned to Abolish Slavery.—The Pennsylvania Abolition Society petitioned Congress, February 12, 1790, to make slavery illegal. It was received favorably, but the 20-year law of 1788 debarred action.

Slave Trade.—March 23, 1790, Con-

among the French Canadians when Detroit and other places were surrendered in 1796. They were Pawnee tribes and their children, who had been sold by other tribes, who had captured them during war.

New York.—In April, 1799, an act was passed for the gradual abolition of slavery. In 1817 the Legislature passed another act providing for the abolition of slavery July 4, 1827.

Territories.—The citizens of Indiana territory in 1802 petitioned Congress to temporarily suspend the ordinance of 1787, prohibiting slavery, until labor became more plentiful in that region. The petition was not granted.

New Jersey.—The Legislature en-

gress voted that the importation of slaves could not be prohibited till 1808, but that Americans could be forbidden to sell slaves to foreigners, and that no foreigner could fit out a slaver in an American port.

National Abolition Convention, held at Philadelphia January 1, 1794, at which all the abolition societies in the country sent delegates, Congress was petitioned to suppress the slave trade.

Fugitive Slave Arrested in Boston in 1794.—While Josiah Quincy was defending a fugitive slave before the court, a confusion arose and the man escaped. His owner threatened Mr. Quincy with a suit, but did not execute his threat.

Indian Slavery was found to exist

acted laws for the gradual abolition of slavery February 15, 1804.

Slave Importation was forbidden by the United States March 2, 1807, after January 1, 1808. The British parliament passed a similar law about the same time.

Anti-Slavery Society. called the "Union Humane," was organized in 1815, at St. Clairsville, Virginia, by Benjamin Lundy.

Connecticut Abolished Slavery in 1818.

Congress declared the slave trade piracy in 1818.

Missouri Compromise.—Missouri applied for admission as a state January, 1820, but was opposed by the anti-slavery men. Maine also asked admission, and the pro-slavery men determined to deny its application unless Missouri was admitted with slavery. Exciting debates followed, until February 16, when, chiefly through the efforts and genius of Henry Clay, the following compromise was effected, viz.: "That Maine should be admitted free, and Missouri with slavery; that slavery should be forever prohibited north of the parallel of 36° 30″. South of that line states were to be admitted with or without slavery, as the people might determine."

Slavery in New York was abolished in 1827, under the statute of 1817. Ten thousand slaves became free, for

1833. John G. Whittier and Lewis Tappan were Secretaries. The American Anti-Slavery Society was formed, with Lewis Tappan as President. Auxiliary State societies were organized, tracts circulated and lectures sent over the country.

Connecticut Black Act.—In 1833 the Legislature enacted a law against schools for colored children, and Miss Prudence Crandall, who had opened one at Canterbury, was imprisoned for violating the law.

Irish Slave.—Mary Gilmore, a young Irish woman, was claimed in 1835 by a Maryland slaveholder as his fugitive slave. At the trial in Philadelphia it

which their owners received no compensation.

Obnoxious Abolitionists.—In 1831 Governor Lumpkin, of Georgia, offered $5,000 for the arrest and trial, under the laws of Georgia, of William L. Garrison. Subsequently $20,000 was offered for Arthur Tappan and $10,000 for Rev. A. A. Phelps.

New England Anti-Slavery Society was organized in Boston January 30, 1832. It demanded *immediate emancipation.*

New York City Anti-Slavery Society was organized October 2, 1833, in the Chatham Street Chapel.

National Anti-Slavery Convention, held at Philadelphia, December 4,

was proved that she had not a drop of negro blood in her veins.

Abolition Documents. — In 1835 President Jackson recommended the passage of a law to prevent the distribution of anti-slavery documents by mail in the South. It was referred to a committee, of which John C. Calhoun was a member, but Congress refused to pass such a law. Shortly after this Congress passed a law to prevent discrimination in mail matters, which the President signed. About this time the Legislatures of the Southern States endeavored to induce Northern Legislatures and Congress to make abolition agitation a penal offense.

Pinckney's Gag Rule was adopted

by the House of Representatives May 26, 1836. By it all petitions relating in whatever way to slavery were laid upon the table and never acted upon. Similar rules were adopted in 1837, '38, '40 and 41, and at one time the rule was made to operate against *all petitions*.

Massachusetts Abolition Society originated May 27, 1839, by secession from the "Anti-Slavery Society," because William L. Garrison advocated non-voting, under the constitution, as long as that instrument made slavery legal.

Census Returns of Slaves in 1840. Maine, Vermont, Massachusetts and Michigan had none. In Ohio were 3; Indiana, 3; Illinois, 331; Wisconsin, 11;

them free because they had landed on English soil.

American Anti-Slavery Society, in 1844, led by Mr. Garrison, formally denounced the United States Constitution as pro-slavery, and "a covenant with death and an agreement with hell." Its motto now was "no union with slave-holders."

"True American" was the name of an anti-slavery paper, issued at Lexington, Ky., in 1845, by Cassius M. Clay. A mob shipped it to Cincinnati, where Clay printed it for some time, but dated the publication office at Lexington.

"Wilmot" Proviso.—In Aug., 1846, David Wimot, a Pennsylvania Democrat, introduced a bill into Congress to pro-

---

---

and Iowa 16. The non-slaveholding states had 46,099 slaves in 1776, and in 1840 1,129. The slaveholding states had 456,000 slaves in 1776, and 2,486,126 in 1840.

False Imprisonment. — In July, 1841, upon a charge of aiding slaves to escape, three Illinois men, who had crossed the river into Missouri, were condemned to 12 years imprisonment.— They were pardoned for good behavior after suffering about five years.

Slaves Secure Their Freedom.— The brig Creole, with a cargo of tobacco and 135 slaves, sailed in 1842 from Richmond, Va., for New Orleans. The slaves overpowered the crew and put into the Bahamas. Nassau authorities pronounced

bibit slavery in all territory which might be secured by treaty from Mexico. It did not pass.

Fugitive Slaves.—In October, 1850, William and Ellen Crafts, who were living in Boston, were arrested as fugitives from Georgia. The claimants themselves were arrested for kidnapping and the Crafts were sent to England. Another fugitive slave named Shadrach, was arrested in Boston Feb. 15, 1851. He was rescued by a mob from the officers of the law in the United States court room. Another named Sims was arrested in Boston April 13, 1851, and returned to his master amid intense excitement.

Detroit.—A fugitive slave was captured in Detroit in October, 1850. The excitement was such that the military was ordered out. The citizens raised $500 and bought him of his claimant.

New York.—A fugitive slave in New York named Henry Long was returned to his owner by United States Judge Judson, December 23, 1850.

Christiana, Pa.—On Sept. 11, 1851, in a conflict between the United States Deputy Marshal's posse and the crowd, a fugitive slave escaped and the owner was killed. Thirty-nine persons were indicted by the United States for "wickedly and traitorously levying war against the United States." $70,000 was expended in these prosecutions, but nobody was convicted.

An Address on Slavery from 576,-

desk. He was so injured that he could not resume his seat for three years. The attack was made for a criticism uttered by Sumner upon Senator Butler, a relative of Brooks, in a debate upon Kansas affairs.

Dred Scott Decision.—March 6th, 1857, the United States Supreme Court gave a decision that widened the gulf between the North and the South. Dred Scott was the slave of Dr. Emerson, of Missouri, a United States army surgeon, who removed to Illinois and afterward to Minnesota, taking Dred Scott with him. He married a negro woman, to whom two children were born, and the whole family were taken to Missouri and sold. Dred Scott brought suit for

ooo English women to the women of America was made November 26, 1852.

Wisconsin.—The fugitive slave law was pronounced unconstitutional by the United States District Court of Wisconsin, February 3, 1855.

The "Echo," a slaver, was captured Aug. 27, 1858, and carried into Charleston, S. C. The negroes were sent to Liberia by the United States government.

Charles Sumner, United States Senator from Massachusetts, was assaulted by Preston S. Brooks, Representative from South Carolina, and beaten over the head with a heavy cane until he fell senseless. This occurred May 22, 1856, in the Senate chamber, after adjournment, while Sumner was seated at his

his freedom. He won his case in Missouri, but upon appeal to the United States Supreme Court it was decided that negroes, whether free or slave, "had no rights which the white people were bound to respect;" that under the constitution a slave was a personal chattel which the owner might move from place to place as he chose, through any state or territory; that the Missouri compromise and the compromise measures of 1850 were unconstitutional and void.— Roger B. Taney was Chief Justice.

African Slaves.—On November 28, 1858, the Yatcht "Wanderer" landed 300 at Brunswick, Georgia.

Re-opening the Slave Trade was

advocated on May 11, 1859, by a convention held at Vicksburg, Mississippi, on May 11, 1859.

Kansas.—A convention held at Wyandotte, Kansas, July 15, 1859, framed a new constitution prohibiting slavery.

John Brown's Raid.—In October, 1859, "Osawattomie Brown," of Kansas, made a mad attempt to incite an insurrection among the slaves of the South. With a party of 21 men (5 of whom were negroes), he made a sudden descent upon the United States arsenal at Harper's Ferry, and held it for nearly two days. The Virginia militia and the United States troops were called out to suppress the revolt. Thirteen of Brown's men were killed, two escaped, and the rest were captured. Brown and six companions were turned over to the authorities of Virginia, tried, condemned and hung. Brown was evidently sincere in the conviction that he was doing God and man a service. He met death calmly and with dignity. This tragedy excited the whole country. His memory was embalmed by the pulpit, the press and in song.

Arkansas.—Free negroes were banished from Arkansas by law passed Jan. 1, 1860.

Maryland.—Slaveholders in Maryland could not lawfully manumit slaves after June 1, 1860.

District of Columbia. — Slavery was abolished in the District of Columbia and prohibited in all future territories of the United States by Congress in July, 1862.

Emancipation Proclamation.—President Lincoln, on January 1, 1863, in accordance with a proclamation issued September 22, 1862, issued another proclamation conferring freedom upon all slaves within the rebellious States. The original draft of this paper was given to a sanitary fair in Chicago, and sold to F. B. Bryan for $3,000. The pen was given to Senator Sumner, who gave it to Geo. Livermore, of Boston.

TARIFF AND TAXES.

Internal Tax on Liquor was first imposed at Manhattan in June, 1644, by the Dutch West India Company.

Poll-Tax in This Country was first levied in Massachusetts in 1646.—First 1s. 8d., and afterward 25s. 6d. was laid upon every male over sixteen years of age.

Taxation in Massachusetts.—In 1661 the general court declared that no taxes should be laid on the colony except with its own consent.

Taxation in Rhode Island.—In 1664 the Assembly declared that "no aid, tax, tallage or custom, loan, benevolence, gift, excise, duty, or imposition whatever, shall be laid, assessed, imposed, levied or required of or on any of his Majesty's subjects within this colony, or upon their estates, upon any manner of pretense or color, but by the assent of the General Assembly of this province."

Custom Houses. — Royal custom houses for collecting taxes were established in 1673, to collect duties levied by the British government on "enumerated articles" of merchandise carried from one colony to another. This was the beginning of internal taxation. It was pronounced unconstitutional by some of the colonists.

Virginia. — In 1676 Virginia declared that its citizens, in common with other Englishmen, ought "not to be taxed but by their own consent, expressed by their representatives."

nated in the first tariff bill passed by Congress, on July 4, 1789, "for the encouragement and protection of manufactures."

Protective Tariff. — July 30, 1827, those favoring it held a national convention at Harrisburg, Pa.

Congressional Action. — Protective tariff upon imported cloths was imposed by Congress in June, 1832, which enraged the cotton planters, particularly in South Carolina.

Enforcing the Tariff. — Congress passed a bill in 1833 for the pupose of enforcing the tariff, against which Southern members, except John Tyler, refused to vote.

New Jersey. — In 1680 the New Jersey Assembly declared that the duties laid on goods without its consent were illegal and unconstitutional.

Taxes on Real Estate during war times, from 1753 to 1758, were at times two-thirds of the income tax.

Tariff Agitation. — The first petition to Congress was from Baltimore mechanics and tradesmen, April, 1789, who asked that government make them "independent in fact as well as in name," by a tariff on foreign articles, which would create a demand for home productions.

The "Protective System" origi-

Compromise Tariff. — A bill introduced by Henry Clay, providing for a gradual reduction of the tariff till 1842, became a law March, 1833.

Increased Duties. — The terrible financial stress for five years caused Congress to pass a bill, on the 30th day of August, 1842, increasing the duties on imported goods thirty-three per cent. and to reduce the free list. Prosperity followed.

An Anti-Free Trade procession of fifteen thousand men took place on the 9th day of February, 1878, in Pittsburg, Pennsylvania.

STEAMBOAT AND RAILROAD NAVIGATION.

"The Griffin" was the first vessel launched on the Great Lakes. She was of forty-five tons burden, and was built in 1679, just above Niagara Falls, by La Salle, who sailed her through Lake Erie, the Straits of Detroit, and Lake St. Clair up to Michillimackinac. He sent her back to Fort Frontenac with a load of furs, but she was never heard from, having doubtless been lost in a heavy gale which arose after she left.

"The Blessing of the Bay," a 30 ton vessel, built by Governor Winthrop, was launched at Medford, Mass., July 4, 1631.

A Steamboat was built by John Fitch in 1788. It made a few trips from

ed by a wheel under water at the stern of the boat. For a boiler it had a twelve gallon pot, with a plank top, secured by an iron bar and clamps. This was Fitch's last attempt to make steamboating a success. During a fit of depression he committed suicide.

Locomotive.—The first steam locomotive, probably in the world, was invented in 1797 by A. Kinsley, and run upon the streets in Hartford, Conn.

Steamboats. — The first effective steam engine after those of Fitch was built in 1798 by Nicholas Rooseveldt, in New York, who experimented in navigation.

Mississippi Steamboat.—A boat

Burlington to Philadelphia at a speed of four miles an hour.

Steamboat in Georgia in 1790. William Longstreet exhibited a steamboat on the Savannah, which sailed five miles an hour up stream.

A Passenger Steamboat was regularly run between Burlington and Philadelphia by John Fitch, in 1790. She was a stern-wheeler and made 7½ miles an hour.

A Stern-Wheel Steamboat was built in 1794 by Samuel Morey, of Hartford, Conn., who run it between Hartford and New York.

First Propeller.—John Fitch exhibited a little steamboat on "Collect Pond," New York City, in 1796, propell-

to navigate the Mississippi was projected in 1803 by Capt. James McKeever, United States Navy, and M. Louis Valcour, who built a boat with 80 feet keel and 18 feet beam in Kentucky, and floated it to New Orleans, where Oliver Evans was to put in a steam engine. Their money being exhausted they could not consummate their plans.

A Steamboat with a Screw Propeller was, in 1804, exhibited on the Hudson River by John C. Stevens. It crossed from Hoboken to New York.— He used a Watts engine and a tubular boiler of his own make.

Robert Fulton's Steamboat Clermont, left New York August 7, 1807, for Albany, making the trip and returning in 72 hours. This was the 16th steamboat which had been built but the first to permanently succeed.

Ocean Steam Navigation.—In 1808, the steamboat Phoenix, built by John Stevens, was sailed from Hoboken, N. J. to Philadelphia, by R. L Stevens. This was the first in the world.

Steamboat on Western Waters.—The first was the "New Orleans" launched at Pittsburg, Pa, March, 1811. It was 138 feet long, 30 feet wide, 300 tons burden, and cost $40,000 It was designed to run between Natchez and New Orleans. It cleared $20,000 the first season, and was snagged near Baton Rouge in 1814.

Steam War Vessel named "Fulton,

Railway.—The first in America was completed in 1827, at Quincy, Mass., for transporting granite for the Bunker Hill monument. It was operated by horse power on iron plated wooden rails.

Railway Charter.—The first in America was given in 1825 to the Mohawk and Hudson Company, N. Y.

Locomotive Trip.—The first in America was made in 1828 by the "Lion," manufactured in England, and run by Horatio Allen over the Carbondale and Honesdale R. R., from the Lackawaxen Canal to the Lackawanna river.

Baltimore & Ohio R. R.—July 4, 1828, Charles Carroll of Carrollton, the last surviving signer of the Declaration of Independence, set the corner stone of

the First," was built by Robert Fulton, and launched at New York October 29, 1814

Steam Ferryboat "Nassau," invented by Robert Fulton, began running between New York and Long Island in 1814.

Steamer on the Great Lakes.—In 1818, the "Walk in the Water," 360 tons burthen, was built at Black Rock, N. Y. She was the first steamer to enter Lake Michigan.

Steam Voyage Across the Atlantic, was first accomplished in 1819, by the Savannah, built in New York. She was a side-wheeler of 380 tons burthen. She sailed to Liverpool, and thence to St. Petersburgh

this road, which was planned for horse cars only. In 1830, Peter Cooper built a steam engine for its use.

Steam Locomotive.—The first made in America was run Dec. 9, 1830, on the South Carolina R. R. for two years. It was built at the West Point foundry on the Hudson. It was named "The Best Friend" and afterward the "Phœnix." A locomotive was built, about the same time, by Peter Cooper, at his iron works, Canton, Md., which was run successfully on the Baltimore and Ohio Railroad.

Locomotive "Ironsides," running on the Germantown R. R. in 1832 was advertised in the Philadelphia papers to "leave the station daily with passenger cars attached when it is pleasant. If rainy horses will be attached." The Ironsides was built by Mr. Baldwin.

Locomotives for Heavy Grades. On July 10th, 1836, the "George Washington," an engine built by M. W. Baldwin, was run up a grade of the Pennsylvania railroad, with a rise of one foot in fourteen, for two thousand eight hundred feet, drawing nine thousand pounds more than the engine, at fifteen miles an hour.

Steamers "Sirius" and "Great Western" both arrived from Great Britain at New York April 23, 1838.

English and Continental Express was organized by W. F. Harnden in 1841 to systematize emigration from Europe to the United States. In three

1855. Its span is 821 feet. The track is 245 feet above water. Its capacity is 12,000 tons.

Steamship Adriatic.—The largest ever built, was launched at New York April 7, 1855.

Panama Railway was completed, and the first train passed over it Jan. 28, 1855. It is 47½ miles long and cost $7,500,000.

Steamship "Great Eastern" arrived at New York June 28, 1860. She is 680 feet long and 18,915 tons burthen, and sails from 12 to 14 knots an hour. Four thousand passengers can be comfortably carried. She rendered efficient service in laying the Atlantic Cable some years afterward.

years 100,000 laborers had been brought over by it.

Steamboats Navigated the St. Lawrence rapids, between Kingston and Montreal, for the first time in 1842.

California Steamship Line.—On March 3, 1847, Congress authorized a line of steamers from New York to Aspinwall, and from Panama to California.

Street Railway in New York City was opened in 1852.

"Great Republic."—This vessel was launched at East Boston, Mass., October 4, 1853. She was the argest merchantman ever built, being 4,000 tons burden.

Niagara Suspension Bridge.—The first train passed over March 14th,

Pullman Sleeping and Parlor Cars were first made by George M. Pullman in 1864.

Pacific Railroad completed May 10, 1869. This grand project was first agitated by Asa Whitney in 1846. Congress passed the first bill in 1862 and a second in 1864. Surveys were begun on three routes in 1853, but the work was not pushed until 1865. The surveys cost $1,000,000. The roads, Union Pacific, and Central Pacific are 2,000 miles long, and cost $112,259,360. They cross nine mountain ranges and the greatest altitude reached is 8,242 feet above the sea, in the Black Hills. The highest grade is 116 feet to the mile. The roads unite at Promontory point, Utah. The last tie of laurel wood plated with silver, was laid, and the last spike of iron, silver and gold was driven in the presence of a large crowd with great rejoicing in San Francisco and Washington, D. C.

Denver and Rio Grande R. R., the first "narrow gauge," was constructed in 1870.

Steamer R. E. Lee sailed from St. Louis, Mo., to New Orleans, La., in July, 1870, in 3 days, 18 hours and 14 minutes.

Narrow Gauge Cars were first used in America on the Denver and Rio Grande Railroad, August 2, 1871. The dimensions were 35 feet long, 7 feet wide and 10½ feet high. Capacity 36 passengers.

and horse power. They can sail over 15½ knots per hour.

Lightning Express Train reached San Francisco, Cal., on June 4th, 1876, in eighty-three hours and thirty-four minutes from New York.

Great Republic, the largest river steamer in the world, was launched at St. Louis, Mo., in 1876. Its dimensions are: Length, 340 feet; beam, 57 feet; width on deck, 103 feet; diameter of wheels, 37 feet. It carries two hundred and eighty passengers and four thousand tons cargo. It cost two hundred thousand dollars.

Trip of the "Uncle Sam."—Aug. 11th, 1879, Captain Goldsmith and wife left St. John's, New Foundland, in a very

Railroad Speed.—May 15, 1872, the directors' car of the New York Central Railroad run from Rochester to Syracuse, eighty-one miles, in eighty-two minutes.

Steamship Line between Philadelphia and Liverpool, viz.: The Pennsylvania, Indiana, Ohio and Illinois, each over 3,000 tons burden, began regular trips in July, 1873.

Largest Iron Steamers in the world were launched at Chester, Pa., in 1874, by John Roach & Sons. They were the City of Pekin and the City of Tokio, built for the Pacific Mail Steamship line. They each carry five thousand tons and one thousand six hundred and fifty passengers, and have engines of five thous-

small boat, for a trip round the world. When a day out Mrs. Goldsmith became ill, but they persisted in going on. The fifth day they encountered heavy gales and would have perished but for their rescue by the "Queen of the Nations," a Liverpool vessel. The "Uncle Sam" was left to her fate.

Mexican Railway Lines were projected in September, 1880, by Gen. U. S. Grant and leading capitalists.—General Grant wrote to General Matias Romers, of Mexico, prophesying immediate and extraordinary prosperity for that country, upon the completion of the proposed railroads, provided she could elect her next president without revolution.

AGRICULTURAL EVENTS.

Sugar Cane.—In 1506 slips of cane were brought from the Canary Islands to Hayti. It was found to flourish and mills were set up, and in a few years it was the chief industry of the island.

Potatoes were first introduced into England from America by Sir John Hawkins in 1563, and into Ireland by Sir Walter Raleigh in 1586.

Tobacco.—Its use was first introduced into England in 1586, by the returned colonists from Roanoke, Virginia. Sir Walter Raleigh became a smoker. On one occasion, his servant seeing a cloud of smoke issuing from his mouth, supposed he was on fire and dashed a pitcher of ale into his face to put it out. It was

Swine and Neat Cattle were first imported into Plymouth in 1624.

Swine and Sheep were introduced into the Dutch colonies at Manhattan in 1625.

Buckwheat began to be cultivated on Manhattan Island in 1626.

Sheep Were First Imported into Massachusetts Bay Colony in 1633.

First Apple Trees in America were on Governor's Island, in Boston Harbor, and bore "10 fair pippins," in 1639.

First Nursery in America, in 1640, was started by Governor Endicott, at Danvers, Massachusetts. It was an apple nursery, and large quantities of trees were sold.

---

first successfully cultivated in Virginia in 1612. Its sale increased so rapidly, and the profits were so great that all the ground, and even the streets of Jamestown were planted with it. Notwithstanding the opposition of King James and his government, it became the staple product and currency of the colony.

Wheat was sown on Long Island in 1605 by a ship's company from London.

Cotton was planted in Virginia in 1621 and was successfully cultivated.

Silk Culture in Virginia. In 1623 the Legislature passed an order for all settlers to plant Mulberry trees, in order to engage them in raising other products beside tobacco.

Bees were introduced into Boston in 1670 by the English.

Over-Production. — Tobacco culture in 1681 in Virginia being in large excess of the demand, bands of men called "Plant Cutters" went among the plantations cutting up young plants, for which some of the leaders were hanged by Lord Culpepper. He tried to remedy the difficulty by inflating the currency, without success.

Rice Culture in America began in 1694 by planting a little package of rice from Madagascar, which was given to Governor Smith, of South Carolina, by a sea captain.

Logwood in Jamaica.—In 1715 seed from Central America was planted in this island, which has since largely supplied the trade of the world with logwood.

Coffee Culture in the West Indies and Brazil. A single plant brought from Marly to Martenique, in 1715, was the parent stock of this great industry in these countries.

Silk and Indigo were introduced into Louisiana in 1718 by John Laws' "Company of the West." Silk cocoons raised in Georgia were shown by Gov. Oglethorpe to Queen Caroline in 1734.—From them she had a birth-day dress made,

Silk Culture in Connecticut.—In 1747 Governor Law wore the first coat

1784, were seized on the ground that "so much cotton could not be produced in the United States."

The First Sea Island Cotton was grown in the United States in 1786, on Sapelo Island, Georgia, from Pernambuco seed sent to Frank Levett by Patrick Walsh, of Jamaica.

Maple Sugar.—On July 17, 1790, a half a ton of maple sugar was shipped to Philadelphia from Stockport, on the Delaware. Later, Albany, New York, sent 40 hogsheads.

Spanish Merino Sheep. — Three were first imported from Cadiz by Wm. Foster, of Boston, in 1793. He pre-sented them to Andrew Cragie, who killed and ate them, and afterward paid

and stockings made from New England silk.

Sugar Cane in Louisiana.—In April, 1751, the Jesuits obtained slips of cane from the West Indies and planted them in gardens in New Orleans. From these slips came the great sugar plantations in the South.

Potatoes from Spain were introduced into New England in 1764.

Improved Breeding Cattle were first imported into the United States in 1783, by Mathew Patton, of Virginia.

South Carolina Agricultural Society was organized in 1784. It was the first in America and still exists.

Exportation of Cotton. — Eight bales of cotton, exported to England in

one thousand dollars per head for the same kind.

A Cast-Iron Plow was invented in 1797, by Charles Newbold, of Burlington, New Jersey. He could not sell them because the farmers believed that they "poisoned the soil, ruined the crops and promoted the growth of rocks."

Merino Buck.—The first full blooded one was imported into New York in 1801.

"Arlington Sheep-Shearing." — April 30, 1803, George Washington Parke Custis, owner of Arlington Heights, opposite Washington, D. C., inaugurated an annual sheep-shearing and banquet on his estate, which was kept up for a number of years. Prizes were given for specimens of fine woolen manufactures.

Reaping Machine.—John J. Hawkins and Richard French patented the first one in 1803. It was not a success.

Agricultural Fair.—In 1804, the first in America was held at Washington, D. C,

Mexican Cotton.—In 1806 Walter Burling, of Natchez, Miss., introduced the seed into the United States. As the Spanish government forbade its importation it was stuffed into a lot of dolls, which were permitted to pass by an understanding with the Viceroy.

Agricultural Society.—The first was organized at Georgetown, D. C., on November 28, 1809, under the name of the "Columbian Society for the Promotion of Rural and Domestic Economy."

given to silkworm culture A specimen of this mulberry tree was brought from France to the United States It was claimed to be hardy, easy of propagation, prolific in foliage, and more profitable than any other in feeding silkworms. In 1834 a great speculation raged. Large plantations were set out in several States, and plants were sold at $5.00 each. In 1839 there was a reaction. They sold at three cents and speculators were ruined.

Pear Tree.—In 1834 a tree near Vincennes, Ill., yielded 184 bushels. In 1840 it bore 140 bushels. Its trunk was 10 feet in circumference.

Strawberries.—In 1834 Mr. Hovey, of Boston, produced his famous seed-

---

Sheep-Shearing.—In 1810 Chancellor R. R. Livingston held a famous sheep-shearing at his place on the Hudson. He had taken great interest in improving the sheep stock of the country, and had imported fine merinos. He sold some of them from $50 to $1,000 per head. A sheep mania arose for several years, but when the excitement passed away a $1,000 buck sold for $12.

Horticultural Society.—The first in the United States was founded in 1829.

Silk Culture.—In 1829 the Mansfield Silk Company was organized in Connecticut, from which a silk worm mania grew that lasted for 10 or 12 years.

"Morus Multicaulis" Mania.— From 1830 to 1840 great attention was

ling. It was the first attempt to improve the culture of this berry.

American Pomological Society was established October 10, 1848, in New York. The North American Pomological Convention was organized about the same time in Buffalo, New York. In 1849 the two were merged into the first one named.

National Agricultural Convention at Washington, D. C., was held June 24, 1852. Delegates from twenty-two States and the District of Columbia were present.

National Agricultural Society was organized in 1852. Since 1863 the Department of Agriculture has done the same work.

American Reapers at Paris in 1855 At a trial between reapers from all nations, England, Algiers and the United States were represented. The American cut an acre of oats in twenty-two minutes, the English did the same in sixty-six, and the Algerine in seventy-two minutes.

Great Mower Contest at Syracuse, New York, in 1857. Forty machines competed. The "Buckeye" was declared the victor.

Department of Agriculture was organized in 1862 by the United States, and buildings have since been erected in the Smithsonian grounds for it.

Grangers.—The National Grange of the Patrons of Husbandry was organized at Washington, D. C., December 4, 1867, by William Saunders, Superintendent of the Gardens of the Department of Agriculture. In 1876 there were nineteen thousand granges.

Wonderful Sale of Short-Horn Cattle at New York Mills, Oneida Co., New York, September 10, 1873. A cow sold for $40,000, a calf for $27,000. For one hundred and nine cattle the sum of $382,000 was paid.

THE REBELLION.

Cheers for a Southern Confederacy.—On November 7th, 1860, the news of Mr. Lincoln's election as President of the United States, was received at Charleston, South Carolina, with cheers for a Southern Confederacy. The "Palmetto" flag was hoisted on the vessels in the harbor.

Aid for a Confederacy.—On November 10th, 1860, a bill was introduced into the South Carolina Legislature to raise and equip 10,000 men. The Legislature also ordered the election of a convention to consider the question of secession.

Appropriation From Georgia.—On November 18, 1860, the Georgia Legislature appropriated $1,000,000 to arm the State.

Right of Secession was denied by President Buchanan, in his message to Congress on December 3, 1860, and the right to coerce the rebellious States was asserted.

First Hostilities.—January 9, 1861, the Union steamer "Star of the West," loaded with supplies for the troops at Fort Sumpter, was fired upon by a battery on Morris Island, Charleston Harbor, South Carolina.

Seizure of Arms.—On January 22, 1861, thirty-eight cases of arms were seized in New York as they were being shipped to Savannah, Georgia. They were afterwards given up, as it could not be proved that they were consigned to disloyal persons.

Confederate Government.—A provisional government of the Southern States was organized at Montgomery, Alabama, February 4, 1861' with Jefferson Davis, of Mississippi, as President, and Alexander H. Stephens, of Georgia, Vice-President. On February 22, 1862, they were inaugurated as President and Vice-President of the Southern Confederacy.

Peace Congress met in Washington on February 4, 1861, with representatives from thirteen Northern States and seven border States. Nothing was accomplished.

Stars and Bars was adopted as the national flag of the Confederate States, March, 1861.

President Calls for Troops. —

20th of June elected Francis H. Pierepont as Governor.

Baltimore Secessionists attempted to take possession of the city June 27, 1861, with the aid of the police. The plot was foiled by ex-Governor Banks, of Massachusetts.

Kentucky Neutrality. — The neutrality of this State was ended September 6, 1861, by General U. S. Grant, who came from Cairo and took possession of Paducah.

"On to Richmond." —On March 10, 1862, President Lincoln ordered McClellan to advance upon Richmond. He started down the Potomac when the Confederates immediately evacuated

President Lincoln issued a proclamation April 15, 1861, calling upon the States for 75,000 troops "to suppress combinations and cause the laws to be duly executed." The Governors of Kentucky, Virginia, Tennessee and Missouri refused to furnish troops under the President's proclamation.

Three Years' Troops. —On May 3, 1861, President Lincoln called for 42,000 three years' volunteers, 22,000 troops for the regular army and 18,000 seamen.

West Virginia. —On May 13, 1861, the inhabitants of the western counties of Virginia met in convention and denounced the secession of Virginia, and agreed to form a new State, and on the

Manassas, so McClellan returned to Alexandria the next day.

Confiscation Proclamation, authorized by Congress, was issued by President Lincoln in July, 1862. It declared the property of all persons remaining in rebellion at the end of 60 days confiscated to the National Government.

Conscription. — Enrolling boards were ordered in each Congressional District by proclamation of the President, May 8, 1863, in accordance with an act of Congress.

SECESSION OF SOUTHERN STATES.

Alabama seceded January 11, 1861.
Arkansas seceded May 6, 1861.

Florida seceded January 11, 1861.

Georgia seceded January 19, 1861.

Louisiana seceded January 26, 1861.

Maryland, at a special session of her Legislature, April 26, 1861, passed resolutions of neutrality.

Mississippi seceded January 9, 1861.

Missouri.—A secession ordinance was passed by a portion of the Missouri Legislature November 2, 1861, who assembled for that purpose. A State Convention held at Jefferson, July 22, 1861, declared all the State offices vacant, and called a new election for Governor, Legislators, etc.

North Carolina seceded May 21, 1861.

South Carolina seceded December 20, 1860. Her United States Senators and Federal officers promptly resigned, and United States property within the State was seized and held.

Tennessee passed an ordinance of secession May 6, 1861, subject to the vote of the people, who ratified it in June.

Texas passed an ordinance of secession at a convention held February 1, 1861, to submit to the people, and on March 4 the State was voted out the Union by 40,000 majority.

Virginia seceded April 17, 1861, and immediately seized upon United States property and began to raise troops.

THE BATTLES OF THE REBELLION.
(Alphabetically arranged. See also Surrenders, etc.)

Antietam.—The battle of Antietam was fought September 17, 1862. Lee's army of 60,000 was collected at Sharpsburg, in the Antietam valley. McClellan came up on the opposite side of the creek with 90,000 Union troops. Four stone bridges spanned the creek, which the Federal forces crossed. The battle raged desperately all day, and at night General Lee's forces were drawn off and retired into Virginia, leaving 3,500 prisoners, 39 stands of colors and 13 guns in the hands of the victors. The Union loss was 2,010 killed, 9,416 wounded and 1,043 missing. Confederate loss, 14,000.

Atlanta, Ga., was captured September 1, 1864. On May 7th General Sherman with 100,000 men, left Chattanooga. At Dalton he met 60,000 Confederates under Johnston. By fighting and flanking he pressed them back from point to point until they made a stand on the Kenesaw mountains, where several bloody battles were fought. Johnston then retired to Atlanta July 10th. Here he was superseded by Gen. J. B. Hood. He made desperate but unsuccessful assaults upon Sherman's lines, losing heavily in each engagement The siege was closely pressed and Hood's supplies were cut off, so that he evacuated the place to save his army.

Arkansas Post Captured January 11, 1862, by the Federals under General McClernand. It was garrisoned by 5,000 Confederates.

Averasboro, N. C. — Battle of Averasboro took place on March 16, 1865. Hardee made an effort to retard Sherman's progress, but was repulsed with considerable loss.

Baker's Creek, Miss.—A battle was fought here May 15, 1863, between Generals Grant and Pemberton. Each army had about 25,000 troops. The Confederates were disastrously defeated, losing twenty-six hundred in killed and wounded, two thousand prisoners and twenty-nine guns.

Ball's Bluff Disaster, October 21,

Farragut ran the Vicksburg batteries and captured this place.

Belmont, Mo.—The battle of Belmont, Missouri, was fought November 7, 1861. General Grant, with 3,000 Illinois volunteers, moved upon Belmont, opposite Columbus, where there was a large force of Confederates, which had been sent by General Polk to reinforce Gen. Price. The camp was well protected by abattis, notwithstanding which it was carried by assault and a large number of men, horses and artillery were captured, and the camp was burned. The Union loss was 485. The Confederates lost 632.

Big Black River, May 17, 1863. Grant, after his victory at Champion Hills, pursued and attacked Pemberton

---

1861. General McClellan sent General C P. Stone, with 4,000 troops, to make a demonstration on Leesburg, Virginia. Colonel Devens was ordered to cross the Potomac at Edward's ferry with 700 men, and Colonel Baker was sent across Conrad's ferry with a force to attract the enemy's attention from Colonel Devens. They had to cross in two old scows and climb a steep bluff 100 to 150 feet high. No sooner had they accomplished this than they were overwhelmed by a superior force, and after a fierce contest, in which Baker was killed, his forces were driven back with great slaughter. The Union loss was 1,000 and the Confederates lost 300.

Baton Ruoge, August 5, 1862.—

at this river, capturing 1,500 prisoners, arms, commissary stores, etc. The Confederates fled to Vicksburg, burning bridges behind them.

Big Bethel, Va.—The battle of Big Bethel was fought June 10, 1861. Gen. Pierce, in command of the Union troops, pushed on to this point where Colonels Hill and Magruder commanded 1,800 Confederates, with 20 heavy cannon, with which they opened fire on General Pierce's forces. The Union troops returned the fire, drove them back until the ammunition of their battery was exhausted, when they in turn retreated.— Reinforcements from Fortress Monroe arrived and covered their retreat. The Confederate cavalry pursued them six miles, and then retired with the whole army to Yorktown. The Union loss was 16 killed, 39 wounded and missing. Both Butler and Pierce were censured for this affair.

Bentonsville, N. C., March 19, 1865. Gen. Johnston suddenly attacked Sherman's flank in force, and but for the tremendous fighting of Gen. Jeff. C. Davis' division would have nearly ruined the Union army. On the 21st it entered Goldsborough, and· Raleigh on the 13th of April, which ended Sherman's grand march.

Blackwater, Mo., December 19th, 1861. General Pope attacked a Confederate force near Milford. Lieut. Gordon led the charge with cavalry, and sup-

ville. Gen. Lyon, with a Union force, put them to flight, June 18, 1861, capturing 20 prisoners, 2 cannon, and a lot of military stores. Jackson fled 50 miles. The Union loss was two killed and nine wounded.

Boston Mountains, Mo., Nov. 27, 1862. The Confederates made an effort to regain Missouri to their cause. Raising an army of 20,000 they advanced northward, but met with a repulse at this point.

Bull Run, July 21, 1861.—After the Union successes in Western Virginia the North became impatient, and "On to Richmond!" was their cry. The Confederates were mainly concentrated at Manassas Junction, 27 miles west of Al-

ported by the infantry, routed a Confederate force of 1,300 infantry and cavalry. They captured 800 horses and mules, 1,000 stand of arms, and 70 wagon loads of supplies.

Bristow Station, Va.—In October, 1863, Lee attempted a demonstration on Washington. He successfully turned Meade's flanks and pushed him back nearly to Manassas. At Bristow station General Hill's corps encountered Gen. Warren's corps of Meade's army, and was defeated with a loss of five hundred prisoners.

Booneville, Mo.—Governor Jackson had called out 50,000 State militia, and placed ex-Governor Price in command, part of whom were encamped at Boone-

exandria, under General Beauregard.— Another large force under Gen. Joseph E. Johnston was within supporting distance in the Shenandoah valley. The Union army under Gen. Irwin McDowell was at Alexandria, while General Patterson's army was in front of Johnston to prevent his junction with Beauregard. On the 16th the Union army advanced and came upon the Confederates on the morning of the 21st, between Bull Run and Manassas Junction. A general engagement ensued, and at noon the advantage was with the Union troops. At that time Johnston, having eluded Patterson, arrived with 6,000 fresh troops. The tide of victory turned, and McDowell's army was hurled back in route and confusion. A panic ensued, and soldiers, civilians and teamsters rushed back pell mell to Washington. The Union loss was 2,952; the Confederates lost 2,050.— The North was now convinced that the war would not "end in 90 days," but that preparations for a long and bloody contest was necessary. Congress voted to raise 500,000 men and $500,000,000 in money.

Bull Run.—The second battle of Bull Run took place August 28, 29 and 31, 1862. Desperate fighting between Pope's worn out army and the Confederates occurred on these days. At one time victory was within Pope's grasp, but Fitz John Porter withheld his reinforcements, and Pope was beaten and

Confederates. He abandoned his baggage and heavy artillery and fled toward St. George. McClellan overtook him at Carrick's ford, where he made a stand, but was defeated and he was killed.

Carthage, Mo., July 5, 1861.—Col. Sigel, commanding a Union force of 1,500, attacked Governor Jackson's army of 5,000 nine miles north of Carthage. Sigel broke the enemy's front with artillery and followed it with an infantry charge. The disparity of forces compelled Sigel to retreat with a loss of 13 killed, 31 wounded, 90 prisoners, 4 cannon, 9 horses and a baggage wagon.— The Confederates lost 35 killed, 125 wounded, 45 prisoners, 80 horses and a number of guns.

forced to retire to Centreville. Porter was court-martialed and forever disqualified from holding any office of trust in the United States Government.

Carnifex Ferry, W. Va.—General Floyd, commanding the Confederate forces, attempted to regain Western Virginia, and surprised and routed Col. Tyler at Cross Lanes on the 9th of September, 1861, but was himself attacked by General Rosecrans at Carnifex ferry. Floyd escaped at night, abandoning a large amount of ammunition and provisions.

Carrick's Ford, W. Va., July 12, 1861. Pegram's defeat at Rich Mountain uncovered General Garnett's position, who commanded the main body of the

Cedar Mountain, August 8, 1862.— General Banks, while endeavoring to effect a junction with Pope, was attacked at this point by "Stonewall" Jackson. Desperate fighting alone saved the Union troops from a rout. 2,000 were lost on each side.

Champion Hills, Miss., May 16, 1863.—After the Confederates were defeated at Jackson, Johnston and Pemberton made an attempt to concentrate their forces at Clinton to crush the rear of the Federal army. While on his way Pemberton was met at Champion Hills by General Grant and forced to battle. The engagement was desperate and lasted for one hour and a half, when the Confederate left gave away and Pemberton's army fell back in confusion with Gen. Grant in pursuit. Grant captured 2,000 prisoners.

Chancellorsville, May 2-3, 1863.—On April 27th, General Hooker, commanding the Union troops, crossed the Rappahannock 10 miles below Fredericksburg and took a position at Chancellorsville. Here he was attacked by Lee. Jackson, with 25,000 men, fell like a thunder cloud upon Hooker's right wing and swept everything before him, but in the twilight "Stonewall" was mortally wounded by a volley from his own men. The conflict was renewed on the 3d. The Confederates forced the Union army back to the river, which it recrossed on the 5th, defeated. The

Charleston, S. C.—The siege of this city commenced April 7, 1863. Admiral Dupont, with a fleet of iron-clads, attempted to pass Fort Sumpter, but was unsuccessful. In June the city was besieged by the land and naval forces of Gen. Gilmore and Admiral Dahlgreen. Batteries were planted on Morris' island, and two unsuccessful attempts to capture Fort Wagner by assault were made, resulting in great loss. On the 7th of September the Confederates evacuated it and retired to Charleston. This enabled Gilmore to plant his guns within 4 miles of the city. Fort Sumpter had been pounded into powder on the side next Morris' island, but it could not be taken. The only gain was to completely

Union loss was 17,000; the Confederates 12,000.

Chantilly, September 1, 1862.—General Lee, after the second battle of Bull Run, sent Jackson to flank Pope's position at Centerville, but Pope anticipated his movements, and fell back to Fairfax Court-house. Gen. Jackson encountered the Union force under General Reno, who was stationed at Chantilly.— A severe battle ensued in which the Union Generals Stevens and Kearney were killed. Colonel Birney then drove Jackson off by a bayonet charge. Pope then retired within the Washington entrenchments and his army was consolidated with the army of the Potomac under General McClellan.

blockade the port, as the harbor and city remained in possession of the Confederates.

Chattanooga, November 23-5, 1863. Bragg was besieging Chattanooga, and had cut the Federal lines of communication, but, with the arrival of Hooker's and Sherman's corps, and with Grant in command, offensive operations were begun by the Union army. The Confederates were in a strong position, with their left wing on Lookout mountain and their right on Missionary ridge. On the 20th Bragg notified Grant to remove all non-combatants from the city, which he proposed to bombard. On the 23d Hooker gained a position at the foot of Lookout mountain, and the next morning charged and captured the Confederate rifle pits before 9 o'clock. A heavy fog hung over the mountain concealing their movements, and Hooker ordered a charge up the ascent, which was successfully made in the face of a heavy fire, and by 2 o'clock the Union flag floated from the summit. The defeated Confederates retreated to Missionary ridge. This was the celebrated "Battle above the clouds." The Confederate loss was about 6,000 in killed, wounded and prisoners. Union loss between 3,-000 and 4,000 in killed and wounded.

Cheat Mountain, Va., Skirmishes September 11-13, 1861.—General Lee, in attempting to open communication with the Shenandoah Valley, attacked the

ing to crush Rosecrans' right, but was out-generaled, and the battle began on the morning of the 20th on the Federal left, commanded by Thomas. The struggle continued with varying success for several hours, when, by a blunder of General Wood, the center of the Union army was weakened, which Longstreet, perceiving, dashed in and cut the Union army in two, capturing Rosecrans and routing the right wing. Thomas, by desperate valor, held the left until nightfall, and then fell back into the intrenchments at Chattanooga. The Union loss was nearly 19,000; that of the Confederates nearly 21,000.

Chickasaw Bluffs, December 28, 1862. Sherman, ignorant of the disaster

Federals under General Reynolds, who was posted at Elkwater, Cheat Mountain Pass and the Summit, with 600 men. Lee's force was 5,000, but he was repulsed at each point with a loss of 190. Reynolds lost 98.

Chickamauga, Tenn., September 19 and 20, 1863. In August, Bragg was at Chattanooga with 40,000 Confederate troops. General Rosecrans, with 60,000, caused him to evacuate the place, which he then occupied. Being reinforced by Buckner and Longstreet, Bragg returned with 80,000, to attack Rosecrans. In the meantime General Burnside had reinforced Rosecrans. The two armies met in the Chickamauga Valley, September 18th. Bragg massed his troops, intend-

at Holly Springs, made an assault upon the Confederate intrenchments at Chickasaw Bayou, but was repulsed with a loss of over 2,000 men, while the Confederate loss was only 200. He retired to the gun-boats and abandoned the enterprise.

Cold Harbor, Va., June 3, 1864.—General Grant, unable to force Lee's front at Spottsylvania, began another flank movement and encountered the Confederates strongly entrenched at this point, 12 miles northeast of Richmond. Repeated assaults upon their position resulted in dreadful repulses, but the Union forces held their lines firmly. During these repeated assaults the Union loss was nearly 10,000, while the Confederate loss was a little over 1,000.

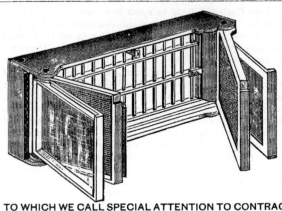

Corinth, April 27, 1862.—The army of the Tennessee, 100,000 strong, commanded by Gen. Halleck, after a delay of several days, moved toward Corinth. The delay had given Beauregard time to reinforce and reorganize his army, and they now numbered 65,000.

Corinth Evacuated, May 30, 1862. When Halleck arrived at Corinth he found nothing but smouldering ruins, Beauregard having fled before his superior force, taking with him all that was valuable.

Corinth, Oct. 3-4, 1862.—General Rosecrans, with 20,000 men, was attacked at this point by Price and Van Dorn with 38,000. They were repulsed after an obstinate contest of two days.

latter was repelled with 186 killed and wounded. The Federal loss was 66.—This closed the campaign of 1861, at the end of which the Confederates were in possession of the immense arsenals at Harper's Ferry, Norfolk and Columbus, Fort Henry, Fort Donelson, Bowling Green, Mill Spring and Cumberland Gap, constituting a strongly fortified line of defense. They had been acknowledged as belligerents and had 350,-000 troops. The Union army had 500,-000, had saved West Virginia, Missouri and Maryland, and thrown the entire South in a state of siege by sea and land. The Federal plan was now to open the Missssppi, blockade the Southern ports and capture Richmond.

Crampton's Gap, Sept. 14, 1862.—General Franklin, marching to relieve Harper's Ferry, encountered three Confederate brigades guarding this gap. After a hard fight they were driven out with a loss of 1,000. Franklin lost 500.

Cross Keys, Va., June 8, 1862.—General McDowell, with 40,000 troops, crossed into the Shenandoah Valley to cut off Stonewall Jackson, who was near Harper's Ferry. Jackson, perceiving his object, fled rapidly up the valley. Fremont pursued and attacked him at Cross Keys unsuccessfully.

Drainsville, Va., Dec. 20, 1861. Gen. McCall, with 4,000 Union troops, was attacked by General Stuart, with 2,500, men while gathering forage. The

Dug Springs, Mo., Aug. 2, 1861. General Lyon, with 5,000 men, met the Confederates nineteen miles southwest of Springfield, as they were advancing on that place, and drove them away, killing and wounding about eighty. His own loss was thirty-eight killed, wounded and missing.

Fair Oaks, Va., June 1, 1862.—McClellan's vast army, lying on both sides of the Chickahominy, within seven miles of Richmond, was suddenly attacked by the Confederates and a two days' battle raged. The latter were driven back with a loss of about 8,000 and their General Johnston seriously wounded. The Federal loss nearly equalled the Confederates.

Falling Waters, Va., July 2, 1861. A battle was fought here between Gen. Patterson's advance, under Colonel J. J. Abercrombie, and a detachment of Gen. Johnston's army under Gen. Jackson. The latter was driven 5 miles to Haines-ville, where he was reinforced heavily, and the United States troops then ceased their pursuit.

Fairfax Court-House, Va., June 1, 1861.—A fight occurred here between 75 cavalrymen under Lieutenant Tompkins and the Confederates. He lost six men, captured five and killed twenty.

Fayetteville, N. C., March 8, 1865. General Kilpatrick was nearly captured by a sudden attack of Wade Hampton, but he escaped on foot into a swamp, closely, as it retreated from the battle of Gaines' Farm, and charged repeatedly upon its rear, but were finally driven back with heavy loss.

Fredericksburg, Va., Dec. 13, 1862. Learning Burnside's plans, Lee massed his forces at Fredericksburg and posted 300 cannon on the heights. The river was crossed on pontoons by the Federal troops, and General Meade began the fight upon Jackson's advance with some success, but with a final repulse and heavy loss. Longstreet was strongly posted behind a stone wall with heavy reserves. He was successively attacked by Generals French, Hancock and Howard, all of whom were beaten back with terrible slaughter. Burnside now de-

and rallying his forces scattered the Confederates by a brilliant charge.

Five Forks. Va., April 1, 1865.— General Sheridan, with 9,000 cavalry and Warren's corps of Infantry, assaulted this fort in Lee's rear, and captured it with 5,000 prisoners. This rendered the position of Lee untenable.

Florida and Georgia Expeditions.— On February 28, 1862, Com. Dupont and Gen. Wright left Port Royal and successively captured Fernandina, Fort Clinch, Jacksonville, Darien and St. Augustine. Mobile, Charleston and Savannah were now the only Atlantic ports held by the Confederates.

Frazier's Farm, June 30, 1862.—The Confederates followed the Union army termined to carry the heights, and repeated charges were made which met with disastrous repulses. Night ended the carnage, and on the 16th Burnside was persuaded by his general officers to withdraw. Burnside lost in this battle in killed, wounded and missing, 12,250. Lee's loss was 5,309.

Fort Donelson was attacked by General Grant, aided by Foote's flotilla, February 16, 1862. It was a strong fort, being defended by 10,000 Confederates under General Buckner. On the 14th the gun-boats were driven back, Com. Foote being among the wounded. On the 15th Buckner endeavored to break through Grant's lines, but was repulsed. On the 16th he asked for an armistice to negotiate terms for a capitulation. Gen. Grant replied that "no terms but unconditional surrender would be accepted," and added : "I propose to move immediately upon your works." Buckner thereupon surrendered. Between 12,000 and 15,000 prisoners, 40 cannon, and a large amount of stores were captured.— Union loss was 321 killed, 1,046 wounded and 150 missing. Kentucky was immediately evacuated by the Confederates.

Fort Donelson was attacked February 3, 1863, by General Wheeler, with a force of 5,000 Confederates. It was garrisoned by only 600 Union troops under Colonel Harding, but he gallantly defended it until the gun boats came and dispersed Wheeler's cavalry.

and Wetzel decided that the attempt would result in the destruction of the army, and returned to Hampton Roads, the fleet remaining. Grant sent another force of 8,000 under Terry. After a heavy bombardment the soldiers and sailors together captured the fort.

Fort Macon, N. C., captured April 26, 1862, by a detachment sent by Gen. Burnside.

Fort Pillow Massacre, April 13, 1864. Gen. Forrest, with 5,000 Confederate cavalry, attacked this fort, which was garrisoned by 560 troops, half of whom were colored. Demanding its surrender under cover of a flag of truce, he surprised the fort and butchered about 300, chiefly negroes, in cold blood.

Fort de Russy, La., March 14, 1864. When Banks' Red River expedition approached this fort, Taylor marched out to attack the land force and prevent its co-operation with the Union fleet. The Union commander, General Franklin, refused battle and slipped into Taylor's entrenchments, capturing 300 prisoners and all his supplies. The fleet passed on and seized Alexandria, 150 miles up the river.

Fort Fisher, N. C., captured January 16, 1865. This last Confederate sea-port was attacked in December, 1864, by a squadron under Admiral Porter, and a land force under Butler. After a heavy bombardment the troops were sent on shore to storm the works, but Butler

Fort Pulaski, Ga., captured April 12, 1862. General Gilmore and Captain Davis left Port Royal with a land and naval force for an expedition up the Savannah river. Erecting a 36-gun battery they besieged Fort Pulaski for three days, when it surrendered. But one life was lost on either side.

Fort Steadman captured March 25, 1865. Lee's situation, in defense of Richmond, was now desperate. He even recommended the emancipation and arming of the slaves. Sheridan had cut off his chief source of supplies by destroying the James river canal. Lee determined to form a junction with Johnston at all hazards. On this day he attacked Fort Steadman, on Grant's extreme right, hoping to draw troops from his left and skip out. The fort was evacuated, but Lee did not promptly follow up his advantage, and the Federals, rallying, repulsed the attacking party with a loss of 5,000 of its number.

Fort Tyler, at West Point, Ga., was assaulted and captured by La Grange, April 16, 1865.

Gaines' Farm, June 27, 1862.—Lee again attacked the retreating Union army after the battle of Oak Grove, and drove them back to the river.

Gettysburg, July 1-3, 1863.—On the 22d of June, Lee with the Confederate army entered Chambersburg, and then pushed on through Carlisle to within a few miles of Harrisburg. The Pennsyl-

the Union army from its position. At night 40,000 dead and wounded lay on the battle-field. On the 3d a tremendous artillery duel was carried on between 115 Confederate and 100 Union cannon, followed by a general charge of Lee's army, which was repelled with terrible slaughter, and the Confederates were defeated with a loss of fully 30,000.— Meade lost 23,000.

Green Briar River, Va., October 3, 1861. General H. R. Jackson, of Ga., was left by General Lee at the foot of Cheat mountain to watch Reynolds, who, with 5,000 men, attempted to flank Jackson. The latter discovered and checkmated the movement with a loss of 200. The Federals lost 42 and retired upon

vania militia and volunteers from other States gathered for defense against the invaders. The army of the Potomac was in hard pursuit. Lee rapidly concentrated his forces near Gettysburg, and General Meade, having superceded Hooker, advanced to the conflict. On the morning of July 1st the Union advance, under Generals Reynolds and Buford, was attacked by Gen. A. P. Hill's division, and driven back to Cemetery ridge, where a stand was made, and during the night the whole Union army was hurried to this strong position, while the Confederate forces occupied an opposite ridge called Seminary ridge. On July 2d the battle was renewed, the Confederates vainly striving all day to drive

learning that the Confederates were to be reinforced.

Galveston recaptured by the Confederates January 1, 1863. Com. Renshaw was sent by General Banks to capture this city, which he did, but General Magruder, having obtained aid of a boat, drove the Federals off with the loss of the Harriet Lane.

Groveton, Va., August 29, 1862.— General Siegel, commanding the Union troops, attacked Jackson and Longstreet near this point. His forces were driven back, when he was reinforced by Heintzleman and Reno. Jackson was also joined by Hood. The contest lasted till dark with heavy loss on both sides.

Hampton, Va., burned August 7th,

1861. The force of General Butler, at Fortress Monroe reduced the forces at Newport News and Hampton to fill drafts made upon him to defend Washington. General Magruder thereupon advanced upon Hampton with 5,000 men. Butler sent a force to repel him, which was beaten, and Magruder burned the town, General Butler was consequently deposed and succeeded by Gen. John E. Wool.

Hanover Court-House, Va., May 27, 1862. McClellan sent Fitz John Porter with part of his corps to this point, to keep an opening for McDowell's troops, who had been ordered to join him. He was attacked there by the Confederates, who, after a sharp fight,

lery, 5,000 stands of small arms, 2,000 hogsheads of sugar, and a large quantity of clothing, tents and ammunition.

Iuka, Miss., September 19, 1862.— This hard fought battle occurred between the Union army under Rosecrans and Grant and the Confederates under Price. The latter was defeated, losing 1,000 prisoners in addition to his killed and wounded. The Union loss was 135 killed and 527 wounded.

Jackson, Miss., May 13th, 1863.— Grant defeated Joseph E. Johnston and captured Jackson, Miss., with 7 cannon and large quantities of military stores, besides 400 prisoners. The State capitol was destroyed by fire by the retreating fugitives.

were driven back with a loss of 1,000. The Federal loss was 350.

Helena, Ark., July 4, 1863.—General Holmes, with 8,000 Confederates, attempted the capture of Helena, Ark., but was defeated by General Prentiss with a loss of one-third of his army.

Island No. 10 surrenders April 7, 1862, to the combined forces of General Pope and Admiral Foote, after withstanding a three week's bombardment. In order to flank the Confederate batteries and unite their forces, the Union troops cut a canal fifty feet wide and twelve miles long across Donald's point, through which the gun-boats passed.— The capitulation embraced 7,000 prisoners, 100 siege guns, 24 pieces field artil-

Kernstown, Va., March 23, 1863.— After Stonewall Jackson had evacuated Manassas, he retired up the Shenandoah pursued by General Shields, who overtook and defeated him at this point. Jackson receiving reinforcements, Gen. Shields retreated.

Knoxville, Tenn.—During the operations at Chattanooga Gen. Burnside was besieged in Knoxville by General Longstreet, who, on November 29, 1863, attempted to carry the town by storm, but was repulsed with heavy loss. After Bragg's defeat at Chattanooga Sherman was sent to Burnside's relief, but on the 4th of December, 1863, Longstreet raised the siege and retreated into Virginia.

Lexington, Mo., Sept. 12th, 1861.—

After the battle of Wilson's creek Price marched upon Lexington, which was defended by Colonel J. A. Mulligan with 2,800 Federals. Price besieged him with 25,000 Confederates. Receiving no succor, and his water supplies being cut off, Mulligan surrendered on the 20th, having lost 160 killed and wounded. The Confederates lost 100.

Little Bethel, Va., June 10, 1861.— General Butler ordered General Pierce to send two regiments from camp near Fortress Monroe to attack this point in conjunction with a detachment from Newport News. Approaching from different directions, and meeting in a thick wood before daylight, they mistook each other for Confederates and fired into

latter, and the capture of Richmond was as far off as ever.

Mechanicsville, Va., June 26, 1862. General Lee ordered Jackson and A. P. Hill to attack the Federal right, with Longstreet's corps in reserve, but were repulsed.

Milliken's Bend, June 6th, 1863.— McCullough encountered a brigade of colored troops here. He ordered a bayonet charge with the cry of "no quarter!" but was repulsed in a desperate hand to hand fight.

Mill Spring, Ky., January 19, 1862. General George H. Thomas was ordered by General Buell to attack 10,000 Confederates, who were strongly posted at Mill Spring, under General Zollikoffer.

each other, killing two and wounding others.

Malvern Hills, Va., July 1, 1862.— General Lee here concentrated his forces for a desperate effort to dislodge the Union army from Malvern Hills, which was on the north bank of the James and under the protection of the Federal gun-boats. The whole army rushed to the assault and continued the fight until 9 o'clock at night, when they fell back exhausted. This ended the 7 days battles before Richmond, commencing with the battle of Oak Grove, Mechanicsville, Gaines' Farm, Savage Station and Frazer's Farm. The Federals lost 15,000 and the Confederates 19,000 men, but the prestige of success was with the

The battle lasted nearly all day with varying success. It was decided at last in favor of the Federals by artillery and a flank bayonet charge. After dark the Confederates slipped away, abandoning artillery, ammunition and supplies.— Their loss was 192 killed including Gen. Zollicoffer, 62 wounded and 80 prisoners. The Federal loss was 30 killed and 208 wounded.

Missionary Ridge, Tenn., November 25, 1863. Generals Hooker and Sherman attacked Bragg's concentrated forces on Missionary Ridge. After several hours hard fighting Grant ordered a general charge, which was promptly and successfully executed, and Bragg was driven from the field. Grant pursued him to Ringgold, Ga., and then returned to aid Burnside in Tennessee. The Confederates lost about 6,000 in killed and prisoners in the engagement, and the Union loss was between 3,000 and 4,000.

Murfreesboro, Tenn., Dec. 31, 1862. Bragg's army was concentrated at this point. The Army of the Cumberland was at Nashville, only 30 miles distant. Rosecrans determined upon an aggressive movement, and on December 30, 1862, had advanced to Stone river, within 6 miles of Murfreesboro, where Bragg's forces were entrenched. Both Generals formed the same plan of battle, which was to mass their forces upon one wing of their opponents and crush it before assistance could arrive. Bragg was first,

Nashville, Tenn., Dec. 16th, 1864.— General Hood advanced northward from Atlanta into Tennessee and defeated Schofield at Franklin, who retreated to Nashville, where General Thomas, now detached from Sherman's command, had concentrated his forces. Hood invested the place, and for two weeks Thomas quietly prepared for the conflict, when suddenly at this date he moved from his works, fell upon Hood's army and routed it with a loss of over 25,000. He then pursued the rest into Alabama, where they became disorganized and the campaign ended.

New Orleans, February 25, 1862.— General Butler, with an expedition composed of 13,700 men, embarked for Ship

---

---

and before daybreak had made a furious charge upon McCook, commanding the Union right, which was shattered to fragments. The centre, under Thomas, gave way, and but for Hazen, who with 1,300 men, held the foe until Rosecrans could form a new line, the Union army would have been entirely defeated. The next day, Jan. 1, 1863, was spent in skirmishing and artillery firing. On the 2nd the armies came together with a terrific crash. The battle raged all day with varying success, but at night, with one tremendous onset, supported by a murderous artillery fire, the Union troops drove the Confederates from the field, and they retreated toward Tullahoma with a loss of about 11,000. The Union loss was nearly 12,000.

Island, where Admiral Farragut was stationed with the navy.

New Orleans Captured.—In April, 1862, a powerful squadron under Admiral Farragut entered the Mississippi and sailed as far as forts Jackson and St. Philip, 30 miles above the gulf. These forts commanded the channel, and an enormous chain was stretched between the two. The 45 vessels of the Federal fleet bombarded the forts furiously from the 18th to the 24th. Farragut then determined to run the batteries. He succeeded in breaking the chain and overpowering the Confederate flotilla of 17 vessels, including several steam rams.— The 25th of April he reached New Orleans and took possession. Gen. Butler became commandant. Three days after Forts Jackson and St. Philip surrendered to Admiral Porter, who had continued the siege.

Newberne, N. C., March 14, 1862.— General Burnside, with 12,000 troops, aided by gunboats, drove the Confederates out of their fortifications. By burning the bridge over the Trent river the Confederates prevented their immediate pursuit by the Federals. Union loss was 600 killed and wounded. The Confederates was considerable less, including 200 prisoners.

New Madrid, Mo., captured by General Pope, March 13, 1862, after a furious artillery duel lasting all day. The Confederates abandoned the place dur-

force under General Cox, February 20, 1865. The Confederates were defeated and lost 375 men.

Oak Grove, Va., June 25, 1862.— General Heintzleman, in reconnoitering the Confederate position at Fair Oaks, was attacked and driven back with heavy loss. McClellan now abandoned all hope of moving on to Richmond.

Pea Ridge, Ark., March 7, 1862.— The consolidated Confederate forces of Price, Van Dorn, McCulloch and Pike, amounting to about 25,000, including 3,000 Indians, made a desperate effort to recover Missouri. General Curtis commanded the Federal army of 11,000. He was attacked by the whole Confederate force on the morning of March 7, and,

ing a thunder-storm that night, leaving 25 pieces of artillery and a large quantity of military stores valued at $1,000,-000.

New Mexico, February 21, 1862.— Col. H. H. Sibley, at the head of 2,300 Texas rangers, invaded New Mexico and defeated 2,000 Federals at Valverde.

Norfolk, Va., captured May 10, 1862, by General John E. Wool. This broke up the blockade of the James river. The Confederate commander fired the navy-yard and blew up the Merrimac before retreating.

Old Town Creek, N. C.—The Confederate garrison had evacuated Fort Anderson and was attacked by a Union

after two days hard fighting, he routed the enemy and drove them back with a loss of 2,000. The Federal loss was 1,400. Price and Van Dorn fled into Tennessee and joined Beauregard at Memphis.

Perryville, Ky., October 8th, 1862. General Bragg, with a Confederate force of 65,000, and a provision train said to be 40 miles long, was overtaken at Perryville, Ky., by Gen. Buell, in command of 100,000 Union troops. Bragg intended to escape with his plunder, but being closely pursued by Buell, was forced to give battle. The engagement lasted, with varying success, from morning until nearly noon, when General Sherman, of Buell's command, made a brilliant charge, and drove the Confederates from their batteries, capturing several guns and a number of prisoners. The battle closed for the day, and during the night Bragg fled towards Tennessee, leaving 1,200 sick and 25,000 barrels of pork behind.

Petersburg, Va., attacked June 18, 1864.—General Grant, after the battle of Coal Harbor, now changed his base to the James river, proposing to capture Petersburg, and then Richmond, from the southeast. Butler, from Fortress Monroe, had captured City Point and Bermuda Hundred on May 5th, but his advance upon Petersburg on the 16th had been defeated by Beauregard. On the 18th, Grant's army having arrived,

the Federal guns an advance was made, and when the Union troops had crowded into the fort a heavy fire was opened upon them by the Confederates and 4,000 were slaughtered. The Confederate loss was but 1,000.

Petersburg and Richmond captured, April 2-3, 1865. After an all-night cannonade a general assault was made, compelling the evacuation of Petersburg and Richmond. With Lee's withdrawal law and order ceased to exist in Richmond. The city was fired, and riot and plunder reigned until the Union army entered when the city was put under martial law.

Philippi, Va., June 3d, 1861 —A fight occurred here between the Union

a general assault was made upon the Confederate works, which was repulsed by Lee's army, which had come to the defence of Petersburg the night before. The Union army lost in this campaign 70,000 and the Confederates 40,000 men, and Grant now begun a regular siege.

Petersburg Mine Explosion, July 30, 1864. One of the strongest forts in front of Petersburg was mined by Burnside's corps. The gallery of the mine was 510 feet long and 18,000 cubic feet of earth was removed in its construction, in cracker-boxes made into wheelbarrows. Eight thousand pounds of powder was deposited in the mine. At dawn it was exploded and the garrison of 300 men destroyed. Under fire of

force, under Colonels Kelly and Dumont and 1,500 Confederates under Colonel Porterfield. The latter was captured, with 380 stand of arms, a regimental flag, valuable papers and a large amount of baggage. The only Union man injured was Col. Kelly, who was wounded.

Piketown, Ky., Nov. 9, 1861.—Gen. Nelson, with 3,000 Unionists, attacked the camp of Colonel Williams with 1,000 Confederates. A sharp skirmish ensued, and after losing 40 killed and a large number wounded the Confederates fled. The Union loss was 6 killed and 24 wounded.

Port Gibson, May 1, 1863.—Grant's canal across Millikin's Bend having proved a failure, he determined to run the fleet past the Vicksburg batteries, which was successfully done the night of April 16. At Port Gibson he encountered a Confederate force, which was defeated after a hard fight.

Port Republic, Va., June 9, 1862.—At this point General Shields attacked the Confederates under Gen. Jackson, but was defeated and driven back five miles. Jackson then crossed the Shenandoah and burned the bridge behind him, thus rendering further pursuit impossible.

Port Royal, S. C., Nov. 7, 1861.—This place was attacked by a combined land and naval force under General W. T. Sherman and Com. S. F. Dupont. It consisted of 15,000 troops and fifty war

them at 1 o'clock and fought them until dark, driving them from their position with a loss of 160. Union loss was 27. Garfield was made a Brigadier General for his skill in this affair.

Prairie Grove, Ark., December 7, 1862. Hindman, with a large force of Confederates, attacked Herron's force of 4,000. He was without cavalry, but his artillery inflicted a heavy loss upon the enemy, so that in preparing to renew the fight in the morning the Confederates had disappeared.

Rappahannock Station, Va.—In October, 1863, General Sedgwick, of Meade's army, met Ewell here and captured 1,600 of his men. Sedgwick lost 300.

vessels and transports. Forts Walker and Beauregard were captured, and Hilton Head, a point most advantageous for operations against Charleston and Savannah, fell into the power of the Federals.

Prestonburg, Ky., January 7, 1862. Colonel J. A. Garfield was sent by Gen. Don Carlos Buel, with two regiments and 300 cavalry to dislodge 2,500 Confederates under Humphrey Marshall from their position in Eastern Kentucky. Upon Garfield's approach Marshall fled up the Big Sandy, but was overtaken and defeated by the United States cavalry at Jennis' creek. The Confederates gained a strong position at Prestonburg and made a stand. Garfield attacked

Richmond, Va., captured April 3d, 1865. (See Petersburg and Richmond.)

Rich Mountain, Va., July 12, 1861. Colonel John Pegram, with 1,500 Confederates, occupied this strongly fortified position, which Gen. McClellan ordered Colonel Rosecrans to reduce. He started from Beverly to attack Pegram's rear, but was himself surprised by the Confederates, who were prepared for him. Rosecrans renewed the fight and drove the enemy before him at the point of the bayonet, killing, wounding and capturing about 400. The Union loss was 18 killed and 40 wounded. Rosecrans was made a Brigadier General for this victory.

Roanoke Island, N. C., February

7-8, 1862. An expedition of land and naval forces under the command of Gen. Burnside and Com. Goldsborough, with 16,000 troops, attacked and carried the Confederate fortifications on this island, capturing 3,000 prisoners and destroying all the Confederate fleet except two vessels. Union loss was 50 killed and 212 wounded.

Romney Bridge, W. Va.—Colonel Lew Wallace, commanding the Indiana Zouaves, left Grafton by an unfrequented mountain road, and on June 11, 1861, surprised the Confederates, compelling them to abandon their battery at Romney Bridge. This caused Gen. Johnston to evacuate Harper's Ferry under the

Fort Pickens committed great havoc with the Confederate navy-yards. This so enraged the Confederates that 1,400 picked men were landed on Santa Rosa Island and surprised 150 zouaves and plundered their camp. The latter were reinforced from the fort and drove back the Confederates and sunk one of their vessels. The Union loss was 64; the Confederates lost 150. The Confederate iron-clad Manassas was then fitted up with an iron prow, and it drove off the bombarding fleet from Fort McRae. It did but little other damage, owing to incompetent management.

Savage Station, Va., June 29, 1862. After the battle of Gaines' Farm, Gen. Lee, finding that McClellan had reached

supposition that a heavier movement was intended.

Sabin Cross Roads, La., April 8, 1864.—Banks' forces were entrapped by the Confederates into a wedge-shaped ambuscade, and were defeated. Finally reinforcements saved the army from destruction, but 2,000 out of 8,000 engaged were lost. The Red river had become so low that dams had to be built to float the fleet over the bars, and the expedition returned to Vicksburg. The result of this expedition disappointed the government, and Banks was suspended by General Canby.

Santa Rosa Island, on the Gulf Coast, October 9, 1861.—Col. Watson, commanding a small Union force at

the James river with his supplies, again attacked him and endeavored to intercept his retreat, but was repulsed by the Federal troops under Sumner.

Selma, Ala., was captured by Gen. Wilson, April 5, 1865, with 2,700 prisoners and 32 guns, from Gen. Forest.

Sheridan's Campaign.—In Aug., 1864, Gen. Sheridan, with 30,000 Union troops, was sent to the Shenandoah valley to stop Early's raids. The armies met near Winchester on September 19, and in the engagement Early was defeated and retreated rapidly through Winchester to the intrenchments at Fisher's Hill. On the 22nd Sheridan defeated him again at Fisher's Hill, and at Port Republic he captured Early's wagon train of seventy-five wagons. Early then concentrated his army at Cedar Creek, but was again routed and driven twenty-six miles. Posting his army strongly, after this engagement, Sheridan made a trip to Washington. In his absence Early surprised his camp, captured his artillery and sent his troops flying toward Winchester, October 19th. Sheridan had just returned, and at that point met the fugitives of his now defeated army. Putting spurs to his horse, he rallied his troops, who, inspired with new courage, rushed upon the Confederates, re-captured his camp and cannon, and routed them with terrible slaughter. Sheridan lost 17,000 men in this campaign, but he destroyed Early's army,

and on the 22d he formerly occupied that city, capturing 150 cannon, 30,000 bales of cotton, and a large amount of munitions of war. Gen. Hardee, with 15,000 troops, fled to Charleston. The capture of Georgia cost Sherman but 567 men. *Sherman in the Carolinas.*—Leaving Gen. Foster at Savannah Sherman started for Columbia, S. C., February 1, 1865.

Shiloh, or Pittsburg Landing, April 6-7, 1862. General Grant, after the battle of Fort Donelson, determined to capture Corinth. While waiting at Shiloh, with 33,000 Union troops, for Gen. Buell, who was on his way from Nashville with reinforcements, he was suddenly surprised by 40,000 Confederates

and put an end to further raids toward Washington.

Sherman's March through Mississippi was made in January and February 1864, as far as Meridian. He destroyed public property and devastated the country in his progress. Multitudes of refugees and negroes returned with him. *Sherman's March to the Sea.*— November 16, 1864, General Sherman burned Atlanta and started, with 60,000 men, to destroy and lay waste the rich agricultural region of Alabama and Georgia to the sea coast. His lines spread out 60 miles wide, living on the country and leaving desolation behind. December 13th he captured Fort McAllister, one of the defenses of Savannah,

under Generals Albert S. Johnston and Beauregard. The Confederates were at first successful. Grant was forced back to the river, and but for the protection of Foote's gun-boats would have been overwhelmed and his army completely demoralized. The battle raged all day and at night was undecided. That night Buell arrived, and in the morning Grant assumed the defensive and compelled the Confederates to retreat to Corinth. Gen. Johnston was killed the first day. Their loss was about 11,000. The Federals lost 13,000.

South Mills, N. C., April 19, 1862.— Gen. Reno, with 4,000 Union troops, left Port Royal to threaten Norfolk from the rear. He landed near Elizabeth City and attacked the Confederates in their chosen position at South Mills, defeating them with considerable loss.

South Mountain, Md., September 14, 1862.—After Lee had defeated Pope's army he advanced to Frederick, Md., and sent Jackson around South Mountain to prevent the escape of Federal troops from Harper's Ferry. He calculated upon McClellan's tardiness, in which he was disappointed, and a battle ensued which lasted all day, resulting in a Federal victory. The fight was severe, and the loss heavy on both sides, the Unionists losing 443 killed and 1,806 wounded. General Reno was among the killed. The Confederates retreated towards the Potomac.

eral force, marched upon Springfield, and sent Major Zagonyi ahead, with 150 cavalrymen, to reconnoiter. He encountered 2,000 Confederates drawn up on the brow of a hill, and charged them.— Notwithstanding a Federal loss of 84 he compelled the Confederates to retreat with a loss of 106 killed and 27 prisoners.

Suffolk, Va., May 3, 1863.—Repeated efforts were made by the Confederates to recapture the Norfolk navy-yard, and early in April Longstreet, with 30,000 troops, laid siege to Suffolk, and endeavored to capture 14,000 Federal troops under General Peck. After a month's siege Longstreet abandoned the attempt.

Triune, Tenn., June 11, 1863.—Gen. Forrest with 5,000 cavalry and 2 batteries

Spottsylvania Court-House, May 10-12, 1864.—General Grant, after the Battle of the Wilderness, ordered a flank movement of his whole army. General Lee's effort to defeat it brought on one of the bloodiest struggles of the war. During the engagement General Hancock made a charge upon the Confederates and captured 3,000 prisoners and 25 pieces of artillery. The Confederate losses were about 10,000, and the Union losses were much larger. It was here that Grant sent his famous despatch to the War Department: "I propose to fight it out on this line if it takes all summer."

Springfield, Mo., October 24, 1861. General Fremont, commanding a Fed-

of artillery attacked the Union cavalry commanded by Colonel R. B. Mitchell, at Triune, Tenn. Forrest was defeated.

Vicksburg, Miss., November, 1862. Measures were first made to capture this place in November, 1862, by Generals Grant and Sherman, and, in accordance with plans agreed upon, Sherman embarked from Memphis with 30,000 troops for the mouth of the Yazoo river, while Grant was to attack the main body of the Confederates and drive them into Vicksburg, and the combined forces were then to lay siege to the place. Meanwhile General Grant had collected $4,000,000 worth of supplies at Holly Springs, Miss., for the Union army to subsist on during the siege. Grant left

Colonel Murphy with 1,000 men to guard these supplies, and ordered 4,000 more to his assistance. Murphy was careless, and was surprised by the Confederate cavalry under Van Dorn, and, after a short conflict, he surrendered before the reinforcements arrived. The victors destroyed what plunder they could not carry with them. This necessitated Gen. Grant's withdrawal and the abandonment of the siege of Vicksburg by this expedition.

Vicksburg Captured, July 4, 1863. May 18, General Grant and Admiral Porter invested this place, and on the 19th General Grant attempted to carry the Confederate works by storm, but was repulsed. Three days later Grant

oners, 132 cannon, and 50,000 stand of arms. The Federal loss during the siege was nearly 10,000 killed, wounded and missing.

Vienna, Va., July 17, 1861.—Gen. McDowell stationed a regiment along the railroad, fifteen miles from Alexandria. While en route on the train 300 of them were fired upon by a Confederate masked battery, as the cars were entering the cut at Vienna. The Union troops returned the fire, inflicting a considerable loss to the Confederates, while they sustained a loss of five killed, six wounded and thirteen missing.

Wilderness, Va., May 5, 6 and 7, 1864.—General Grant, on assuming command of the entire Union army, decided

---

---

determined to renew the attack along the whole line, which was twelve miles long, but again suffered another repulse more disastrous than the first. These two assaults resulted in a Union loss of 3,000 men. It was evident now to Grant that Vicksburg could not be taken by storm, and he now prepared to approach it by a regular siege. In the meanwhile Porter kept up a continuous bombardment from his fleet, and Grant pressed closer every day to the doomed city. Grant's forces were about 30,000. After a siege of forty-five days, during which time the Confederates and inhabitants of Vicksburg were reduced to a condition of starvation, Pemberton surrendered to General Grant 27,000 pris-

upon two important campaigns. The Army of the Potomac to advance on Richmond, and that of Gen. Sherman to march against Atlanta to engage the Confederates under General Johnston. Both armies were to move in concert to prevent the co-operation of Lee and Johnston. Grant's army advanced across the Rapidan to the Wilderness, where a terrible battle with the Confederates ensued, lasting three days, with indecisive results, both armies holding the same ground as when the battle commenced. In this engagement the Confederates lost 10,000 and the Federals 20,000.

Williamsburg, Va., May 5, 1862.— The Confederates, 10,000 in number, in command of Magruder, evacuated York-town May 3d, and retreated towards Williamsburg. They were pursued by General Stoneman's cavalry, supported by the divisions of Generals Hooker and Kearney. On the morning of the 5th they made a stand and were attacked by the Federals, and a furious battle en-sued, lasting all day, when the Confederates were driven from the field by a charge made by General Hancock. The Union loss was 2,000, four hundred of whom were killed. The Confederates lost about 1,000. McClellan, the following day, occupied Williamsburg.

Wilson's Creek, Mo., August 10th, 1861.—General McCulloch, commanding about 23,000 Confederates, ordered an advance on Springfield. General Lyon, with only 5,000 troops, met him at Wilson's Creek. He divided his army into two divisions, one of which, under Gen. Siegel, assailed the Confederates in the rear, while he attacked him in front.—

The battle was a desperate one, but the Confederates held the field at a cost of 3,000 men. The Federals returned to Springfield, losing about 1,300, including General Lyon.

Winchester, Va. May 25th, 1862.—General Banks, with 5,000 Union troops, was attacked by Ewell with 20,000 Confederates at this point. Notwithstanding his inferior force, Banks held the Confederates at bay 5 hours. Jackson then reinforced Ewell, and Banks was forced to make a hasty retreat and reached the Potomac safely.

Winchester, June 15, 1863.—Ewell's corps arrived at this point, which was occupied by Milroy with 10,000 Union troops. After a heavy skirmish, finding the odds were too great, Milroy retreated to Harrisburg, Pa. This was the beginning of Lee's invasion of Pennsylvania and Maryland, which finally terminated in the battle of Gettysburg.

SURRENDERS, INVASIONS, ETC., DURING THE REBELLION.
(Numerically Arranged.)

Fort Moultrie, in Charleston Harbor, was evacuated by General Anderson, December 26, 1860, and Fort Sumter occupied. His force was 111 Federal soldiers.

United States Property and munitions, valued at $1,209,500, was surrendered to Texas by General Twiggs, on February 18, 1861.

Fort Sumter was evacuated by Maj. Anderson, April 14, 1861. On the 11th

General Beauregard demanded its surrender, and, on being refused, commenced the bombardment on the 12th, and continued it during the 13th, until terms of evacuation were agreed upon. The soldiers retained their arms and fired a salute of 50 guns before taking down the Union flag, which they carried with them.

Gosport Navy-Yard, at Norfolk, Va., was evacuated, and shipping destroyed by the Union forces, April 21, 1861.

Arlington Heights Occupied.— May 24, 1861, thirteen thousand Union troops under General McDowell occupied Arlington Heights. This was the first great move of Union troops into Virginia.

General Pegram, with 900 Confederate troops, surrendered to General McClellan, July 14th, 1861, near Beverly, W. Va.

Kanawha Valley Evacuated on July 29, 1861, by General Wise, who retreated before the Federals under Gen. Cox.

Illinois Threatened by General Pillow, with 12,000 Confederates, July 31,

seize Louisville at the same time, but was foiled by General Anderson, the hero of Fort Sumter, who was in command of Camp Joe Holt, near that city.

Kentucky was invaded by seven regiments of Confederates commanded by General Zollicoffer, October 21, 1861. While raiding through the State he came upon a Union force just mustered under Colonel Garrard. He made two attacks upon them at Camp Wildcat, in Rose Castle Hills, but was driven off. Gen. W. T. Sherman was now appointed to command the Department of the Cumberland.

Beaufort, N. C., was occupied by the Union forces December 6, 1861.

Nashville Evacuated, February 16,

1861. This danger was averted by Gen. Fremont, who took 3,800 volunteers from St. Louis, on 8 steamboats, to Cairo, the point intended to be invaded. Gen. Pillow abandoned his project and retreated.

Forts Hatteras and Clark, at Hatteras Inlet, surrendered to a combined land and naval force under Gen. Butler and Com. Stringham, after a two days' contest, August 28-29, 1861. The trophies were 715 prisoners, 25 cannon and 1,000 stand of arms.

Columbus and Hickman, Ky., were seized September 4, 1861, and fortified by the Confederates under General Polk. General Simon Buckner started with three regiments of Confederates to

1862.—Upon the news of the fall of Fort Donelson a regular stampede began from Nashville for Chattanooga. Stores were thrown open, bank vaults were emptied, and $25 per hour was paid for hack hire.

Price was Driven from Missouri February 25, 1862, by General S. R. Curtis, after a series of skirmishes and manœvers.

Army of the Potomac changes its base.—April 1, 1862, General McClellan, with 120,000 troops, embarked for Fortress Monroe, intending to march upon Richmond from that point.

Tennessee and Mississippi was raided in April, 1862.—General Mitchell conducted an expedition through these

States, capturing 160 prisoners and 117 locomotives and coaches at Huntsville, on the Memphis and Charleston R. R.

Yorktown Evacuated, May 3, 1862. After withstanding McClellan's siege, with but 10,000 men, for a whole month, Magruder retired to Williamsburg.

Memphis Captured, June 6, 1862.— Commodores Davis and Ellet attacked the Confederate fleet, causing all the vessels to be sunk or abandoned. Memphis was then occupied by Gen. Wallace from Grant's army.

Confederate Congress adjourned in a panic May 8, 1862, because of the approach of the Federal army To save Richmond, General Johnston ordered "Stonewall" Jackson, who was in the

Cincinnati Threatened.—Guerillas roved through Kentucky and Tennessee during July and August, 1862, destroying public and private property. Gen. J. H. Morgan was the most dreaded of these, and after dispersing some Federal cavalry and destroying several miles of railway, he began to threaten Cincinnati. Green Clay Smith organized a superior force, aided by the business men, and drove him back into Tennessee.

Texas Loyalists Massacred, August 9, 1862. Sixty Germans, while attempting to flee the State, were overtaken and fiendishly murdered in a cane brake on the Nueces river, by Lieut. Lilley's band of guerillas.

Pope and Lee on the Rappahan-

Shenandoah Valley with 15,000 troops, to make a demonstration toward Washington and prevent the junction of 30,000 troops, under McDowell, with Gen. McClellan. Fremont and Banks were also in the mountains with 15,000 troops each. By a series of rapid and brilliant manœuvers Jackson accomplished his purpose, and finally joined the army defending Richmond.

Stuart's Raid. — While McClellan lay inactive on the banks of the Chickahominy General J. E. B. Stuart, with 1,500 cavalry, made a daring raid. He dispersed two squadrons of cavalry, captured 165 prisoners, a number of horses and mules, a large quantity of supplies, and returned to Richmond unharmed, June 14, 1862.

nock.—August 23, 1862. Lee attempted to crush Pope before he could be reinforced. The Rappahannock was between them, which Lee crossed and attempted to flank Pope. A heavy rain foiled him.

Bragg Invades Kentucky. — In August, 1862, Bragg, with 65,000 men, started from Chattanooga to Louisville. Buell, learning his design, began pursuit. Reaching Mumfordsville on the 17th of September, Bragg captured a Federal division of 4,500 men. Meantime Buell had reached Louisville, and the Confederates turned back, plundering as they retreated, without hindrance from Buell. The United States government ordered Buell to act on the offensive. His army was now 100,000. He followed Bragg to Perryville, where a severe but indecisive battle was fought. Bragg fled during the night, leaving 1,200 sick and 25,000 barrels of pork, but he took with him 4,000 wagons loaded with plunder.

Manassas Junction Seized by Stuart, August 26, 1862. He captured 300 Federals and a large quantity of railroad rolling stock and supplies.

Maryland Invaded. — Gen. Lee moved up the Potomac and crossed into Maryland at Point of Rocks, September 2, 1862.

Cincinnati, Ohio, Defended.—On September 12, 1862, General Lew Wallace, by vigorous action, had gathered 40,000 volunteers from Cincinnati, Cov-

ton, crossed the Blue Ridge mountains in pursuit, but so slowly that Lee escaped to Gordonsville.

Banks' Raid through Western Louisiana.—Leaving Baton Rouge on the 11th of January, 1863, Banks marched to Pattersonville and defeated 1,100 Confederates and destroyed a gun-boat. He made another expedition up the Red River, April 12, 1863, to devastate the region West of the Mississippi. The Confederates were driven back to Pattersonville, and at Bisland Gen. Dick Taylor was forced from his position.— Taylor then burnt several steamers, transports of supplies and bridges, then fled. The ram Queen of the West was captured and burnt by the Federals.—

ington and Newport, who had thrown up entrenchments and prepared to receive Kirby Smith's attack. At this date 15,000 of his men under General Heath appeared before the city, but, frightened by its bold front, he retreated under cover of night.

Frankfort Seized. September 12, 1862, by Kirby Smith, from which he planned the capture of Louisville, Ky.

Harper's Ferry Surrendered.— September 14, 1862, Colonel Miles, with 12,000 Federals, surrendered this important place without much resistance. Miles was killed after the surrender.

Lee Retreated Into Virginia on November 4, 1862, followed by McClellan, who, under orders from Washing-

Banks then pushed on and captured Alexandria on the Red River.

Grierson's Cavalry Raid.—Starting from La Grange, Georgia, April 17, 1863, he went down through Ripley, Macon, Montrose and Hazlehurst to Baton Rouge, where he arrived May 2. He destroyed telegraphs, railroads and other property to the amount of about $6,000,000 on this raid.

Stoneman's Cavalry Raid, May 3rd, 1863.—This General, with 10,000 troopers, crossed the Rappahannock, tore up the Virginia Central Railroad, swept round to within a few miles of Richmond and returned in safety.

Colonel Streight and one thousand seven hundred Union troops was captured by Forrest's cavalry at Cedar Bluff, Ga., on May 8, 1863.

Raymond, Miss., was captured May 12, 1863, by General McPherson, after a hard fight.

Lee's Second Northern Invasion, June 13, 1863.—Organizing his army into three corps under Longstreet, Ewell and A. P. Hill, and leaving the latter to hold Fredericksburg, General Lee began his march into Maryland and Pennsylvania.

Port Hudson Surrendered July 9, 1863.—This place had been first invested by General Banks, May 24. Numerous unsuccessful attempts had been been made to take it by storm. The garrison was reduced to starvation, and

were helpless women and children; 581 were wounded, many of them mortally. About 80 of the murderers were killed.

Little Rock, Ark., surrendered to General Grant's forces, September 10, 1863.

Kilpatrick's Raid with 5,000 cavalry, to release prisoners on Belle Isle and in Libby Prison, was made February 28, 1864. He failed to accomplish it, but captured 500 prisoners. Colonel Ulric Dahlgreen was killed on this raid.

Sheridan's Raid.—On May 9, 1864, General Grant sent Sheridan, with a large force of cavalry, to cut Lee's communications. He destroyed part of the Virginia Central Railroad and 1,500,000 rations, liberated 400 Union prisoners,

was compelled to subsist on rats and mule meat for food. In this desperate state, and hearing of the fall of Vicksburg, Gardner surrendered, with 6,400 prisoners of war. The Mississippi was now open.

John Morgan and his gang of four thousand guerrillas was captured by the Home Guards in Ohio, July 26, 1863.

Quantrell's Raid. — The town of Lawrence, Kansas, was surprised in the middle of the night of August 13, 1863, by 300 guerillas under the leadership of Quantrell. The town was set on fire and 182 buildings burned to the ground, and $2,000,000 worth of property destroyed. One hundred and ninety-one persons were killed, many of whom

assaulted the outer defences of Richmond and mortally wounded the Confederate General Stuart, returning to the Army of the Potomac May 25th.

Fight for the Weldon Railroad, June 24, 1864.—A Union cavalry force of 8,000 attempted to seize this railway, but was defeated by a superior Confederate force.

Early's Northern Raid.—To compel Grant to raise the siege of Petersburg, Lee sent Early with 20,000 men to invade Maryland and threaten Washington City. He crossed the Potomac on July 5, 1864. On the 9th he defeated General Wallace on the Monocacy, who was there to check his advance on the capitol. Early pushed up within gunshot of Washington, but finding a large army defending it—Grant having sent Smith's corps for that purpose—he retired with large booty, first sending a detachment of cavalry northward to Pennsylvania.

Chambersburg, Pa., burned July 30, 1864, by Jubal Early's cavalry, because his demand for $200,000 in gold or $500,000 in greenbacks was refused.

Last Invasion of Missouri.—Oct. 25, 1864, Sterling Price attempted to recover this State for the Confederacy. He was defeated at the Little Osage River by Generals Curtis and Pleasanton.

Columbia, S. C., Surrendered to Sherman, February 17, 1865. By order

General Sheridan Captured a large quantity of Lee's supplies and some prisoners at Appomatox Station, April 6, 1865.

Lee's Surrender was demanded by Grant, April 7, 1865. He replied that "the occasion for the surrender of the Army of Northern Virginia had not yet arrived."

Lee's Capitulation, April 9, 1865. Seeing that a further struggle was useless, General Lee sent a note to General Grant, asking a meeting. It took place at William McLean's residence at Appomattox Court-House on Sunday at 2 P. M., when the army of Northern Virginia was surrendered.

Mobile Evacuated, April 11, 1865.

of Wade Hampton, a large quantity of cotton was burned, from which the city was speedily in flames.

Charleston, S. C., was evacuated February 18, 1865, and the city fired by the Confederates. When Sherman's troops marched in they aided the citizens to save the city from the flames. Two hundred persons were killed by the explosion of powder at the depot.

Wilmington, N. C., was evacuated by the Confederates and occupied by General Schofield, February 22, 1865.

Wilson Invaded Alabama and Georgia in March, 1865, with a large cavalry force. He had captured five cities, 288 pieces of artillery, 6,820 prisoners, losing but 725 men.

This city did not fall when Farragut closed its harbor. It was yet defended by Forts Spanish and Blakely, commanded by General Dick Taylor, who had marched from Louisiana with 15,000 men to assist Gen. Maury in the defense. Gen. Canby, with 40,000 Union troops, besieged them on the 27th of March, and had possession of them by the 11th of April.

Montgomery, Ala., the first capitol of the Southern Confederacy, surrendered to General Wilson April 12, 1865.

Columbus, Ga., was seized by Gen. Wilson, April 16, 1865.

Sherman's Truce with Johnston, April 18, 1865.—Learning of Lee's surrender, Johnston sent a note to his pursuer asking a truce. A paper was drawn up between them recognizing the governments of the States in rebellion and according them political privileges. It was rejected at Washington, and Sherman was ordered to grant no terms but those granted to Lee.

Macon, Ga., Surrendered to Gen. Wilson, April 20, 1865. Wilson here received the first information of Lee's surrender from Howell Cobb.

Johnston's Surrender to Sherman took place April 26, 1865, upon the terms accorded to Lee. Wade Hampton, with with his cavalry, refused to surrender and withdrew. About 25,000 troops were here given up, and the surrender included all the soldiers in the seaboard States under Johnston's command.

Jefferson Davis Captured May 11, 1865, while fleeing to the Florida coast, near Irwinsville, Georgia, by two troops of cavalry under Lieutenant Colonels Pritchard and Hardin. He was taken in female disguise.

General Kirby Smith surrendered to General Canby, May 26, 1865, the last regular army movement of the war.

General Richard Taylor surrendered to General Canby at Citronville, Ala., May 4th, 1865, upon the terms granted to Lee.

Last Battle of the War, at Palmetto Ranche, Texas, May, 13, 1865, between a Union force under Col. Barrett and Confederates under Colonel J. E. Slaughter. The last volley was fired by a colored regiment of United States troops.

NAVAL ENGAGEMENTS, ETC., DURING THE REBELLION.

The Blockade of Southern ports was declared April 17, 1861, by a proclamation from President Lincoln.

Sewell's Point, May 20, 1861.—A Confederate battery at Sewell's Point, and 2,000 Virginia troops, fired upon the Potomac flotilla, consisting of four armed propellers and the flag-ship Thos. Freeborn. The battery was silenced and the Confederates retreated. On May 29, after reducing this battery, Captain Ward, who commanded the flotilla, captured two schooners with 50 Confederate soldiers.

Aquia Creek. — The Confederate batteries here were shelled May 31 and June 1, 1861, by four gunboats commanded by Captain Ward.

A Confederate Battery at Pig Point was attacked by the Harriet Lane June 5, 1861, by order of General Butler, who wished to ascertain its strength. Owing to shallow water he could not approach nearer than 1,800 yards, and could not reach the battery with her guns. She was struck twice by the long range guns of the Confederates, and had five men wounded.

Matthias Point, June 27th, 1861.— Captain Ward, with the Potomac flotilla,

reduced the Confederate battery at this point without loss; but while sighting a cannon he was mortally wounded from a shot fired from the shore.

Sumter. — This privateer ran the blockade at New Orleans, June 30, 1861, and preyed upon the United States merchantmen in the West Indies. Entering the port of Gibraltar, she was guarded by the United States gunboats Tuscarora and Kearsage. Her crew here abandoned her and escaped to Liverpool, where they joined the Alabama.

Confederate Privateer Savannah was captured June 3, 1861, by the Perry, off Charleston harbor. This was the first vessel bearing the Confederate flag that was captured.

Confederate government had appointed Mason and Slidell (former United States Senators), as ambassadors to England. They ran the blockade, and at Havana sailed on the British mail steamer Trent for Europe. On November 8th, 1861, they were overtaken by the United States frigate San Jacinto, Capt. Wilkes commanding. The Trent was stopped and boarded, and the envoys were seized and carried to Boston and imprisoned. England demanded their release. Secretary Seward conceded that the arrest was in violation of the law of nations, and the ambassadors were liberated.

Charleston Harbor Blockaded. December 20, 1861, the United States government loaded 25 condemned mer-

---

Petrel Recaptured, July 28, 1861.— This vessel, which had been captured by the Confederates in December, 1860, slipped out of Charleston harbor as a privateer. Sighting the St. Lawrence, she gave chase, supposing her to be a merchantman. The St. Lawrence pretended flight, but when the Petrel was near enough she discharged three shots and sunk her. Part of her crew were saved and taken prisoners.

Pamlico Sound. — United States gunboat Monticello shelled a Confederate force with great slaughter, October 5, 1861, defeating their attempt to land in Pamlico Sound and attack a Union camp.

Mason and Slidell Affair.—The

chantmen with granite and sunk them at the entrance of Charleston harbor. The vessels either sunk in the sand, or were carried out to sea by strong currents, thus failing to accomplish the desired result.

Mason and Slidell were released January 2, 1862, by order of the United States government, and sailed for Europe to obtain aid for the Confederacy.

Com. Foote's Flotilla, consisting of 12 gunboats (7 of them iron-clads), carrying 126 heavy guns, was fitted out at St. Louis January 31, 1862.

Fort Henry Captured.—February 6, 1862, Foote's fleet bombarded this fort, which was armed with 17 heavy guns and flanked by rifle pits. It was reduced in less than an hour and the garrison fled to Fort Donelson.

Elizabeth City, February, 1862.— The Confederate flotilla sailed up the Albemarle Sound, from Roanoke, where it was attacked by the United States fleet. After a fierce engagement of 30 minutes all the Confederate vessels but one were burnt or captured.

The Confederate Privateer Nashville was destroyed, after a fierce conflict with the Montauk, Captain Worden commanding, February 28, 1862. The Nashville was built in a Confederate port for the Confederates, and was famous for the number of American merchantmen she had destroyed.

Merrimac and Monitor. — The

destroyed the entire United States fleet and had the Atlantic seaports at her mercy.

Fort Pillow, May 10, 1862.—A naval engagement occurred here between part of Foote's flotilla and Com. Hollins' Confederate fleet of rams, aided by the fort. The Confederate fleet was driven back to the protection of the fort, and finally escaped down the river.

Drewry's Bluff Fight.—Com. John Rogers, with a fleet of five Federal vessels pursued Huger, who had commanded Norfolk, up the James river. He was stopped by a battery at Drewry's Bluff, and, after a combat of three hours, was compelled to withdraw, on the 15th of May, 1862. Federal loss was 27 and the Confederate 15.

Confederates had raised the United States frigate Merrimac, which was scuttled and sunk in the Norfolk navy-yard, plated her with railroad iron, and fitted an immense iron beak to her prow.—This done she attacked the Union fleet at Fortress Monroe and sunk the Cumberland and Congress, on the 9th of March, 1862. That night the Monitor, an iron-clad vessel with a single revolving tower, containing two 11-inch guns (an invention of Capt. John Errickson), sailed into Hampton Roads. When the Merrimac reappeared in the morning she was assailed by this "Cheese Box," and after five hours severe conflict, was compelled to return to Norfolk badly damaged. But for this the Merrimac might have

Farragut Attempts to Run the Port Hudson batteries, March 13, 1863. Farragut's fleet, consisting of 4 frigates, 5 gunboats and 6 mortars, attempted to move silently up the Mississippi river one very dark night. They were seen, and, by the light of a bonfire, were under heavy fire for an hour and a half, when they retired, leaving the frigate Mississippi in flames.

The Ram Atlanta was captured, June 17, 1863, by the Monitor Weehawken, Com. John Rogers, commander, off South Carolina.

Alabama Destroyed by the Kearsage, June 14, 1864. This formidable British built Confederate privateer, Semmes, commander, was caught in

Cherbourg harbor, France, and being ordered to leave port, was sunk by the United States war vessel Kearsage, Captain Winslow, after an hour's contest.

Mobile Blockaded, Aug. 5, 1864.—This harbor was defended by Forts Gaines and Morgan, a fleet, the iron-clad ram Tennessee, and sunken torpedoes. Admiral Farragut's squadron undertook its capture. Passing the forts after an hour's severe fighting, the fleet engaged the Confederates. In order to direct the movements of his vessels, Admiral Farragut had mounted to the maintop of the Hartford and lashed himself to the rigging. After a desperate conflict the fleet and the forts surrendered.

Privateer Florida Captured Oct. 7, 1864, in the Port of Bahia, S. A., by the United States steamer Wachusett, Capt. Collins. She was taken to Hampton Roads, where she was sunk.

The Blockade of Southern Ports ended June 23d, 1865, by proclamation of President Johnson.

Privateer Shenandoah delivered up at Liverpool, June 28, 1865. She was built in Scotland and manned by Englishmen. She destroyed thirty vessels worth $1,354,958.

MISCELLANEOUS ITEMS OF THE REBELLION.

Army Medical Department. — From May, 1861, until the final mustering out of the service, 5,825,000 soldiers were treated in field and hospital. Of these 166,623 were fatal.

Disbanding United States Army began June 2d, 1865. It took several months, as there were 1,034,064 volunteers upon the rolls. The total enlistments during the war was 2,678,967.— The Confederates had about 2,000,000. The entire loss of both armies was about 600,000 killed and 400,000 disabled and crippled.

United States Navy had 7,600 men at the beginning of the war and 51,500 at its close. Government had built 208 war vessels and bought 418. C. Vanderbilt gave the United States a steamer worth $1,000,000. The navy captured 1,504 blockade runners.

United States Pay Department. The disbursements during the war were $1,100,000,000. Losses from defalcations and accidents less than $1,000,000. Expense of paying the army $6,000,000, or less than ¼ of 1 per cent.

Confederate Flag.—The first captured during the war was taken from Alexandria, Va. May 23, 1861.

Col. E. E. Ellsworth, May 24, 1861, was shot by Jackson, proprietor of the Marshall House, Alexandria, Va., while hauling down the Confederate flag from that hotel. Jackson was shot dead on the spot by Frank E. Brownell, one of Ellsworth's companions.

"Contrabands." —— This famous phraze originated with General Butler May 24, 1861. Three negroes escaped from the Confederates and came into the

Union lines at Fortress Monroe. Butler pronounced them "contrabands of war."

Halleck's Blunder.—Nov. 18, 1861, Gen. Halleck succeeded Gen. Hunter in Missouri. Thousands of refugees flocked into the Union lines. As the Confederates obtained early information of the movements of the Union armies, General Halleck, by proclamation, on November 29th, forbade fugitive slaves to enter the lines upon the ground that they were the offenders. This proclamation was speedily countermanded.

Bell Metal Cannon.—March 8th, 1862, artillery had become so scarce in the Confedercy that General Beauregard appealed to the people to donate bells

first cartel was signed July 22, 1862, but it was a source of much contention throughout the war.

"Quaker" Gunboat. — In March, 1863, the Confederates had captured the "Indianola," a powerful iron-clad of Porter's fleet; also the Union ram "Queen of the West." The former was disabled and her captors were repairing her. Com. Porter rigged up an old flat-boat in resemblance of a ram, and set up pork barrels on her deck to imitate smoke-stacks. This "Quaker" was started at night past the Vicksburg batteries, from which it received a heavy fire. As it did not respond it was thought to be some new formidable Federal monster, and at its approach

---

---

and iron. The result was that churches, public institutions, plantations and families responded with such liberality as nearly to strip the country of iron and brass.

Butler's Famous "Woman Order," May 15, 1862.—The women of New Orleans insulted Union officers and soldiers grossly and without provocation, until to stop it General Butler in an order declared that "any female who shall, by word, gesture or movement, insult or show contempt for any officer or soldier of the United States shall be regarded and held liable to be treated as a woman of the town plying her vocation." This order was effectual.

Exchange of Prisoners. — The

the "Queen of the West" fled, and the Indianola was blown to fragments to prevent her recapture.

Veteran Reserve Corps was organized April 28, 1863, for light garrison and hospital duty, by soldiers who, from wounds and disease, were incapable of active service. Over 60,000 men entered this corps.

Andersonville.—November 27, 1863, Captain Winder established a military prison at this point, which became notorious in the annals of suffering under the management of Henry Wirz. It was enclosed by a strong stockade surrounded by a line of earthworks. The famous "dead line" was about 19 feet inside the stockade. If prisoners crossed it they were shot. 49,485 Union prisoners were registered here, of whom 12,-462 died and 328 escaped. Aug. 9, 1864, 33,006 were in the pen.

Peace Commissioners at Niagara. In July, 1864, Horace Greely met some Confederate envoys on the Canada side of Niagara Falls, to propose terms of peace, but as Mr. Lincoln would listen to no terms involving the independence of the South, and as Mr. Davis insisted upon that, the attempt came to naught.

Amnesty Proclamation issued by President Johnson, May 29, 1865, offered full pardon to all engaged in the late rebellion, with fourteen exceptions.

Alexander H. Stevens and other Confederate prisoners were released on parole from Fort Warren, Boston, Oct. 11, 1865.

War Ended.—April 2, 1866, President Johnson, by proclamation, announced the close of the war.

UNION AND CONFEDERATE OFFICERS.

George B. McClellan, May 14th, 1861, appointed Major General of the Ohio River Volunteers, including those from West Virginia.

Benj. F. Butler, May 16, 1861, appointed Major General of the Department of East Virginia, with headquarters at Fortress Monroe.

Joseph E. Johnson was appointed to command the Confederate troops at Harper's Ferry, May 23, 1861.

Major General Patterson was superceded in the command of the Army of the Shenandoah on the 19th of July, 1861, by General N. P. Banks.

General George B. McClellan was appointed to command the Army of the Potomac July 22, 1861, in place of Gen. McDowell. Rosecrans succeeded McClellan in West Virginia. General Lee took Garnett's place in the Confederate army. General Garnett was killed at the battle of Carrick's Ford.

General Fremont was superseded in his command November 2, 1861, by General Hunter.

General Beauregard was ordered to the command of the Confederate army in the West, January 27, 1862.

Buell was relieved October 30, 1862, for his unsatisfactory conduct of the campaign, and General Rosecrans appointed to the command of what was now called the "Army of the Cumberland."

General McClellan superseded by Burnside, November 5, 1862, because of his failure to destroy Lee's army. Burnside planned to act against Richmond, making Acquia Creek his base of supplies.

Butler Superseded by Banks Nov. 9, 1862. Butler's administration of the government of New Orleans was marked with great ability and he left the city in a better condition than had ever been known before.

Burnside Superseded by Hooker in command of the army on the Rappabannock, January 26, 1863.

General Hunter Superseded in command of the, Department of the South by General Gilmore, June 1, 1863.

Military Affairs in the West.— October 16, 1863, General Grant was appointed commander of the consolidated armies of the Ohio, Cumberland and Tennessee. Sherman was appointed to the Tennessee army and Thomas to succeed Rosecrans.

Robert E. Lee was made General of all the Confederate armies February 1, 1865.

Allentown, Pa.—*Hotels Continued.*

PENNSYLVANIA HOTEL,
BITTNER & HARTMAN, Proprietors.

SEVENTH, COR. LINDEN ST.,
ALLENTOWN, PA.

Boarding by the Day or Week.   Stabling for 150 Horses.

Marble Works.

ROMIG MARBLE & GRANITE WORKS.
MRS. ELIZA WEISS, Proprietress.

JACOB M. ROMIG, Manager.

NINTH, COR. LINDEN ST., ALLENTOWN, PA.

Machinists.

GEO. L. KNAUSS & CO.
MACHINISTS,

Manufacturers and Repairers of Light Machinery, Screw Cutting. Foot Lathes, Models, Tower Clocks, Knitting Machines, Printing Presses, Engines, Ventilating Fans, Show Windows, Racks, Brackets, Sewing Machines, &c.

14 and 16 S. Church St., Allentown, Pa.

CHARLES SPANGLE,
Manufacturing Machinist,
BRASS AND IRON FOUNDER,
Cor. Third and Walnut Sts., Allentown, Pa.

Machinery Manufactured. Models made to Order. General Repairing a Specialty. Castings of every Description made. Small Stationery Engines, Mining and Hoisting Machinery made.

RECONSTRUCTION.

Secession Ordinance of Mississippi was repealed August 22, 1865, by a Constitutional Convention, which also declared slavery abolished.

Alabama, by a Constitutional Convention held September 10, 1865, nullified her secession ordinance, repudiated her Confederate war debt and declared slavery abolished.

South Carolina held a Constitutional Convention September 13, 1865, which nullified her ordinance of secession and declared slavery abolished.

North Carolina held a Constitutional Convention October 2, 1865, which nullified her ordinance of secession, declared slavery abolished and repudiated her State war debt.

Georgia held a Constitutional Convention October 25, 1865, which nullified her ordinance of secession, repudiated its State war debt, and declared slavery abolished.

Florida held a Constitutional Convention and nullified her ordinance of secession, October 28, 1865.

Texas held a Constitutional Convention February 10, 1866, which nullified its ordinance of secession, repudiated its State war debt, and declared slavery abolished.

Tennessee was readmitted to the Union, and her Senators and Representatives admitted to Congress, July 23rd, 1866.

Virginia was readmitted into the Union January 26, 1870.

Mississippi was readmitted into the Union February 17, 1870.

Texas readmitted to the Union March 29, 1870.

Test-Oath abolished by House of Representatives February 1, 1871.

Amnesty Debate in the United States House of Representatives occurred in January, 1876, creating great excitement. It was proposed to remove all political disabilities from citizens of the South except Jefferson Davis,

Packard Government in Louisiana was recognized January 14, 1877, over the rival Nichols government.— Each had been inaugurated January 8.

United States Troops entirely withdrawn from the South in 1877.

ARMY AND NAVY OF THE UNITED STATES.

Washington took command of the army July 3, 1775, under a large elm standing on Cambridge Common, Mass. It numbered less than 14,000 men. Military supplies, especially powder, were scarce, and discipline was almost unknown. Washington at once introduced the latter.

Congress Called upon the States, February 5, 1780, to fill up their quotas so as to make an army of 35,000, which did not then exceed 10,000 men.

Uniform Militia System for the United States was adopted by Congress May 8, 1792, which has, with slight variations, continued until now.

United States Navy.—The Alger-

Washington's request Alexander Hamilton was made Major General.

Provisional Army Disbanded, May 10, 1800, by order of Congress, because of the favorable reception of our envoys by France.

West Point United States Military Academy founed March 16, 1802.

War of the Epaulettes.—In 1839 the medical corps of the United States army protested against wearing an aiguilette instead of an epaulette upon the shoulder. Considerable excitement followed, which was ended by the triumph of the epaulettes.

Mutiny in the U. S. Navy.—In 1842 Captain Alexander S. Mackenzie,

---

---

ine troubles caused Congress, March 27, 1794, to authorize the building of six frigates of 32 guns each.

War Measures in 1797.—Congress arranged to raise 80,000 militia and a small navy, but forbid privateering under heavy penalties.

Navy Department created by Congress April 30, 1798, and Benjamin Stoddert, of Maryland, appointed Secretary.

Provisional Army.—Congress, on May 28, 1798, authorized the President to enlist 10,000 men for three years.

Commander-in-Chief. — General Washington was nominated Lieutenant General of all the United States armies by the President July 2, 1798, and unanimously confirmed by Congress. At

hanged Philip H. Spencer, son of the Secretary of War, and two others of his crew for mutiny. A naval court of inquiry justified his act.

Naval School at Annapolis, Md., was opened October 10, 1845, under direction of Hon. George Bancroft, Secretary of the Navy.

Army Rations.—The orignal soldier's ration was one pound of beef or three-quarters of a pound of pork, one pound of bread or flour, one-half gill of spirits or its value, and at the rate of one quart salt, two quarts vinegar, two pounds soap and one pound candles to every one hundred rations. In 1832 four pounds of coffee and eight pounds of sugar to every 100 rations was substituted for the liquor. August 3, 1861, it was increased one and one-half pounds of bread or flour, or one pound of hard bread, fresh beef as often as may be possible in place of salt beef; beans, rice and hominy twice a week, one pound of potatoes three times a week; tea to be substituted for coffee if desired, and other food to be provided for to some extent. This ration being found too large was afterward diminished, but the army was well fed through the war

Grand Army of the Potomac was fully organized, equipped and disciplined and in July, 1861, numbered 125,000. It was increased by the following March to 220,000.

enlist negroes for camp duty, constructing intrenchments, or any other service for which they were found competent. In 1864 they were unconditionally enlisted as troops. The whole number in service was one hundred and eighty-six thousand and seventeen.

Army of Virginia was organized July 20, 1862, for the defense of Washington. It consisted of 50,000 efficient troops under Major Generals Sigel, McDowell and Banks. When ready for action General Pope asked McClellan to co-operate with him, but he refused, whereupon Pope recommended that a General-in-Chief be appointed superior to both. General Halleck received this

---

Iron-Clad Steam Rams were first constructed for the United States service upon the Mississippi by James B. Eads, of St. Louis, Mo., in 1861.

Army of the Potomac, at Harrison's Landing, July 8, 1862, was visited by President Lincoln. McClellan reported his strength at 50,000 after the battle of Malvern Hills, with only 9,000 present and fit for duty. Thus had a splendid army of 160,000 been reduced by the disastrous peninsula campaign. A council decided to transfer the army to Washington.

Colored Troops.—July 17th, 1862, Congress authorized the President to

appointment. He ordered McClellan to transfer his army to Acquia Creek.

Lieutenant General Grant.—This office had expired with Washington. On March 4, 1863, Congress created it again, and conferred it upon Grant, who was thereby placed in command of all the United States armies, numbering 800,000 men. The Confederates numbered 400,000.

General of the Armies of the United States was the title created and conferred upon U. S. Grant, July 25, 1866.—General W. T. Sherman was promoted to be Lieutenant General in Grant's place.

PRESIDENTIAL ELECTIONS AND CONVENTIONS.

First President.—George Washington was unanimously elected first President of the United States in February, 1789, and John Adams was chosen Vice-President. They were inaugurated on April 30th, 1789, in Federal Hall, New York City.

The Second Presidential Campaign, in 1792, resulted in the re-election of George Washington as President and John Adams as Vice-President. The anti-Federalists supported George Clinton, Thomas Jefferson and Aaron Burr for Vice-President. Washington and Adams were inaugurated March 4, 1793, each for a second term.

Third Presidential Campaign,

ists. Thomas Jefferson, of Virginia, and Aaron Burr, of New York, received a similar Democrat-Republican nomination. The two latter received 73 votes apiece, but, being equal in number, it devolved upon the House of Representatives to choose which should be President. Adams had 65, Pinckney 64 and Jay 1 vote. Feb. 17, 1801, on the 36th ballot, the House of Representatives elected Thomas Jefferson President and Aaron Burr Vice-President. They were inaugurated March 4, 1801.

Fifth Presidential Campaign.— In 1804 Thomas Jefferson, of Virginia, and George Clinton, of New York, were the candidates of the Democrat-Repub-

---

1796.—The Federalists supported John Adams, of Massachusetts, for President, and Thomas Pinckney, of Maryland, for Vice-President. The Democrat-Republicans supported Thomas Jefferson, of Virginia, and Aaron Burr, of New York. Of the electoral votes John Adams had 71, Thomas Pinckney 59, Thomas Jefferson 68, Aaron Burr, 30. According to the Constitution, John Adams was elected President and Thomas Jefferson Vice-President. They were inaugurated March 4, 1797.

Fourth Presidental Campaign. The fourth occurred in 1800. John Adams, of Massachusetts, and C. C. Pinckney, of South Carolina, were nominated by a Congressional caucus of Federal-

licans, and C. C. Pinckney, of South Carolina, and Rufus King, of New York, of the Federalists. The former received 162, and the latter 14 electoral votes. Thos. Jefferson as President, and George Clinton, as Vice-President, were inaugurated March 4, 1805.

Sixth Presidential Campaign was in 1808. James Madison, of Virginia, and George Clinton, of New York, were the successful candidates of the Democrat-Republicans, and C. C. Pinckney, of South Carolina, and Rufus King, of New York, were supported by the Federalists. Madison received 122 and Clinton 113 electoral votes. Pinckney and King received 47 votes. The inauguration of James Madison, of Virginia, and Rufus King, of New York, as President and Vice-President of the United States took place March 4, 1809. Madison wore a suit of American broad-cloth on the occasion.

Seventh Presidential Campaign —First Political Convention.—In May, 1812, at a Congressional caucus, James Madison was renominated for President, and Elbridge Gerry, of Massachusetts, for Vice-President, by the Democrat-Re-publicans. A political convention, in which eleven States were represented, the first ever held in the United States, assembled in New York and nominated, as opposition candidates, De Witt Clin-ton, of New York, and Jared Ingersoll, of Pennsylvania, for President and Vice-

Vice-President were inaugurated March 4, 1817.

Ninth Presidential Campaign in 1820.—Monroe and Tompkins were re-elected with but slight opposition. Out of 235 electoral votes Monroe re-ceived 231. Three electors had died and one voted for John Q. Adams. The inauguration of James Monroe, of Vir-ginia, as President, and Daniel D. Tomp-kins, of New York, as Vice-President, occurred March 4, 1821.

Tenth Presidential Campaign.— In 1824 four candidates were in the field: John Quincy Adams of Massachusetts, William H. Crawford of Georgia, Henry Clay of Kentucky, and Andrew Jackson of Tennessee. Neither candidate re-

President. Madison received 128, Gerry 131, Clinton 89, and Ingersoll 86 electo-ral votes. James Madison, of Virginia, as President, and Elbridge Gerry, of Massachusetts, as Vice-President, were inaugurated March 4, 1813.

Eighth Presidential Campaign, 1816. — In Congressional caucus the Democrat-Republicans nominated James Monroe, of Virginia, for President, and Daniel D. Tompkins, of New York, for Vice-President. The Federalists nomi-nated Rufus King, of New York, and John E. Howard. Monroe and Tomp-kins received 183 electoral votes, King 34 and Howard 22. James Monroe as President and James D. Tompkins as

ceived a majority of the electoral vote, hence the election devolved upon the House of Representatives, by whom John Quincy Adams was elected Presi-dent and John C. Calhoun Vice-Presi-dent. The popular vote stood as fol-lows: Andrew Jackson, 155,872; John Q. Adams, 105,321; Henry Clay, 46,587; William H. Crawford, 44,282. The in-auguration of John Quincy Adams of Massachusetts as President, and John C. Calhoun of South Carolina as Vice-President, occurred March 4, 1825.

Eleventh Presidential Campaign in 1828, resulted in the election of An-drew Jackson of Tennessee and John C. Calhoun of South Carolina. They were the candidates of the Democrats, as they now called themselves. Their opponents, the National Republicans, supported John Quincy Adams of Massachusetts, and Richard Rush of Pennsylvania. General Jackson received 178 and Calhoun 171 electoral votes; Adams and Rush 83 votes each. The popular vote was 647,231 for Jackson and 509,097 for Adams. The inauguration of Andrew Jackson of Tennessee as President, and John C. Calhoun of South Carolina as Vice-President of the United States occurred March 4, 1829.

Political National Convention. The second in the country (the first was in 1812), was held at Philadelphia in September, 1830, by the Anti-Masons.— Ninety-six delegates were present. The

Martin Van Buren of New York for Vice-President of the United States. They made no nomination for President because Jackson was the unanimous choice of the party for re-election.

Twelfth Presidential Campaign, 1832.—Andrew Jackson of Tennessee, and Martin Van Buren of New York, were the Democratic candidates, except in South Carolina, where they supported John Floyd of Virginia, and Henry Lee of Massachusetts. The National Republicans supported Henry Clay of Kentucky and John Sergeant of Pennsylvania. The Anti-Masons supported William Wirt of Maryland and Amos Ellmaker of Pennsylvania. Jackson had 219 electoral votes, Van Buren 189.

presiding officer was Francis Granger of New York. It adjourned to hold another the following year to nominate Presidential candidates.

National Anti-Masonic Convention was held in Baltimore, Md., in 1831. It nominated William Wirt of Maryland for President, and Amos Ellmaker of Pennsylvania for Vice-President of the United States.

National Republicans assembled in convention at Baltimore December 12, 1831, and nominated Henry Clay of Kentucky for President, and John Sergeant of Pennsylvania for Vice-President of the United States.

Democratic Convention assembled at Baltimore in May, 1832, and nominated

Their popular vote was 687,502. Clay and Sergeant had 49 electoral and 530,-189 popular votes. Floyd and Lee had 11 electoral votes, Wirt and Ellmaker had 7, and their combined popular vote was 33,108. The inauguration of Andrew Jackson of Tennessee as President, and Martin Van Buren of New York as Vice-President of the United States, occurred March 4, 1833.

Democratic National Convention was held at Baltimore Md., in May, 1835, which nominated Martin Van Buren for President, and Richard M. Johnson of Kentucky for Vice-President. The two-thirds rule was first adopted in this convention.

Thirteenth Presidential campaign

occurred in 1836. The Democratic candidates were Martin Van Buren of New York and Richard M. Johnson of Kentucky. The National Republicans, now known as Whigs, supported General William H. Harrison of Ohio, and Francis Granger of New York. The result gave Van Buren 170 electoral votes, Johnson 147, and a popular vote of 761,-549. General Harrison had 73 electoral votes and Granger had 77. The popular Whig vote was 736,656. The inauguration of Martin Van Buren as President, and Richard M. Johnson as Vice President, occurred March 4, 1837.

Liberty Party Convention was held at Warsaw, New York, November 13, 1839, by the Abolitionists, who nomi-

Martin Van Buren and R. M. Johnson were the Democratic, and James G. Birney and Francis J. Lemoyne were the "Liberty" party, or Abolition candidates. This was known as the "log cabin and hard cider" campaign. Gen. Harrison had 294 and John Tyler 234 electoral votes, and a popular vote of 1,275,015. Van Buren had 60 and Johnson 48 electoral and 1,128,702 popular votes. The "Liberty" party cast a popular vote of 7,059. General William Henry Harrison of Ohio, and John Tyler of Virginia, were inaugurated as President and Vice-President of the United States March 4, 1841.

Presidential Inauguration of John Tyler.—William Henry Harrison,

nated James G. Birney of New York for President, and Francis J. Leymoyne of Pennsylvania for Vice-President.

Whig National Convention.—The first was held December 4, 1839, at Harrisburg, Penna., and nominated General William Henry Harrison of Ohio as President, and John Tyler of Virginia as Vice-President.

Democratic National Convention at Baltimore, held May 5, 1840, nominated Martin Van Buren for President, but made no nomination for Vice-President.

Fourteenth Presidential Campaign.—In 1840 General William Henry Harrison of Ohio, and John Tyler of Virginia, were the Whig candidates,

President of the United States, died on April 4, 1841, and John Tyler, Vice-President, was inaugurated President on April 6, 1841.

Whig Convention met at Baltimore on May 1st, 1844, and nominated Henry Clay of Kentucky for President, and Theodore Frelinghuysen of New Jersey, for Vice-President.

Democratic Convention met at Baltimore on May 27, 1844, and nominated James K. Polk of Tennessee for President, and George M. Dallas of Pennsylvania for Vice-President.

Fifteenth Presidential Campaign. In 1844 James K. Polk and George M. Dallas, the Democratic candidates for President and Vice-President, received

170 electoral and 1,337,243 popular votes. Clay and Frelinghuysen received 105 electoral and 1,299,068 popular votes. Birney and Morris, supported by the Liberty party, received 62,300 votes. The inauguration of James K. Polk of Tennessee as President, and George M. Dallas as Vice-President of the United States, occurred March 4, 1845.

Democratic National Convention met at Baltimore May 22, 1848, and nominated Lewis Cass for President and William O. Butler for Vice-President. This convention split into two sections, the "Barnburners," or free-soil Democrats, who opposed the extension of slavery, and the "Hunkers," who wished to let slavery alone. The former finally withdrew from the party.

Butler, 1,220,544 popular, 127 electoral; Van Buren and Adams, 291,263 popular, and no electoral votes. The inauguration of Zachary Taylor of Louisiana as President, and Millard Fillmore of New York as Vice-President of the United States, occurred March 4, 1849.

Millard Fillmore was inaugurated President of the United States July 10, 1850; vice, President Taylor, who died July 9, 1850.

Democratic Convention met at Baltimore June 1, 1852, and nominated Franklin Pierce of New Hampshire for President, and William R. King of Alabama for Vice-President.

Whig Convention met June 16, 1852, and nominated General Winfield Scott

Whig National Convention met at Philadelphia July 7, 1848, and nominated General Zachary Taylor of Louisiana for President, and Millard Fillmore of New York for Vice-President.

Sixteenth Presidential Campaign. In 1848 Lewis Cass of Michigan, and William O. Butler of Kentucky, were the nominees of the Democrats for President and Vice-president. The Whigs supported General Zachary Taylor of Louisiana, and Millard Fillmore of New York. The candidates of the Free-Soilers were Martin Van Buren of New York, and Charles Francis Adams of Massachusetts. The votes were as follows, viz.: Taylor and Fillmore, 1,360,-101 popular and 163 electoral; Cass and

of Virginia for President, and William A. Graham of North Carolina for Vice-President. This was the last Whig convention.

Free-Soil Party, August 11, 1852, nominated John P. Hale of New Hampshire for President, and Geo. W. Julian of Indiana for Vice-President. It denounced slavery as a "sin against God and a crime against man."

Seventeenth Presidential Campaign.—In 1852 the campaign occurred with the following result, viz.: Pierce and King, Democrats, had 1,601,474 popular and 254 electoral votes; Scott and Graham, Whigs, had 1,386,578 popular and 42 electoral votes; Hale and Julian, Free-Soilers, had 156,149 popular votes. The right of secession had been discussed in several Southern conventions this year. The inauguration of Franklin Pierce of New Hampshire as President of the United States took place March 4, 1853. William R. King was in Cuba, and was sworn in as Vice-President March 24 by United States Consul Sharkey.

Republican Convention met at Philadelphia June 17, 1856, and nominated John C. Fremont of California as President, and William L. Dayton, of New Jersey, as Vice-President. It declared in favor of internal improvements, the right to prohibit slavery and polygamy in the Territories, and of admitting Kansas as a free State.

anan and Breckinridge had 1,838,169 popular and 174 electoral votes; Fremont and Dayton had 1,341,264 popular and 114 electoral votes; Fillmore and Donelson had 874,534 popular and 8 electoral votes. The latter carried the State of Maryland. The inauguration of James Buchanan as President, and John C. Breckinridge as Vice-President of the United States, took place March 4, 1857.

Republican Convention met at Chicago May 16, 1860, and nominated Abraham Lincoln of Illinois for President, and Hannibal Hamlin of Maine for Vice-President.

Constitutional Union Party, at its convention in Baltimore May 19 1860,

---

Know-Nothing Convention met February 22, 1856, and nominated Millard Fillmore of New York for President, and Andrew J. Donelson of Tennessee for Vice-President. This party was a secret organization, opposed to foreigners, and favored a naturalization only after 21 years residence. This was the only campaign in which the party presented candidates for President and Vice-President.

Democratic Convention met at Cincinnati June 2, 1856, and nominated James Buchanan of Pennsylvania for President, and John C. Breckinridge of Kentucky for Vice-President.

Eighteenth Presidential Campaign of 1856 resulted as follows, viz.: Buch-

nominated John Bell of Tennessee for President, and Edward Everett of Massachusetts as Vice-President.

Democratic National Convention held at Charleston, S. C., April 23, 1860, split upon the doctrine of "popular sovereignty." The delegates from several slave States seceded and adjourned to meet at Richmond, Va.; the Northern delegates adjourned to meet at Baltimore, Md. The latter held their convention at Baltimore, June 18, 1860, and nominated for President Stephen A. Douglas of Illinois, and for Vice-President Hershel V. Johnson of Georgia. The Democratic seceders met in convention at Baltimore, June 28, 1860, and nominated John C. Breckinridge of Kentucky for President, and Joseph Lane of Oregon for Vice-President.

Nineteenth Presidential Campaign, Nov. 6th, 1860.—As the result of this election Abraham Lincoln and Hannibal Hamlin were the successful candidates, receiving 180 electoral votes and a popular vote of 1,866.352; Breckinridge and Lane 72 electoral and 845,763 popular votes; Bell and Everett 39 electoral and 589,581 popular votes, and Douglas and Johnson 12 electoral and 1,375,157 popular votes. Lincoln and Hamlin carried all the Northern States except New Jersey, which cast three electorals for Lincoln and four for Douglas. The inauguration of Abraham Lincoln as President, and Hannibal Hamlin as Vice-President

tion of Lincoln and Johnson, who received 2,216,067 popular and 212 electoral votes; McClellan and Pendleton had 1,808,725 popular and 21 electoral votes. Eleven States in the Confederacy had 81 electoral votes, which would not have changed the result if they had all been cast for the defeated candidates. Abraham Lincoln was inaugurated as President, and Andrew Johnson as Vice-President of the United States, March 4, 1865.

Andrew Johnson was sworn in as President of the United States April 15, 1865, by Chief Justice Chase, vice, President Lincoln, who was assassinated on April 14, 1865.

Republican National Convention.

of the United States, took place at Washington, D. C., March 4, 1861, notwithstanding fears of violence.

Republican National Convention, held at Baltimore June 7th, 1864, nominated Abraham Lincoln of Illinois for President, and Andrew Johnson of Tennessee for Vice-President. It took a decided stand and opposed any compromise upon the question of the rebellion.

Democratic National Convention met at Chicago August 29th, 1864, and nominated George B. McClellan of New Jersey for President, and George H. Pendleton of Ohio for Vice-President of the United States.

Twentieth Presidential Campaign, November 8, 1864, resulted in the elec-

met at Chicago, Ill., May 20, 1868, and nominated U. S. Grant of Illinois for President, and Schuyler Colfax of Indiana for Vice-President of the United States.

Democratic National Convention met at New York, July 4, 1868, and nominated Horatio Seymour of New York for President, and Francis P. Blair of Missouri as Vice-President of the United States.

Twenty-first Presidential Campaign. November 3, 1868, General Grant and Schuyler Colfax, the Republican nominees, were elected President and Vice-President of the United States. They received 214 electoral and 3,015,071 popular votes; Seymour and Blair received

80 electoral and 2,709,613 popular votes. Nine of the electoral votes cast for the latter candidates were from the State of Georgia. U. S. Grant was inaugurated President, and Schuyler Colfax Vice-President of the United States March 4, 1869.

Liberal Republican Convention.— Horace Greely of New York and B. Gratz Brown of Missouri, were nominated May 1, 1872, for President and Vice-President of the United States by the "Liberal Republicans," in convention at Cincinnati, Ohio.

National Democratic Convention was held at Baltimore July 9th, 1872, and adopted the candidates and platform of the Liberal Republicans.

Ohio for President, and William A. Wheeler, of New York for Vice-President of the United States.

National Greenback Convention met at Indianapolis, Ind., May 17, 1876, and nominated Peter Cooper of New York for President, and Samuel F. Carey of Ohio for Vice-President of the United States.

Democratic National Convention met at St. Louis, Mo., June 27, 1876, and nominated Samuel J. Tilden of New York for President, and Thomas A. Hendricks of Indiana for Vice-President of the United States.

Twenty-third Presidential Campaign, November 7, 1876.—The votes were as follows, viz.: Tilden and Hend-

---

National Republican Convention met at Philadelphia June 5, 1872, and nominated U. S. Grant for President, and Henry Wilson of Massachusetts for Vice-President of the United States.

Twenty-second Presidential Campaign, November 5, 1872, resulted in the election of Grant and Wilson, Republicans. They received 286 electoral and 3,597,070 popular votes. The Democrats and Liberals received 47 electoral and 2,834,079 popular votes. U. S. Grant and Henry Wilson were inaugurated President and Vice-President of the United States March 4, 1873.

Republican National Convention met at Cincinnati, Ohio, June 14, 1876, and nominated Rutherford B. Hayes of

ricks, Democrats, received 184 electoral and 4,284,885 popular votes. Hayes and Wheeler, Republicans, received 166 electoral votes. Peter Cooper, Greenback, 81,740 popular votes, and Green Clay Smith, Prohibitionist, 9,522. Louisiana, Florida and South Carolina were in doubt. If the electoral vote of any one of the doubtful States should be given to Tilden and Hendricks it would elect them, but if *all* of the doubtful States should be given to the Republicans Hayes and Wheeler would have 185 electoral votes, and would be elected President and Vice-President.

Electoral Commission Bill.—To settle the dispute of the doubtful States, and to avoid all further controversy,

Congress passed a bill January 29, 1877, which was signed by the President, entitled the "Electoral Commission Bill." It provided that in the case where double returns were made by several States they should be referred to a commission composed of five Senators, five Congressmen and five Justices of the Supreme Court. The Senate vote on the bill was yeas 47, nays 17. The House vote was yeas 191, nays 96. January 30, 1877, Senators Edmunds, Morton, Frelinghuysen, Thurman and Bayard, and Represesentatives Payne, Hunter, Abbott, Garfield and Hoar were elected members. January 31, 1877, Chief Justices Clifford, Miller, Field, Strong and Bradley were also chosen to serve on

New York for Vice-President. A strong effort was made to nominate Gen. Grant for a third term, over 300 delegates voting solidly for him 36 times.

Greenback Convention met at Chicago, Ill., June 11, 1880, and nominated General J. B. Weaver of Iowa for President, and B. J. Chambers of Texas for Vice-President of the United States. The same party held a convention in St. Louis March 5, 1880, and nominated Stephen B. Dillaye of New Hampshire for President, and B. J. Chambers of Texas for Vice-President.

Democratic National Convention met at Cincinnati, O., June 24, 1880, and nominated Winfield S. Hancock of New York for President, and William H.

this Commission. It gave the votes of the doubtful States, by a vote of 8 to 7—Judge Bradley voting with the Republicans—to Hayes and Wheeler, and on March 2, 1877, they were declared elected President and Vice-President of the United States. President Hayes and Vice-President Wheeler were inaugurated March 5, 1877, as the 4th occurred on Sunday. Hayes' title to the office was pronounced irrevocable by Mr. Burchard's (of Illinois) bill, which passed the House of Representatives June 14, 1878, by a vote of 215 to 21.

National Republican Convention met at Chicago June 8, 1880, and nominated James A. Garfield of Ohio for President, and Chester A. Arthur of

English of Indiana for Vice-President of the United States.

Independent Labor Party met in Convention at Sharon, Penna., July 29, 1880, and nominated Garfield and Arthur as their presidential ticket.

Twenty-fourth Presidential Campaign ended November 2, 1880. Garfield and Arthur, the Republican candidates were elected, receiving 214 electoral and 4,449,053 popular votes; Hancock and English, 155 electoral and 4,442,035 popular votes; Weaver and Chambers received 307,306 popular votes and no electoral votes. The inauguration of President Garfield and Vice-President Arthur took place March 4th, 1881.

Chester A. Arthur was sworn in as President of the United States September 20, 1881, vice, President Garfield, who was assassinated by Charles Guiteau on July 2, and died at Elberon, New Jersey, September 19, 1881.

Republican National Convention met at Chicago, Ill., June 3, 1884, and nominated James G. Blaine of Maine for President, and John A. Logan of Illinois for Vice-President.

Democratic National Convention met at Chicago, Ill., July 8, 1884, and nominated Grover Cleveland of New York for President, and Thos. A. Hendricks of Indiana for Vice-President.

The Prohibitionists, or Temperance party, nominated John P. St. John of Kansas for President, and William Daniel of Maryland for Vice-President.

The Greenback, or Labor party, supported Benjamin F. Butler of Massachusetts for President, and A. M. West for Vice-President.

Twenty-fifth Presidential Campaign.—The election took place November 4, 1884, and the Democrats succeeded in electing Grover Cleveland, President, and Thomas A. Hendricks, Vice-President. This was the first success of the Democrats in twenty-four years, Buchanan being the last President elected by them. Cleveland and Hendricks secured 219 electoral and 4,911,017 popular votes; Blaine and Logan received 182 electoral and 4,848,334 popular votes; St. John and Daniel received 151,809 popular and no electoral vote; Butler and West received 133,825 popular and no electoral vote. Belva A. Lockwood, a female Equal Rights candidate, received twelve votes in Texas. The inauguration of Grover Cleveland President, and Thos. A. Hendricks, Vice-President, occurred on March 4, 1885.

DUELS BETWEEN NOTED PERSONS.

Duel in New England.—June 18, 1621, Edward Doty and Edward Leister, servants of Mr Hopkins, fought upon a challenge of single combat with sword and dagger. One was wounded in the hand, the other in the thigh. The punishment adjudged by the whole company was that "they should lie with head and feet tied together for 24 hours, without meat and drink." They were released at the end of an hour upon their own and their masters' request and promise of better carriage."

Duel on Boston Commons.—In 1728 a duel was fought on Boston Commons between two young men named Woodbridge and Phillips. They met alone in the night and used short swords in the fight. Woodbridge was killed, and Phillips fled to France to escape the penalties of the law.

Button Gwinnett, of Georgia, a signer of the Declaration of Independence, and General Lackland McIntosh, a Revolutionary officer, fought a duel with pistols at a distance of twelve feet,

May 27, 1777. Gwinnett was killed and McIntosh was wounded. The quarrel grew out of a rivalry for a brigadier generalship.

Generals Cadwallader and Conway fought a duel July 4, 1778. It grew out of the opposition of Conway to Washington. Conway was wounded, and thinking he was going to die, wrote a penitent letter to Washington for his dishonorable attacks upon his character.

Major General Charles Lee and Colonel John Laurens, an aid of Washington, fought a duel in 1778. Laurens challenged Lee on account of slanderous remarks made by him concerning Washington, defending his conduct at Monmouth in courtmartialing Lee. The

punishment, at the discretion of a court-martial." The practice of dueling had become at this time so frequent in the army that it demanded legal measures for its suppression, and the erroneous impression of honor made it impossible for one to decline a challenge without socially ruining his character.

Henry Clay and Humphrey Marshall fought a duel in 1808. Both were wounded. They were both members of the Kentucky Legislature at the time.

Gen. Andrew Jackson and Senator Thomas H. Benton fought a duel in 1813.

Gen. Armistead T. Mason, United States Senator from Virginia, and John M. McCarty fought a duel near Washington, D. C., in 1819. The former was killed and the latter wounded.

affair terminated in the wounding of Lee.

Alexander Hamilton and Aaron Burr, then Vice-President of the United States, fought a duel at Weehawken, N. J., July 11, 1804. Hamilton fired into the air and was mortally wounded by Burr. The challenge was given by Burr because of Hamilton's successful opposition to Burr's political aspirations.

Congressional Action Against Dueling.—In 1806 Congress passed a law "that no officer or soldier should send a challenge to another officer or soldier to fight a duel, or accept a challenge if sent, upon pain, if a commissioned officer, of being cashiered; if a non-commissioned officer of suffering corporeal

Lieut. Francis B. White, of the Marine Corps, and Lieut. William B. Finch, of the United States Navy, fought a duel on an island in Boston harbor in 1819. The former was killed, and Finch afterward assumed the name of Bolton.

Stephen Decatur, Jr., and Commodore James Barron fought a duel at Bladensburg, Md., March 22, 1820. Decatur was killed and Barron wounded. The latter was commander of the Chesapeake who surrendered to the Leopard in 1807. The duel grew out of a discussion of that affair. Decatur was a brave naval officer, and celebrated for his gallant conduct in the Mediterranean against the Algerine pirates.

Dueling Treated as Murder in

Illinois.—In 1820 William Bennett was hung for killing Alphonso Stewart, at Belleville, St. Clair County, Ill., in a duel. This fatal case made dueling forever discreditable in Illinois. It is the only case where a man has been hung in this country for killing another in a duel.

George T. Wetmore and George F. Street, attorneys at law, fought a duel in New Brunswick in 1821. They had a difficulty in court. Wetmore was killed and Street was tried for murder and acquitted.

Henry Clay, of Kentucky, Secretary of State, and John Randolph, United

account of being near-sighted. Their pistols overlapped one another when the duelists were in position. The quarrel grew out of politics. Both were killed.

Congressmen Jonathan Cilley, of Maine, and William J. Graves, of Kentucky, fought a duel near Washington, D. C., February 24th, 1838. The former was killed at the third fire. The trouble originated in a quarrel with Jas. Watson Webb, who was determined upon the death of Cilley.

Dueling in the District of Columbia.—In 1839 Congress passed a law pro-

States Senator from Virginia, fought a duel April 8th, 1826, near Little Falls Bridge, on the Potomac. The duel grew out of a speech made in the Senate, in which Randolph used insulting language in referring to Mr. Clay. The latter demanded satisfaction, and on being refused, challenged Randolph. The parties met and exchanged fire without any effect, and on the second call Clay fired again without hitting Randolph, who then fired in the air. As neither were hurt a reconciliation took place.

Thomas Biddle and Spencer Pettis fought a duel in Missouri in 1831. Pistols were used at a distance of five feet, which was chosen by Mr. Biddle on

hibiting the giving or accepting a challenge within the District of Columbia.

United States Senator David C. Broderick and Judge D. S. Terry, both of California, fought a duel September 21, 1859. Broderick was killed. The cause was Broderick's outspoken anti-slavery sentiments. Terry was upon the Democratic list of electors in 1880, and was the only one not elected, owing to the remembrance of that duel.

A Duel Between Ex-Speaker Carter of the Louisiana Legislature, and Chief of Police Badger of New Orleans, with rifles, occurred February 15th, 1872, at Bay St. Louis, Mississippi. Nobody hurt.

PIRATES AND PIRACIES.

Havana, Cuba, was destroyed in 1554 by French buccaneers. Santiago had been compelled to pay a ransom of $80,000 for its safety but a short time before.

Pirates Captured on New England Coast in 1689.—Thomas Hawkins and Thomas Pound, pirates, had ravaged the coast when Captain Samuel Pease, of the sloop Mary, captured them near Woods Hall, after severe fighting. During the engagement Captain Pease was wounded, from the effects of which he shortly afterward died.

Pirates.—In 1696 many buccaneers were capturing valuable prizes. It was thought great wealth could be obtained tion broken up, by Dutch, English and Spanish ships.

Capt. William Kidd was arrested in Boston July 6th, 1699, by Governor Bellemont, who sent him to England to be tried for piracy. He was tried, convicted and executed in London May 24, 1701. He was the son of Rev. John Kidd, of Scotland. He went to sea when a boy and became an excellent navigator. In 1691 New York paid him £150 for protecting it against freebooters. He was commissioned and furnished with a vessel to capture pirates. In 1696-7 he went to Madagascar and turned pirate himself. He captured the Quidah Merchant, in which he sailed to the West

by recapturing them, for which purpose a company in England, under royal sanction, fitted out the Adventure, giving the command to Captain William Kidd. He sailed from New York on his mission, with instructions forbidding him to leave the Atlantic waters, but failing to find the object of his search, he went to Madagascar, which was at this time a noted resort for pirates.

Cartagena, S. A., taken by pirates. In 1697 Pointis, with seven ships and 1,200 men, captured Cartagena, S. A. The booty amounted to $8,000,000, but Pointis kept most of the plunder, and his disappointed men robbed the city again. His fleet was afterward nearly destroyed, and the buccaneer organiza- Indies, and leaving it near Hayti came to the New England coast in a sloop. He opened a correspondence with Gov. Bellemont with a view to reinstate himself with the government. Upon the Governor's promise of protection he visited Boston and was arrested. He had buried £14,000 on Gardiner's Island, which Bellemont afterward secured.— Hundreds of persons have wasted time and money in the vain effort to discover other treasure reputed to have been buried by Kidd.

Pirate Black Beard.—This notorious freebooter was captured and slain upon the Carolina coast in 1718.

Capt. Phillips, a pirate, captured the fishing sloop Dolphin off Cape Ann, and impressed her crew, among whom were John Fillmore (great grand sire of Millard Fillmore), Edward Cheeseman and an Indian. These three successfully plotted to take the pirate. They killed Phillips and two others and carried the vessel into Boston, May 3, 1724.

Pirates Hanged in Boston. — In 1726 Fly, Cole and Greenville were executed for piracy, before which Dr. Coleman preached a sermon to them in old Brattle Street Church. Captain Fly did not go in the church, and submitted smilingly to the penalty of the law.

War was Declared upon the United

Malayan Outrages punished. — The United States frigate "Potomac" destroyed Quallah Batoo, in Sumatra, Feb. 6, 1832, because the natives had massacered the crew of the Friendship and seized the ship and cargo.

Pirates Hung. — Gibbs and Wansley, two bloodthirsty pirates, who for 18 years had been a terror to seamen, were executed by the United States Government April 30, 1831.

"Buccaneer of the Lakes." — "Bill Johnson," a notorious character claiming the above title, seized, robbed and burned the new steamer Robert Peel, upon

States by Tripoli in 1801, and the Tripolians immediately commenced piratical depredations.

The Squadron Under Commodore Richard V. Morris was, in 1802, ordered to the Mediterranean to protect American vessels against Algerine pirates.

Algiers Declared War against the United States in 1812, and commenced pirating American merchantmen.

Commodore Perry was ordered to West India waters in 1819 to break up piratical expeditions, but his death prevented success.

West India Pirates were exterminated in 1823 by the United States fleet under Com. Porter.

Lake Ontario, May 30, 1838. The steamer plied between Kingston and Ogdensburg.

Mexican Pirates captured the American bark "Brothers," August 27, 1871, off Santa Anna. The crew escaped and were picked up by the bark "Harvest," which the pirates had also attacked unsuccessfully.

Piracy in New York Harbor. — November 30th, 1878, the brig Mattano was boarded by river thieves, the Captain wounded, the watchman bound, and the cabin robbed. Two of the robbers were subsequently sentenced to twenty years each in State prison.

INTERNAL IMPROVEMENTS.

Levee Along the Mississippi.—In 1727 a mile of levee was constructed at New Orleans for protection against overflows.

Canals.—In 1762 the first canal route was surveyed between the Swatara and Tulpehacken creeks in Pennsylvania.

Streets Graded and paved in Albany, N. Y.—In 1790 Elkanah Watson, an enterprising Yankee, took up his residence in Albany, N. Y., and, by persistent efforts, succeeded in getting a contract to grade and pave the streets of that city. He narrates the following as

zons, although I did not run, as some of my friends insisted, but walked off at a quick pace."

First Turnpike in the United States was begun in June, 1792, between Lancaster and Philadelphia. Two thousand two hundred and sixty-seven shares of stock were sold the first day.

Canals.—The South Hadley and the Montague canals were chartered and begun in 1792. They were dug around the Connecticut river rapids. New York chartered two companies, one from the Hudson to Lake Ontario and

some of the dangers he had to contend with: "Just after State Street had been paved at heavy expense, I sauntered into it, immediately after a heavy thunder storm, and whilst regretting the disturbance in the sidewalk, and observing the cellars filling with water, for in that section, which was in the present locality of the State Bank, the street in grading had been elevated about two feet, I heard two women in the act of clearing their invaded premises from the accumulation of mud and water, cry out, 'Here comes that infernal paving Yankee.' They approached me in a menacing attitude, broomsticks erect. Prudence dictated a retreat, to avoid being broomsticked by the infuriated Ama-

Seneca Lake, and another from the Hudson to Lake Champlain.

Public Turnpikes.—Many companies had been chartered, especially in Connecticut, where fifty had been incorporated since 1803. The cost varied from $1,000 to $14,000 per mile.

Middlesex Canal.—Completed in 1804. It connected Boston Harbor with the Concord River. It was 27 miles long and had 22 locks.

National Road, from Cumberland, Md., to Ohio. In 1806 Congress authorized and provided for its construction at public expense. It was the first great internal improvement constructed at the expense of the government.

Erie Canal.—April 15th, 1817, the New York Legislature authorized and appropriated for its construction. Its estimated cost was $5 752,738. The canal was completed and opened in 1825 with imposing ceremonies. It was 363 miles long and cost $8,401,394.

Croton Aqueduct, which supplies New York City with water from Croton River, forty miles distant, was completed in 1842. It cost $12,500.000.

Suspension Bridge over Niagara was erected in 1846 by John A. Rœbling, an American engineer.

Wheeling Bridge.—The suspension bridge over the Ohio at Wheeling, W. Va., was built in 1848 by C. Ellett. It

upper part of New York City was dedicated for a permanent free park by act of Legislature.

Steubenville Iron Bridge. — An iron bridge, with a span 320 feet long, was built across the Ohio at Steubenville in 1862.

Chicago Water Works.—Mar. 25, 1867, water was admitted through the great tunnel, which is 62 inches high and 60 inches wide. It runs two miles out under Lake Michigan, and 72,000,000 gallons daily can be pumped into the city.

East River Bridge, New York, was begun in 1870. Its span across the water reaches 1,595 feet, and it is 135 feet high above the river. It was finished

had a span of 1,010 feet. It was blown down in 1854.

Ariesian Well at St. Louis, Mo., was begun in 1849 and completed in 1854. Its depth is 2,199 feet. It discharges 75 gallons per minute. It cost over $10,000.

Hoosac Tunnel through the Green Mountains, in Western Massachusetts, was begun in 1852, and after several failures was finally completed by F. Shandley & Co., of Canada, who, by the use of compressed air drills and nitro-glycerine, effected an opening through the mountain November 27, 1873. The tunnel is nearly five miles long and cost the State nearly $10,000,000.

Central Park, N. Y.—In 1857 the

and opened to the public May 24, 1883, with appropriate ceremonies. President Arthur and Governor Cleveland were present on the occasion.

Great St. Louis Bridge across the Mississippi was completed April, 1874. It cost $12,000,000. It was begun in August, 1869. It has two spans, one 502 feet and the other 520 feet long. It is built of iron. Captain James B. Eads was the inventor and engineer.

Sutro Tunnel completed July 8th, 1878. It was begun in 1869 and cost $3,500,000 in gold. It was constructed by Adolph Sutro to drain the Comstock silver mine. It is 2,000 feet below the surface and is four miles long.

THEATER AND DRAMA.

Theater at Lima, Peru, was built in 1614, and was about the first erected on the continent.

Theatrical Performances in Boston first took place in 1750. The play performed was Otway's "Orphan."

In New York.—Theatrical performances, under the management of Thos. Kean, were given in 1750.

Theatrical Troupe.—The first in America commenced giving regular performances at Williamsburg, Va., Sept. 5, 1752. They continued to play in the larger cities until the revolution.

Theatrical Exhibitions were forbidden by law in Pennsylvania in 1786. Massachusetts had enacted a similar law just before.

First American Play was written in 1786 by Royal Tyler, afterward Chief Justice of Vermont. It was entitled "The Contrast," and was not a success.

" Vagrants."—Actors were classed as "vagrants subject to arrest," by an act passed in South Carolina in 1787. The law classing them as such was repealed in 1791.

Pennsylvania.—The act which forbade theatrical performances in Pennsylvania was repealed in 1789.

Actors Arrested.—In 1792 a theater was opened in Boston in defiance of the law prohibiting them. During the performance the company were arrested on the stage, but were discharged from some legal defect in the papers. A second arrest was made, however, and the company disbanded.

Massachusetts repealed her law prohibiting theatrical performances in 1793.

Charlotte Cushman bid farewell to the stage, received a popular ovation, and was crowned with laurels, November 7, 1874.

Booth's Theater, New York, was sold for $385,000 to Oliver Ames, Dec. 6, 1874.

MANUFACTURES AND ARTS.

(See also Inventions and Improvements.)

Manufactures at Jamestown, Va.— In 1608 a glass-house was erected near the settlement. Clapboards and wainscotting were also cut and exported to England. These were the first humble beginnings of American industries. One hundred and twenty persons arrived this year.

Bricks.—The first manufactured in the English colonies were made in Virginia in 1612.

Wine was exported to England from Virginia in 1612.

Iron Works were established near Jamestown in 1620, the money for the purpose having been raised in England, and forty skilled workmen were sent out.

Rope-Making from hemp began in Jamestown in 1621.

Bricks and Lime were manufactured and mills were erected in New Amsterdam in 1628.

Cloth-Making was begun in Rowley, Mass, in 1638, by a company of Yorkshire clothiers who settled there.

Brandy in the colonies was first made in Manhattan, now New York, in 1640.

Iron Works in New England.—In 1643 John Winthrop, Jr., established works at Saugus, now Lynn, Mass. A small quart pot was the first article made, which is preserved in the family of Thomas Hudson, upon whose land

Works, contracted to build for the city of Boston an "engine to carry water in case of fire." This was the first built in America.

Paper-Mill.—The first in America was built at Roxborough, near Philadelphia, by Wm. Rittenhouse, Wm. Bradford and Thomas Tresse in 1690. One was erected in Massachusetts in 1717.

New England Rum was first distilled in America from West India molasses at Boston in 1700.

Engraving on Copper-Plate.—The first in America was a portrait of Increase Mather in 1718.

Tobacco-Pipes were advertised in the *Mercury*, published in Philadelphia in 1719, as follows: "Good, long Tay-

---

Reading, Pa.—*Carriage and Wagon Builders Continued.*

SHADELL & FEGLEY,
Manufacturers of
DRAYS, CARTS, ICE and FARMERS' WAGONS,
REPAIRING A SPECIALTY,
340 Church Street, Reading, Pa.

Carriage Repainter.

Horn, Robt. A., 420 Court St.

Carriage Bolt Manufacturer.

ALBERT KNABB,
Manufacturer of
PHILADELPHIA CARRIAGE BOLTS,
Third, Cor. Lebanon V. R. R.,
READING, PA.

Carpet Cleaning.

DILVAN ROBBINS, Prop.
Reading Automatic Carpet Cleaning. Manufacturer and Dealer in all kinds of Awnings, etc. Carpets cleaned without injury to fabric or loss of color.
100 South Fifth Street, Reading, Pa.

Cigars and Tobacco.

JOHN KALBACH,
Manufacturer of Pure Havana and Domestic Cigars, and Dealer in Standard Brands of Tobacco and Smoker's supplies.
701 Walnut Street, Reading, Pa.

WM. J. SCHEIFLEY,
Dealer in
PURE HAVANA AND DOMESTIC CIGARS,
Tobacco and Smoker's Supplies,
919 PENN STREET, READING, PA.

---

the works stood. Bog iron ore was used.

Scythes and Edged Tools. — In 1646 Joseph Jenks received a patent for fourteen years for making them in Massachusetts.

Copper-Smelting Works were set up by Gov. Endicott, at Salem, Mass., in 1648.

Wines and Hemp.—In 1651 premiums were offered by Virginia to encourage the manufacture and cultivation of these articles.

Iron Bloomery and Forge were erected at Taunton, Mass., in 1652 by Henry and James Leonard.

American Fire Engine.—In 1654 Mr. Joseph Jenks, of the Lynn Iron

lern tobacco-pipes sold at 4s. per gross by the single gross, and 3s. for a larger quantity, by Richard Warden, tobacco-pipe maker, living under the same roof with Philip Syng, goldsmith, near the market-place, where any that have occasion may have their pipes burned at 8d. per gross."

Repeating Fire-Arm, that would fire eleven times without reloading, was exhibited in Boston in 1725 by its maker, Mr. Pim.

Steel.—In 1727 good steel was made from common iron by a Connecticut blacksmith.

Bell Foundry at New Haven, Conn., established in 1736 by Abel Parmalee.

Steam Engine for the New Jersey

copper mines was built in 1736. It was the first built in America.

Paper Hangings were first advertised and sold in America in 1737.

Type Foundry.—The first in America was established at Germantown, Penna., in 1740, by Christopher Sower.

Muskets and Cannon were first manufactured in America in 1748 by Hugh Orr, at Bridgewater, Mass.

Steam Navigation was unsuccessfully attempted by a Pennsylvania farmer in 1750.

Sugar Mill.—The first in the United States was built near New Orleans in 1758 by M. Debrenieul.

Horn Combs were first made in

was made by John Belmont, Philadelphia, in 1775.

Cotton Factory.—The first in America, being also the *first joint-stock manufacturing Company in the world*, was organized and began operations in Philadelphia in 1775.

Stocking Factory.—The "Committee of Safety" donated £300 in 1776 to Mr. Coxenfinder, of Maryland, to assist in its establishment. This was the first in America.

Wool Card Teeth.—In 1777 Oliver Evans invented a machine for making 300 a minute.

Stocking-Frames were forbidden by law to be exported from England to

---

America in 1759, at New Westbury, Mass.

Wall Paper.—In 1763 paper hangings were first manufactured and used in the United States in New York. The sheets were thirty miles long, and were stamped by means of blocks of wood.

Carriages.—In 1768 the manufacture of carriages was begun in New York by Elkanah and William Deane, from Dublin. They offered to make coaches, chariots, laudaus, phætons, post-chaises, curricle-chairs, sedans and sleighs at five per cent. less than the cost of importation. Few carriages had heretofore been used in the colonies.

Piano Forte.—The first in America

the United States under penalty of £40, in 1784.

Cotton Mill.—The first in New England was started at Beverly, Mass., in 1787. Corduroys and bed-tickings were made.

Salt Works at Syracuse, N. Y., began in 1787 to manufacture about ten bushels per day.

Dentist.—The first American dentist was John Greenwood, of New York, in 1788. He carved a complete set of ivory teeth for General Washington.

Water-Power Cotton Mill. — The first successful one in America was set up in Providence, R. I., in December, 1790, for Almy & Brown, by Samuel Slater, a young English mechanic, who constructed the Arkwright machinery, with which the mill was equipped, from memory, as it could not be imported.

Jewelry.—The first manufactured in the United States was in 1790 by Epaphras Hinsdale, at Newark, N. J.

Salt Manufactured from sea water in 1790 by John Sears, at Dennis, Mass. The water was raised by a wind-mill and pump. His success caused the formation of numerous companies.

Carpet Factory.—The first in America was established in 1791 at Philadelphia by William P. Sprague

Silk Dress.—The first manufactured in the United States was made by the family of Rev. Mr. Atwater, Beauford,

the straw with scissors, split it with her thumb nail, and bleached it in burning sulphur fumes. It was the foundation of a business.

Academy of Fine Arts incorporated in New York in 1802.

Piano-Fortes were manufactured at Boston in 1803 by Adam and William Brent.

Broadcloth.—The first of fine quality made in America was at Pittsfield, Mass., in 1804, by Arthur Scholfield, who also constructed his own machinery.

Printing Cotton Goods by engraved rollers, run by water power, was first done in 1810 by Thorp, Siddall & Co., Philadelphia.

Silk was First manufactured by ma-

Conn., in 1792. He raised the silk himself.

Clocks.—The first in the world, with wooden wheels, was made by Eli Terry, of Connecticut, in 1792. He first manufactured them by shaping the wheels with a penknife. He traveled through the country twice a year to sell them.

Cotton Sewing-Thread was first manufactured at Pawtucket, R. I., by Samuel Slater in 1794. Flax had everywhere been used before.

United States Armory at Springfield, Mass., for the manufacture of muskets, was established in 1795.

Bonnets were made of oat straw in 1798 by Betsey Metcalf, a girl 12 years old, at Dedham, Mass. She smoothed

chinery in 1810 at Mansfield, Conn., by Rodney and Horatio Hanks.

Power Looms, for weaving cloth, were constructed at Waltham, Mass., in 1813.

Stereotyping was first done in America in 1813 at Bruce's foundry, New York; also by John Watts.

British Efforts to break down American manufactures.—In 1815 Lord Brougham said in Parliament that "it was worth while to incur a loss upon the first exportations in order to stifle the rising manufactures in the United States," thereupon large stocks of English goods were shipped to America and sold at auction. The purchasers lost heavily, one man losing $80,000 on a single speculation.

Remington Fire-Arms.—In 1816 Eliphalet Remington, living near Rochester, N. Y., forged a rifle barrel in a blacksmith shop. It was so skillfully done that others were ordered, and from this sprung the great factory at Illion, N. Y., and the Remington breech-loader is now one of the leading rifles of the world.

Lithographing.—The first executed in America was the work of Mr. Otis, of Philadelphia, in July, 1819. It was first conducted as a business in the United

Canterbury, Conn., by William Mason, in 1829.

Horse Shoes were first made by machinery in 1835 by Henry Burden, of Troy, N. Y.

Gold Pens were first manufactured in America in 1835 by Levi Brown, of Detroit, Mich.

Beet Sugar was first successfully manufactured at Northampton, Mass., by David L. Child, in 1838. A manufactory was erected at Chatsworth, Ill., in 1864.

American Watches were first made by machinery in 1850, at Roxbury, Mass.

Reading, Pa.—*Continued.*

Flour, Feed, Grain, Etc.

Eighth Street Roller Mills and Coal Yard

Manufacturer Roller Patent Vienna Flour, Flour, Feed, Grains, Wood and Coal.

244 and 246 Eighth St., Reading, Pa.

AARON YOCOM, Propr.

Mountz, J. M., Franklin, Cor. Second.

Groceries and Provisions.

C. A. COLE,

Dealer in Groceries, Foreign and Domestic Fruits. Confectionery and Farmers Produce. Canned Goods a Specialty.

148 Franklin St., Reading, Pa.

Harness and Saddles.

H. D. SANDS,

Manufacturer of Light and Heavy, Single and Double Harness, and Dealer in Saddles, Collars, Whips, Robes, Blankets, &c.

20 N. Eighth St., Reading, Pa.

Heaters, Ranges, Stoves, &c.

JOHN P. DAUTH,

Manufacturer of and Dealer in Stoves, Heaters, Ranges, &c. Steam and Hot Air Combination Furnaces a Specialty. Tin Roofing and Repairing Promptly Attended to.

754 Penn Street, Reading, Pa.

LEWIS DAUTH,

Stoves, Ranges, Heaters, Tin and Sheet Iron Worker. Metalic Roofing a Specialty.

23 N. Eighth St., Reading, Pa.

States in 1822, by Barnett & Doolittle, in New York.

Hats and Bonnets were first made in 1821 out of a grass resembling leghorn, that grew in the Connecticut valley, by Sophia Woodhouse, of Wethersfield, Conn. The Society of Arts in London, to whom she sent specimens, advised its cultivation.

Axes were First manufactured in America in 1826, at Collinsville, Conn. The company at first made eight broadaxes in a day, but the increase of business has been so great that it now uses 600 tons of grindstones in a year.

Power Looms for manufacturing diaper linen were first made and run at

The process was invented by Aaron Dennison and Edward Howard. In 1854 the manufactory was removed to Waltham, Mass.

Cheese Factory.—In 1851 Jesse Williams started the first in the world in Oneida county, N. Y.

Paper Collars were first sold in New York in 1853.

Kerosene Oil was manufactured from coal at Newton Creek, L. I., in 1854.

Rodman Gun, of 15-inch bore, and weighing 49,000 pounds, was cast in 1859 at the Fort Pitt Iron Works, Pittsburg, Pa., and placed in Fortress Monroe. A 20-inch gun, throwing a 1,000 pound shot, has since been cast at the same works.

Philanthropic Enterprises and Benevolent Institutions.

Jesuit Mission in Florida, for the conversion of the natives, was first established in 1566.

Six Jesuits were sent to the Potomac in Virginia in 1570, by Menendez, to found a mission. They were killed by the Indians.

First Hospital.—"Hotel Dieu" was founded in Quebec, August 1, 1639, by three nuns, who came for the purpose, under the patronage of the Duchess d' Aiguillon, neice of Richelieu. This was the first hospital in America.

Green Bay Mission.—In 1669 Father Claude Allouez was sent to Green Bay, Wisconsin, to found an Indian mission.

taught them himself every Sunday evening.

George Whitefield established the "Bethesda Orphanage" at Savannah, Ga., in 1740. He raised money in England and America for this purpose, and had sixty-eight orphans under its care in a year.

Seventh-Day Dunkers' Sunday School was established in 1740 at Ephrata, Penn. It lasted 30 years.

Fanieul Hall, Boston, was built in 1742, and given to the town by Peter Fanieul, a Hugenot merchant. It was built as a market and hall. In 1760 it was destroyed by fire and rebuilt, and

---

Hospital at Boston.—The first in the colonies was opened in Boston in 1717, for the cure of persons afflicted with contagious diseases.

Subscription Library.—The first in the country was originated in 1731, by Benjamin Franklin, in Philadelphia.— Fifty subscribers at forty shillings apiece were the original stockholders. In addition to this they agreed to pay ten shillings annually for fifty years.

"Dr. Bray's Associates" were organized in England in 1731, to instruct negro children in the Southern colonies.

Sunday School of forty children was established by John Wesley in Savannah in 1736. He catechised and

afterward became famous as the "cradle of American Liberty."

Pennsylvania Hospital was chartered in 1751. It was the first general hospital in the colonies.

Society for "Promoting Industry Among the Poor" set three hundred young women to work on Boston Common, each at a spinning wheel, at its anniversary in 1753.

Insane Asylum.—The first in the country was opened at Williamsburg, Va., in 1773.

Army Hospital.—The first one in America was established at Cambridge, June 17, 1775, under charge of Dr. John Warren, a brother of Dr. Joseph Warren.

Harmony Society, consisting of twenty families from Wirtemberg, under the leadership of George Rapp, settled in Harmony, Butler county, Penn., as a business community, in 1804. They cultivated the soil on a large scale, and engaged in manufactures. It removed, in 1814, from Butler county, Penn., to Indiana, and erected a village and factories on the Wabash River, which they called New Harmony. Within ten years they again removed to Economy, Penn.

" Sisters of Charity " were first founded in the United States at Emmettsburg, Md., in 1809, by Mrs. Eliza Seton, who was their first Mother Superior.

Apprentices' Library.—The first was organized in Philadelphia in 1819.

Society for the "Reformation of Juvenile Delinquents" was incorporated by the State of New York in 1823.

Robert Owen, of England, having bought the Rappirt village and 30,000 acres of land at New Harmony, Ind., began his social communistic experiment with 900 persons, April 27, 1825. The community lasted but a few years.

Reform School opened in New York in 1825 by the "Society for the Reformation of Juvenile Delinquents." It is now upon Randall's Island.

New England Asylum for the Blind was incorporated in Boston in

School for Deaf Mutes started in New York in 1811, but failed.

American Colonization Society was organized in December, 1816, by Southerners at Washington, D. C. Its object was to colonize free negroes from the United States in some other country. It founded Liberia, in Africa, for that purpose.

Asylum for Deaf Mutes.--The first in America was opened April 15, 1817, by Rev. T. H. Gallandet, in Hartford, Conn. A New York school was chartered the same day. Attempts to instruct idiots were made in 1818 at the Deaf and Dumb Asylum at Hartford, Conn.

1829. In 1831 another was founded in York.

Smithsonian Institute, Washington, D C., originated in a bequest from James Smithson, of England, to the United States Government, for the "diffusion of knowledge." The amount was nearly $600,000, and was accepted by Congress July 1, 1836.

Aid for Ireland.—In March, 1847, the United States war steamer "Jamestown" was sent with a cargo of provisions to the starving population of Ireland.

Astor Library.—In May, 1848, John Jacob Astor's bequest was fulfilled. Dr. Joseph B. Cogswell was sent to Europe to purchase books. When the building was opened in 1854 70,000 volumes were placed on its shelves.

School for Idiot Children was opened in July, 1848, at Barre, Mass., by Dr. Hervy B. Williams. The same year one was opened at Perkins' Institution for the Blind at Boston. Dr. Seguin, of Paris, an instructor of idiots, visited the United States this year.

George Peabody donated $300,000 to establish a free literary and scientific institute at Baltimore, Feb. 12, 1857.

Sanitary Commission.—The first organization of the kind was at Bridgeport, Conn., April 15th, 1861. Others speedily followed. Its work was in conjunction with the medical force of the army during the civil war. By it trained nurses, delicacies and help of all kinds

with $200,000 worth of provisions contributed by New York merchants for the starving operatives of Lancashire. To protect it from Confederate privateers, fitted out in English ports, she was convoyed by an American ship of war.

Freedman's Bureau for relieving the wants of emancipated slaves, and educating them, was established by act of Congress March 3, 1865, and General O. O. Howard was made commissioner.

Soldiers' Homes, or asylums for soldiers disabled in the war of 1812, the Mexican war, and in the rebellion, were established by Congress in 1865. They are supported by the United States government.

Elect Surds, a society for the improvement of deaf mutes, was founded in 1866. It has now a number of lodges.

were afforded to invalid soldiers.— Through fairs and other agencies $5,000,-000 in money and $15,000,000 in supplies were contributed.

Christian Commission began with the labors of Mr. Vincent Colyer, of the Young Men's Christian Association of New York in 1861, after the first Bull Run battle. It aimed at elevating the moral and religious welfare of the troops, and also in supplying their physical wants. The money and supplies raised were about $6,000,000. The first year it had 1,069 ministers and laymen at work, and held 3,445 meetings in camp and hospital.

Aid for Starving Englishmen.— February 9, 1863, the ship George Griswold reached Liverpool from New York

Peabody Fund, for the cause of education in the South, was founded February 7, 1867, by a gift of $2,100,000 from George Peabody.

Penikese Island, off the coast of Massachusetts, was donated by John Anderson, of New York, to Prof. Agassis, for a summer school of natural history, in April, 1873. Fifty thousand dollars cash accompanied the gift.

Moody and Sankey began their labors October 24, 1875, in a Brooklyn rink, to congregations of 5,000. A great religious revival was the result. On Nov. 21 they began services in Philadelphia, in an old freight depot at 13th and Market streets, to an audience of about ten thousand. Great success has always attended their efforts.

ADVENTURES AND EXPLOITS.

Pacific Ocean was first navigated by Balboa in 1516. Several brigantines were built and launched through the energy of Balboa. The timber was cut on the Atlantic coast and dragged through forests and over mountains by Indians, negroes and Spaniards. Many of the former died from the severe labor. Balboa at last spread his sails upon the sea he had discovered. He cruised beyond the Gulf of St. Michael and heard more of the wonderful wealth of Peru.

First Voyage around the world was accomplished by the Victoria, of Magellan's fleet. After his death she sailed by way of the spice Islands and Cape of Good Hope, arriving in Spain Sept. 6,

Antonia de Espejo started with an expedition to find Ruyz and his companions. They failed in this, but found the curious cities. of which they brought back wonderful accounts. Part of the expedition remained at Santa Fe, N. M.

Cathedral in the City of Mexico was begun in 1573. It was not finished until 1667, nearly 100 years afterward.

Laselle's 1,000-Mile Journey, from Fort Crevecœur to Fort Frontenac was accomplished by May 6, 1680—65 days.

Sunken Treasure Secured.—£300,-000 was raised from a sunken vessel, on the Haytien coast, by William Phipps, of New England, in 1687.

1522. Her commander was Juan Sebastian Cano.

Florida to Mexico.—July 22, 1536, Cabaca de Vaca and three companions, survivors of the ill-starred expedition of Narvaez into Florida, reached Mexico, after a journey of eight years across the continent. They were held prisoners by the Indians for a long time. They gave the first account of the Pueblo Indians, and their statements brought about the subsequent explorations of New Mexico and California.

Mississippi River was first navigated in 1543 by the seven frail brigantines built by the followers of De Soto, and in which they floated to the Gulf of Mexico.

Cliff Cities of New Mexico.—In 1582

Governor Fletcher, of New York, in 1693, having been authorized by the King to command the Connecticut militia, went to Hartford on this business. In order not to hear his commission read, Captain Wadsworth, of the militia, ordered the drums to be beaten. Gov. Fletcher ordered silence, but upon Captain Wadsworth's saying: "If I am interrupted again I will make the sun shine through you in a moment," he gave up the attempt.

Remarkable Pedestrian.—Robert Metlin died in 1787, at Wakfield, Mass., aged 115 years. He was formerly a baker at Portsmouth, N. H., and used to walk to Boston in a day—60 miles—

to buy flour. This he did until he was 80 years old.

Kit Carson successfully drove 6,500 sheep across the Rocky Mountains into California in 1853.

Atlantic Ocean was crossed on a raft by three men in 1867. It was made of three-pointed cylinders 24 feet long and 12½ feet wide, lashed together with boards and covered with canvass. It was called the Nonpariel, or American Life Raft.

Type-Setting Extraordinary.— On Feb. 19, 1870, George Arensburg, in New York, set two thousand and sixty-

N. Y., was blown up September 25, 1876, by dynamite, under the supervision of General Newton. It was the consumation of seven years' work.

Atlantic Ocean Crossed in a whale-boat, by Captain Crapo and his wife, who reached Liverpool July 21st, 1877, from New Bedford, Mass. They had weathered three gales on the voyage.

Quebec Harbor Obstructions in the St. Lawrence river were finally removed in August, 1877, by the Harbor Commission, after several years' work. The obstructions were tangled cables and anchors, the first of which were dropped

four ems solid minion, six break lines, in one hour.

Blossom Rock, at the entrance of San Francisco Harbor, was blown up April 24, 1870, by 23 tons of powder, removing 40,000 tons of rock, at a cost of $75,000.

Brick-Laying Extraordinary.— November 4, 1870, in Philadelphia, W. D. Cozzens laid 702 brick in 12 minutes.

Enormous Strength. — December 13, 1870, in New York, R. A. Pennell put up a 10-pound dumb-bell 8,431 times.

Balloon Ascension at Philadelphia, September 5, 1874, carrying six lady passengers.

Hell-Gate Reef, in the East River,

by Wolf's fleet in 1759, when they were about to attack the city. Others were caught and abandoned from time to time. One mass contained 2,000 fathoms o chain and 70 anchors.

The Nautilus, a little dory, crossed the Atlantic in 45 days, arriving in London July 31, 1878.

Pike's Peak, Colorado, was ascended in 1860 by two ladies, at great risk. One of them, Mrs. W. J. Williams, from Milford, N. H., was killed in Kansas on May 30, 1879, by a tornado.

Dr. Tanner's Fast.—On August 7, 1880, Dr. Tanner, of Minnesota, completed a fast of forty days in New York. The experiment was made under the charge of physicians.

TRADE AND COMMERCE.

Boston.—In 1634 the first merchant's shop was opened.

West Indies Trade was opened in 1636, by the sailing of a thirty-ton vessel from Massachusetts to the West Indies.

Free-Trade between England and New England was decreed by the House of Commons in May, 1643.

Navigation Act.—In 1651 the House of Commons enacted that all imports and exports to and from the colonies must be shipped in English vessels, and the latter must sail to the English dominions only. This act stimulated colonial ship-building.

Book-Seller in Boston in 1652.—

Cuba.—In 1762 the United States first opened trade with Cuba. Cuba heretofore traded with no country and lived by smuggling.

Furs.—In 1762 a fur company was founded in New Orleans, which led to early settlements along the Mississippi and Missouri rivers.

Chamber of Commerce, of New York, was founded in 1768 and was chartered in 1770.

Shipment of Wheat.—In 1771 John Stevenson, of Baltimore, began the first shipment of wheat to Europe. This was the beginning of our present foreign grain trade.

American Fur Company.—John

Hezekiah Usher was the first regular book-seller in the colonies.

Canadian Business.—In 1667 Intendent Talon built the first brewery, established trade with the West Indies, encouraged manufactures and arranged for a more regular emigration from France. Large bounties were offered to soldiers to settle in the province.

Cotton Exported.—In 1748 seven bags were shipped from Charleston, South Carolina.

Granite was used in the construction of King's Chapel, Boston, in 1752. This was the first built of American stone.

Tobacco amounting to 70,000 hogsheads, were exported from Virginia in 1758.

Jacob Astor, chief owner, began operations in 1784.

Wood Engraving was introduced into the United States in 1794 by Alexander Anderson. He made the pictures for Webster's spelling book.

Book-Trade Sale.—The first in America was held in June, 1802, at New York, by the American Company of Booksellers.

The Miami Exporting Company was organized in 1803, to provide improved transportation for the produce of the N. W. Territory. Crops were marketed in New Orleans, La., being floated down the Ohio and Mississippi in flat boats, the owners returning on foot about 1,000 miles, the trip taking six months. Afterward large canoes, propelled by oars and then by sails, shortened the time. The Miami Company existed for several years, but was not a permanent success.

Artificial Propagation of fish was first attempted in the United States in in South Carolina in 1804.

Ice Exported from the United States to Martenique, W. I., from Charleston, Mass., in 1806. A cargo of 130 tons was shipped, per brig Favorite, by Frederick Tudor, of Boston. The venture was unprofitable. A cargo of ice was shipped

parcels for the accommodation of business men. He first carried them in a satchel, but his business grew until he had offices in both cities, and sent daily messengers each way. The next year Alvin Adams began running between New York and Boston, via Norwich and Worcester. Thus originated the whole modern express traffic.

Chicago, a city of one year's growth, made its first shipment of wheat to the seaboard, via the lakes, in 1839. The amount forwarded was 78 bushels.

Whaling Extraordinary.—In the

---

to New Orleans from Boston, in 1820.— The strange material so alarmed the inhabitants that a mob was excited, who threw one cargo overboard.

Advertising Agency.—The first in America was established in 1828.

Duty on American Products.—Peru, in 1828, laid a ninety per cent. duty on American cottons, hats, shoes, soaps, tobacco, etc., which was practically probibitory. It was repealed in 1829.

Express Business.—March 4, 1839, William F. Harnden started to travel between New York and Boston with small

year 1853 the cargoes of two whalers from New Bedford and Fair Haven sold for $400,000.

War of Sewing Machines.—Oct. 10, 1856, numerous suits having arisen between the Singer Company and the Wheeler and Wilson and Grover and Baker Companies, an agreement was entered into to use each other's features and combine against all other infringers.

American Bank-Note Company was organized in 1858 by a combination of the engraving companies in the United States.

ATMOSPHERIC PHENOMENONS.
STORMS, TORNADOES, CYCLONES, EARTHQUAKES, ETC.

Guatemala, in Central America, was destroyed in 1541 by a flood of water from a volcano. A new city was built further down the valley.

Great Wind and Rain in New England in 1635. The tide rose perpendicularly twenty feet.

Earthquakes were felt for twenty days in New England in 1638.

Storms.—Two tremendous storms occurred in August and December, 1638. The tide rose fourteen feet above the spring tide in Narragansett, and flowed over twice in six hours.

Severe Winter.—In 1641 Boston and

February, 1717. It impeded all modes of travel.

Aurora Borealis was for the first time seen in New England December 17, 1719, and created considerable apprehension.

Earthquakes occurred in New England in 1727 and November 18, 1755, of great severity.

Drought.—One hundred and twenty-three days without rain, in 1762, the longest drought ever known in America, occurred the summer of this year.

Dark Day in Detroit.—October 19, 1762, a dark day prevailed at Detroit,

Chesapeake Bays were frozen, the latter passable for horses, carts, etc., for five weeks.

Hurricane in Barbadoes, August 10, 1674, was of such terrific power that scarce a house or tree was left and many lives were lost.

Mobile, Ala., was almost destroyed by a hurricane and flood in 1711. It was removed to its present site for greater safety.

Dark Day in New England October 21, 1716. People were compelled to use artificial lights to do the ordinary work of the day.

Snow Storm.—The greatest ever known in New England occurred in

Mich. Rain fell, which is said to have been of a "dirty, sulphurous smell."

Dark Day in New England, May 19, 1780. The approach of darkness began about 10 A. M., and increased until it became so dark that it was impossible to read ordinary print. Men and beasts were alarmed. The Connecticut Legislature was in session. Some of the members, thinking the day of judgment was at hand, called for adjournment. Col. Abraham Davenport said: "The day of judgment is approaching, or it is not. If it is not there is no cause for adjournment; if it is I choose to be found doing my duty. I wish, therefore, that candles be brought."

Dark Day in Canada, October 16, 1783. It began at 2 P. M. and continned one hour. The darkness was extreme while it lasted.

Aerolite fell in Texas in 1808, weighing 1,635 pounds. It is now in Yale College.

Earthquake, December 16, 1811, at New Madrid, Mo. Boats and houses were destroyed. The ground rose and fell in undulations, and lakes and swamps were formed in Tennessee.

Storm in New England.—September 23, 1815, a severe storm prevailed. In thirty-five hours eight inches of rain fell. The streets of Providence, R. I., and other cities on the coast, were filled with streams of water. Houses were

peared in March, 1843. It could be seen by daylight part of the time.

Heated Term.—From August 11 to 14, 1853, intense heat prevailed through-out the United States. Four hundred deaths occurred in New York City in four days.

Lowest Temperature ever recorded was by Dr. Kane, in Smith's Sound, on February 5, 1854, in latitude 78° 37' N. His spirit thermometer registered 100° below freezing point of water.

Earthquake in Central America, April 16, 1854, destroyed the city of San Salvador, with two hundred lives and $4,000,000, in less time than one minute.

Lost Island, a summer resort on the coast of Louisiana, was completely en-

wrecked, shipping destroyed, and many cattle and other stock were killed.

Meteors.—A grand shower of shooting stars occurred in America on the night of November 13, 1833. It occasioned great fear among the inhabitants, especially the negroes in the South, who thought that the world was about to be burnt up.

Cold Weather.—The winter of 1834-35 was so severe that the waters of the South were frozen, and snow fell a foot deep there. Orange trees in Florida, and fig trees 100 years old in Georgia, were killed.

Comet.—A great comet suddenly ap-

gulfed for three days, during a violent storm in August, 1856. One hundred and seventy-eight persons were drowned.

Intense Heat prevailed in California in June and July, 1859.

Tornado.—A terrific tornado visited Iowa and Illinois June 3, 1860. It almost annihilated a number of towns and a large amount of property was destroyed.

Eclipse.—The sun was totally eclipsed on August 7, 1869. It was visible in various parts of the United States.

Deluge in Virginia, September, 1869. The flood rose until in Richmond ferryboats plied in the streets. Much property was destroyed, and at Harper's Ferry forty lives were lost.

Yellowstone Geysers were first

visited in 1869 by tourists, led by Cook and Folsom.

Earthquake, October 19, 1870.—The greatest ever known in this country occurred, extending from Canada across New England and the Middle States as far West as Michigan. There were two distinct shocks, each lasting a few seconds.

Tornado destroys most of Helena, Ark., February 18, 1871.

Nitro-Glycerine explosion at Titusville, Penn., May 19, 1871, shattered everything in the vicinity, and excavated a hole 12 feet wide and 5 feet deep.

Galveston, Texas, was damaged by a heavy storm, June 12, 1871. Much shipping was wrecked.

1872, which destroyed a brick market house.

Hot Weather.—On 1st day of July, 1872, the thermometer at Washington, D. C., indicated 151 degrees. Over seventy deaths in New York and twenty in the city of Boston occurred from sunstroke.

Earthquake felt on Long Island and in Westchester county, New York, July 11, 1872.

Tornado at Harrisburg, Pa., August 5, 1872, unroofed buildings and did much damage.

Cold Wave in New England January 30, 1873. Prof. Loomis, of Yale College, reported that there was no record of any colder day in the last 100 years. The

Labrador devastated by a hurricane June 13, 1871. Settlements destroyed, vessels were wrecked and three hundred lives lost.

Earthquake on Long Island and Staten Island, N. Y., June 18, 1871. Also at Visalis, Cal., July 5, 1871. Another occurred in California, March 26, 1872. Its duration was four hours. Many lives were lost. In the valley of the Sierras a chasm 35 miles long opened in the earth.

Dayton, O., suffered severely from a terrible storm, July 9, 1871. Many lives lost.

Tornado in Cincinnati, O., May 23, 1872, did great damage to the city. One occurred in St. Louis, Mo., March 30,

thermometer averaged 21.9° below zero in 29 towns in Massachusetts.

Tornadoes occurred July 4, 1873, in Indiana, Ohio, Wisconsin and Missouri, destroying many lives and much property.

Delaware and Chesapeake Canal burst its banks August 21, 1873, and the inundation destroyed $1,800,000 of property.

Destructive Floods along the Mississippi submerged hundreds of square miles of land above and below New Orleans, in April, 1874.

Ice-Break in the St. Lawrence river, May 8, 1874, caused enormous destruction to the shipping. The river had not been so long ice-bound in 38 years.

Mill River Reservoir. near Northampton, Mass., broke on May 16th, 1874, sweeping away the manufacturing villages of Williamsburg, Haydensville, Skinnersville and Leeds. Loss, 150 lives and millions worth of property.—Cause, faulty construction.

Blush Hollow Reservoir, on Middlesex brook, near Chester, Mass., burst July 12, 1874. Loss, $1,000,000.

Water-Spout burst in Nevada, July 24, 1874, destroying the town of Eureka and killing twenty persons.

Rain Storm, of a very destructive character, visited Pittsburg and Alleghany City, July 26, 1874. Great amount of property swept away and 200 lives lost.

State legislators and the citizens of Richmond.

Tornado in Illinois, March 10, 1876, seriously damaged Quincy and other towns. Many lives were lost and a large amount of property was destroyed.

Storms of a terrible character prevailed throughout the United States and Europe from the 19th to the 25th of Mar., 1876, seriously interfering with railroad and telegraphic communications, wrecking vessels and destroying property and lives. In Hungary $10,000,000 worth of property was destroyed.

Reservoir of Water-Works at Worcester, Mass., bursted March 30, 1876, depriving the city of water and destroy-$1,500,000 of property.

Tornado at Tuscumbia, Ala., Nov. 22, 1874, destroyed over 100 buildings and killed twelve persons.

Ice-Break in Delaware Valley, Mar. 16, 1875, caused great destruction in and around Port Jervis, N. Y.

Detroit was visited by a terrific tornado, which destroyed thirty buildings and a large number of lives, June 27th, 1875.

Cyclone in Texas, September 20th, 1875, destroyed Indianola, leaving but five out of three hundred houses standing, and nearly four hundred lives were lost. Galveston suffered severely.

Earthquake on December 22, 1875, in Virginia, created a panic among the

Ice-Break in the Ohio river January 14, 1877, damaged vessels and property to the amount of $2,000,000.

Dam at Staffordsville, Conn., in the Williamantic Valley, burst March 27th, 1877. Ten persons lost their lives, and $1,000,000 worth of property was destroyed.

Tornado at Mt. Carmel, Ill., June 4, 1877, destroyed one hundred and twenty buildings and property worth $500,000 and twenty-two lives.

Connecticut River Bridge, between Northampton and Hadley, Mass., was blown down by a hurricane June 14th 1877. Fifteen persons and a number of teams went down with the ruins.

Cyclone in Georgia, February 8th,

1878, destroyed considerable property and many lives.

Rain Storms raged over all the United States in February, 1878, causing great damage. In Providence, R. I., streets were flooded to the depth of four feet, and in California the Sacramento river flooded the country.

Tornado in Kentucky, Mar. 2, 1878, destroyed a great amount of property and seven lives in Carey county.

Cottonwood, Kansas.—A tornado prevailed here April 13, 1878. It destroyed much property and several lives were lost.

Tornado through the interior of the United States, April 21, 1878, did vast damage, especially in Illinois and Iowa.

a height greater than at any time since. 1844.

Heated Term.—In July, 1878, intense heat prevailed throughout the United States. In St. Louis there were 145 deaths from sun-stroke in seven days, and on July 15 over one hundred horses fell dead on the street. In Milwaukee the thermometer stood at 101° in the shade, and one hundred and three persons were prostrated July 17th. In Chicago, Ill., many persons and over fifty horses died. Farmers in the West worked by moonlight. In New York the thermometer was 100° in the shade, and thirty sun-strokes. Throughout Massachusetts the thermometer stood from 90° to 100° in the shade, and many

The track of the tornado was a mile wide and forty miles long. It was accompanied with hail, one stone of which measured fourteen inches in circumference.

Explosion of Washburn Flouring Mills, at Minneapolis, Minn., May 2nd, 1878, originated in gases from the mill dust. It caused the destruction of several mills, seventeen lives were lost, and $1,500,000 in property was destroyed.

Cyclone in Southern Wisconsin, May 23, 1877, began at Mineral Point and swept across the State nearly to Milwaukee, leaving great ruin in its track. Thirty persons were killed and a large number injured.

Missouri River rose, July 3, 1878, to

persons died. Habitual beer and whisky drinkers suffered most.

Tornadoes, Hail and Rain Storms, of great violence, occurred in many parts of the United States in August, 1878. A large amount of property was destroyed, and many lives were lost.

Wallingford, Conn., August 9th, 1878.—A tornado destroyed ninety buildings and killed thirty persons.

Philadelphia, October 23, 1878.—A tornado demolished four hundred buildings and property worth $2,000,000. Six lives were lost.

Terrible Tornado swept over parts of Minnesota, Wisconsin, Iowa and Dakota, causing vast destruction of life and property, July 3, 1879.

. *Ohio and Canada* was visited by a tornado, July 11, 1879. It destroyed hundreds of thousands of dollars worth of crops, many public buildings, and a large amount of private property.

Massachusetts suffered from a tornado July 16th, 1879. It was felt with great severity upon the coast, and destroyed many vessels. More than thirty lives were lost. Some of the beautiful towns in the central part of the State were rid of the magnificent elms which had been shading them for many years.

Storm on the Atlantic coast, August 18, 1879, caused great destruction. Vessels were driven ashore, and the velocity of the wind was sixty miles an hour. New England suffered severely, and the

inches. The orange groves in Florida were seriously damaged.

Storms raged throughout the United States during the week ending February 7, 1881. Railroads were blockaded in the Northwest. New Orleans was flooded by the bursting of levees, and 3,500 square miles were overflowed in the Sacramento Valley. On the 8th the roof of the New York Central depot at Buffalo, N. Y., fell with the weight of snow, killing five persons. Later great floods were reported in Oregon, at Toledo, Ohio, Washington, D. C., and at other points.

Snow Storms prevailed throughout the United States, especially in the Northwest, February 26 and March 5, 1881. Blockades ensued, and provisions

damage to the shipping was great. At Norfolk, Va., the streets were flooded, and buildings unroofed, causing a loss of over $200,000.

Cyclone, April 18, 1880.—The worst ever known in this country, swept through Indiana, Illinois, Wisconsin, Iowa, Kansas and Missouri. At Marshfield, Mo., all but twenty or thirty buildings were wrecked and one hundred persons were killed. A child was found in the crotch of a tree, unhurt, three miles from home.

Cold and Snow in the South, December 29, 1880. Severe cold prevailed throughout the United States. At Greensborough, N. C., snow fell fifteen

and feed were exhausted in certain localities. Chicago was cut off almost entirely. In some places railroad ties and telegraph poles were used for fuel.

Iowa, Kansas, Minnesota and Missouri were visited with violent storms, June 12, 1881. Many lives were lost and much property was destroyed.

New Ulm, Minn., was completely wrecked by a cyclone, July 16, 1881. The town contained a population of between two and three thousand, and of those thirty persons were killed and wounded, and more than one hundred homes demolished.

Georgia and South Carolina suffered from a severe hurricane along the coast,

August 27, 1881. Many lives were lost and much property destroyed.

A Blizzard was reported to have occurred March 29, 1882, along the line of the Winona and St. Peter Railroad, Dakota. Many lives were lost and a large amount of property destroyed.

A Tornado prevailed in the Western States, April 6th, 1882, by which twelve lives were lost and great destruction of property occurred.

McAllister, Indian Territory, was visited by a cyclone, May 16, 1882, and one hundred and twenty persons were killed and wounded.

Grinnell, Iowa, a town with a population of 2,415, was struck by a cyclone and Southern States about the 22nd of April, 1883. Nearly three hundred lives were lost and a large amount of property destroyed.

Missouri was struck by a cyclone on May 13, 1883, and many persons were killed and much property was destroyed. The town of Oronogo was entirely demolished.

Rochester, Minnesota, a city with a population of nearly 6,000, was struck by a cyclone August 21, 1883, and one-third of the town destroyed. A railroad train, on its way from Rochester to Zumbrota, was lifted from the track and completely demolished. Thirty persons were killed and fifty wounded.

Springfield, Missouri, was visited by

June 18, 1882, and one-half the town destroyed, and more than one hundred persons were killed. About the same time very destructive storms also visited Kansas, Missouri and Iowa.

Coalville, Pa., was visited by a cyclone June 30, 1882, and several persons were wounded.

Overflow of the Mississippi.—During the spring of 1882 the Mississippi River and its tributaries overflowed, causing many deaths and the destruction of a vast amount of property. By a report made to the Secretary of War, dated March 17, eighty-five thousand persons were rendered homeless and destitute by the floods.

Tornadoes prevailed in the Western a tornado November 5, 1883. Five persons were killed and many wounded.

Floods in the Ohio Valley. — The spring of 1883 witnessed heavy floods in the Ohio Valley, which caused great destruction of property and the loss of several lives. Large tracts of country were submerged, railway bridges swept away, mills damaged and thousand of families driven from home. The cities of Cincinnati and Louisville suffered greatly. In February, 1884, these floods were repeated, but were more disastrous than the preceding year. At Cincinnati the water was seventy feet deep. Among the disastrous incidents was the fall of a large boarding-house at Cincinnati, killing fourteen of the inmates.

Wind Storms, of a furious character, visited the South and West April 1, 1884. The town of Oakville, Indiana, was entirely destroyed, and four of the inhabitants killed and fifty wounded.

Mississippi, Georgia, South and North Carolina, and many other Southern States, suffered from a destructive cyclone, February 19, 1884. Many lives were lost and much property destroyed.

Indiana, Ohio, Pennsylvania, South Carolina, Alabama and Tennessee.—Destructive storms prevailed in these States April 1, 1884, with great loss of life.

Jamestown, O., was destroyed by a cyclone on April 27, 1884. Six persons were killed and a number wounded.— Extensive damages were suffered in other portions of the State.

Baltimore, Washington, New York, Philadelphia, and other portions of the country, experienced earthquake shocks on August 10, 1884. It was felt from Richmond, Va., to Portland, Me., and from the Atlantic coast to the Ohio.

Clear Lake, Wis., was struck by a cyclone, September 9, 1884. Three lives were lost and the greater part of the town laid in ruins. Several other towns in Wisconsin and Minnesota were damaged.

GREAT FIRES.

Plymouth.—The first great fire occurred here on November 5, 1624. It destroyed several houses, with goods and provisions.

Boston.—Two wooden houses were destroyed by fire in Boston, March 16, 1631. The fire caught in a wooden chimney. Such chimneys and thatched roofs were thereafter forbidden. This was the first fire in Boston. Another great fire occurred here in 1771, which destroyed 100 buildings.

Charleston, S. C.—A destructive fire raged here in 1740. Parliament voted £20,000 for its relief. January 16, 1778, Charleston suffered from another great fire. It raged for 24 hours. The shipping and boats in the harbor were filled with unfortunate families.

New York.—A great fire occurred here September 21, 1776. It burnt Trinity Church and 500 dwellings near by.— Some lives were lost. Another and greater fire occurred December 16, 1835. It raged fourteen hours, and the burnt district covered over forty-five acres. It destroyed $20,000,000 of property. The thermometer stood at zero, and gunpowder was used to blow up buildings and arrest the flames. It wrecked twenty-three insurance companies.

Detroit, Mich., was destroyed by fire in 1805. At that time it was a prominent fur-trading post.

Richmond, Va., Theater burned, December 24, 1811. Over sixty persons, including the Governor of the State, perished in the flames.

Patent and Postoffices.—A great fire consumed the Patent and Postoffices, with valuable models and records, in Washington, D. C., December 15, 1836.

New York. — Forty-six buildings and $10,000,000 worth of property were destroyed by fire, September 6th, 1839.

Charleston, S. C.—A large fire here, April 27, 1838, destroyed 1,158 buildings and $3,000,000 worth of property. The city was burned, December 14, 1861, and several millions of dollars' worth of property were destroyed.

Pittsburg, Penn.—A great conflagration prevailed here, April 10, 1845, which destroyed 1,800 buildings, $6,000,000 of property, and burned over fifty-six acres.

city. Another occurred May 3-5, 1851, by which $3,500,000 worth of property was destroyed and many lives were lost. June 22nd, 1851, witnessed still another, which destroyed five hundred buildings and $3,000,000 worth of property.

St. Louis, May 4, 1851.--Three-fourths of the city and $11,000,000 worth of property were destroyed by fire.

Library of the United States, in the Capitol at Washington, was burned December 24, 1851. Out of 55,000 volumes 3,500 were destroyed, besides valuable paintings, medals and statuary.

Columbus, O., February 1, 1852.— The State-House and most of the records were destroyed by fire.

Crystal Palace in New York burned

New York, July 19, 1845.—Between Broadway, Exchange Place, Broad and Stone streets, 450 buildings and $6,000,000 of property were destroyed by fire.

Louisville, Ky.—A great fire here consumed several hundred buildings in 1846.

Albany, N. Y., August 17, 1848.—Six hundred houses and $3,000,000 worth of property were destroyed by fire.

St. Louis.—A great fire occurred here in 1849. One-third of the city and much shipping on the river was destroyed.

San Francisco, Cal., May 3, 1850.— A fire here destroyed $10,000,000 worth of property, including the Custom-House and many of the finest buildings in the

October 5, 1858, consuming its entire contents.

Key West, May 16, 1859.—A fire here destroyed 110 buildings and $2,750,000 worth of property.

Nashville, Tenn., June 10, 1865.—A fire consumed $10,000,000 worth of Union supplies. Another, on July 24, 1866, destroyed $1,000,000 worth of property.

Barnum's Museum was burned in New York July 13, 1865.

Fort Riley, Kansas, January 31, 1866.—A fire consumed $1,000,000 worth of United States quartermaster and commissary stores.

Academy of Music and University Medical College in New York were burned May 21, 1866.

Portland, Me., burned July 4, 1866. A fire-cracker exploded by a boy in a cooper-shop, originated a conflagration which destroyed one thousand six hundred buildings and $15,000,000 worth of property.

Theater Burnings in New York.— In 1866 the American, the Academy of Music and the New Bowery Theaters were destroyed by fire. In 1867 Winter Garden and the disused Mechanics' Hall were burned, and the Theater Comique was singed. In 1872 Kelly & Leon's Minstrel Hall, Niblo's Garden and the Hippo Theater were destroyed. In 1873 Daly's Fifth Avenue Theater floated to the skies. In 1882 the Park theater fol-

September 16, 1871. Loss, $300,000. Six persons were killed.

Wisconsin.—Great fires prevailed in this State October 8, 1871. An appalling conflagration occurred in the lumber region, which swept out of existence the towns of Peshtigo, Manistee, Williamsonville, Menekaumee, Marinette and Brussels, with over six hundred lives and $4,000,000 of property.

Chicago Fire, October 8-9, 1871.— About 10 o'clock on a windy night a cow kicked over a lamp while she was being milked, in DeKoven street, which exploded and caused one of the most disastrous fires in modern times. It swept over 2,124 acres, destroyed 17,450 build-

lowed, and in 1883 the Windsor and the Standard were consumed.

Adelphia Theater, Boston, was destroyed February 4, 1871.

Troy Opera House and P. E. Church of Messiah, destroyed by fire April 1, 1871.

Albany, N. Y., April 7, 1871.— A fire destroyed the great printing house of Weed, Parsons & Co. Loss half a million.

Williamsport, Penn., had a great fire August 20th, 1871, which destroyed $2,000,000 worth of property.

Saratoga, N. Y., September 14th, 1871.—The Park Place and Columbia Hotels were consumed by fire.

Pioche, Nev., was destroyed by fire

ings and 250 lives; 98,000 were made homeless, of whom 50,000 left the city. The loss was $175,000,000, insured in two hundred insurance companies for $98,000,000, sixty-four of which failed.

Little Rock, Ark., December 28th, 1871.—A fire destroyed $100,000 worth of property.

Monroe, La., December 30th, 1871, $580,000 worth of property was destroyed by fire.

The Library of Edwin Forrest was burned January 15, 1872, in Philadelphia. It was worth $20,000.

Reading, Penn., January 16, 1872, a great fire destroyed $250,000 worth of property.

Jayne's Granite Block, in Philadelphia, was nearly destroyed by fire on March 4, 1872. Loss, $478,000.

State Lunatic Asylum at Newburg, Ohio, burned September 27, 1872, Five lives were lost and $500,000 in property.

Sing-Sing, N. Y.—A fire destroyed a great part of the business section on October 8, 1872.

Cambria Iron Works, at Johnstown, Pa., were burned October 13, 1872. Loss, $400,000.

Boston Fire. — Sixty-five acres in the heart of the city were burned over, destroying four hundred and forty-six buildings, November 9th, 1872. Fourteen lives were lost and $73,600,000 in property consumed.

pletely destroyed, and a number of lives lost, in consequence of the burning of the woods surrounding the village, June 19, 1873.

Portland, Oregon, August 2, 1873.— A great fire occurred here, which consumed twenty-three blocks of two hundred and fifty dwellings, and destroyed $1,500,000 worth of property.

Valuable Relics and documents of the Long Island Historical Society were lost by the burning of the Hamilton building in Brooklyn, N. Y., January 15, 1874.

State Prison at Charleston, Mass., was partially burned March 21, 1874.— Loss, $50,000.

Chicago. — Another great fire pre-

Rand & Avery's printing establishment, Boston, Mass., was burned Nov. 20, 1872. Loss, $250,000.

Galva, Ill., November 21, 1872.—A fire here destroyed $218,000 in property.

Fifth Avenue Hotel, New York, burned and suffocated eleven servant girls, December 11, 1872.

Barnum's Museum, in New York, burned December 24, 1872. Loss, $1.-000,000.

At Chicago, January 17, 1873, the First Congregational Church was destroyed by fire.

Marshall House, in which Colonel Ellsworth was killed, at Alexandria, Va., burned February 25, 1873.

Michagamme, Michigan, was com-

vailed here, July 14th, 1874, which destroyed fifteen squares of three hundred and forty-six buildings and $4,000,000 of property.

Fall River, Mass., September 19th, 1874. — Granite Woolen Mills burned, killing twenty and wounding thirty-eight operatives.

Boston, December 15th, 1874.—Over $1,000,000 was destroyed by fire.

Holyoke, Mass., May 27, 1875.—The French Catholic Church was burned and seventy-five lives lost.

Oshkosh, Wisconsin, April 28, 1875.— A fire destroyed a large part of the city. Loss, $3,000,000.

Forest Fires raged in May and June, 1875, in Canada, Michigan, Pennsylvania, and New York, destroying whole villages and many lives.

Home for the Aged, at Williamsburg, N. Y., an institution of the Sisters of Charity, was burned, with twenty-eight inmates, March 4, 1876.

Castle Garden, New York, was burned July 9th, 1876. It was erected in 1807 as a fortification.

Brooklyn Theater burned December 5, 1876, causing the death of three hundred persons.

Fox's New American Theater, at Philadelphia, was burned February 25, 1877. Loss, $250,000.

Forest Fires raged in parts of New England, Pennsylvania and New York, and in Michigan and Wisconsin, in May,

partially destroyed by fire September 24, 1877, causing a loss of $1,000,000, besides models and papers that money cannot replace.

Daniel Webster's House at Marshfield, Mass., was burned February 14th, 1878.

Hot Springs, Arkansas, suffered from a great fire March 5th, 1878. One hundred and fifty buildings were burned.

Philadelphia, Penn., suffered to the extent of $1,000,000, by a great fire, March 25, 1878.

Bishop Mansion, on the Hudson River, New York, burned April 16, 1878, destroying valuable paintings, one of which was valued at $30,000.

Alta, a town in Utah, was nearly all

1877, destroying millions of lumber, whole villages and many lives.

Southern Hotel at St. Louis, Mo., was burned April 11, 1877. It was a six-story building, and seven persons jumped from the upper windows. The whole number of lives lost was fourteen. Property lost, $750,000.

St. John, N. B., June 20, 1877.—A destructive fire burned over five hundred acres of buildings in the main part of the city. Many lives were lost and fifteen thousand people made homeless. Property valued at $20,000,000 was destroyed.

Gayville, Dakota, was consumed by fire August 18th, 1877. Three hundred buildings were burned.

Patent Office at Washington was

burnt August 1st, 1878. Loss, $200,000. The fire originated from a man who fell asleep with a cigar in his mouth.

Cape May, New Jersey, November 9, 1878, eight hotels and many cottages were consumed by fire.

New York, January 17, 1879.—Nineteen dry goods firms, involving a loss of $3,000,000, were consumed by fire.

Insane Asylum, near St. Joseph, Missouri, burned January 25, 1879. Loss, $200,000.

San Reno, Nevada, was almost consumed by fire, March 2, 1879. Five lives lost and $1,000,000 was destroyed.

Forest Fires in Lincoln Co., Kansas, raged in March, 1879, attended with loss of life.

Columbus, O.—Patrol of one thousand citizens served each night in Mar., 1879, at Columbus, O., to guard against incendiary fires, of which there had been great numbers.

South Bend, Indiana.—The Notre Dame Roman Catholic University at South Bend, Indiana, was burned April 23, 1879. Loss, $1,000,000.

Deadwood, Black Hills, was burned, September 26th, 1879. Two thousand people were made homelesss. Loss, $3,000,000.

Titusville, Penn.—Oil fire at Titusville, Penn., August 16, 1879. A tank of oil was struck by lightning, and the flames spread from tank to tank until 85,000 barrels, worth $100,000, were con-

Three hundred persons burned to death, and many villages and an immense amount of property was destroyed.

Haverill, Mass.—A destructive fire occurred here February 17th, 1882, by which the business part of the town was destroyed. Loss, over $2,000,000.

Newhall House, Milwaukee, Wis., was destroyed by fire, January 10, 1883. Over one hundred lives were lost in the conflagration.

Kimball House, in Atlanta, Ga., was destroyed by fire August 12th, 1883. It was one of the finest and largest hotels in the South. Loss, $1,000,000.

Exposition Building, Pittsburg, Penna, was destroyed by fire October 3, 1883. Loss, $1,000,000.

sumed. A change of wind saved the city.

New York, January 4, 1881.—Ten women and children were burned to death by a fire in the rear tenement house, No. 35 Madison street.

Stafford County, New Hampshire, Poor-House destroyed by fire, January 7th, 1881. Thirteen persons burned to death.

Catholic Orphanage, at Scranton, Penna., destroyed by fire February 27th, 1881. Fifteen children were burned to death.

Eastern Michigan suffered terribly from forest fires September 4, 1881. They spread over a large portion of Huron, Sanilac and Tuscola counties.

Park Theater, New York, was destroyed by fire early in the evening, October 30th, 1883. Mrs. Langtry was to make her first appearance in America at this theater the same evening. Two lives were lost.

Roman Catholic Convetn at Belleville, Ill., was destroyed by fire January 5, 1884. Twenty-six nuns and pupils were burned to death.

Park Theater, Cleveland, O., was destroyed by fire January 5, 1884.

Hampton, Va., suffered from a destructive fire, April 9th, 1884, causing a loss of $100,000.

Forest Fires.—Late in April and May, 1884, extensive forest fires raged in New York, New Jersey and Pennsylvania, burning several villages and many square miles of timber land. A number of persons perished in the flames.

Erie, Penn., suffered from a fire, August 13th, 1884. Two-thirds of the business portion of the city was destroyed.

Orton's Anglo-American Circus. — One of its cars containing sixty men caught fire near Greeley, Col., August 29th, 1884. Many persons were fatally burned.

Cleveland, O., was visited by a large fire, September 7, 1884. Loss aggregated over $2,000,000.

Liberty, Va., had an incendiary fire, October 12th, 1884. Fourteen business houses were destroyed, involving a loss of nearly $150,000.

Goldsboro, N. C., was visited by a fire, November 16th, 1884. Loss, over $250,000.

St. John's Male Orphan Asylum, Brooklyn, New York, was destroyed by fire, December 16th, 1884. Many lives were lost.

Harrigan & Hart's Theater Comique, New York, was destroyed by fire, December 23, 1884.

Blake Opera House and hotel at Racine, Wis., destroyed by fire, December 28, 1884. Three lives lost.

POSTOFFICE DEPARTMENT.

Mail Route established in 1672 between Boston and New York. The round trip was to be made once a month. Postage, four pence a letter for sixty miles, and two pence extra for each additional hundred miles. This was the first mail route in the country.

Government Postoffices were first established in America by act of Parliament in 1710. The main office was to be at New York, and the other offices were scattered through the country at convenient places.

Postmasters.—Colonel Spottswood was Postmaster, with Benjamin Franklin Assistant Postmaster, from 1737 to 1753. At his death Franklin was made Postmaster, with William Hunter, Assistant. Their joint salary was £600, if they could make it out of the office. In 1757 it owed them £900. After this date it paid.

Philadelphia and Boston Mail.—In 1754 Franklin issued a notice that the New England mail, which used to leave Philadelphia "once a fortnight in winter, would start once a week all the year, whereby answers might be obtained to letters between Philadelphia and Boston in three weeks, which used to require six."

New York and Philadelphia mail

was run weekly each way by coaches in 1760.

Benjamin Franklin, Postmaster General of the Colonies, made a trip in 1763, through the country in a chaise, to perfect the arrangements of the department. The trip, which can now be made in five days, took five months.

Postoffice Department was established by Congress, July 26, 1775. Benjamin Franklin was chosen Postmaster General, with a salary of $1,000 per annum. It was reorganized by the United States Government September 22d, 1789. Samuel Osgood, of Massachusetts, was First Postmaster General, who was not a member of the President's Cabinet until 1829.

cents; for any distance not exceeding ninety miles, ten cents; not exceeding one hundred and fifty miles, 12½ cents; not exceeding three hundred miles, 17 cents; not exceeding five hundred miles, 20 cents; any distance over five hundred miles, 25 cents. These rates were held in force till 1816, when they were changed without changing the awkward unit of mail matter. The rate that went into effect in 1826 made the charge for a single letter carried not to exceed 30 miles, 6¼ cents; not to exceed 80 miles, 10 cents; not to exceed 150 miles, 12½ cts.; not to exceed 400 miles, 18¾ cents, and for any distance over 400 miles, 25 cents. Newspapers were carried for one cent for 100 miles or less, and 1½ cents for longer

Postal Service.—In 1790 there were only seventy-five postoffices in the United States and 7,375 miles of service. In five years there were 1,799,720 miles, and in 1845, 35,634,269 miles.

Mail Wagon.—The first mail wagon west of Albany, New York, was run in 1791. It carried the mail and passengers to Canajoharie, and the enterprise ultimately developed into the great stage lines of Central New York and Western Pennsylvania.

Postage in 1792.—The first schedule of rates, which was established by the law that organized the postoffice, was as follows: For every letter consisting of one piece of paper for any distance not exceeding forty miles, eight

distances. Congressmen could frank letters during, and for twenty days after, sessions. The unit of charge for letters was one sheet of paper. There were no envelopes at that time. A letter was so written on a piece of paper that one side of one part of it was left blank. When folded this blank side became the back of the letter, on which the address was written.

Cabinet Officer.—The Postmaster General was, in 1829, first invited to a seat in the President's Cabinet.

Reduced to Five Cents—In 1845 an act was passed reducing the letter rate to five cents per half ounce, regardless of the number of pieces of paper contained in a letter. The scale of distances was so simplified that for any distance under 300 miles the rate of five cents was charged, and for any distance over 300 miles 10 cents. By the same act carrying letters by private enterprise, which had been indulged in up to the present time, on account of the high rate of postage, was prohibited on all post-roads unless postage had been prepaid. Here was relief in both directions in which it was demanded. A person could, by ascertaining whether his letter was to go 300 miles or more than that, and whether it weighed one-half ounce or more than that, tell precisely what the sending of his missive would cost. From this change of rate the expenditures of the depart-

age rate has ever been increased after a reduction has once been made.

Reduced to Three Cents in 1851. The prepayment of all letters came about through the operation of the Optional law of 1851, by which the rate of domestic letter postage was further reduced to three cents, provided payment was made in advance. If paid by the recipient the old rate, five cents, was charged. People who had respect for their correspondents paid in advance. Those who sent letters grudgingly, as the payers of bills by mail, or who were naturally stingy and small-souled, sent letters without prepaying them. Under this law many letters were not taken

---

---

ment began to exceed the receipts so largely that repeated efforts were made to return to higher rates. But the fact seems to be that the department began to run behind in 1843. From the time it was organized in 1789, to 1843, there was an annual surplus. The first year of the Government this was $5,795 profit. Ten years later, 1800, the surplus was $66,-810. The falling off of revenue under the rates of 1845, not so much as the increase of expenditures on account of contracts with railroads and steamboats about that time, contributed to swell the annual deficits, and sent the statesmen of the period on the back track. The clamor of the people, however, was too loud to be disregarded. No letter-post-

from the office. Finally, in 1855, the law requiring all postage in advance, at the uniform rate of three cents, went into effect. It took people a long time to get used to this innovation. They would persist in dropping their letters in without stamps, which had been adopted by the department in 1847, seven years after they had been shown in England to be practicable and convenient. The Postmaster-General, in his report next after the Three-Cent Prepayment, by Stamp act went into effect, deplored the stupidity of people as shown by their neglect to affix the stamp. "Through the press," said he, "and by placards on the letter-boxes, every possible publicity has been given to this law, yet from inadvertence, fraud, or other causes, letters continue to be deposited without prepayment." For some time Postmasters all over the country informed people that letters addressed to them were waiting for stamps, but after his patience was exhausted the Postmaster-General, James Holt, ordered all unprepaid letters to go to the Dead-Letter Office.

Overland Mail to California started from St. Louis, Mo., September 16, 1858.

"Pony Express," between St. Joseph, Mo., and Sacramento, Cal., was established in April, 1860, as a link in the mail line between New York and San Francisco, which was made in fourteen days. Fleet horsemen carrying ten pounds, rode sixty miles each, for which they received $1,200 per month. The postage was $5,00 in gold for each quarter of an ounce.

New York and Chicago.—A fast mail between these two cities left New York, September 16th, 1875, from the Grand Central Depot, at 4:15 A. M., with thirty-three tons of mail, in mail bags, which were taken on and dropped at almost every station. It reached Chicago at 6:27 A. M., September 17th, being less than twenty-six hours on the way, averaging 41¼ miles per hour.

Postal Bill, reducing rates on third-class matter to one cent per ounce, on packages of four pounds and under, and on transient newspapers and magazines to one cent for three ounces or less, and one cent for each two additional ounces, passed the United States Senate April 12, 1876.

Transit of the Australian Mail to England, in October, 1880, was made in 41 days via San Francisco, thence by special train to New York, and by the Guion steamer to England. The old route, via the Suez canal, usually took 45 days.

Two-Cent Postage.—The reduction of postage in the United States from three to two cents went into operation October 1, 1883.

MATRIMONIAL AND SOCIAL EVENTS.

Virginia Dare, the first American child of English parentage, was born in Roanoke Colony, August 18, 1587.

Wives Bought with Tobacco.—In 1619 the London Company sent ninety respectable young women to Jamestown, where the planters bought them for wives, at one hundred pounds of tobacco each, to pay for their passage. This conduced so greatly to the contentment of the colonists that others were afterward sent out, and the price advanced to one hundred and fifty pounds each.

Wedding in Plymouth.—The first wedding was between Edward Winslow and Mrs. Susanna White, May 12, 1621.

Courtship of Miles Standish.—Captain Standish became a widower shortly after the arrival of the colony. One day, in the spring of 1621, he sent his young friend, John Alden, with an offer of marriage to Priscilla Mullens, a fair young maiden. Upon hearing the request, Priscilla archly replied: "Prithee, John, why do you not speak for yourself?" The bashful messenger blushed and retired, but in due time a happy wedding took place between them. The poet Longfellow has made this incident famous.

"Merry Mount."—In 1626 Thomas Morton, a "pettifogger of Furmval's Inn," got control of a plantation known

violation of law, but the matter was dropped.

First Ball in Canada.—The Jesuit *Journal* records the first ball in Canada, February 4, 1667, and adds: "God grant that nothing more may come of it."

Wives for Canadians.—In 1667 a large number of maidens were sent over to become wives to the settlers. Over one thousand came by 1673 It frequently occurred that as many as thirty were married at one time, and sometimes it was discovered that a few of the young women had left lawful husbands at home. None were sold, as at Jamestown.

---

as "Mount Wallaston," near Boston. He changed the name to "Merry Mount," sold ammunition to Indians, gave refuge to runaway servants and set up a May pole, broached a cask of wine and a hogshead of ale, and held high revel and carousal. This went on for two years, until, at the complaint of a number of settlements, he was arrested by Miles Standish and sent prisoner to England.

Queer Wedding.—In 1641 Governor Richard Bellingham, of Massachusetts, married a young lady by performing his own marriage ceremony, he being a magistrate, and without publishing the bans, as required by the colony rules. He was brought before the courts for his

Ball at Washington, D. C.—Mrs. John Quincy Adams gave a famous ball, January 8, 1824, at Washington, D. C., in commemoration of Jackson's victory at New Orleans.

Ball at New York.—Magnificent ball at the Academy of Music, New York, October 12, 1860, in honor of the Prince of Wales. A similar ball was given in Boston.

Spelling Mania reached its height in April, 1875. It extended all over the country.

Frederick Douglass, a prominent and eloquent colored politician, was married to Mrs. Helen M. Pitts, a white woman, of Washington, D. C., January 24, 1884.

CENSUS RETURNS.

Population of the Colonies of Virginia, New England and Maryland in 1660 was about 80,000.

Population of English Colonies in 1688 was about 200,000, while that of New France was but 11,000.

New York City had a population of 12,000 in 1756.

First Census.—The first systematic census ever taken in the United States was in 1790. It cost $44,377.18, and enrolled 3,929,827 persons, excluding Indians, and 700,000 slaves.

Fifth Census.—The fifth was taken in 1830, and gave a population of 12,866,020, an increase since 1820 of 32.51 per cent. It cost $378,543.13. This census, for the first time, included some returns of the fruit crop.

Sixth Census.—The sixth was taken in 1840, and showed a population of 17,069,453, an increase from 1830 of 33.52 per cent. It cost $833,370.95.

Seventh Census.—In 1850 the seventh census gave a population in the United States of 23,191,876. The in-

---

Second Census.—The second census was taken in 1800 at a cost of $66,609.04. The population was 5,308,483, an increase of 35.10 per cent since 1790.

Third Census.—The third was taken in 1810, and gave a population of 7,239,881. It had increased 36.38 per cent. since 1800. These returns showed some valuable, although imperfect, statistics of manufactures. The cost of the census was $178,444.67.

Fourth Census.—The fourth was taken in 1820. and gave a population of 9,633,822, an increase since 1810 of 33.06 per cent. The cost was $208,525.99.

crease since 1840 had been 35.83 per cent. It cost $1,329,027.53.

Eighth Census.—The eighth, taken in 1860, returned a population of 31,443,321. The rate of increase since 1850 had been 35.11 per cent. The cost of the census was $1,922,272.42.

Ninth Census.—The ninth was taken in 1870, giving a population of 38,558,371, or 22.65 per cent. increase since 1860. It cost $3,336,511.41.

Tenth Census.—The tenth census, taken 1880, showed a population of 50,155,866. There were 6,677,360 foreign born persons and 6,577,151 blacks.

FILLIBUSTERS.

Lopez's Expedition against Cuba in 1849.—Narciso Lopez, a prominent office-holder in Cuba, disgusted with the Spanish policy toward her colonies, organized his "Round Island Expedition" in the United States for overthrowing Spanish authority in Cuba. It was a ridiculous failure.

The Second Expedition of Lopez against Cuba, from the United States, captured Cardenas, May 19, 1849. He had about six hundred men, who speedily fell into the hands of the Cuban authorities, but Lopez escaped.

Third Expedition of Lopez, with five hundred men, landed at Morillo, Cuba, August 11, 1851. He was speedily defeated, captured and garroted by the Cuban authorities. A great riot occurred

against him, and on May 1st, 1857, he was again a prisoner. Released at New Orleans, he organized a third company of adventurers, but was compelled to surrender to Com. Paulding, who carried him to New York. There he gathered another band and made a descent upon Hondurus, in June, 1860. Aided by a British man-of-war, the President of that country captured the whole gang. On the 3rd of September Walker was court-martialed at Truxillo and shot.

Cuban Expeditions.—June 26th, 1869, the steamer Catharine Whiting was seized at the east end of Long Island, upon the eve of starting with an armed force to aid the Cuban insurrectionists. Two other expeditions succeeded in landing upon that island. Gen. Thomas

---

---

in New Orleans this month, in which Spaniards were assaulted by the sympathizers with Lopez.

Walker's Expeditions.—Gen. William Walker, an audacious and unscrupulous adventurer, began operations in 1853 in Lower California. In 1854, with one hundred men, he attempted the conquest of Sonora, but failed. He was made prisoner, tried by the United States authorities and acquitted. In 1855, with sixty-two followers, he proceeded to Central America, and being joined by a regiment of natives, fought and won a battle at Rivas, June 29, 1855; also one at Virgin Bay. He made himself President of Nicaragua, but the other Central American States, aided by the Vanderbilt Steamship Company, combined

Jordon, a West Point graduate and an ex-Confederate officer, was the leader of one of them, and was afterward commander of all the Cuban revolutionists.

Blockade of the American steamer Virginius by the Spanish man-of war Pizarro, was raised April 26, 1872, by the United States war vessel Kansas.

American Steamer Virginius captured October 30th, 1873, by the Spanish man-of-war Tornado, and fifty-four of her men were afterward shot upon suspicion of being fillibusters, nothwithstanding the protests of the American and British Consuls. In December the steamer and survivors were surrendered to United States authorities and Spain paid $80,000 indemnity to the United States in 1875.

ARCTIC EXPEDITIONS.

"Grinnell" Arctic Expedition, in search of Sir John Franklin, sailed from New York in 1850, commanded by Lieut. E. J. DeHaven, with Dr. Elisha Kent Kane as surgeon and naturalist. The expedition returned in 1851 without accomplishing its object.

Kane's Arctic Expedition.—In 1853 Dr. Kane and seventeen men, one of whom was Dr. Hayes, sailed from Boston in the "Advance." They reached Rensselaer Bay, where they were frozen in for two seasons. The third season they escaped in open boats, and reached Boston on October 11, 1855.

Sir John Franklin's expedition were found in a cairn at Point Victory. Sir John died June 11, 1847. The ships were abandoned April 22, 1848, and 105 survivors started for Great Fish River, and all probably starved to death.

Francis Hall's Expedition.—The Arctic Expedition of Charles Francis Hall sailed from New London, Conn., May 29th, 1860, to search for Sir John Franklin, and, after an absence of two years, he returned with no tidings from the object of his search.

Hall's Second Arctic Trip.—July 30, 1864, Charles Francis Hall sailed for the

Sir John Franklin's name was found upon some articles, and bodies were discovered, not far from Great Fish River, by Dr. Rae, in 1854.

British Arctic vessel "Resolute," abandoned in the Arctic seas while in search of Sir John Franklin, in December, 1855, was brought into New London, Conn., by a whaler. She was refitted by the United States Government and returned to the English Government as a gift. In November, 1880, an elaborate and beautiful writing-table, made of the wood of the "Resolute," was sent to the White House as a present from England to President Hayes.

Records Found.—In 1858 records of

Polar regions again, accompanied by the two Esquimaux who returned with him from his first trip. He spent four winters there, returning in 1869. On June 29, 1871, he made another expedition in the Polaris, from New York, for the North Pole. This was Hall's last voyage, as he died in Greenland. Some of the survivors of this expedition were rescued. A party of nineteen had drifted from the Polaris by the breaking up of the ice. They were afloat on the ice 195 days, drifting 2,000 miles. The Tigress, a Nova Scotia whaler, picked them up, April 30, 1873. The others abandoned the Polaris in June in two boats, and were picked up by a Scotch whaler and carried to Dundee. They reached the United States in December, 1873.

Jeanette Expedition.—On July 8, 1879, this steamer, fitted out by James Gordon Bennett, sailed from San Francisco for an Arctic trip through Behring's Strait. June 11th, 1881, it was reported that the Jeanette was destroyed by the ice in the Siberian seas. One boat's crew was never heard from.

Franklin Arctic Expedition.—In September, 1880, the party of Lieut. Frederick Schwatka, U. S. A., returned from a trip of four months, eleven days, of 3,000 miles in sledges. They buried

the officers of the expedition were Lieut. James B. Lockwood, Second Lieutenant Frederick F. Kislingbury, and Dr. Octave Pavy, Surgeon. The colony numbered twenty-five men all told. They were landed at a point in Discovery Harbor, where a station was established and named Fort Conger. The Proteus left the party on August 18, 1881, and returned to the United States, after which time nothing was heard of the colony until July 17, 1884. On that day Secretary Chandler received a telegram from Captain W. S. Schley, commanding a relief expedition sent out by the United

twenty skeletons of Sir John Franklin's party, and brought home relics, including a medal found on the skeleton of Lieut. John Irving.

The Greeley Expedition.—On the 7th of July, 1881, an expedition under the command of Lieutenant Adolphus W. Greely, U. S. A., departed from St. John, N. F , on the steamer Proteus, for the Arctic regions. Its main object was to establish an international polar station in Lady Franklin Bay, which all future expeditions could use as a base of supplies. He was to remain until the fall of 1883. Besides Lieutenant Greely,

States Government, announcing that the Greeley party had been found in a starving condition. Of the twenty-five men who set out only seven were living, one of whom, Joseph Ellison, died soon after being found. The survivors were Lieut. Greely, Sergeants David L. Brainerd, Julius Frederick and Francis Long, and Privates Henry Biederbick and Maurice Connell. They were brought home safely by Commander Schley. Two attempts to relieve the Greely expedition were unsuccessful. Cannibalism was charged against the members of the Greely expedition, August 12, 1884.

WITCHCRAFT, DELUSION and SUPERSTITION.

Painted House.—Rev. Thos. Allen, of Charlestown, Mass., was, in 1639, charged with painting his dwelling.— Upon showing that the house was painted before he owned it, and that he disapproved of such a thing, the magistrate discharged him.

Tobacco. — The use of tobacco was prohibited in 1640, by the General Court of Massachusetts.

Witchcraft in Massachusetts. — In 1645 four persons were executed as witches. In 1648 Margaret Jones, of Charlestown, was hung in Boston for witchcraft.

Long Hair worn by men was denounced as unscriptural by the government of Massachusetts in 1649.

delusion originated in the family of Rev. Samuel Parris, whose niece and daughter, being afflicted with a nervous disorder, he charged his Indian servant, Tituba, with having bewitched them, and tied and whipped her until she confessed herself a witch. From this the delusion spread, being strengthened by the fanatical zeal of Parris and the Rev. Cotton Mather, of Boston. Through their influence Gov. Phipps appointed a special court to go to Salem and sit in judgment upon accused persons. English law punished witchcraft with death, and in June executions began, and by the 20th of September twenty victims were hung,

nounced as unscriptural by the government of Massachusetts in 1649.

Extravagance in dress was prohibited by law in Massachusetts in 1651.

Mrs. Ann Hibbins was hung as a witch in Massachusetts in 1655.

Connecticut Witchcraft.—In 1662 three persons were executed as witches in Connecticut.

Pennsylvania. — Witchcraft was charged against a woman in Pennsylvania in 1684. She was acquitted.

Boston Witchcraft. — In 1688 an Irish woman was executed in Boston for this crime. Cotton Mather was deceived by the case, and issued an account of it, which produced a great impression.

Salem Witchcraft, 1692. — This

including some of the most exemplary Christians in the community. Fifty-five others had been tortured into confessing abominable falsehoods, and one hundred and fifty lay in prison. Two hundred were accused or suspected, when the frenzy reached its heighth, and a reaction began to take place in the popular mind. The veto of the witchcraft act by King William stopped further trials, and the prisoners were all set free by order of Governor Phipps.

Public Whipper.—In New York in 1750, the public whipper being dead, £20 a year was offered by the mayor for some one to fill the office. In some cases through New England and elsewhere, certain things were made the subject of discipline, among them the gagging of women known as common scolds. This did not come within the range of legal action, but was numbered as one of the duties of the "Public Whipper."

Blue Laws of Connecticut.—Rev. Samuel A. Peters died April 19, 1826.— He was a Tory who fled to England in 1774, where he published a "History of Connecticut," which was "the most unscrupulous and malicious of lying narratives." In it he pulished "laws enacted in the Dominion of New Haven," which by many were thought to be genuine, but were chiefly fabrications.

Millerism.—During the year 1843 a religious delusion originated with a Mr. Miller, a plain, uneducated farmer, who for ten years had predicted the second coming of Christ and the world's destruction in 1843. Fifty thousand disciples believed the prediction and confidently awaited its fulfillment. A feverish excitement prevailed among them, any many became almost insane. Miller died in 1849. Some of his followers are now known as Seventh-Day Adventists.

"Spirit Rappings" originated in 1848 in the family of John D. Fox, Hydeville, New York. His two daughters, after considerable experimenting, gave public exhibitions in 1849. Other phenomenas were added to the raps, and mediums and believers multiplied.

INSURRECTIONS, MOBS AND RIOTS.

Negro Insurrection in Hayti.—On December 27th, 1522, the slaves rose against their oppressors, but were speedily overcome by the vigor and promptitude of the Spaniards.

Maryland.—In April, 1635, Lord Baltimore's suthority on Kent Island was resisted by William Clayborne.— Clayborne fled to Virginia and his estates were confiscated.

New Jersey.—Insurrection among anti-renters arose in New Jersey in 1672, who resisted the demand of the proprietors of the province, for half penny an acre quit-rent on lands bought of Indians.

Bacon's Rebellion against Berkeley's government in Virginia in 1676 was caused by his weak measures in suppressing Indian outrages. Jamestown was burned, but Bacon died, and the rebellion ceased. Berkeley hanged twenty-two of Bacon's comrades.

Virginia.—An insurrection in Virginia in 1688 was caused by financial troubles and an unpopular government. It was speedily suppressed.

South Carolina.—By an insurrection in 1688 Governor Seth Sothell was deposed because of his avarice and tyrany.

"Petticoat Insurrection."—In Mo-

bile in 1706 the colony suffered for want of supplies, and the women threatened rebellion because they were obliged to live on Indian corn.

Charleston, S. C.—Slave insurrection, instigated by the Spaniards of St. Augustine, broke out near Charleston, S. C., in 1738. After killing some whites and destroying property they were subdued by the planters.

" Negro Plot " in New York in 1741. Slavery existed in the province, and the negroes were naturally distrusted. Several incendiary fires aroused suspicion, and credit was given to an absurd story that the negroes intended to burn the city, kill the whites and set up a negro as governor. A panic ensued. One

cause he sympathized with the scheme of taxation. The records of the Admiralty Court were burned. Mobs in other colonies compelled stamp distributors to resign.

Boston Massacre.—March 2, 1770, a rope-maker quarreled with a soldier and struck him. From this a fight ensued between several soldiers and ropemakers, in which the latter were beaten. A few evenings afterward (March 5), about seven hundred excited inhabitants assembled in the streets for the purpose of attacking the soldiers. A sentinel was attacked near the custom-house, when Captain Preston, commander of the guard, went to his rescue with eight armed men. Irritated and assailed by

hundred and fifty negroes were made prisoners; one hundred were convicted as conspirators; twelve were burned; twenty-two, including four whites, were hung and twelve transported to be sold as slaves. The subsequent verdict was that *there was no plot at all.*

Boston.—A riot occurred in Boston, August 14th, 1765. The effigy of Andrew Oliver, a stamp distributor, was hung on Liberty tree. That evening the Sons of Liberty bore the effigy in procession, and before dispersing attacked Oliver's house and office, injuring them seriously.

Taxation Mobs.—Mob violence was manifested against Chief Justice Hutchinson, of Massachusetts, whose residence was attacked August 26, 1765, be-

the mob, the soldiers fired upon the citizens, killed three and dangerously wounded five. The mob instantly retreated, when all the bells of the city rang an alarm, and in less than an hour several thousand exasperated citizens were on the streets. Governor Hutchinson assured the people that justice would be done in the morning, and thus prevented further bloodshed. Captain Preston and six of his men were tried and acquitted by a Boston jury. Two other soldiers were found guilty of manslaughter, and the troops were removed to Castle William.

Rivington's New York Gazetteer, a tory paper, was demolished in 1775, by one hundred patriots under Isaac

Sears, who came from New Haven for the purpose.

Mutinous Soldiers, June 21, 1783, demand of Congress immediate pay for services. The Philadelphia militia, refusing protection, Congress adjourned to Princeton.

Shay's Rebellion broke out in December, 1786, in Massachusetts, under Daniel Shay, formerly an army officer. The country was poor, taxes high, and no money in circulation. The courts were burdened with suits for debt. The people thought that State officials received too high salaries and heavy fees. Conventions were held to obtain relief by legal measures, but failed. Armed bands of "Regulators" prevented the

who had robbed graves for subjects for dissection. There was intense excitement, and the doctors fled for their lives.

Whiskey Insurrection in Pennsylvania.—A law was passed in 1791, which imposed duties on domestic distilled liquors, and when officers of the government were sent to enforce it, July 16, 1794, they were fired upon in the Monongahela valley, and a force of 16,000 men threatened to march to Pittsburg to take the United States arsenal and fort. Many outrages were committed. Buildings were burned, mails were robbed, and Government officers were insulted and abused. President Washington finally issued a call for troops, to which several States responded with a large force,

sitting of the courts, held Worcester and attempted to secure the arsenal at Springfield. In January, 1787, General Lincoln called out the militia and fired upon the malcontents, killing three or four, and by vigorous measures suppressed the insurrection.

Financial Distress in 1786 caused an excited mob to attempt to frighten the Legislature of New Hampshire, at Exeter, into issuing paper money for public relief.

Newspaper Mobbed.—Greenfield's Political *Register*, a New York newspaper opposing the new constitution, was mobbed July 27, 1788.

"The Doctors' Riot" in New York in 1788 was caused by some physicians

upon which the leaders of the rebellion hastened to make terms of peace, and the matter was settled without war.

House-Tax Insurrection.—In 1799 armed resistance was made against taxing houses in Bethlehem, Pa., by about fifty men led by one Fries. Arrests followed. Fries was condemned for treason, but was soon after pardoned by President Adams.

Baltimore. Md.—In June, 1811, a newspaper called the *Federal Republican*, was destroyed by a mob for uttering sentiments of censure on the conduct of the Government. Shortly after this affair the paper made its appearance again, containing severe allusions to the mayor, police and people of Baltimore, for the depredations that had been committed upon the establishment. The office was again mobbed, and during the frequent discharge of muskets, Dr. Gale was killed, when the party in the office were finally escorted by the military to the county jail for protection against further violence. Shortly after dark the mob assembled at the jail, carried the mayor away by force and compelled the turnkey to open the door. General Lingan was killed; eleven were beaten and mangled with such weapons as stones, bludgeons, sledge-hammers, etc., and thrown as dead into one pile. Mr. Hanson, editor of the paper, fainting from repeated wounds, was carried away by a gentleman of opposite political senti-

melee the darkies fired upon them, killing one man and wounding two others. As soon as it was discovered the following day that a white man was killed by the blacks it occasioned great excitement, and a mob assembled, when the sheriff arrested seven and committed them to jail, but in three or four instances the mob made the rescue. On the 23d the mob renewed their attack at Snowtown, stoning and destroying houses. The military were called out to preserve order, but were met with defiance by the mob. Stones were hurled at them with such force by the mob as to split the socks of several muskets, and, as a matter of self-protection, they were compelled to fire. Four of the rioters

ments, at the risk of his life. No effectual inquiry was ever made into this violation of the law, and the guilty escaped punishment.

Opposition to Machinery. — The hand-weavers of Manayunk, Pa., in 1830 attempted to destroy a power loom invented by Alfred Jenks. They were prevented by an armed force.

New York.—October 13th, 1831, Anderson, an English vocalist, was driven from the stage of the Park Theater, New York, for disrespectful remarks concerning the United States.

Providence, R. I.—September 21, 22 and 23, 1831, a serious riot occurred here, between negroes and a party of sailors and steamboat men. During the

were killed and the mob dispersed. A committee of the citizens of Providence appointed to investigate the matter were unanimous in their opinion that the infantry were justified in firing, and that it was strictly in defense of their lives.

Nat. Turner's Insurrection occurred August 21, 1831, in Southampton, Va. Turner was a Baptist preacher who headed sixty other slaves in an indiscriminate massacre of the whites. They started on their work of destruction in the night. Nat. Turner had arranged with only five other slaves to meet him and begin their depredations. But finding at their place of meeting a sixth, he asked, with surprise, what he was there for. The man said: "My life is worth no more than that of others, and my liberty is dear to me." By morning a regular massacre was in progress. United States troops quelled it, with considerable bloodshed.

Political Riots in Philadelphia, October 4, 1833.

Election Riot New York City, April, 1834. The mob seized all the weapons in the gunshops and tried to capture the arsenel. Bloodshed followed.

Anti-Abolition Mob. — Hatred of Abolitionists culminated in a riot in New York, July 4, 1834. Houses of prominent Abolitionists and churches were broken open. Lives were endangered, and for a few days the mob seemed to have complete sway.

lishing a censorship of the press by which such documents could be excluded from Southern mails.

Academy at Canaan, N. H., was destroyed August 10, 1835, because negroes were among its pupils.

Boston Female Anti-Slavery Society was mobbed October 21, 1835, by 5,000 persons. Mr. Garrison was pulled through the streets with a rope around him. To save him the Mayor lodged him in jail. The New York Anti-Slavery Society was mobbed the same day, at Utica, N. Y.

Irish Mob in New York in 1835 attacked a militia company called the "O'Connell Guard." The riot continued three days. A prominent physician was

Stonemason's Mob. — In August, 1834, convicts employed as stonemasons in New York were mobbed by a band of marblecutters and others. Troops were on duty constantly for four days to preserve the peace.

Ursaline Convent, near Boston, was mobbed and burned in 1834. One of the nuns died from fright and exposure.

Canal Riot occurred between some Irish laborers in New Orleans, La., in 1834, to quell which troops were called out and blood was shed.

Postoffice at Charleston, S. C., mobbed, July 29, 1835, and anti-slavery documents seized and publicly burned. A bill was introduced into Congress estab-

killed, others were injured and property was destroyed.

Flour Mob in New York.—In Feb., 1837, owing to short crops, flour was scarce, and was held by a few capitalists at high prices. Several warehouses were broken open by a mob of about 6,000, and the flour dumped into the streets.

Bailey's Anti-Slavery Press at Cincinnati, O., was destroyed by a mob at midnight, July 12, 1836.

Pro-Slavery Mob at Alton, Ills., November 7, 1837, destroyed the press which had just been set up by Rev. Elijah P. Lovejoy, for the publication of an Abolition paper called the *Alton Observer.* This was the fourth press which had been destroyed, and in defending it Lovejoy was killed. No one was ever brought to justice for this murder.

Insurrection in Canada.—In 1837 a revolt and an effort to establish independence occurred among some disaffected Canadians, who seized and fortified Navy Island. They had some aid from sympathizers in New York. The Canadian loyalists set fire to the "Caroline," the supply steamer of the adventurers, and cutting her loose she drifted over Niagara Falls. The insurgents soon surrendered.

Pro-Slavery Mob burned Pennsylvania Hall, Philadelphia, May 17, 1838, because an Abolitionist meeting had been held therein. The riot lasted four days. Another Pro-Slavery mob occurred in Philadelphia, August 1, 1842. The colored people undertook to celebrate emancipation in the West Indies by a procession. A great mob assailed them, and for two days violence reigned. Negroes were beaten, a church, a hall and many houses were destroyed. The city authorities took no steps for their protection.

Dorr's Rebellion.—For two hundred years Rhode Island had been governed under a charter granted by Charles II., by which the right of suffrage was restricted to property-holders. In 1842 a party, wishing to abrogate the charter, elected Thomas M. Dorr, Governor.—Another party chose Samuel W. King.

Both parties claimed the election, and rival governments were organized, which led to a conflict of authority. The Dorrites were ultimately suppressed, and their leader convicted of treason and sentenced to imprisonment for life. He was pardoned in 1847.

"Weavers' Riots" in Philadelphia, January 11, 1843.

"Know-Nothing" Riot.—In May, 1844, the Native American party held a meeting in Kensington, a district of Philadelphia, in a market opposite a building filled with foreigners. From this building a gun was fired into the crowd in the market, which caused a riot that lasted two days. A Catholic female seminary, two churches and thirty buildings were demolished. Fourteen persons were killed and thirty-nine wounded. The authorities were powerless.—Martial law was proclaimed, and order was finally restored by United States troops.

Joe Smith, the Mormon prophet, was shot by a mob, June 27, 1844, at Carthage, Ill. Brigham Young was chosen his successor.

Anti-Rent Riots in New York.—In 1845, some of the tenants on the Van Rensselaer estates, near Albany, refused to pay rent, which consisted of only "a few bushels of wheat, three or four fat fowls, and a day's work with a team each year." The anti-renters considered it illegal, and disguised as Indians, tarred and feathered those who paid, and even killed the Sheriff. The trouble was suppressed by the military.

Revolt Against the United States Government.—Governor Bent and other Americans were murdered at Fernando de Taos, January 19, 1847.

Astor-Place Opera House Riots occurred May 7th and 10th, 1849. They were instigated by friends of Edwin Forrest, an American actor, to prevent the performances of W. E. Macready, an English actor, in retaliation for the alleged opposition by the latter to the performances of the former when he visited England. The mob stoned the Opera House, and had to be dispersed by the

War." Mobs of women renewed the riots along the Erie Railroad several times in the month of January, 1854.

Boston.—A riot occurred here on May 26th, 1854, caused by an attempt to arrest a fugitive slave. A deputy marshal was shot dead. United States troops from Rhode Island and the local militia were called out to sustain the government. The fugitive slave was finally returned to his master in Virginia without further violence.

Louisville, Ky.—An election riot occurred in Louisville, Kentucky, Aug. 6th, 1855, between Americans and foreigners.

Baltimore, Md. — Election riot in

militia, who killed twenty-two persons and wounded others.

Hoboken, N. J.—A riot occurred here May 26th, 1851, between Germans and New York "Short Boys." Several were killed.

Cleveland, O.—Homœpathic Medical College at Cleveland, Ohio, was destroyed by a mob, February 16th, 1852, because subjects for dissection had been taken from a cemetery.

Erie, Pa.—A mob of both men and women, at Erie, Pa., destroyed the railroad track, December 9-27, 1853. This was because the railway companies proposed a continuous gauge, to avoid transferring freight and passengers at Erie. It was known as the "Peanut

Baltimore October 8, 1856, in which nine persons were killed.

Mormon Difficulties.—In February, 1856, an armed Mormon force compelled Judge Drummond, of the United States District Court to adjourn sine die. The United States officials all fled the territory. Brigham Young openly defied the United States Government.

"Dead Rabbit" Riot in New York, July 4, 1857.—In resistance to legal measures to oust corrupt members of the police force, the rowdies of "Five Points," calling themselves "Dead Rabbits," created a riot in which eleven persons were killed.

Mormon Rebellion in Utah.—In 1857 President Buchanan appointed Alfred Cumming, Governor, vice, Brigham Young, removed, and sent an army of 2,500 men to repress lawlessness. The Mormons prepared for resistance and harassed the "invaders," cutting off their supply trains. Colonel Albert Sydney Johnston, the commanding officer, was compelled to go into winter quarters on Black's fork, near Fort Bridger.

Harper's Ferry, Va.—October 17, 1859, a negro insurrection took place here. John Brown, with a score of followers, crossed the Potomac at Harper's Ferry and entered Virginia, where he incited the slaves to take up arms against their masters. After a short time Brown was captured, tried for treason and found guilty. He bore his misfortune with the greatest composure, and when asked upon the scaffold to give a sign when he was ready, he answered, "I am always ready." He was executed at Charlestown, Va., in the midst of slaves and slave-owners—his countrymen—and now no countryman of his can look at his place of execution and call himself a slave owner or a slave.

Union Troops attacked in Baltimore.—April 19th, 1861, while the 6th Massachusetts regiment was passing through Baltimore on its way to Washington, it was attacked by a mob. A severe fight occurred in which three soldiers were killed, one mortally wounded and many others injured. The soldiers fired upon the mob, killing nine and wounding many.

Draft Riot in New York, July 13-15, 1863.—The conscription ordered by the United States Government began, and a riot raged for three days in New York York City. Buildings were destroyed, including a colored orphan asylum containing two hundred children. One thousand persons were killed and injured. Troops finally quelled the riot by severe measures. The city paid over $1,500,000 as indemnity for losses that occurred during the riot.

New Orleans.—A great riot occurred here on July 30, 1866, between whites and negroes, in which many were killed. It arose from difficulties concerning a State Convention held two years before.

Coal Riots in Pennsylvania, March 3, 1871.—Mr. Hoffman was killed and his house was blown up by miners.

Meridian, Miss.—A riot took place here on March 6, 1871, in which Judge Bramlette and two negroes were killed in the court-room, and others were killed outside.

Scranton, Pa.—Coal riots here had reached such magnitude that on April 7, 1871, Governor Geary ordered out the militia for their suppression.

Orangemen and Catholic riot occurred in New York on July 12, 1871. A parade of the former was attacked by a mob of Roman Catholic Irish. The militia defended them, and sixty-seven persons were killed and one hundred and thirty-seven wounded.

Ogdensburg.—A religious riot occurred in Ogdensburg, N. Y., on August 15th, 1871. A lecturer was assaulted and his audience dispersed by Roman Catholics for denouncing their faith.

Philadelphia.—An election riot occurred in Philadelphia, Pa., on October 10th, 1871, between negroes and white roughs, in which the latter attempted to

killed. A Congressional investigating committee made two reports: one charging the "White Leaguers" with instigating the riot, and the other denying it.

Chicago.—Rioting occurred in Chicago, Ill., on July 26, 1877. Police and troops were fighting the mob all day.— Fifteen persons were killed and many wounded. At San Francisco incendiary fires were started. At Philadelphia conflicts occurred. Trains began running on the Erie, the Delaware, Lackawana and Great Western, the Morris and Essex, and the American division of the Canada Southern Railroads.

destroy the *Press* newspaper office.— Four men were killed.

Holden, Mo.—April 24. 1872, Judge Stevenson and Messrs. Cline and Dutro, of Cass County, Mo., were taken from a train and hanged by a mob, for issuing fraudulent county bonds, with the proceeds of which they were escaping.

Vicksburg Riot, December 7, 1874, between whites and negroes, was caused by a request of the tax-payers to Peter Crosby, the Sheriff, to resign, he being charged with official abuses. Between fifty and one hundred negroes were

Salt Springs War, in El Paso County, Texas, December 14, 1877, between Americans and Mexicans, for possession of the springs. State troops interfered, but were beaten by the mob, who afterward shot Judge Howard, the agent of the mines, and two other Americans, and then departed.

Railroad Rioters.—On January 26, 1878, five leaders of the Pittsburg riots were convicted.

Sunday Riot in Chicago, between a pic-nic party and a military company, occurred June 22, 1879. Several were killed.

Murraysville, Pa.—A riot occurred on the 26th of November, 1883, at a natural-gas well in Murraysville, Westmoreland County, Pa., forty miles from Pittsburg. It was a bloody and desperate affair, and resulted in the death of one man and the wounding of several others. Milton Weston, a Chicago millionaire, who incited the riot, was tried, convicted and sentenced to five years hard labor in the penitentiary.

Cincinnati Riot.—March 28, 1884, one of the most serious and bloody riots ever witnessed in this country occurred in Cincinnati. It grew out of the dissatisfaction of the people with the verdict rendered in the case of William Berner, tried on the charge of murdering Wm. H. Kirk. The evidence against Berner was complete and positive, and the failure of the jury to convict him so outraged the feelings of the people that they attacked the public buildings. The Court-House was burned, and much other property was destroyed by the mob. It lasted three days. The entire State militia was called out to suppress the riot, and in the conflict that followed forty-five of the people were killed and one hundred and thirty-eight wounded.

EPIDEMICS AND PESTILENCE.

A Destructive Pestilence raged among the Indians of New England in 1616-18, and carried them off by hundreds.

Philadelphia.—Yellow fever broke out in Philadelphia in 1699 for the first time. In 1762 it again prevailed here with great severity. Again, in August, 1792, this scourge appeared, and lasted until about the 9th of November, during which time 4,000 persons died out of a population of 60,000, as many as 119 in a single day. More than one-half of the houses were closed, business was entirely suspended, and about one-third the inhabitants fled the city. The streets were almost entirely deserted, except a few persons who were in quest of a physician, a nurse, a bleeder, or the men who bury the dead. In 1793 it appeared again in a most violent form, causing great consternation, the suspension of business, etc. By October 20th, over 4,000 had died.

New York.—Yellow fever in New York in 1702. It was brought from St. Thomas and carried off six hundred persons, or about one-tenth of the population. It appeared again in New York in 1791, 1822 and 1833.

Atlantic Coast.—In 1797 yellow fever raged on the Atlantic coast.

Asiatic Cholera.—This epidemic first appeared in New York, June 27th, 1832. The number of deaths from the 1st of July to the middle of October, when the pestilence ceased, is reported at 4,000. During this time the population was reduced from 225,000, by removals, to 140,000. The ratio of deaths to cases was one to two, and the greatest number dying in one day was 311, on the 21st of July. The first case appeared in Philadelphia, July 5th, and the number of cases to September 13 was 2,314; the number of deaths 935. In Baltimore the number of deaths to September 29th was 710; in Norfolk, to September 11, 400; in Cincinnati, from May 1 to Aug. 7th, 1833, 307; in Nashville, from March

out at New Orleans in 1853, and 15,000 lives were lost in the coast cities.

Cholera in the United States in 1854, and 2,500 persons died in New York City.

Colorado Potato Bug.—In 1859 this pest began to attract public attention, as the beetle was migrating through Kansas and Nebraska. In 1865 it crossed the Mississippi, and in 1875 it reached the Atlantic seaboard. No effective means have been found for its eradication.

Grasshopper Ravages occurred in 1864 to a greater extent than ever before in the west. Hundreds of farmers lost their entire crops.

27 to July 12th, 27 whites and 50 blacks. The disease appeared in New Orleans October 27, 1832, and raged with great severity among the blacks, occasioning a pecuniary loss to slave owners of nearly $4,000,000. General Scott had nine companies of artillery at Chicago attacked with the scourge and broken up. In 1849 this disease again raged throughout the United States and Mexico, with fatal violence. St. Louis and Cincinnati each lost 6,000 persons.

"Cattle Disease," or pleuro-pneumonia, was introduced into the United States by a sick cow from Germany in 1843.

New Orleans.—Yellow fever broke

Cholera destroyed about 20,000 lives in 1865 in the United States.

Southern States. — Yellow fever raged in the South in 1867. There were twenty deaths a day in New Orleans alone. It appeared again in the South in June, 1873.

New York.—August 12th, 1872, the Spanish iron-clad Numanci arrived at New York with yellow fever on board.

Epizootic.—In October, 1872, 40,000 horses in New York were attacked in ten days, and 13,000 in Brooklyn, causing an almost entire suspension of public conveyances. It spread all over the United States. This disease is an old one. It was known in the third century before Christ.

Louisiana.—Yellow fever raged in Louisiana, and on September 17th, 1873, there were not enough well persons in some places to care for the sick.

Savannah, Ga. — Twenty-two to twenty-seven deaths per day occurred here in September, 1876, from yellow fever. As many as two thousand were afflicted with the disease at one time, and one hundred and eighty new cases were reported in a single day.

Florida. — Yellow fever raged in Florida, September, 1877, chiefly among the negroes at Fernandina.

Memphis.—Yellow fever broke out in Memphis, Tenn., July 9, 1879.

Southern States. — Yellow fever raged in the South in August, 1878, causing 7,000 deaths. The region of the Mississippi river suffered most. Neglect of sanitary precautions caused its rapid spread. Relief societies were organized North and West, and past animosities were forgotten. Money and nurses were freely sent to aid the sick and dying, but villages and cities were almost depopulated, and commerce stopped. Not until frost came did the plague cease.

CRIMES, TRIALS AND PUNISHMENT.

Columbus was sent in chains to Spain in October, 1500, by Bobadilla, who had been sent out by the government to investigate charges against him. He reached Spain November 23d, 1500, where the spectacle of his chains produced a reaction. The sovereigns restored him to liberty, received him with honor, and promised to remove Bobadilla for his injustice.

Plymouth Punishment. — In the month of March, 1621, John Billington spoke with disrespect of the lawful authority of Captain Standish, for which, in town meeting, he was sentenced to have his neck and heels tied together.

First Execution in New England. In October, 1630, John Billington was condemned and executed at Plymouth, Mass., for the murder of John Newcomer. In 1638 three Englishmen were executed in Plymouth for killing an Indian.

Benjamin Franklin Robbed.—In 1738 Franklin advertised for the following stolen property, viz.: "Broadcloth breeches lined with leather, sogathee coat lined with silk, and fine homespun linen shirts."

Benedict Arnold's Treason.—On September 23d, 1780, at Tarrytown-on-the-Hudson, the British officer, John

Andre, was halted by three militiamen, named David Williams, John Paulding, and Isaac Van Wart. He exhibited a pass as John Anderson from Arnold. He was, however, searched, and in his boots were found papers detailing the condition of West Point, and exposing Arnold's treachery. Arnold, learning of the capture, fled to the British ship of war Vulture, in the Hudson. He received gold and emoluments from the British, but was ever after held in contempt by all honorable men.

Trades Unions.—In 1806 eight persons were tried in the courts and fined $8.00 each and costs on the charge of combining to increase wages, and to prevent non-union men from working,

Helen Jewett was murdered in New York, April 9, 1836, by Richard P. Robinson.

Samuel Adams was murdered in New York City in September, 1841, by John C. Colt, a brother of Samuel Colt, who invented the revolver. Colt committed suicide in the Tombs the day before he would have been hung.

Parkman and Webster Murder. November 23, 1849, Dr. Parkman, of Boston, was murdered by Prof. John W. Webster, in the Cambridge Medical College, for which he was hung.

California Vigilance Committee was organized in 1851, because thieves and murderers were committing atrocious crimes "unwhipt of justice,"

and establishing arbitrary rules over workmen.

Aaron Burr's Treason.—In 1806 Burr's military preparations and western expeditions excited suspicions that he was plotting to dismember the government and establish an empire west of the Alleghanies. He was arrested on the Tombigbee river, State of Alabama, in February, 1807, on the charge of treason. He was tried at Richmond, Va., but the testimony showed that his probable design was an invasion of Mexican provinces, and then to establish an independent government. He was acquitted.

Richard Lawrence, while insane, tried to assault President Jackson, Jan. 30th, 1835.

through connivance of officers and judges. After several executions law and order reigned and lives and property became secure. The Vigilance Committee was reorganized again in 1856 because of the alarming prevalence of crime. Thousands of the leading citizens were members of it, and a number of executions took place. Criminals were less audacious thereafter.

Burdell Murder.—January 30, 1857, Mrs. Cunningham was tried for the murder of Dr. Harvey Burdell, at his own residence. She was acquitted, although the evidence indicated strongly that she murdered him to secure his property through a pretended marriage with him in New York City.

Mountain Meadow Massacre.—This foul deed of 1857 was charged upon the Mormons, April 18, 1872, by Philip Klingon Smith, of Nevada, an ex-Mormon Bishop.

Hon. Daniel E. Sickles, on February 27, 1859, killed Philip Barton Key, District Attorney for the District of Columbia, in Washington, for alleged intimacy with his wife. Intense excitement prevailed. Sickles was tried and acquitted. He afterward became Major General in the United States army and then Minister to Spain.

Assassination of President Lincoln.—On the evening of April 14th, 1865, at Ford's Theater, Washington, D. C., John Wilkes Booth, an actor, stole south of Fredericksburg. Refusing to surrender, he was shot by Boston Corbett, and dragged from the burning building to die.

Rewards for Supposed Conspirators.—May 2, 1865, President Johnson. by proclamation, offered $100,000 for Jefferson Davis, $25,000 each for Jacob Thompson, C. C. Clay, George N. Saunders and Beverly Tucker, and $10,000 for William C. Cleary, upon the supposition that they conspired for the assassination of the President and Secretary Seward.

Execution of Booth's Accomplices. David E. Harold, George A. Atzerott, Lewis Payne Powell and Mrs. Mary E. Surratt, convicted by a military commission of complicity in the assassination of

into the President's private box unnoticed and shot him in the back of the head, then, leaping over the front of the box upon the stage, he shouted: "*Sic semper tyrannis,*" and in the confusion escaped into the outer darkness. Mr. Lincoln died at twenty-two minutes past seven o'clock the next morning.

Secretary Seward's Murder Attempted.—At the hour when the President was shot, Lewis Payne Powell burst into the bed chamber of Mr. Seward, who was ill, sprang upon his couch and stabbed him nigh unto death and made his escape in the night.

Death of Booth.—April 26th, 1865, Booth the assassin, was found concealed in a barn at Garrett's farm, twenty miles President Lincoln, were hung, July 7th, 1865. Michael O'Laughlin, Samuel A. Mudd and Samuel Arnold were sentenced to hard labor for life upon the Dry Tortugas, and Edward Spangler to hard labor for six years.

Henry Wirz, the commandant at Andersonville Prison, was tried by military commission and hung for cruelty to Union prisoners, November 10, 1865.

Jefferson Davis, ex-President of the Southern Confederacy, after two years imprisonment in Fortress Monroe, was bailed in the sum of $100,000, May 13, 1867. Horace Greeley was one of his bondsmen.

Reno Gang.—In 1868 several bold robberies were committed in Indiana by a band led by the Reno brothers, against whom no conviction could be had. They robbed an express car at Jeffersonville, Ind., of $90,000, on May 22. A second attempt was made July 10, but the company being prepared, captured several of the outlaws. On July 20, while being taken to Jackson county for trial, a vigilance committee took them from the train and hung them. In October the three Reno brothers and an accomplice were arrested in Canada, brought back to the United States, and placed in jail at New Albany. Seventy-five vigilants broke into the jail and hung them in the corridors. This broke up the gang.

Nathan Murder.—On July 29, 1870, Benjamin Nathan, a wealthy New York

Mulberry Creek, Ark.—November 26th, 1881.—Two youug ruffians named Joseph Forbish and William Chenoweth, outraged and murdered a child four years old at Mulberry Creek, Ark. They were arrested, and having attempted to escape, were shot dead by their captors.

Lake City, Ark.—On December 15, 1871, a band of negroes took possession of Lake City, Ark,, and shot three residents, whom they charged with murdering a negro lawyer.

Fisk Tragedy.—January 7th, 1872, James Fisk, Jr., was shot by Edward S. Stokes, because of a quarrel about a woman known as Josie Mansfield, who was intimate with both men. Fisk died, and Stokes was sentenced, after trial, to

citizen, was mysteriously murdered in his own house. Notwithstanding the heavy rewards offered, the perpetrator has never been found.

Kensington National Bank, of Philadelphia, robbed of $100,000, Feb. 3, 1871, by thieves disguised as policemen.

Express Robbery in St. Louis, Mo., July 25th, 1871. A driver of the United States Express Company was gagged and robbed of $90,000.

Tweed Ring in New York.—Legal operations against this gang of thieves began October 23, 1871, by the arrest of William M. Tweed, who gave bail for $1,000,000. His confederates mostly fled.

be hung, but obtaining a new trial, was sent to Sing Sing prison until 1876.— James Fisk, Jr., was born in Vermont, April 1, 1835. He began life as a hotel waiter, and afterward was a pedler, then salesman, and finally partner in the Boston house of Jordan, Marsh & Co. They bought his interest, and he next appeared in Wall street in connection with Daniel Drew, who had a great contest with C. Vanderbilt, for possession of the Erie Railway. Fisk and Jay Gould finally captured it, and used its revenues for their own ends, boldly and unsorupulously plundering it of millions. The audacity of the pair was unbounded.— Together they engineered the "Black Friday" in September, 1869. Fisk was manager of two lines of Long Island Sound steamers and Colonel of the 9th regiment of the New York State Guard.

William M. Tweed, Mayor A. Oakley Hall, Comptroller R. B. Connelly, Nathaniel Sands and others were indicted by a Grand Jury in New York, February 10th, 1872, for embezzling the city's funds.

Celina, O., July 8, 1872.—Absalom and Jacob Kimball and Alexander McLeod, who outraged and murdered a young girl named Secor, were taken from jail at Celina, Ohio, by a mob, and Absalom Kimball and McLeod were hanged at the scene of their crime.

Blackstone National Bank robbery, at Uxbridge, Mass., July 12, 1872.

Des Moines, Ia.—Train wreckers removed a rail and threw the California mail train from the track, 60 miles west of Des Moines, July 21, 1873. The desperadoes killed the engineer and escaped with three tons of bullion and considerable cash.

Tweed Ring.—William M. Tweed was found guilty of defrauding the New York City treasury on 204 counts, Nov. 19, 1873, and sentenced to pay a fine of $12,550, and to the penitentiary for 12 years. On the 26th of the same month James H. Ingersoll and John D. Farrington, confederates of William M. Tweed, in robbing the New York City treasury, were convicted and sentenced to State Prison. Henry W. Genet was

Burglars compelled Charles Wesson, the teller, to open the safe, from which they took $13,000.

Third National Bank, Baltimore, Md., was robbed of $500,000, August 18, 1872.

Judge C. G. Barnard, of the Supreme Court of New York, was impeached for high crimes, removed from the bench, and declared ineligible to ever hold office in the State, August 18, 1872.

Saratoga County Bank, at Waterford, New York, was robbed by burglars of $500,000, October 14, 1872. Binding and gagging the Cashier's family, they compelled him, by threats, to divulge the combination of the vault lock.

convicted of fraud on the New York City treasury, December 19, 1873. On the 22d he escaped from the Sheriff and was not recaptured.

Beecher's Trial began January 11, 1874. The suit was instituted by Theodore Tilton, upon a charge of improper relations between the defendant and Mrs. Tilton. It lasted six months and resulted in a disagreement of the jury, who were out seven days, and stood nine for acquittal and three for conviction.

Boy Murderer. — At Dorchester, Mass., young Edward Pomeroy shockingly murdered the lad Horace Mullen, April 22, 1874.

Charlie Ross abducted, July 1, 1874,.

in Germantown, Penna. He was about four years old. Two men in a buggy stole him to obtain a ransom of $20,000. They were both killed in burglarizing the house of Judge Van Brunt, at Bay Ridge, L. I., and the secret of the boy's whereabouts died with them.

Theodore Tilton was arrested on July 28th, 1874, on the charge of slander against H. W. Beecher.

Kansas.—A vigilance committee in Kansas hung three horse thieves, July 30, 1874.

Edward Spangler, noted as one of the assassins of President Lincoln, died near Baltimore, Md., February 14, 1875. He was 55 years of age.

Mutiny at Sea, on the American schooner Jefferson Borden, from New Orleans to Liverpool, in March, 1875.— Three sailors killed the two mates and tried to seize the vessel, but were foiled by the vigilance of the Captain's wife. The mutineers were confined, and on reaching America tried and convicted of murder and mutiny.

William M. Tweed was released from the Penitentiary, June 21, 1875, but in default of $3,000,000 bail upon civil suits against him, was committed to Ludlow Street Jail. He escaped from the custody of his keepers, while out for a drive, December 4, 1875.

Northampton, Mass., bank robbery of $750,000, occurred January 25, 1876. The robbery was committed between three and four o'clock in the morning by a gang of masked men, who entered the house of the cashier, bound and gagged seven members of the family, and forced Mr. Whitlessey to give up the key to the bank vault and disclose the combination.

Winslow, the Forger.—January 28, 1876, discovery was made that Rev. E. D. Winslow, an eloquent Boston clergyman, had committed forgeries for hundreds of thousands of dollars. He fled to Rotterdam and London, but owing to technicalities in the extradition treaty with England, he escaped.

Younger Brothers atttempted to rob the Northfield, Minn., bank, Sept. 7, 1876, at midday. There were eight highwaymen. Three of the robbers entered, while five remained outside the bank to defend themselves from the citizens who came upon them. The cashier refused to open the safe and was shot. The citizens had now begun to fire upon them, and in the affray two of the highwaymen were killed. The rest escaped, but vigorous pursuit was made without success till the last of the month, when four of the criminals stopped at a house to secure food. The citizens of a neighboring place named Medalia were aroused, and followed the robbers to a marsh, where they were taken after a conflict in which one of them was killed and the other three wounded.

"Boss" Tweed was arrested Sept.

8, 1876, at Vigo, Spain, where he had just arrived from Cuba. He was returned to New York and lodged in Ludlow Street Jail.

General Babcock was tried at Washington, D. C., for complicity in a safe burglary conspiracy.

Edward S. Stokes, having served out his term of imprisonment in Auburn State Prison, New York, for the killing of James Fisk, Jr., was released October 28, 1876.

Springfield, Ills.—Grave robbers made an unsuccessful attempt to steal the remains of President Lincoln from

Parlan, one of Pinkerton's detectives.

Jail Delivery in Rio Grande City, Texas, August 12, 1877, by twenty armed men from Mexico, who released the criminals and escaped.

Big Springs, Neb.—Train robbery at Big Springs, Neb., September 18th, 1877, by which the Pacific express train lost $75,000.

"Boss" Tweed's Confession, Oct. 10th, 1877, occupied eighteen columns of the New York *Herald.* He detailed his methods of corrupt legislation, implicating a great number of legislators and others, and offered to turn State's evi-

the vault, at Springfield, Illinois, Nov. 7, 1876.

Streator, Ill.—Wholesale poisoning by arsenic, which was put into the food of miners at Streator, Ills, caused sixty deaths, May 14, 1877. Strikers were suspected.

Tweed Ring.—The city of New York sued Peter B. Sweeney, one of Tweed's allies, for $7,000,000, and compromised it for $4,000,000, June 6, 1877.

"Molly McGuires" Hung.—June 21, 1877, ten of this gang were executed for murder, at Pottsville, Pa. Evidence to convict was obtained by James Mc-

dence if released. His offer was not accepted. February 13, 1878, judgment was entered against him in New York for $10,857,197.09.

Dexter, Me.—Cashier Barron, of the Dexter, Maine, Savings Bank, was murdered, February 22d, 1878, by unknown persons, for whom it was supposed that he refused to open the safe. The robbers got only $100.

William M. Tweed, famous for the enormity of his frauds, died April 12th, 1878, in Ludlow Street Jail, New York. He was born in New York, April 3, 1823. He was first a chair-maker, then a lawyer, a city and State office-holder, a member of Congress, a State Senator, and finally Commissioner of Public Works, in which position he and his "ring" stole vast sums of public money. On October 28, 1871, Charles O'Connor began the series of suits against him in behalf of the citizens of New York, which culminated in his downfall and incarceration as a felon.

Manhattan Bank Robbery in New York occurred October 29, 1878.— Masked men entered the bank in day light and carried off $11,000 in cash and $2,700,000 in securities.

A. T. Stewart's Body was stolen from its vault in St. Mark's church yard, New York, November 6, 1878. His ex-

mand and promise to raise her to life on the third day. He and some of his followers defended his act. He was committed to an insane asylum.

Trial of Talmage, the Presbyterian preacher of Brooklyn, May 2, 1879, for immoral conduct in inducing a party to subscribe a large sum for his Tabernacle, with the understanding that he should never pay it, but allow the use of his name to influence others to subscribe. The fact was admitted, but he was acquitted of intentional wrong by a vote of 24 to 20.

Indecent Literature. — June 5th, 1879, D. M. Bennett, of New York, was sentenced to a fine of $300 and thirteen months hard labor in the penitentiary

ecutor, Judge Hilton, refused to pay the amount demanded by the robbers, viz.: $250,000. It has never been recovered.

"Molly Maguires" Executed.— January 14, 1879, McDonnell and Sharp were hung at Mauch Chunk, Pa., about one minute before Governor Hartranft's messenger bearing a reprieve reached the scene.

Assassination of Edwin Booth was attempted at McVicar's Theater, in Chicago, while he was playing Richard III., April 23, 1879, by a lunatic named Gray, who was sent to an asylum.

Religious Fanatic's Crime.—May 1, 1879, Charles F. Freeman, a Second Adventist, killed his daughter under the delusion of obedience to a divine com-

for sending immoral publications thro' the United States mails.

Mrs. Hull was murdered in New York by Chastine Cox, a negro, for her jewelry, June 11, 1879. He was afterward executed.

West Point Outrage.—April 6th, 1880, J. C. Whittaker, a colored cadet, was found bound and bruised in his room. He said it was done by masked men, presumably on account of his color. A court of inquiry reached no satisfactory conclusion, the Recorder deciding that he did it himself. He was, however, cleared by a court-martial, and the outcome was that General Schofield was removed from the head of the Academy and Gen. Howard appointed in his stead.

Wolf in Sheep's Clothing.—On February 20, 1880, Rev. Edward Cowley, manager of the "Shepherd's Fold," a New York institution for rearing orphans, was sentenced to a fine of $200 and one year's imprisonment, for starving and abusing the little ones.

"Billy, the Kid," gang of outlaws, in New Mexico, was broken up by the authorities, December 27, 1880. He and his followers had made themselves a great terror. Two were killed and four lodged in prison. At first the enraged citizens seemed determined to lynch them, but this step was prevented.

buried in Lake View Cemetery, Cleveland, Ohio, September 26, 1881. On the occasion business was suspended and memorial services were held all over the country.

Spotted Tail, a head chief of the Sioux tribe, was murdered by another Indian, July 5, 1881.

Charles J. Guiteau's trial for the murder of President Garfield, commenced November 14, 1881, in the District Supreme Court, at Washington, D. C. On January 25, 1882, he was found guilty of murder and sentenced to be hung. On June 30, of the same year, he

President Garfield Assassinated.—An attempt was made to assassinate President James A. Garfield in the city of Washington, D. C., July 2, 1881, by a disappointed office-seeker named Chas. J. Guiteau. The President was in the the waiting-room of the Baltimore and Potomac Railroad Depot, about to take the train for New York, when his assailant approached him from behind and fired two shots, one of which passed through his coat sleeve and the other entered his body. Guiteau was immediately arrested and conveyed to jail.—President Garfield died at Elberon, N. J., on September 19, 1881, from the effects of the wound received. He was fifty years of age. His remains were

was executed in the corridor of the jail-yard, Washington, D. C.

Assassination of Captain Thomas Phelan.—January 9, 1885, Richard Short, an alleged dynamiter, assaulted Captain Thomas Phelan, in the office of O'Donovan Rossa, New York City. Phelan received numerous severe cuts, and for some time it was doubtful whether he would survive his wounds, but he finally recovered. Short was not injured. It was claimed that Phelan was assaulted for exposing, in a Kansas city paper, some of the secrets of the dynamiters. Short was tried and acquitted on the ground of self-defense. A great deal of dissatisfaction was expressed by the people and the press at the verdict.

FRAUDS, DEFALCATIONS, ETC.

"Mississippi Bubble." — In 1717 the French Government granted to John Laws' "Company of the West" the exclusive commerce of Louisiana, and a monopoly of the Canada free trade for twenty-five years. In 1720, by bad management and unscrupulous dealings, this scheme brought ruin upon thousands, including Laws himself. He had issued an enormous amount of shares and bonds, which sold during the excitement at fabulous prices, but with the loss of public confidence, suddenly became worthless. Several thousand immigrants had, however, settled in Louisiana through Laws' influence, and the colony raged crowd destroyed the machinery.

Samuel Swartout, Collector of the port of New York, was discovered, on March 29, 1838, to be a defaulter to the United States in the sum of $1,225,705, which he had sunk in Wall Street speculations.

Insurance Frauds.—In 1853 numerous bogus mutual insurance companies failed, swindling their patrons out of hundreds of thousands of dollars.

John B. Floyd, Secretary of War, was indicted, January 28th, 1861, by the Grand Jury of Washington, for defrauding the government. He fled to Virginia.

was firmly established and became a royal province.

"Yazoo Fraud."—This fraud was perpetrated by the Georgia Legislature in 1795, in selling the Western lands belonging to that State. It produced great excitement, and after much controversy the sales were expunged from the State records, but the United States courts subsequently declared the claims of the purchasers valid.

Perpetual Motion.—In 1812 one Redhiffer claimed to have invented it, but refused to permit his apparatus to be tested. Robert Fulton was one of his visitors and detected the fraud. An old man in an upper room turning a crank was the motive power. The en-

Shoddy.—In 1861 some contractors supplied clothing to the regiments made of refuse matter, pressed into a cloth, which was fine in appearance, but would not wear because it had no strength.— From this originated "shoddy."

Ketchum Forgery.—A great forgery of $2,000,000, by one Ketchum, of New York, was discovered August 14th, 1865.

Credit Mobilier of America, which was organized as a banking institution, sold its charter in January, 1867, to the company which proposed to build the Union Pacific Railroad. Its stock was increased to $3,750,000.

United States Government defaulter.—September 9th, 1870, Major L.

Hodge, Assistant Paymaster General, confessed that he had robbed the United States of $500,000.

Philadelphia Defalcation. — On November 2d, 1871, City Treasurer Mercer and C. T. Yerks, banker, were arrested for stealing $478,000 city funds.— They were pardoned by Gov. Geary, September 26th, 1872.

Jay Gould was arrested November 22d, 1872, for swindling the Erie Railway Company out of $9,726,555, but was bailed in $1,000,000. On December 17, of the same year, he compromised the claim of the Erie Railway Company by restoring about $9,000,000 "*for the sake of peace.*"

Custom-House Frauds.—November 29, 1872, the United States Government recovered $480,000 from Weld & Co., East India merchants, who were charged with defrauding the customs.

Credit Mobilier Exposure.—On February 27, 1873, a Congressional committee of investigation damaged the reputation of a number of public men. Great frauds in constructing the Pacific Railroads were unearthed, and Oakes Ames (the principal manager), and Jas. Brooks (a Government Director of the Railroad), were censured by the House of Representatives, of which both were members

"*Salary Grab.*"—March 3d, 1873, Congress passed a law increasing the pay of the members of the Legislative, Executive and Judicial Departments of the Government, and providing that the increased pay for Senators and Representatives should begin with the first session of that Congress, which gave the Senators and Representatives two years back pay. Great indignation was caused among the people. Some never drew it, others drew it and returned it, but most of the members and officials pocketed the amount.

F. L. Taintor, Cashier of the Atlantic National Bank, New York, was arrested April 26th, 1873, he being a defaulter for $400,000.

New York, November 26th, 1873.— James H. Ingersoll and John D. Farrington, convicted of defrauding the city treasury of New York, and sentenced, Ingersoll to four years; Farrington in the Court of Oyer and Terminer, to one year and six months in the State Prison.

Revenue Frauds were charged against Jordan, Marsh & Co., of Boston, and their books were seized by the United States officers, December 27, 1873.

Emma Mine Scandal.—In 1874 the British stockholders discovered that the stock sold them by one Albert Grant, an English agent for the Emma mine, was worthless. Gen. Robert C. Schenck, United States Minister to England, being one of the Trustees, was largely blamed.

Pacific Mail Investigation. — In February, 1875, the United States Senate Judiciary Committee reported that the subsidy granted by Congress to this line had been procured by the corrupt use of great sums of money among its members. The contract was thereupon abrogated by a heavy vote.

Whiskey Ring.—On May 17th, 1875, United States Treasury Agents made a sudden raid upon "crooked" whiskey distillers in Chicago, Milwaukee and St. Louis. The fact was revealed that high officials of the Government were in complicity with the "Ring," which was extensive and powerful, but, by Secretary Bristow's efforts, it was completely broken up. In February, 1876, General E. O. Babcock, Private Secretary to President Grant, was tried at St. Louis for complicity in these whiskey frauds,

Smuggled Diamonds and Jewelry, valued at $20,000, were seized at New York by Custom-House officers from the person of a woman, October 14, 1876.

Philadelphia.—Fraud confessed on September 22d, 1877, by John S. Morton, President of the West Philadelphia Passenger Railway, who acknowledged to the over issue of 10,000 shares, valued at $1,000,000, since 1870.

Gilman Forgeries.—The forgeries of W. C. Gilman, New York, were discovered October 2d, 1877. Two certificates of the Atlantic Mutual Insurance Company's scrip had been raised from $100 to $10,000 each. He confessed to having carried on similar frauds for two years, and to the amount of $247,000.—

but the evidence was insufficient to convict him.

Keeley Motor was brought to public notice in 1875. The inventor claimed that he could obtain a power of 50,000 pounds to the square inch by condensed air, and that it would supersede steam. He has never yet demonstrated this.

Washington Ring.—In February, 1876, exposures were made to Congress of the methods of "Boss" Shephard and his ring in improving Washington City, D. C., and legislation was had which put a stop to them.

W. W. Belknap, Secretary of War, was impeached by the House of Representatives, March 2d, 1876, for official misconduct and corruption.

He was sentenced to Sing Sing for five years.

"Petrified Man" from Colorado. In March, 1878, one who helped to manufacture this "stone man" made public the fact that it was cast in a lime kiln at Elkland, Penna., by George Hull, the originator of the "Cardiff Giant," at the expense of P. T. Barnum, the showman.

Great Defalcations in Massachusetts.—April 10, 1878, it became known that S. A. Chase, Treasurer of the Union Mills, Fall River, Mass., had robbed the company of half a million dollars.— Within a fortnight George T. Hathaway, treasurer of another large corporation, was discovered to be a defaulter for a million. Both men were sent to State prison.

Pacific Mills Defalcation. — At Lawrence, Mass., May 10, 1878, George F. Waterman, Assistant Paymaster of the Pacific Mills, was found to have stolen $100,000. He was sent to State Prison for twelve years.

New York.—Defalcation of $100,000 in the Bank of North America, New York, was confessed, February 5, 1878, by A. M. Turney, teller. The crime had been kept secret nine years.

Fall River, Mass.—Defalcation in the Manufacturers' Gas Company, Fall River, Mass., September 7th, 1878, by Charles P. Stickney, a leading citizen and ex-State Senator, for over fifty thousand dollars. He was sent to State Prison.

Chicago, Ills. — Defalcation in the Pullman Palace Car Company, at Chicago, Ills., August 17th, 1878, Charles W. Angell had robbed the Company of $120,000.

Evils of Speculation.—In August, 1879, George B. Durfee, ex-Treasurer of the Mechanics' Mill, at Fall River, Mass., was found to be a defaulter; also Walter Paine, Treasurer of the American Linen Mill, and George H. Eddy, Treasurer of the Flint Mill; James W. Wilbur, at Lawrence, and Wm. M. Roach, Cashier Citizens' National Bank at Washington. These all speculated with other people's money.

Missouri. — State Treasurer Gates, of Missouri, was found to be a defaulter in the sum of $343,000, in February, 1879.

War Upon Lotteries by the Post-office Department.—In November, 1879, an order was issued forbidding the payment of money or delivery of registered letters to persons connected with these swindles, it being evident that thousands of persons were being cheated out of their money.

Halifax Award of $5,500,000 to England was made upon the basis of manufactured evidence, according to charges made by Prof. H. T. Hinds, an eminent Canadian scholar. He stated that the facts did not justify such an award, and demanded an investigation.

Ladie's Deposit Company, of Boston, was shown to be a swindle, October 16, 1880, and the managers, Mrs. Sarah E. Howe and Miss Julia A. Gould, were arrested. They induced large deposits by paying 8 per cent. per month out of the depositor's own money.

Marine National Bank, of New York, suspended May 6, 1884, involving the failure of the banking house of Grant & Ward, of which firm ex-President Grant was a member. The failure of the latter firm brought to light one of the most audacious frauds ever practiced, by which ex-President Grant, Colonel Fred Grant and U. S. Grant, Jr., with many other prominent and wealthy men, were innocent sufferers, by the crafty and fraudulent misrepresentations of Ferdinand Ward. Ward's plan of operations was to represent that he had profitable contracts from the government, and was able to pay 30 and 40 per cent. on the investments he made. He practically done no business, but rendered sufficient dividends from the money borrowed to keep the confidence of his victims, and appropriated the remainder to his personal use. He was assisted in his schemes by James D. Fish, President of the Marine National Bank. Fish was tried and found guilty of fraud, and Ward is now in the Tombs prison awaiting trial.

TEMPERANCE MOVEMENTS.

Sunday Liquor Law.—In April, 1641, a law was passed by the authorities of New Amsterdam, forbidding the "tapping of beer during divine service, or after 10 o'clock at night," because "complaints are made that some of our inhabitants have commenced to tap beer during divine service, and use a small kind of measure, which is in contempt of our religion, and must ruin the State." The penalty for violating the law was twenty-five guilders, or ten dollars for each offense, besides the forfeiture of the beer for the use of the Attorney-General.

Maryland.—Drunkenness was punished in Maryland, in 1642, by a fine of one hundred pounds of tobacco, and swearing by a fine of five pounds.

License Law—Massachusetts passed the first one in 1646.

Temperance Meeting at Sillery, near Quebec, was held in 1648. A converted Algonquin chief was the principal speaker, who exhorted his people to total abstinence. This was the first temperance meeting in America, and it originated with the Catholic priests.

Brandy-Sellers Excommunicated. In 1660 Vicar General Laval, of Canada, issued an excommunication against those in the liquor traffic with Indians.

Notwithstanding this, and the whipping of one offender and shooting of another, prohibition could not be enforced.

Drunkards Posted.—In 1694, the Legislature of Massachusetts caused the names of drunkards in several towns, to be posted up in public houses, and imposed a fine for giving them entertainment.

Indian Potest Against Rum.—In April, 1730, Governor Thomas, at Philadelphia, received a petition from "The Chieffs of ye Delaware," that the business might be stopped, as rum had caused some recent outrages upon white men.

Georgia.—Importation of rum was forbidden by the Trustees of Georgia in 1733. They however established alehouses and provided for wines and for brewing beer, because these drinks would be more wholesome and refreshing to the people. It was intended to make a temperance colony of Georgia. But violations of this occured even among the officers of the colony.—There were constant evasions of the law till its appeal took place in 1742.

New York.—In 1772 intemperance was punished in New York by compelling the offenders to "drink three quarts of warm water with salt enough to act as an emetic, and lamp oil to act as a a purge." This dose killed a drunken negro.

Litchfield, Conn.—The first temperance association in the United States was formed in Litchfield, Conn., in 1789, where two hundred farmers agreed not to use distilled liquor in doing their farm work that season.

Total Abstinence Pledge.—The first one used in America was drawn up by Micajah Pendleton, of Nelson county, Virginia, in 1800.

Temperance Society.—The first in America was organized in 1808, in Moreau, Saratoga county, New York, by Dr. Billy J. Clarke and Rev. Lebbeus Armstrong. Forty-seven male members signed the pledge. A fine of twenty-five cents was imposed for every violation of the pledge. It prohibited rum, gin, whisky, wine, or any distilled liquors whatever. It did not, therefore, go as far as a total abstinence pledge of the present day.

"The Well Conducted Farm" was the title of an essay by Dr. Justin Edwards, published in 1825, detailing the operations of a large farm in Worcester county, Mass., on which no intoxicating drinks were used.

"American Temperance Union" was organized at Boston in 1826, based on Micajah Pendleton's pledge, which permitted the use of cider, wines and malt liquors, but required total abstinence from distilled liquors. In six years 4,000 societies were organized, with which 20,000 families united, and the distillation of liquor nearly ceased.

Temperance Convention.—A National Convention was held in May, 1833, at Philadelphia, Penna. Four hundred delegates from twenty-one States were present. It was " *Resolved*, That the trade in ardent spirits is morally wrong and ought to be abandoned."

Total Abstinence " was voted d. .n at the annual meeting, in 1833, of the American Temperance Union. The moderate use of wines, cider and malt liquors were permitted.

American Congressional Temperance Society was formed in Washington in 1833. Lewis Cass, Secretary of War, was chosen President. The use of ardent spirits in the army was prohibited.

in the year 1835 by the American Temperance Society, and in 1836 the American Temperance Union was organized on this basis, and since then "total abstinence" has become the bulwark of all temperance societies.

Massachusetts' Fifteen Gallon Law. In April, 1838, a law was enacted by the Legislature which prohibited the sale of alcoholic liquors except by druggists and physicians, and then in not less than fifteen gallons.

Evasion of the Fifteen Gallon Law. In April, 1838, at a militia muster in Massachusetts a man exhibited a striped pig at ten cents admission. The persons who entered found a pig with stripes painted around his body, and also found

Teetotalism originated in England in 1834. A member of a Lancashire Society said: "Tee" is a provincialism for "going the whole figure." He said: "We must have a teetotal abstinence from every kind of drink that will produce drunkenness, if we wish to get rid of drunkenness itself." This saying gave the temperance cause a new watchword. The idea was adopted this year by many American societies, which changed the words "ardent spirits" in their former pledges, to "intoxicating liquors."— Much opposition at first arrayed itself against this principle. But it was adopted

a free drink. Nobody could prevent a man from giving away liquor, if he chose.

"Washingtonians."—April 2, 1840, six boon companions met in Chase's tavern, Baltimore, for their customary carousal. They were William K. Mitchell, tailor; John F. Hoss, carpenter; David Anderson, blacksmith; George Steers, wheelwright; James McCurly, coachman; and Archibald Campbell, silverplater.— It had been their practice to drink together. This night they were unusually sober, and seemed to delay calling for liquors. At last they found that each

was distressed about his habit of becoming intoxicated. In a short time they agreed to band themselves together into a "Washington Temperance Society," whose principle should be teetotalism from all which can intoxicate. They began to work among their companions, and by simple power of earnest effort, soon found hundreds joining their ranks. Thus originated one of the most wonderful temperance movements known to the world.

Anniversary of the Washingtonian Society in 1841. One thousand reformed drunkards marched in procession.

Woman's Temperance Crusade, February 10, 1874, began in Ohio by the efforts of Christian ladies to break up the sale of intoxicants by public prayer within and in front of saloons. Success attended their efforts, and the excitement spread throughout the State, resulting in largely reducing the liquor traffic.

Reynolds Reform Club, organized at Bangor, Maine, September 10, 1874, by eleven reformed drunkards. It has met every Sunday afternoon since its organization, and similar clubs have spread all over the State.

Congressional Total Abstinence Temperance Society was organized in Washington, D. C., February 9, 1842.

Six Hundred Thousand sign the pledge.—Father Mathew, the great Irish "Apostle of Temperance," visited America in 1849, creating great enthusiasm, and administering the pledge to 600,000 persons.

Maine Liquor Law.—In 1851 Gen. Neal Dow influenced the Legislature to pass a law prohibiting the sale of intoxicating liquors in that State.

National Temperance Convention met at Chicago September 1, 1869.

Red Ribbon Temperance Badges.—In June, 1875, Dr. Reynolds, of the Reynolds Reform Clubs, suggested this badge at a convention of delegates at Bangor, Maine, as a means of mutual recognition. It subsequently became a badge of loyalty.

The Blue Ribbon was adopted later by a temperance organization in Vermont, and the white ribbon by the Woman's Christian Temperance Union in Massachusetts.

Francis Murphy, a reformed drunkard, inaugurated a temperance movement which in 1877 swept over New York

State and influenced thousands to sign the pledge

Illinois.—A monster temperance petition signed by 110,000 persons was presented to the Illinois Legislature March 6, 1879, asking that women might vote on all questions pertaining to liquor licenses. On investigation it was found that an amendment to the constitution of the State would have to be made before such a law could be passed.

Commission of Inquiry into the effects of the liquor traffic was appointed by Congress, May, 1879. A similar commission had been appointed by the House of Lords, England, which had made a valuable report.

National Prohibitionist Convention met at Cleveland, July 17, 1880, and nominated General Neal Dow, of Maine, for President, and A. W. Thompson, of Westville, Ohio, for Vice-President, of the United States.

Kansas.—A prohibitory amendment to the constitution of Kansas was affirmed by the Supreme Court of the State, February 23, 1881.

Iowa passed a prohibitory liquor law by a vote of the people, June 27, 1882, by a majority of 29,751.

MARINE DISASTERS, ETC.

Steamer Ben Sherrod, of New Orleans, was lost, with one hundred and seventy-five persons, opposite Natchez, May 9, 1837.

Steamer Home, a new vessel of New York, was wrecked, and one hundred lives lost, in Pamlico sound, N. C., October 9, 1837.

Steamer Monmouth was lost, October 29th, 1837, with two hundred and thirty-four persons, on the Mississippi River.

Shipwrecks of the Bristol and Mexico, and loss of one hundred and thirty-nine lives during the winter of 1837.—The cold was so intense that passengers froze to death in the rigging. These disasters occurred on Far Rockaway and Hempstead beach.

Steamer Moselle burned at the wharf at Cincinnati, Ohio, April 25th, 1838. One hundred and thirty-one lives were lost.

Steam Packet Pulaski, of Savannah, exploded June 14th, 1838, off the North Carolina coast and killed one hundred persons.

Steamer Lexington was burned on Long Island Sound one bitter cold night in January, 1840. Two hundred lives were lost.

The President, a steamship, sailed

from New York to Liverpool in 1841, and was never heard from. One hundred and nine persons perished.

Steamer Erie, of Buffalo New York, was burned on Lake Erie, August 9th, 1841. One hundred and seventy-five lives were lost.

Queen Victoria sent six gold medals to six New York sea captains in 1842, who had saved a British vessel in 1840.

Big Hatchee, a Mississippi river steamer, exploded in 1845, and twenty or thirty persons were killed.

Steamboat Swallow was lost on the Hudson River in 1845, and fourteen persons perished.

Terrible Gale on the New England coast, September 19th, 1846, destroyed

hundred and seventy-seven lives, on December 30, 1853.

United States and Paraguay Navigation Company.—The first steamer of this line sailed from New York March 21, 1853, but was wrecked on the coast of Brazil.

Steamer San Francisco, with United States troops, foundered at sea, January 5th, 1854. Two hundred and forty perished and seven hundred were saved.

Steamer Tayleure, of the White Star Line, was wrecked on the Irish coast January 20, 1854. Three hundred and seventy lives were lost.

Steamer Powhatan, from Havre to the United States, was lost at sea on

many ships and lives. From Marblehead alone forty-five husbands were lost, leaving one hundred and fifty-five children fatherless.

Steamer Phœnix lost November 21, 1847, on Lake Michigan, with two hundred and forty lives.

The Griffith, with three hundred lives, was lost June 17th, 1850, on Lake Erie.

Steamer Oregon exploded and burned on the Mississippi in March, 1851. Sixty lives lost.

The Atlantic was lost on Lake Erie, August 20, 1852, with two hundred and fifty lives.

Ocean Disaster. — The Staffordshire was lost near Cape Sable with one

April 15, 1854, with three hundred and eleven lives.

Steamer City of Philadelphia, from Liverpool, was lost off Cape Race, September 17th, 1854. Loss of life unknown.

United States Mail Steamer Arctic was run down by the French steamer Vesta, off New Foundland, September 27, 1854. Loss of life three hundred and sixty.

Ocean, of Boston, was burned in the harbor, November 24th, 1854, with a loss of thirty-five lives.

Steamer City of Glasgow, from Liverpool to Philadelphia, was lost at sea with four hundred and eighty lives.

Steamer Pacific left Liverpool for

New York, January 23, 1856, and never was heard from.

The John Rutledge, from Liverpool to New York, was sunk by an iceberg, February 19th, 1856. Loss of life unknown.

Camden Ferry-boat, from New York, was wrecked March 16, 1856, and thirty lives were lost.

Steamer Lyonnais, from New York, was lost in the Atlantic November 2d, 1856, with one hundred and thirty-four lives.

Steamer Central America, from Aspinwall to New York, foundered off Cape Hatteras, September 8, 1857. Four hundred and twenty seven lives and $2,000,000 of treasure were lost.

Steamer Austria, of the New York and Hamburg line, was burned Sept. 13, 1858, in mid ocean. Out of five hundred and thirty-eight persons only sixty-seven were saved.

Steamer Lady Elgin, with a Sunday School excursion aboard from Milwaukee, collided with the sailing vessel Augusta on Lake Michigan, September 8, 1860. Two hundred and ninety-seven persons were lost.

Steamer Golden Gate, of San Francisco, was lost on the coast of Mexico, July 27, 1862, with two hundred and and four lives.

General Lyon, a steamer of Wilmingtou, N. C., was lost off Cape Hatteras, March 31, 1865, with a loss of five hundred lives.

Steamer Sultana exploded upon the Mississippi, April 28th, 1865, killing 1,320 returned Union prisoners. There were 2,106 on board.

Six Steamboats burned at Cincinnati, Ohio, March 6, 1872. Loss, $250,000.

Great Republic, an American clipper ship, was abandoned in a sinking condition off Bermuda, March 4, 1872.

Pacific Mail Steamer America was burned August 24th, 1872, at Yokohama, Japan. Sixty lives and a large amount of specie were lost.

Collision on Long Island Sound, August 30, 1872, between the propeller Metis and a schooner. The latter instantly sank, and the steamer shortly broke up. Twenty-two lives were lost.

Steamer Missouri, from New York to Havana, burned October 22, 1872, off Abaco. Eighty-eight persons, out of one hundred on board, perished.

Great Storm throughout the United States, December 26th, 1872, which was very severe on the Atlantic coast. Bark Kadosh wrecked in Massachusetts Bay and seven lives lost. Ship Peruvian lost on Massachusetts coast, and all hands on board, twenty-five in number, were drowned.

Steamer Harry A. Jones burned at Galveston, Texas, February 15, 1873. Twenty-one persons perished.

Alaska Mail Steamer George S. Wright was wrecked at Portland, Oregon, March 4, 1873, with a loss of twenty-three lives.

Anglo-American Cable Steamer, Robert Lowe was lost November 20th, 1873. Commander Tidmarsh and sixteen of the officers and crew were drowned.

French Steamer Ville de Havre collided with British ship Loch Earn, November 22d, 1873, and sunk in mid ocean with a loss of two hundred and twenty-seven lives.

Mississippi Steamer Pat Rogers was burned near Aurora, Ind., August 5, 1874. Fifty passengers perished.

Pacific Mail Steamer Japan burned near Yokohama, December 17, 1874, with great loss of life.

Steamer Atlantic, of the White Star Line, was wrecked on March 30th, 1873, off the coast of Halifax. Seven hundred lives lost.

Steamer Wawasset burned on the Potomac with seventy lives, August 8th, 1873.

Terrible Storm on the Atlantic coast, in August, 1873, caused immense damage. Fifty American and two hundred and eighty ·fishing vessels were lost.

Propeller Ironsides foundered on Lake Michigan, September 15th, 1873, with great loss of life.

Three Steamers burned at New Orleans, April 23d, 1875, and fifty lives were lost.

Steamer Vicksburg, from Montreal to Liverpool, was lost in an icefield, May 30th, 1875, with eighty-three persons.

United States Steamer Saranac, lost off Vancouver's Island, June 21st, 1875.

Steamer Pacific was· wrecked on the California coast November 4th, 1875, and nearly two hundred lives were lost.

Steamer City of Waco was burned

November 9th, 1875, off Galveston bar, and nearly seventy lives were lost.

Propeller St. Clair was burned on Lake Superior July 10, 1876. Upwards of thirty lives were lost.

Arctic Whaling Fleet of twelve vessels was lost in the ice with many lives. The barque Florence arrived at San Francisco October 21, 1876, with the intelligence.

Heavy Gales on the Atlantic coast November 24th, 1877, caused immense damage. The United States man-of-war Huron was lost, with one hundred lives, off the coast of North Carolina.

Steamer Metropolis was lost in a gale January 31st, 1878, on Currittuck beach, North Carolina. On board were

at sea December 27th, 1878. Only two persons were saved. This was the steamer that carried yellow fever to New Orleans.

Fishing Fleet, of Gloucester, Mass., lost fourteen vessels and one hundred and fifty-five lives, February 20, 1879.

Excursion Steamer Seawanhaka, of New York, burned in East River on June 29, 1880, and fifty persons perished. A colored singer and his wife had floated together in the water some time, when she began to be exhausted. To encourage her he said: "Let us try and sing Rock of Ages." They made the effort, and were joined by others in the water, which stimulated some to new efforts, and they were saved.

200 laborers and 500 tons of railroad iron for the Maderia and Mamore railroad, in Brazil. Eighty lives were lost.

Whaling Bark Sarah, of New Bedford, capsized October 12, 1878, in a hurricane. Eighteen of the crew were lost. Seven were imprisoned in the forecastle by the overturn of the hull of the vessel, four of whom died from lack of food and pain from being thrown about by the rolling of the vessel. Two dived and came up outside and climbed on the bottom of the hull. They were rescued by a pilot boat, and cutting a hole in the hull they saved the last man, who was yet imprisoned.

Steamer Emily B. Souder, from New York to Turk's Island, foundered

Steamer Vera Cruz was lost off the Florida coast in a hurricane, August 29, 1880. Out of eighty-two persons but eleven reached land. The same storm destroyed $1,500,000 of the Florida orange crop.

Disasters on the Great Lakes.—On October 16-18, 1880, a fearful storm destroyed numerous vessels and lives.— The shores of Lake Michigan were strewn with wrecks. The greatest loss was the steamer Alpena, of the Goodrich line, which went down with all on board, some seventy persons, near Holland, Mich.

Elgin, Ill., April 28th, 1881, twelve persons were drowned by the capsizing of a Ferry boat in the Fox River.

Steamer Columbia, September 11, 1881, foundered off Frankfort, Mich.— Fifteen persons were drowned

Steamer Golden City was burned at Memphis, April 3, 1882. Thirty lives were lost.

Schooner Industry capsized on Lake Michigan June 4, 1882, and all on board perished.

Steamer Sciota, while carrying an excursion party, collided with a tugboat, near Mingo Junction, Ohio, July 4, 1882. Fifty-nine lives were lost.

Steamer Gold Dust exploded its boiler, August 7, 1882, on the Ohio river, near Hickman, Ky. Seventeen lives were lost.

West Point, Va.—December 25th, 1882, a steamboat explosion occurred at West Point, Va., by which nineteen lives were lost.

Propeller Morning Star exploded her boiler, December 6th, 1883, on the Mississippi River, by which sixteen men were killed.

Steamship City of Columbus, of the Boston and Savannah line, was wrecked off Gay Head, Mass., January 18, 1884. One hundred and three lives were lost.

SPORTING EVENTS.

Unlawful Entertainments.—The first Congress met October 26, 1774, and took action discountenancing gaming, cock fighting, exhibitions, plays, shows and other expensive diversions and entertainments.

Messenger, an English thoroughbred horse, was imported into the United States in May, 1788. He was sire of many fast horses of this century. He died at Oyster Bay, Long Island, in the year 1808. Over his grave a volley of musketry was fired in honor of his long popularity.

Pugilistic.—In 1816 the first pugilistic encounter, between trained men, occurred in the United States. It was between Jacob Hyer (father of Tom Hyer), and Tom Beasley. The match was declared a draw.

Morgan Horses.—The progenitor of this celebrated breed died in 1821 from a kick from another horse. He was twenty-nine years old.

Horse-Racing in America was inaugurated by trotting. "Boston Blue" against time. It was the result of a wager by Major William Jones, of Long Island, with Colonel Bond, of Maryland, that no horse could trot a mile in three minutes. "Boston Blue" did it.

Trotting Horses.—In 1836 "Dutchman" made three miles in 7 minutes 31½ seconds "Awful," another horse, was noted for speed and his vicious disposition.

Yacht Club.—The first in the United States was organized in New York in 1844. It consisted of nine members and nine yachts.

Regatta in New York harbor held July 17th, 1845. Ten yachts competed. The Cygnet won. This was the first regatta in America.

Base Ball.—The "Knickerbocker" club was organized in New York in 1845. It was the first permanent club in this country.

Trustee's "Twenty-Mile Trot" was

nine years old he trotted five miles in 16 minutes, winning $1,000. He was twenty three years old when he died.

Base Ball Players of various States first organized the National Association in 1857, and established a uniform system of rules.

Champion Chess Player of the World.—In 1858 Paul C. Murphy, of New Orleans, then twenty-one years of age, having beaten every noted chess player in the United States, visited Europe, and was victorious over the best players of the Old World.

College Regatta Association was organized in May, 1858, by a convention from Yale, Harvard, Brown and Trinity Colleges.

made in 59 minutes and 35½ seconds.— It took place in October, 1848.

Yacht America won the prize, the "Cup of all Nations," at the international regatta, at Cowes, England, Aug. 22d, 1851. She was built by George Steers, at Brooklyn, New York, and commanded by Com. John C. Stevens, and was the first yacht to cross the ocean.

College Boat Race, August 3, 1852. Harvard and Yale crews rowed their first race, in eight-oared barges, on Lake Winnipeseogee, N. H. Harvard won.

Black Hawk.—This famous horse died at Bridgeport, Vt., in 1856. He was the first of that breed, and was sold for $150.00 when four years old. When

Prize Fight between John C. Heenan and John Morissey took place October 20, 1858, at Long Point Island, Lake Erie, for a wager of $2,500. The latter was victor, and was declared champion of America.

Flora Temple trotted two miles in harness in 4 minutes and 50½ seconds, August 16th, 1859, on the Long Island track.

Rarey, the horse-tamer, created great excitement in 1861 by his public exhibitions, in which he made the wildest and most vicious steeds obey his will. He claimed that kindness was the basis of his system.

Cincinnati Base Ball Club played, during the season of 1869, with all first class clubs in the United States and won every game.

National Association of American Colleges for rowing was organized in 1870.

Boat Race on the Connecticut river, at Holyoke, Mass., July 19th, 1871, between the Atlantics, of New York, and the Harvard crew. The former were victors.

Goldsmith Maid trotted a mile in 2 minutes 17 seconds, at Milwaukee, Wis., September 6, 1871.

Jim Mace and Joe Coburn fought a prize fight near New Orleans, November 30, 1871. Twelve rounds were fought in four hours. Neither was victor.

Yacht Race in New York harbor in

John Hatfield threw a regulation ball 133 yards, 1 foot and 7½ inches, in Brooklyn, New York, October 15, 1872.

Goldsmith Maid and Occident ran a race at Sacramento, Cal., October 16, 1872. It was won by Goldsmith Maid in three straight heats. Best time, 2:20¼.

Great Strength.—Dr. Winship, in 1872, in Boston, lifted 2,600 pounds in harness.

"True Blue" ran two miles in 3 minutes 32½ seconds, at a horse race in Saratoga, N. Y., July 12, 1873.

Harvard-Yale Regatta, July 16th, 1873, on the Connecticut River. Yale was victor.

Prize Fight between Mike McCool and Tom Allen, near St. Louis, Mo.,

1871. The American sloop Magic won the Queen's cup, running forty-three miles in 4 hours, seven minutes and 54 seconds.

Boat Race, June 10, 1872, between the London (Eng.), Rowing Club, and the Atlanta, of New York, on the river Thames. The Englishmen won.

Great Race at Saratoga, between Longfellow and Harry Bassett, July 16, 1872, won by the latter because of an injury to the former during the race.

College Regatta at Springfield, Mass., between Amherst and Harvard crews, July 24, 1872. The former won, rowing three miles in 16 minutes and 32 seconds.

Ball Throwing Extraordinary. —

September 22, 1873. The latter won on the ninth round.

Feats of Strength.—November 18, 1873, in New York, R. A. Pennell lifted 1,210 pounds dead weight, and W. B. Curtis lifted 3,300 in harness.

Jack Lewis and Jim Rogers fought a prize fight, near Ottawa, Ill., Nov. 19, 1873, which resulted fatally for Lewis, who died after the 36th round.

Skating Extraordinary.—In 1873 William Clark, at Madison, Wisconsin, skated one mile in one minute and fifty-six seconds.

Steamboat Mary Powell ran from New York to Poughkeepsie, seventy-six miles, in 3 hours and 3 minutes, in 1873.

Corinthian Yacht Race at Newport,

August 9th, 1874. The cup was won by the "Idler."

Swimming Match between Trantz and Johnson, at Pleasure Bay, August 28, 1874. The latter won.

International Rifle Match at Creedmoor, September 26th, 1874, between Irish and American teams. The latter won.

Irish Team won the Bennett prize in long range contest at Creedmoor, October 2, 1874.

Boston and Athletic base ball clubs visited England in 1874 and played cricket with the English elevens.

New York August 11, 1876. The American yacht Madeline beat the Canadian yacht Countess of Dufferin.

International Rifle Match at Creedmoor, September 14th, 1876, between teams from Australia, America, Ireland and Canada. The Americans won by twenty-three points.

Polo, a game played upon horseback with a ball and crooked mallets, was introduced into this country in 1876 by James Gordon Bennett.

Red Stocking base ball club of Boston, won the championship in 1876 for five years successively from 1871.

Daniel O'Leary, of Chicago, Ills., walked 115 miles in 24 hours, April 24, 1875.

International Rifle Match at Dollymount, Ireland, June 29, 1875, was won by the American over the Irish team by a score of 968 to 929.

Saratoga Regatta, July 13th, 1875, was won by Cornell.

Ocean Race between the Dauntless and Mohawk was won by the former, October 26th, 1875, and on October 28th the Dauntless beat the resolute in a race from Cape May.

Yacht Race for the Queen's cup at

International Rifle Match between American and British teams at Creedmore range, Long Island, September 14, 1877, resulted in a brilliant victory for the Americans. The score beat the world.

International Walking Match in London, March 23d, 1878, was won by O'Leary, an Irish-American, who walked two hundred and fifty miles between 1 A. M. on the 18th and 10 P. M. on the 23d. He obtained the champion pedestrian belt of the world.

Cricket Match played October 2d, 1878, between an Australian and New

York eleven. The former won by a score of 162 to 161.

International Sculling Match at Montreal, October 3, 1878, between Hanlan, a Canadian, and Courtney an American, was won by Hanlan.

International Walking Match at Gilmore's Garden, New York, ended March 15, 1879, with the victory of Rowell, the Englishman, The distance was 500 miles. It lasted six days and the receipts were over fifty thousand dollars.

Paul Boynton made a successful trip in his rubber suit down the Connecticut river and over Bellows' falls, October 29, 1879. One night in the month of May, 1885, Boynton attached a baloon-

International Walking Match in London, Eng., was won, June 21, 1879, by E. P Weston, an American, who who walked five hundred and fifty miles in six days.

"Sleepy Tom," the blind pacer, made the fastest record in the world at Chicago, July 25, 1879. Time, a mile in 2:12¼.

Champion Walker.—Hart, a negro, made the best distance on record, April 10th, 1880. He walked 565 miles in six days, twelve more miles than had ever been recorded.

Fast Trotting by St. Julien and Maud S., at Rochester, New York, Aug. 12, 1880. This team made a mile in 2 minutes 11¾ seconds.

shaped dynamite torpedo to the British man-of-war Garnet, while she lay in New York harbor. He was not detected in the work until after he had rowed out of danger, when the splashing of his oars arrested the attention of one of the sentinels on the Garnet. The torpedo was harmless, but for the failure of the officers of the Garnet in arresting him they were courtmartialed by the British government.

International Sculling Race on the Tyne in England, May 5, 1879. Edward Hanlan, of Toronto, Canada, defeated John Hawdon, of Delaval, Eng.

St. Julien, the California trotter, beat his own record by trotting a mile in 2:11¼ at Hartford, Conn., August 27th, 1880.

"Maud S" trotted a mile in 2:10¾ on the track of the Chicago Jockey Club, September 18, 1880, thus beating the record of the world.

Jay-Eye-See trotted a mile in 2:10, at Narragansett park, R. I., August 1, 1884, beating all previous records.

Maud S trotted a mile at Cleveland, Ohio, August 2, 1884, in 2:09¾, beating Jay-Eye-See's record. November 19th she trotted a mile in 2:09¼.

ACCIDENTS—MISCELLANEOUS.

Whaleship Essex, of Nantucket, was sunk November 13, 1820, by a whale. Its calf had been captured, when the enraged dam dashed against the ship twice with such force as to crush in its bows.

Crawford Notch disaster in White Mountains, August 28, 1826. Samuel Willey, Jr., kept a little inn in the notch. A fearful tempest arose and the Saco river became a raging torrent. An avalanche swept down the mountain. Willey and his family rushed out for safety and were overwhelmed. The house escaped destruction, being protected by an enormous boulder, which split the

sher and Secretary of Navy T. W. Gilmer and eighteen others were killed and injured.

New York.—A frightful catastrophe occured in Ward School, No. 26, in New York City, November 20, 1851. A panic among the children was created by the fainting of a teacher. In their struggle to escape from the building fifty lost their lives.

New York and New Haven Railroad Accident, May 6th, 1853. A train ran into an open drawbridge, killing and wounding a large number.

Pemberton Mill Horror.—January 10, 1860, one of the great mills at Law-

avalanche. A Bible opened at the 18th Psalm was found on the table.

Steamboat Explosion.—In 1833 the Lioness was blown up at the mouth of Red River by gunpowder, carelessly stowed, killing Senator Johnson of Louisiana, and fourteen others.

Hon. J. Blair, of South Carolina, committed suicide in 1834, at Washington, D. C., while insane.

Drawbridge at Albany, New York, fell in 1840, and twenty persons were drowned.

Explosion of the "Peacemaker," a large cannon, occurred February 28th, 1844, on the United States steamer Princeton, while on an excursion on the Potomac. Secretary of State A. P. Up-

rence, Mass., filled with operatives, fell in with a crash, leaving no time for escape. The mass of ruins quickly caught fire, and about one hundred persons lost their lives.

Oil City, Pa.—In December, 1862, 50,000 barrels of petroleum were lost at Oil City, Pa., the boats with which it was loaded being crushed in an ice gorge.

Indianapolis, Ind.—The explosion of an engine on the fair grounds, at Indianapolis, October 1st, 1869, killed thirty persons and injured many others.

Steamer W. R. Arthur exploded near Memphis, Tenn., January 28, 1871, and killed eighty persons.

Revere Station.—A railway disaster

occurred August 26th, 1871, at Revere Station, near Boston, Mass., caused by an express train running into the rear of a crowded excursion train. Thirty-three were killed and many injured.

Bridge on Cincinnati and Louisville Railroad, near Elliston, gave way February 23, 1872. A train fell twenty-five feet and sixty-five passengers were killed or wounded.

Ashland, Pa.—Colliery explosion occurred near Ashland, Penn., March 26, 1872, fatally injuring ten men.

Steamer "Oceanus" exploded her boiler on the Mississippi, near Cairo, April 11, 1872, killing seventy persons.

Niagara Falls, April 24th, 1872.—

Williamsport, Pa.—Baptist church disaster, near Williamsport, Pa., occurred December 25, 1872. The floor gave way and precipitated three hundred persons into the cellar. Eleven were killed and many wounded.

Stonington and Providence Railroad.—April 19, 1873, a passenger train broke through a bridge, killing and wounding a large number.

Dixon, Ill.—Iron bridge at Dixon, Ills., gave way May 4th, 1873, under a crowd of spectators to a baptism, and one hundred lives were lost.

Arctic Steamer Tigress exploded April 9th, 1874, killing twenty-one persons.

Three unknown men from Chippewa were carried over the falls.

Tug Boat Epsilon exploded at her pier in New York harbor, May 27, 1872, killing every man on board.

Nitro-Glycerine explosion at Yonkers, New York, November 25th, 1872, caused by the foolhardy "fun" of four young men, who threw stones at the cans containing it to see what would happen. Two were blown to atoms and two crippled for life.

Buffalo and Pittsburg Railroad disaster. Dec. 24th, 1872, a train fell through a trestle bridge near Prospect, New York. Twenty persons were killed or burned to death.

Baloon Ascension took place at Chicago, July 15th, 1875, by Professor Donaldson and Grimwood, a newspaper reporter. Both were lost.

Yacht Mohawk was capsized July 20, 1876, off Stapleton, Staten Island.—The owner, Commodore Garner, his wife, Mr. Frost Thorne, Miss Adele Hunter and a cabin boy were drowned.

Mine Disaster at Scranton, Penna., November 16th, 1871.—The props of the roof of a mine under Hyde Park gave way, and twenty acres covered with buildings dropped three feet, causing $50,000 damage.

Opera House disaster at Sacramento, Cal., November 18, 1876. The Peak

Family Swiss Bell Ringers were performing, when the floor gave way, killing seven and injuring fifty-four.

Ashtabula, Ohio, Horror.—Dec. 29, 1876, a train of eleven cars and two engines, with one hundred and sixty passengers, were precipitated into a creek by the breaking of a bridge. A terrible storm, intense cold, and the burning of the wreck made it a scene of horror. One hundred were killed, and of the rescued sixty several died. P. P. Bliss, the revival singer, and his wife, were among the victims.

Dome of Court-House at Rock-

boiler between New York and Norwalk, Conn., on September 28th, 1878, killing twelve and injuring twenty persons.— The accident was in consequence of the parsimony of the owners, who used an old unsafe boiler.

Excursion Train on the Old Colony Railroad, near Wollaston, Mass., was wrecked, October 8, 1878, by a misplaced switch. Twenty-one persons were killed and one hundred and fifty injured.

Pottsville, Pa.—The explosion of a powder magazine, August 17, 1878, with 1,100 barrels of powder, occurred at

ford, Ill., fell May 11th, 1877, before the building was completed, killing ten men.

Niagara Falls Catastrophe.—July 1st, 1877, two men in a row boat were caught in the rapids and swept over the falls.

Hartford, Conn.—January 15, 1878, an excursion train from a Moody and Sankey meeting in Hartford, Conn., fell through a bridge over the Farmington river, near Tariffville, killing thirteen and injuring many other persons.

Steubenville, O.—A railway collision at Steubenville, Ohio, August 7th, 1878, occasioned the death of fifteen persons and injury of fifty.

Steamer Adelphia exploded her

Pottsville, Penna., by a stroke of lightning. Several persons were killed.

New Albany, Ind.—Ice break in the Ohio river at New Albany, Ind., January 14, 1879, caused great damage upon the river banks for miles.

Aeronaut Professor John Wise made an ascension in a baloon and was lost in Lake Michigan, October 13, 1879.

Madison Square Garden disaster in New York occurred April 21st, 1880.— While a large hospital fair was in progress part of the building fell and crushed about twenty-five persons. Many valnable paintings loaned for the occasion were destroyed. The cause was faulty construction of the building.

Hudson River Railroad.—A collision between passenger trains occurred on this road January 13, 1882, near Spuyten Duyvil. Eight persons wers killed, including Webster Wagner, the inventor of Wagner's Palace Cars.

New Albion, Ia., January 16, 1882.— An accident occurred on the railroad here by which twenty-one persons were killed.

Chester, Pa., February 17, 1882, the fireworks factory at this place exploded and fourteen lives were lost by the accident.

Texarkana, Ark.—A house was struck by lightning July 12th, 1882, and beneath its walls thirty persons were crushed to death.

Greenville, Texas. — Thirteen persons were killed by the collapse of a hotel, April 6, 1883.

North Point.—Tivoli, near Baltimore, was the scene of a serious disaster, July 23d, 1883. Sixty-five persons were drowned by the breaking of the wharf, which gave way while a large excursion party were waiting to embark on the boat.

Alliance, O.—February 1st, 1884, an explosion of gasoline occurred, by which eight persons were killed.

FOREIGN VISITORS OF NOTE.

Jerome Bonaparte, nineteen years of age, brother of Napoleon, visited the United States in 1803 and wedded Miss Patterson, of Baltimore, Md. In 1805 he returns to France, leaving his wife to follow. The Emperor forbids her to enter France, and had the marriage annulled by the French Council. Jerome then married the daughter of the King of Wurtemberg, and six days after was made King of Westphalia.

Joseph Bonaparte, brother of the Emperor, came to the United States as Count de Survilliers, in 1815, and purchased 1,500 acres of land in Bordentown, N. J., and settled down to the life of an opulent gentleman. In 1830 he returned to France, and died in Florence in 1844.

Napoleon Murat, nephew of Napoleon I., arrived in the United States in 1820. He was of a scientific turn of mind, and took great interest in our educational institutions. He married a grand niece of George Washington, and died in Tallahassee in 1847.

Lafayette revisits the United States August 15, 1824, and returned to France September 7, 1825.

Napoleon Lucien Charles, nephew of Napoleon I., came to America and married a Yankee school mistress, in 1825. He went to France in 1848 and received the title of Prince of the Imperial Family.

Charles Louis Napoleon, the late Emperor of the French, was banished to the United States for attempting to gain the throne of his uncle, the First Consul, by revolutionary means. He landed in Norfolk in March, 1827, and then came to New York, where he remained until May, when he sailed for Switzerland to see his dying mother.

Charles Dickens and wife landed in Boston June 22, 1842.

Martin Koszta, a leader in the Hungarian revolt of 1849, had taken out partial naturalization papers in the United States and visited Smyrna, where he was seized by the Austrian Consul as a rebel refugee, and put on board an Austrian frigate. His release was demanded by the American Consul, which was refused, thereupon Capt. Ingraham, commanding the American sloop of war St. Louis, July 2d, 1853, threatened to fire upon the Austrian vessel unless Koszta was surrendered. It was then agreed that he should be placed in charge of the French Consul to await the action of the respective governments. The question was discussed by Baron Hulseman, the Austrian minister at Washington, and William L. Marcy, Secretary of State. Koszta was ultimately surrendered to the United States.

Prince of Wales arrived at St. Johns, July 24, 1860. He afterward visited some of the chief cities in the United States, and was received with great enthusiasm. He returned to England in October of the same year.

Queen Emma, widow of a former King of the Sandwich Islands, arrived in San Francisco in 1866, and after making a thorough inspection of our institutions and religious and educational systems, she went to England via New York.

Prince Arthur, third son of Queen Victoria, arrived in New York January 21, 1870. Three days later he was introduced to President Grant by the British Minister, and was honored with a grand ball in the Masonic Temple in Washington.

Grand Duke Alexis, son of the Czar of Russia, arrived in New York November 18th, 1871. After a grand reception there he visited the President at Washington.

Japanese Embassy was received by President Grant at Washington on the 4th of March, 1872.

Henry M. Stanley, the discoverer of Livingston, arrived in New York on the 20th of November, 1872.

King Kalakaua, of the Sandwich Islands, arrived in Washington and was received by the President and Congress December 12, 1874.

Dom Pedro, the Emperor of Brazil, arrived in New York for a tour of the United States, April 15, 1876.

Centennial Celebrations and Holidays.

Thanksgiving was appointed and held in the fall of 1621 at Plymouth, in gratitude of an abundant harvest. Three days were occupied in the festivities, to which Massasoit and some of his tribe were invited.

Fast Day.—In July, 1623, the Plymouth colonists observed their first fast day. A long drouth had prevailed, and the crops were endangered. A failure meant starvation. The day set in clear and hot, but in eight or nine hours a gentle rain fell, which saved the crops.

First Celebration of the Fourth of July occurred at Philadelphia in 1777.— A Hessian band, captured at Trenton,

Peace Jubilee at Boston, June 15-20, 1869, lead by P. S. Gilmore, in a building covering four acres. An orchestra of 1,000 pieces and a chorus of 10,000 singers participated. Parepa Rosa's wonderful voice created a great sensation. One hundred firemen beat the anvil chorus on one hundred anvils, and a battery of cannon outside was fired by electricity in unison with the music. Wonderful enthusiasm pervaded throughout the vast audience.

Decoration Day.—May 30th, 1872, was observed by impressive ceremonies in honor of the dead soldiers of the civil war.

N. J., played excellent music on this occasion.

Great Celebration in Philadelphia, July 4th, 1788, in honor of the newly adopted constitution. A similar celebration at Providence, R. I., was prevented by a mob from neighboring towns who opposed the constitution.

Washington's Birthday was celebrated February 22d, 1793, and excited criticism among some who feared an attempt to make him King.

World's Fair opened in New York July 14, 1853, in a crystal palace built of glass and iron in the form of a Greek cross, 365 feet long each way and 150 feet wide. Three thousand exhibitors came from foreign countries.

World's Peace Jubilee.—The second jubilee, directed by Gilmore, was held at Boston June 17, 1872. The chorus consisted of 20,000 voices and the orchestra of 2,000 musicians.

Centennial Celebration of the discovery of oxygen gas by Dr. Joseph Priestly was held at Northumberland, Penn., in 1874.

Bunker Hill Centennial occurred June 17, 1875. Hon Charles Devens, Jr., delivered the oration. Among the many military organizations participating was the Washington Light Infantry, of Charleston, S. C., which had fought in the rebellion. Three hundred thousand visitors were present.

Centennial Appropriation Bill

of $1,500,000 was signed by the President of the United States February 16, 1876, with the quill of an eagle found near Mount Hope, Oregon.

Centennial Exhibition at Philadelphia, May 10, 1876. The opening of this exhibition, celebrating the 100th anniversary of American independence, occurred. Forty foreign nations had responded to the invitation of the United States to send commissioners and make exhibits. The President and Cabinet, the Diplomatic Corps, Senators and Representatives frem every State in the Union, and also Dom Pedro, Emperor of Brazil, were present. The grounds embraced sixty acres. Three hundred thousand persons

17, 1877, by 60,000 people and a procession four miles long. Speeches were made by President Hayes and Secretary Evarts.

Lynn, Mass., celebrated its 250th anniversary, June 17th, 1879.

Exposition at Louisville, Ky., was opened by President Arthur, August 1, 1883.

Newburgh, N. Y., Centennial was celebrated October 18th, 1883, with imposing ceremonies.

Maryland Pilgrims. — In Baltimore, Md., March 25, 1884, was witnessed the celebration of the two hundred and fiftieth anniversary of the landing of Maryland Pilgrims.

International Electrical Exhibition

were present, and the day's receipts were $75,000. The exhibition closed Nov. 10, 1876. The following comparison with other great exhibitions shows its success:—

Year.	Place.	Number of visitors.	Receipts.	Days open.
1851....	London.	6,039,195	$2,530,000	141
1855....	Paris	5,162,330	640,500	200
1862....	London.........	6,211,103	2,300,000	171
1867....	Paris...........	10,000,000	2,822,932	210
1873....	Vienna	7,254,687	2,000,000	186
1876...	Philadelphia....	9,786,151	3,761,598	158

Centennial Fourth of July, 1876, was celebrated in all parts of the United States with extraordinary enthusiasm.

Centenary of the Battle of Bennington, Vermont, was celebrated Aug.

opened in Philadelphia, Pa., September 2d, 1884.

Franklin County, Pa., Centennial was celebrated at Chambersburg, Sept. 8, 1884.

Methodist Centenary.—A Methodist Centennial Conference, to celebrate the organization of the Methodist church in America in 1784, at the Christmas Conference in Baltimore, was held in Mount Vernon Place M. E. Church, December 10-17, 1884. Eight branches of Methodism were represented—the Methodist Episcopal, Methodist Episcopal South, African Methodist Episcopal, African Methodist Episcopal Zion, Colored Methodist Episcopal Church of America, Primitive Methodist, Canada

Methodist Episcopal, and the Independent Methodist Churches. About five hundred delegates were present. Statistics were read, showing that in all the branches cf Methodism in the United States there were 25,239 traveling preachers, 32,937 local preachers, 3,488,000 members, and 189,328 probationers.

New Orleans Exposition.—The World's Industrial and Cotton Centennial Exposition at New Orleans was opened December 16th, 1884, by the President of the United States in Washington City, setting the machinery in the halls in motion by the touch of an electric key. The funds guaranteed for the Exposition in advance were $1,650,000 by the United States Government, $500,-

ooo by the citizens of New Orleans, and $100,000 by the State of Louisiana. The principal buildings, five in number, were located in the City Park. The dimensions of the main building were 1,378 feet by 905 feet, without courts and with continuous roof composed largely of glass. A building for the United States Government and State exhibits was 885 by 565 feet; the Horticultural Hall 600 by 194 feet; the Art Gallery 250 by 100 feet, and an iron building, 350 by 120 feet, for factory and milling machinery. There was also a building belonging to the Republic of Mexico, which country, as well as Central and South America and the West Indies, was largely represented.

TELEGRAPHIC INVENTIONS.

Telegraphic Experiments. — In 1748 Dr. Benjamin Franklin stretched a wire across the Schuylkill river and transmitted electric shocks over it.

Electricity and lightning were first proven to be identical by Dr. Franklin's well known experiment with a kite made in the year 1752.

Boston and Martha's Vineyard were connected by telegraph October 14th, 1800, by a patent made and operated by Jonathan Grant, Jr., of Belchertown, Mass. The distance between the places was ninety miles, and a question had been sent over the line and answered in less than ten minutes.

Telegraph on Long Island.—In 1827 a line two miles long was operated on the race track. Signals were transmitted through the chemical action of electricity on litmus paper.

Morse's Telegraph.—The idea of an electric recording telegraph originated in 1832 with Prof. S. F. B. Morse. In 1834 Dr. Charles T. Jackson, of Boston, claimed that Morse had got the idea of a recording telegraph from him; also that he had first discovered the use of anæsthetics for relieving pain. He had a prolonged controversy with Morse over the first, and with Dr. W. T. G. Morton over the second. The French Academy of Sciences awarded prizes of 2,500 francs each to Drs. Jackson and Morton. Morse first exhibited his invention in a room in New York in 1835. In 1837 he filed a ceveat for a patent upon the American magnetic telegraph.

Submarine Cable was first laid between New York and Governor's Island October 18, 1842, by Prof. S. F. B. Morse, through which signals were successfully transmitted. Another was laid in 1843, between Cony Island, N. Y., and New York City, by Samuel Colt,

Baltimore and Washington.—A telegraph line between Baltimore and Washington was completed May 27, 1844. Miss Anna Ellsworth dictated the first message: "What hath God wrought?" Morse's original idea was to lay the wire in pipes, but a test resulted in failure.— Ezra Cornell then erected the wire on poles, which was his own idea.

Submarine Telegraph was laid August, 1849, across the Hudson at Fort Lee. The wire was coated with gutta percha.

of fire-arms fame, which worked successfully.

Appropriation for Morse's telegraph.—An appropriation of $30,000 was voted by Congress, March 3, 1843, to Samuel F. B. Morse, for the purpose of establishing an experimental telegraph line. After weary waiting and working, the appropriation was made on the last night of the session. Morse had gone away to his bed disappointed and sore. But fresh faith was given by the news of the morning.

Atlantic Cable.—In October, 1851, the United States brig Dolphin began a line of soundings across the Atlantic preliminary to laying a cable. The first attempt to lay one ocross the ocean began August 5, 1857, at Valentia, Ireland, by the English ships Leopard and Agamemnon, and the American ships Niagara and Susquehanna. The cable parted three hundred miles from land, and the enterprise was abandoned for this year. It was successfully laid August 13, 1858, between Valentia, Ireland, and Newfoundland. On the 17th congratulatory messages were passed between Queen Victoria and President Buchanan. It ceased working about Sept. 1st. The Atlantic cable was successfully laid July 27, 1866, by the steamer Great Eastern. She then returned to the mid-Atlantic, grappled the end of the cable of 1865, spliced it and continued the line to Newfoundland. These lines have never since failed. The persevering efforts of Mr. Cyrus W. Field were crowned with success.

Rocky Mountains. — Telegraph over the Rocky Mountains across the continent was established in 1862.

French Cable between Duxbury, Mass., and Brest, France, via the Island of St. Pierre, was completed July 14th, 1869.

Sixth Atlantic Cable.—November 16, 1879, a new Franco-American trans-Atlantic cable was landed at North Eastham, Mass., from Brest, France.

Telegraph Monopoly was consummated January 12, 1881, by the consolidation of the Western Union, the American Union, and the Atlantic and Pacific Companies.

IMPORTANT INVENTIONS.

Alphabetically Arranged. (See also Manufactures and Arts.)

Artificial Limbs.—In 1846 a patent was issued to Benj. F. Palmer, of Meredith, N. H., for artificial legs and feet. In 1857 he patented hands and arms.

Automatic Fire Signal Telegraph was first exhibited in New York at H. B. Claflin & Co.'s store in December, 1873.

"Babbitt Metal."—Isaac Babbitt, of Taunton, Mass., began to manufacture it in 1825. It is also known as "Brittania" and "white metal."

Babcock's Fire Extinguisher was patented in December, 1869.

Beef Shipping.—American beef was first shipped to England on February 11, 1875. It was kept fresh and cool by fan blowers, first operated by hand, afterward by steam, which sent air currents, first passed over ice, through the refrigerators containing the meat.

Beer —Ale invented 1404 B. C.; ale-booths set up in England in 728, and laws passed for their regulation. Beer was first introduced into England in 1492; in Scotland as early as 1482. By the statute of James I, one full quart of the best beer or ale was to be sold for one penny, and two quarts of small beer for one penny.

Bomb-shell, invented by Robert L. Stevens in 1813, was purchased by the United States for an annuity.

Bows and arrows introduced in 1066.

Bread.—First made with yeast in England in the year 1754. The quarter loaf was sold for about eight cents; three years after it rose to about twenty cents, and in March, 1800, to about thirty-four cents, when new bread was forbidden, under the penalty of $1.20 per loaf, if the baker sold it until twenty-four hours old.

Breech-Loading Rifle invented in 1811 by John Hall. The United States Government ordered some made at

Cannon were first used in ships of war in 1539.

Carding and Spinning. — Machinery for weaving, carding and spinning cotton was first constructed in the United States by Alexander and Robert Barr in 1786. Massachusetts voted £200 toward setting it up at East Bridgewater.

Carte de Visite. — (Photographic) first made by M. Ferrier, in Paris, 1857.

Carpet Weaving.—In 1845 E. B. Bigelow patented his methods of matching figures in weaving carpets by the automatic power loom.

Chimneys. — First introduced into buildings in the year 1200. In England

Harper's Ferry, under Hall's supervision.

Bridges.—A model for an iron bridge of 400 feet span, to be built across the Schuylkill river, was exhibited in 1787, by Thomas Paine, author of "Common Sense." He got his idea from a spider's web. It was deemed too hazardous, and a wooden bridge was built instead.

Buckles.—Invented about this time in 1680.

Calicos.—First made in Lancashire in 1771.

Cannon.—Invented in 1330, and were first used by the English in 1346; first used in England in 1445; first made of iron in England in 1547; of brass in 1635.

only in the kitchen, or large hall, where the family sat round a large stove, the funnel of which passed through the ceiling, 1300.

Circular Saw.—Invented by Gen. Bentham, in England, in 1790; improved by Trotter, 1804; by Brunel, 1805 and 1809.

Clocks.—With wheels of metal, were made by Chauncey Jerome in 1837. They speedily superseded wooden wheeled clocks.

Coal.—Was discovered in 1234 near Newcastle; first dug at Newcastle by a charter granted the town by Henry III.; first used in 1280 by driers, brewers, etc. In the reign of Edward I , began to use sea-coal for fire in 1350, and he published a proclamation against its use in 1398 as a public nuisance.

Collodian.—Used in photography.— Originated by F. S. Archer in 1851.

"*Columbiad*," a long gun for throwing shells, was invented in 1814 by Col. Bomford, of the Ordinance Department. It was afterward improved in France and called "Paixhans."

Columbian Printing Press was invented in 1817 by George Clymer, of Philadelphia. It would print 250 impressions per hour.

Condensed Milk was patented by Charles Alden in 1857. He has since invented processes for evaporating the moisture in fruit.

received no permanent benefit from his invention.

Daguerreotype. — Definite experiments looking to the production of a picture by the action of light upon a sensitized surface were made as early as 1802, but the production of a permanent picture was not accomplished until 1838, by M. Daguerre, an optician of Paris, France, from whom such pictures were named.

Edison's Electric Light.—In Jan., 1880, a stock company was formed, and on the announcement of the success of his experiments shares advanced until they reached $3,300 each. Unexpected difficulties caused them to drop to $1,500.

Electrotyping was first introduced

Corn Sheller.—Invented by Phinney in 1815; improved by James in 1819.

Corn Starch from Indian corn was first produced by Thomas Kingsford in 1842. Now, at Oswego, N. Y., alone, 1,000,000 pounds are annually made.

Cotton Gin.—M. Debreuil, of Louisiana, invented one in 1742 It was used to some extent, but was not a success.— Eli Whitney's Cotton Gin was invented in 1793. He was a Yankee schoolteacher in Savannah, Ga. Cotton was comparatively a worthless crop before this, owing to the difficulty of separating the seeds from the cotton From a production of 487,600 pounds in 1793 it increased to 6,276,300 pounds in 1796. It also gave great impetus to slave labor. Whitney

in 1839 by Joseph A. Adams. It has taken the place of stereotyping in all fine work.

Elevated Railway. — Invented by Sargent in 1825; improved by Andrew in 1861.

Electric Light.—Invented by Stalte & Petrie about 1846; improved by Jules Dubosq in 1855; by M. Lerrin, 1862; by Holmes, 1858; by Dumas & Benoit, 1862.

Electric Telegraph was proposed in 1816 by Dr. John Rodman Coxe, Professor of Chemistry in the University of Pennsylvania. He suggested that signals be transmitted by the decomposition of water and metalic salts, which would produce a change of color.

Fairs and Markets.—First instituted in 886 in England by Alfred. The first fairs took their rise from wakes, when the number of people then assembled brought together a variety of traders annually on these days. From these holidays they were called fairs.

Fairbanks' Scales.—E. & T. Fairbanks, of St. Johnsburg, Vt., obtained patents on scales for weighing heavy bodies, June 13, 1831.

Fire Alarm Telegraph constructed in Boston in 1852.

Fire Engines.—In 1841 Mr. Hughes built a steam fire engine in New York after a model made by Captain John Er-

Flying Machine was exhibited in Tremont Temple, Boston, by Professor Ritchel, of Connecticut, June 24, 1878.

Friction Matches were introduced into America in 1831.

Gas. From Coal.—In 1802 Benjamin Henfrey proposed to light Central Square, in Philadelphia, with it. He had obtained a patent "for a cheap mode of obtaining light from fuel," and had already lighted Richmond with gas from wood.

Gas for Illumination was used in Baltimore, Philadelphia and New York in 1816. It was made from stone coal.

ricsson. Captain Ericsson also fitted the first screw propeller in America to the United States steamer Princeton.

Fire-Proof Safe.—Jesse Deland, of New York, obtained a patent in 1826 on an "Improved Paris Fire-Proof Safe."

Fire Service.—In 1853 a steam fire engine was built and put into effective use in Cincinnati by A. B. Latta. It weighed ten tons and was partly propelled by its own steam.

Flour Mill Machinery.—In 1783 Oliver Evans invented the endless chain, conveyor hopper-boy, drill and kiln drier, upon which all subsequent mill improvements have been based.

Gatling Gun was patented in 1862. It fires four hundred shots per minute.— It was afterward used by the United States army.

Gun Cotton.—Invented by M. Schonbein in 1845-46.

Hats.—First made in London in 1510.

High Towers.—First high towers or steeples were erected on churches in the year 1000.

India Rubber Manufacture. —Invented by Chaffee in 1836; improved by Charles Goodyear in 1844.

Iron Armor for protecting vessels was suggested in 1811 by Robert L. Stevens, of Hoboken, N. J.

Iron Boat.—The first in America was built at York, Penn., in 1825. It was named the "Codurus."

Iron Clad Steamship.—Patented in 1814 by Thomas Gregg, of Penna.

Iron Clad Steamers.—In 1842 the Government authorized R. L. Stevens, of Hoboken, N. J., to construct one as an experiment for coast defense. It was not begun until 1856, and was sold for old iron in 1880.

Knives.—First made in England in 1563.

Lamp for preventing explosion by fire-damp in coal mines, first invented in 1815.

Lanterns.—First invented by King Alfred in 890.

lock that no English locksmith could pick, but Linus Yale, Jr., of Pennsylvania, did it.

Locomotive.—William Howard, of Baltimore, Md., obtained the first recorded patent in the United States for a locomotive steam engine, Dec. 10, 1828.

Mould Board for plows, which would turn a furrow without breaking it, was invented by Thomas Jefferson in 1793.

Nail Cutting Machine.—The first one was patented in America in August, 1791, by Saml. Briggs, of Philadelphia.

Nail Cutting and Heading Machine.—The first one was patented in 1796 by Isaac Garrettson, of Philadelphia.

Lathe.—The irregular form lathe, a wonderful invention, was patented January 20, 1820, by Thomas Blanchard.

Leaden Pipes for carrying water invented in 1236.

Life Boats invented in 1802.

Life Car, invented by Captain Ottinger, of the United States revenue marine, was adopted by the United States in 1849. By it persons can be saved from wrecks upon the coast.

Lightning Rods.—Invented in 1752 by Benjamin Franklin.

Locks.—Hobbs, an American, picked an English lock on exhibition at the World's Fair in London in 1851, winning £200 reward from the makers, Messrs. Bramah & Co. Hobbs then invented a

Nail Machines of American invention were patented in England by Joseph C. Dyer, of Boston. In 1811 he patented the American card making machine.

Oleomargerine was first patented in 1871 by William H. Bradley.

Organs.—Improved organs were patented in 1818 by A. M. Peasley. Over thirty years after Emmons Hamlin discovered the art of voicing reeds. Mr. Hamlin and Henry Mason, son of Dr. Lowell Mason, founded the house of Mason & Hamlin, for maufacturing organs.

Parlor Skates.—Invented by Plymton in 1863; improved by Pollitt in 1870.

Parrott Guns were invented by Mr. Parrott, at Cold Spring, N. Y., in 1860.

One of them known as "Swamp Angel," threw a ball five miles into Charleston, South Carolina.

Percussion Locks were first used for the muskets of the United States infantry in 1842.

Phonograph, an instrument for recording and reproducing sounds, was invented in 1878 by Thomas A. Edison.

Pianos.—The great American pianoforte, "of his own invention," was advertised by James Juliann, of Philadelphia, 1785. Portable Grand Pianos were patented in 1800 by John J. Hawkins, Philadelphia.

Planing Machine patented in 1828 by William Woodworth, of New York.

Plows.—An improved plow was patented in 1819, by Jethro Wood. It is the basis of all modern plows. A steam plow, the first in the United States, was patented in 1833 by E. C. Bellinger, of North Carolina. Daniel Webster's mammoth plow, which he invented in 1836, was twelve feet long and turned a furrow twenty-four inches wide. He was enthusiastic over its success.

Postmark Stamp.—Invented by M. P. Norton in 1859.

Power Looms, for weaving ingrain carpets, were invented in 1839 by E. H. Bigelow of Boston, for the Lowell Manufacturing Company. Ten yards per day were produced against eight yards by hand looms.

Power Loom for weaving Axmins-

ter carpets was patented by Alexander Smith and Halcyon Skinner in 1856. The factory is at Yonkers, N. Y.

Printing Presses.—Bullock's Web printing press was patented in 1861. It receives the paper from a roll and cuts off each sheet as it proceeds and prints both sides before the sheet leaves the cylinders.

Propellers.—John Ericsson patented an improved propeller in 1838, which is in extensive use on all waters.

Putnam forged horse-shoe nails by a machine invented by Silas S. Putnam, which was put in operation at Neponset, Mass., in 1859. This nail was adopted by the United States Government as a standard nail.

Railways. — Charles Williams, of Boston, patented an improvement in 1821. He claimed that in 1817 he had been the first to apply steam to locomotives. and that Robert Stevenson had copied his invention.

Reaping Machine, patented by Obed Hussey, of Cincinnati, O., made a public trial July 2d, 1833. It was a success and took the lead. Cyrus W. McCormick, of Rockbridge County, Va., patented his reaper June 21st, 1834. It took the great medal at the World's fair in 1851.

Reflecting Quadrant, invented by Thomas Godfrey, of Pennsylvania, came into use in 1731. It is wrongly known as "Hadley's Quadrant" in England.

Revolvers.—Colt's revolvers were patented February 25, 1836. His first model was made when he was fifteen years old. It was improved by Sharp in 1850; Pettingill, 1859; Smith & Wesson and T. Remington, 1863; Kittridge, Palmer, Joslyn, Reynolds, Wood and E. T. Starr, 1864; A. M. White, 1875.

Revolving Turrets.—In 1841 T. R. Timby, of New York, produced a model of a metalic revolving turret, for use in warfare. At the outbreak of the civil war he was paid for the use of his idea in the Monitors constructed for the government.

Rifles were invented by Whitworth about 1800. Sharps' Rifle, an improved breech-loading gun, was patented Sept. 12, 1848, by Christian Sharps, of Cincinnati, O. The Spencer Repeating Rifle was patented in 1860. It has a magazine in the butt of the gun containing seven cartridges, which can be discharged in twelve seconds.

Rifled Guns.—Mr. Cyrus Alger, of the South Boston Iron Works, produced the first in America in 1834.

Rubber Goods.—Goodyear's rubber patent was granted February 24, 1839.— It was based upon the use of sulphur in drying rubber, but the goods were not durable. By experiments he found that rubber impregnated with sulphur did not melt, but charred and hardened when touched to a hot stove. He finally succeeded in vulcanizing rubber.

Sawing Machine.—A rotary sawing machine was patented in 1820 by Robert Eastman and J. Jaquith, of Brunswick, Me.

Scenes first introduced into theatres in 1533.

Scythes were invented by Mr. Joseph Jenks, of Lynn, Mass., in May, 1655, who obtained a patent in it for seven years.

Sewing Machines.—In 1834 Walter Hunt, of New York, invented a sewing machine with an eye-pointed needle at the end of a vibrating arm, and a lockstitch shuttle. In 1854 he applied for a patent, but his claim was already covered by the patent of Elias Howe. John J. Greenough obtained the first patent February 21, 1841. The eye was in the centre of the needle, which was pointed at each end. The Howe sewing machine was patented September 10, 1846, by Elias Howe, of Cambridge, Mass. It was the first practicable sewing machine.

Shoes, of the present fashion were first worn in England in 1633.

Shoe Pegs were invented in 1818 by Joseph Walker, of Hopkinton, Mass.— They were made at first by hand and subsequently by machinery. The pegging machine has since been invented.

Sleeping Cars were run on American railroads for the first time in 1858.

Spike Machine was patented in 1839 by Henry Burden, of Troy, N. Y.— It made fifty complete spikes per minute, and most of the railroad spikes in the United States are made by Burden's machines

Starch.—A process for making starch from potatoes was invented. and patented in 1802 by John Biddis, of Pennsylvania.

Steamboats. — First steamboat was exhibited July, 1786, on the Delaware by John Fitch and Henry Voight. It was a skiff with paddles at the stern, propelled by a steam engine with a 3-inch cylinder. Another steamboat was exhibited on the Delaware river in 1787 by John Fitch. It was a larger boat than that of the last year. It had a 12-inch cylinder and obtained a speed of eight miles an hour in dead water. James Rumsey, in December, 1787, floated a steamboat on the Potomac river, which was propelled by pumping water in at the bow and forcibly expelling it at the stern directly into the river, thus pushing the boat ahead.

Steam Heating was successfully accomplished at Lockport, N.Y., in February, 1878. The steam was furnished to dwellings from a central station on the plan of water and gas supply.

Steel Engravings.—In 1814 Jacob Perkins, of Newburyport, Mass., first decarbonized steel so that it could be engraved.

Steel Pens.—Invented about 1820.

Stereoscope.— Invented by Charles Wheatstone in 1838.

Stereotype Printing.—Invented by William Ged, a goldsmith, of Edinburgh, Scotland, in 1735.

Stoves.—The Franklin stove was invented by Benjamin Franklin, in 1742 as a substitute for the old brick fireplace.—Franklin refused to patent it, affirming that "as we are benefitted by the inventions of others we ought to devote ours to the general good." A man patented it and made money on it in England.—Improvements in stoves were made in 1785 by Count Rumford, a scientific American. He encountered much prejudice.

Street Sweeper.—Invented by R. A. Smith in 1855.

Tack and Nail Machine.—Invented in 1786 by Ezekiel Reed, Bridgewater, Mass.

Tallow Candles. — First used in 1290, and were so great a luxury that splinters of wood were used for lights. There was no idea of wax candles in the year 1300.

Telephone. — This instrument rests upon the "resonator," invented in 1873 by Elisha Gray, of Chicago. In 1876 Professors Bell and Dolbear and Thomas A. Edison experimented upon it, and from their various attempts came the modern instrument.

Theater Seat (to turn up out of the way).—Invented by A. A. Allen in 1854.

Time automatically regulated by telegraph was achieved by Dr. John Locke, of Cincinnati, Ohio, in 1848, for which Congress donated to him ten thousand dollars.

Type-Casting Machine. — David Bruce, Jr., patented the only successful one ever invented in 1831.

Type-Setting Machine was invented by Timothy Alden in 1856.

Velocipede. — Patented by William K. Clarkson, Jr., of New York, June 26, 1819.

Watches.—Said to have been invented at Nuremburg in 1477.

Water-Power.—In 1646, in Massachusetts, Joseph Jenks patented "the making of engines for mills to go by water."

Water-Proof Clothing. — In 1833 a company for its manufacture was chartered at Roxbury, Mass.

Westinghouse Brakes proved their efficacy, March 7, 1872, on a New York and Boston train, which was partially derailed near Springfield, Mass. They prevented any sleeping car from leaving the track, although part of the train had gone over into the river.

Window Glass.—First made in England in 1557.

Yale's Locks.—In 1843 Linus Yale, of Philadelphia, patented a lock which was never picked until some years afterward. The feat was accomplished by his son, Linus Yale, Jr.

NOTED MISCELLANEOUS EVENTS.

[Alphabetically Arranged.]

America received its name in 1507 by the suggestion of a geographer of Freiburg, who called it America Terra, in honor of Amerigo Vespucci, whose account of his voyage in 1499 had just been published.

American Flag in China.—It was first displayed in 1784 by the "Empress of China," a New York ship commanded by Captain Green.

Grand Duke Alexis gave $5,000 to the poor of New York City, December 11, 1871.

Beacon Hill, Boston, got its name in 1635, because a pole was erected thereon, to the top of which a barrel of burning tar could be elevated as a signal to the surrounding country.

Bunker Hill Monument Association was incorporated by the Massachusetts Legislature, June 7th, 1823. The corner stone for the monument was laid June 17th, 1825, by Lafayette. Daniel Webster delivered an oration.

Bunker Hill Survivor. — Ralph Farnam, who fought at Bunker Hill, died December 26, 1861, at Acton, Me He was born at Lebanon, Me., July 17, 1756, and was 105 years, 5 months and 19 days old.

Cemeteries.—July 17, 1862, Congress authorized the purchase of grounds for the interment of those who should die in the national service. There are now about eighty of these cemeteries, containing 350,000 soldiers.

——Stonewall Jackson Cemetery was dedicated at Winchester, Va., October 23, 1866.

Chinese-American Citizen.—Nov. 27, 1878, Wong Ah Lee was naturalized, the first instance on record.

Charter Oak, at Hartford, Conn., being Hollow, was, in 1687, made a hiding-place for the charter of Connecticut from Sir Edmund Andross, who went there to secure it. The oak was blown down during a heavy gale, August 21st, 1856.

City "Wards."—In 1637 train bands were organized in Boston to *"watch and ward"* over separate parts of the town. They also originated the "training days" so well known in New England. From this early date city wards first originated.

Civil Service Reform.—March 3, 1871, in accordance with an act of Congress, President Grant appointed a board of commissioners, George William Curtis, of New York, chairman, to investigate and reform government appointments.

Colored Senator.—H. R. Revels was elected United States Senator from Mississippi January 20th, 1870. He was made presiding officer pro tem. of the Senate, February 14, 1879.

Confederate Dead from Gettysburg were removed and carried in mournful procession through Richmond, Va., June 20, 1872.

Copyright Law.—The first in America was granted by the General Court of Massachusetts to John Upsher, in 1672.

Cremation.—December 6, 1876, at Dr. F. J. Le Moyne's furnace, Washington, Penna., the body of Baron D. Palm was cremated in two hours ten minutes, and the ashes gathered into an urn. This was the first cremation, and it created a wide-spread interest.

——Remains of the corpse of Mrs. Ben. Pitman were cremated February 15, 1875, at Dr. Le Moyne's furnace, at Washington, Penna.

——Crematory at Lancaster, Pa., was dedicated November 25, 1884.

Egyptian Obelisk, which hau been transported to America by Commander Gorringe, at the expense of W. H. Vanderbilt, was set upon its pedestal in Central Park, New York, January 22, 1881.

Fatal Leaps.—Sam Patch made his famous leap into the Genesee Falls, at Rochester, N. Y., November 13, 1829.— The Falls were 100 feet high, but in addition he had a scaffold 25 feet erected, from which he jumped, making the distance 125 feet. He advertised it as "Sam Patch's Last Jump," and as such it proved to be, as he never arose to life again.

——Robert Odlum, an expert swimmer, of Washington, D. C., jumped from the Brooklyn bridge, May 19, 1885. The height was 145 feet, and the jump resulted in his death in 43 minutes after he made the leap.

"Flying Machine."—This was the name of a passenger coach advertised in 1772, to run between New York and Philadelphia, "in the remarkably short time of two days."

Fountain of Youth.—Juan Ponce de Leon, being told by the Indians of a fountain whose waters restored youth to the old, sailed March 3, 1572, to find it.

Grand Jury.—The first Grand Jury in America met in Boston, September 1, 1635, and prepared a list of one hundred names, which they presented to the magistrates for trial.

Geological Surveys. — Massachusetts was the first State to have its territory completely surveyed. In 1830 Dr. Edward Hitchcock was charged with the work.

Grand Review of the United States army took place in Washington, D. C., May 22-3, 1865.

Gas.—For illumination was first made a permanent success in 1822 at Boston.

"Hail Columbia."—This national ode was composed in 1798 by Joseph Hopkinson, of Philadelphia.

Imprisonment for debts due to the United States was abolished January 14, 1841.

International Fish Commission met at Halifax Nov. 23, 1877, and awarded $5,500,000 to Great Britain for fishing privileges given to the United States.

Lotteries.—In 1612 the new charter of Virginia authorized the raising of money by lotteries and £29,000 was realized from them in a few years. This was the first lottery in America.

——In Massachusetts lotteries were suppressed by law in 1719.

——In Baltimore a lottery was established in 1753 to raise money enough to build a public wharf.

——They were authorized by Massachusetts in 1759 to aid in constructing public works.

——Dismal Swamp Lottery Company, of Norfolk, Va., was chartered in 1787, for the purpose of raising $50,000 for the improvement of internal navigation between the waters of North Carolina and those of Virginia, through the Dismal Swamp. The company never done anything, and in 1882 its charter was forfeited.

——Congress authorized lotteries in 1776 to raise funds to defray the expenses of the campaign of 1777, but it was a failure.

——Lotteries in the United States had, in 1834, multiplied to such an extent that efforts were made to break them up by wholesome laws. .

Louisiana ceded to France by Spain in 1802, pending which the Spanish commander at New Orleans closed the navigation of the Mississippi river to United States citizens. Congress thereupon sent James Monroe to Paris to negotiate for its reopening.

ing no word. Returning and finding her lover gone she started after him on foot, in a snow storm, with night coming on. Her road was a path with blazed trees, which led through Crawford Notch in the White Mountains, thirty miles distant, where dwelt the only inhabitants on the route. She tried to kindle a fire in the warm ashes, where her lover had recently camped. Exhausted by her rough journey, and in fording the Saco river, she perished in the storm. Her affianced died a madman.

Niagara Falls.—The first known mention of this cataract was made in the year 1648, in the Jesuit relation, by Ragueneau.

Marquet.—Father Marquet died on May 19th, 1675, on the shore of Lake Michigan, on his homeward trip. He was one of the noblest pioneers of the Northwest.

Militia Organization. — Ancient and Honorable Artillery Company, of Boston, was organized in 1637. It was armed with pikes, "hand-gounes" and "snap-hances." It is the oldest militia organization in America, and still has an annual "training day."

"Nancy's Rock."—In 1778 a young couple in Jeffer n, N. H., were engaged to be married. During the girl's temporary absence the young man started with his employer to Portsmouth, leav-

Omnibus.—The first in America was built and run in New York in 1830.

"Penn Treaty Tree" was blown down in 1810 by a severe gale.

Pension Act.—The first Pension Act was passed by Congress August 26th, 1776.

Plymouth Rock.—In 1774 an attempt was made to remove this famous rock from its bed to a place in town. While being raised it broke apart. Only a portion was removed, but in 1880 it was restored to its original position. A beautiful granite canopy now covers it.

Post-Bellum Courtesies.—November 12, 1879, the Duke of Northumberland, England, presented a portrait of

Lord Percy, who led the British in their march on Lexington, Mass., April 19th, 1775, to that town. In return the citizens voted to present to the Duke a painting of Monroe tavern, where Lord Percy made his headquarters during his brief stay in Lexington.

Polygamy was decided by the United States Supreme Court to be illegal and subject to prohibition by Congress on January 6, 1879.

Potosi is the highest city in the world. It is 13,300 feet above the sea. Two hundred years ago the population was 150,000. It has now less than 30,000, yet the mint coins $2,000,000 annually.

Powder Mill was erected in Massa-

Rev. Dr. Hall, an Episcopalian, and Mr. Lincoln's pastor, Rev. Dr. Gurley, Presbyterian. Afterward, from city to city, in one vast funeral procession, the mourning people followed his remains to their last resting place at Springfield, Ills., where on May 4, 1865, Bishop Simpson pronounced the funeral oration, and a choir of 250 voices sang requiems.

President Van Buren received costly presents from the Imaum of Muscat in 1840, which were sold, and the price converted into the United States Treasury. Congress appropriated $15,000 for return presents.

Rodman Gun was cast at the Fort Pitt Iron Works, Pittsburg, Pa., in 1863.

chusetts in 1640, but it was afterward suppressed by English law.

Powder Houses in Massachusetts. In 1642 the General Court passed a law obliging every town to keep a supply of powder on hand, which led to the erection of powder houses on lonely hills.

Presidential Fund of $250,000, the interest of which is presented to Gen. Grant during life, was completed Feb. 2, 1881. After his death it will be presented to the senior ex-President of the United States then living.

President Lincoln's funeral occurred April 19, 1865. The ceremonies in the White House were conducted by Bishop Simpson, a Methodist clergyman, and

Its weight when cast was 17,000 pounds, and when finished 115,000 pounds. It was 243 inches long, with a bore 210 inches long. It would throw a 1,000 pound solid shot, or a 700 pound shell. In casting three furnaces were charged with eighty-six tons of metal, which required 6 hours in melting and 25 minutes in drawing off into the mould.

Saving Service.—The United States Life Saving Service originated March 3, 1847, by an appropriation from Congress to equip light-houses with the means of assisting wrecked vessels.

Sewing Machine patents expired in 1877, ending the monopoly and reducing the price one-half.

Ship Canal, to connect the Atlantic and Pacific oceans via Lake Nicaragua, was proposed in 1527.

Statues. — The Benjamin Franklin statue was unveiled January 17, 1882, in Printing-House Square, New York.

——The statue of Abraham Lincoln, by Thomas Ball, was unveiled at Washington, D. C., April 14th, 1876. It was erected by the colored people of the United States.

Stuyvesant Pear Tree, corner of Third avenue and Thirteenth street, N. Y., died in 1867. It was over 200 years old and bore fruit till shortly before its death.

Table Rock, Niagara Falls, May 24, 1877. The last half, weighing sixty tons, fell with a shock which was felt for several miles.

Testimonial to Lafayette.—In December, 1824, Congress voted $200,000 and a township of land to Lafayette, as a slight return for his efforts in behalf of American liberty.

Trades Societies.—The Carpenters' Society, organized in Philadelphia in 1724, was the first of a long list of trade societies in America.

" Tramps " had been roving about the northern States ever since the close of the civil war. Their numbers increased so rapidly as to create alarm.— In August, 1875, there were 30,000 in Massachusetts alone. Several States passed severe laws against them. Gradually the nuisance decreased.

"Uncle Sam."—This phrase originated in 1812, at Troy, New York, where a large number of provisions had been contracted for by the United States.— They were inspected by two brothers, Ebenezer and Samuel Wilson, the latter of whom was familiarly known as Uncle Sam. The packages were all branded E. A.—U. S. A jocose workman, being asked what the letters meant, replied: "It must be Elbert Anderson and Uncle Sam," which latter term became current for the United States.

Vallandigham.—Clement L. Vallandigham, of Dayton, O., was arrested by General Burnside, May 4th, 1867, for treasonable speeches, courtmartialed and sent within the Confederate lines under penalty of execution if he returned.

Washington.—President Washington was maligned by the press, October 1795. It was charged that he had overdrawn his salary, etc., by the Secretary of the Treasury, but Alexander Hamilton proved it to be false.

——His farewell address was issued September 17, 1796. It was his last direct utterance to his countrymen. Its wisdom and patriotism showed that he truly merited the title " Father of his country."

Washington National Monument.—The building of the Washington National Monument at Washington, D. C., was completed on Saturday, December 6th, 1884. The idea of this National Monument took definite shape in 1833, when citizens of Washington formed an association to build it by popular subscriptions of individual sums not to exceed one dollar each. In 1847 the collections footed up only $87,000. With this sum it was determined to begin the work. On the 4th of July, 1848, the corner stone of the monument was laid; in 1854 the funds of the National Monument Society, amounting to $230,000, were exhausted. The monument had then reached a height of 170 feet, and during the succeeding twenty-four years only four feet were added. On August 22d, 1876, Congress passed an act creating a joint commission for the continuance and completion of the monument, and made the necessary appropriation, which was continued annually. The monument is a marble obelisk. The shaft from the floor is 555 feet 4 inches high, being 30 feet 5 inches higher than the spires of the great Cathedral at Cologne, Germany. The present foundations are 36 feet 8 inches deep, making an aggregate height from the foundation bed of 592 feet. The base of the obelisk is 55 feet 1½ inches square, the walls 15 feet ¼ inch thick, and at the five hundred feet mark, where the pyramidal top begins, 34 feet 5½ inches square and 18 inches thick. The amounts expended for the monument to the date of December 6th, 1884, were as follows: By the Monument Society, $230,000; appropriated by Congress $900,000, making a total of $1,130,000. Within the obelisk (the walls being vertical), is an elevator and stairway. From the top of the wall of the obelisk to the bottom are 900 steps, requiring about twenty minutes to make the descent.

Weighty Man.—Miles Darden died January 23, 1857, in Tennessee, weighing over one thousand pounds. He was born in North Carolina in 1798 and grew to be 7 feet 6 inches high. When 47 he weighed 871 pounds. He worked until he was 55 years old.

Whale Fisheries were first begun on a large scale in America in 1690 by Nantucket sailors.

White Mountains, in New Hampshire, were ascended for the first time in 1642 by the first white man, an Irishman named Darby Field, accompanied by two Indians.

Women of Note.—Female attorneys were allowed to practice in the United States Supreme Court by a law passed February 7, 1879. The bill had passed the House a year before, and was called up in the Senate through the persistent efforts of Mrs. Belva A. Lockwood.

——In January, 1849, Elizabeth Blackwell, an English woman, graduated from the medical school at Geneva, N. Y.—Other schools had refused to admit her on account of her sex.

——Anna Dickinson delivered her first public address in Philadelphia in 1860, upon Woman's Rights and Woman's Wrongs."

——Dr. Mary P. Jacobi, of New York, graduated from the Paris Ecole de Medecine in 1871, of which she was the first female graduate. She had previously been the first woman to graduate from the College of Pharmacy, New York.—She won the second prize for her graduating thesis in Paris.

——Dr. Mercy B. Jackson, of Boston, was the first woman admitted to the American Institute of Homœpathy in Philadelphia, June, 1871.

——Fanny Wright, a Scotch woman, lectured extensively in the United States in the year 1820, upon politics, slavery and woman.

LABOR STRIKES.

Coal Miners great strike began in Pennsylvania, January 10, 1871.

Eight-Hour Movement.—In 1872 workmen all over the United States loudly clamored for a reduction from 10 to 8 working hours at the same pay.— The problem began to look serious, until solved by the panic of 1873, during which time work of any kind was scarce.

Miners' Strikes in Pennsylvania suppressed by the militia June 5, 1875.

Belleville, Ills.—The coal miners struck here May 7th, 1878. Four thousane stopped work. In a short time 1,500 men were on the verge of starvation.

Lynn, Mass.—The strike of the Lynn shoemakers occurred January 14, 1877. Work almost entirely stopped and a long conflict was begun.

Baltimore & Ohio R. R.—A strike began among the employees of this road July 16th, 1877, because of a 10 per cent. reduction of wages. The strikers had stopped 1,200 cars at Martinsburg, W. Va., by July 17, 1877, and fired upon the militia, who had been ordered by the Governor to suppress rioting. Federal troops were ordered to Martinsburg, Va., by President Hayes, July 18, 1877, to quell the railroad riot, by request of the Governor of West Virginia, the strikers having got possession of the entire railroad.

Erie Railway.—A strike occurred on the Erie Railway, July 20, 1877. All trains were stopped. The Sixth Maryland Regiment was assaulted in Baltimore by the mob with stones and brickbats. The soldiers fired upon the mob and killed 9 and wounded about 50 of them.

Conflict at Pittsburg, Pa., between strikers and the military, July 21, 1877, resulted in the killing of Sheriff Fife and a number of others, and the wounding of many, including General Pearson.—

as they marched out hastily, they were attacked by the strikers, who followed them as they double-quicked toward the Arsenal, firing shots and hurling all sorts of missiles at the soldiers, many of whom were badly hurt and others shot down and left in the streets. Once the military turned and fired into their pursuers, twenty or more persons being killed by the discharge. The commandant at the Arsenal refused to allow the troops admission, saying that he had but twenty men with him, and if he allowed them to enter he could not protect the place against the mob. They then hur-

The mob sacked all gun stores. President Hayes issued a proclamation ordering all to desist and to retire to their homes by noon of July 22. On the morning of the 22d the rioters continued their work of destruction by completely destroying the Round House of the Pennsylvania Railroad Company, together with 125 first-class locomotives, hundreds of loaded freight cars and other property, aggregating in value, according to a rough estimate, $3,000,000. The troops, who had been penned up in the Round House all night, were forced to attempt to escape when the building was fired, and,

ried on to the bridge over the Allegheny at Sharpsburg, after crossing which they separated in squads and took to the woods. The civil authorities were totally powerless, and thieves, who took advantage of the reign of terror, broke open and plundered the cars and carried off the stolen goods with perfect impunity. The strike in Philadelphia was inaugurated at 6 o'clock P. M., by the men abandoning their places. Trouble occurred at Hornellsville, N. Y., on the Erie road, the strikers preventing trains departing.

Railroad Strikers were joined by

the Central New Jersey, Lehigh Valley and Texas Pacific freight men. July 25, 1877, conflicts occurred between the rioters and police at Chicago, St. Louis and San Francisco. The Erie strikers at Hornellsville and at Rochester, N. Y., agreed to resume work.

Erie Railroad and canal men at Buffalo, N.Y., on July 25, 1877, took possession of the New York Central stock yards and stopped the movement of trains. On the Cleveland and Pittsburg Railroad and Lake Shore and Southern Michigan Railroad all trains were abandoned. The Vandalia Railroad men at Indianapolis, Ind., and the Niagara division of the Erie Railroad employees

Compromise with Firemen and brakemen on the Pittsburg, Ft. Wayne and Chicago Railroad was partially effected July 29, 1877. Troops were concentrated at East St. Louis, Ills., for fear of an attack upon the bridge.

Strikers Resume Work.—Striking trainmen of the Lake Shore, Texas Pacific, Delaware, Lackawanna and Great Western Railroads, and of several lines centering at Pittsburg, Pa., went back to work July 30th, 1877, at the reduced wages, the question of pay to come up for future discussion. Freight trains in large numbers were moved on the Pennsylvania and Baltimore and Ohio roads. Regular trains were running on the

joined the strike. A vigilance committee was formed at Pittsburg to protect property. At Reading, Pa., troops killed seven and wounded thirty rioters engaged in tearing up tracks.

Railroad Strikes.—At Baltimore, Md., July 28, 1877, seven freight trains moved and five hundred cars from Cumberland, over the Baltimore and Ohio Railroad, all under the protection of troops. At Pittsburg, Pa., Governor Hartranft, with 4,000 United States troops, took possession of the Pennsylvania Company's territory. At Johnstown mobs stoned moving trains and wrecked five cars. At Fort Wayne, Ind., the mob prevented two attempts of the authorities to move trains.

Morris and Essex and New Jersey Central Railroads. No fresh outbreaks occurred on the railroads, and dispatches from various points indicated a speedy resumption of work. At Baltimore many of the old men were returning, more offering than could be made use of.

Labor War Ended.—August 3d, 1877, freight trains were running, or were about to be started, on all the roads.— The striking miners in the coal regions of Pennsylvania were kept quiet by the presence of troops. The coronor's jury at Baltimore, Maryland, exonerated the Sixth Regiment from all blame for the riot.

MISCELLANEOUS INFORMATION.

THE FENIANS.

"Fenians."—This organization was founded in 1857 in New York by Michael Corcoran and others, as the "Emmet Monument Association." Similar societies in Ireland were known as Phœnix societies. The name "Fenian" was afterward taken from Finn, the commander of Irish militia in the third century.

Fenian National Congress was held at Chicago on November 3d, 1863. About 15,000 of the brotherhood were represented, and James Stephens was declared to be the "head centre."

Raid on Canada.—June 1st, 1866, Notwithstanding the watchfulness of the President Grant, and the leader, Colonel O'Neill and his officers, were captured and imprisoned.

Irish National Congress convened at Cincinnati, O., August 23, 1870.

O'Donovan Rossa and other Fenian exiles arrived in New York in January, 1871.

Fenians under Gen. O'Neill seized the Canadian Custom-House and Hudson Bay post at Pembina, Manitoba, Oct. 7, 1871. The United States troops capture them.

Irish Cause.—C. S. Parnell, member of Parliament from Meath, Ireland, and John Dillon, arrived in this country Jan.

United States authorities, 1,500 Irishmen crossed into Canada at Buffalo. They encountered the Canadian militia June 2nd, and lost heavily in wounded and prisoners, and a few killed. At night they attempted to recross and 700 of them were captured by a United States steamer. This failure discouraged further attempts.

Erin's Hope was the name of a vessel sent to Ireland in April, 1867, by the Fenians, with military supplies. Owing to the watchfulness of the British government she did not land and returned to America.

Expedition against Canada by the Fenians, May 24th, 1870, was broken up by General Meade, under orders from 1, 1880, to promote the cause of Irish home rule, and procure money for their famished countrymen and for political purposes.

Charles S. Parnell, the Irish agitator, received a farewell banquet March 11, 1880, on the eve of his departure for Ireland.

INSURANCE COMPANIES.

Marine Insurance.—John Copson, of Philadelphia, first engaged in this business in 1721, but failed because ship owners preferred to insure in other countries. In 1759 the first office in America for this business was opened in New York.

Fire Insurance Company.—"The

Philadelphia Contributionship for the insurance of houses from loss by fire,'' was organized, with Dr. Franklin as President, in 1752. It still does buiness in Philadelphia.

First Life Insurance Co. in America was chartered in 1769. It was called the "Protestant Episcopal Association for the benefit of Widows and Children of the Commonwealth of Pennsylvania."

Philadelphia Company for life insurance, with a capital of $500,000, was organized in 1812

Traveller's Insurance Company was organized by Mr. James G. Batterson in 1863. The first policy issued was to Mr.

tories, were paralyzed, and financial distress prevailed. Consequently they were opposed to the war policy of the administration. They were in secret session about three weeks, and accomplished little, except to create an impression that they meditated a disruption of the Union, and thereby they made a final wreck of the Federal party.

Women's Rights Convention, July 19, 1848, was held at Seneca Falls, N.Y., by Lucretia Mott, Elizabeth Cady Stanton, Martha C. Wright, Mary Ann McClintock, and others.

National Teacher's Association held its first annual convention at Cincinnati, August 11, 1858.

James Boltes, in Hartford, Conn., who asked Mr. Batterson: "What will you take to insure me for $5,000, if I get killed by accident, in going from here to my house in Buckingham street?" "Two cents," was the reply. The two cents were paid, and are now exhibited by the company as the first "accident" premium taken in America.

CONVENTIONS.

Hartford Convention met on the 14th of December, 1814, in response to a call from the Masachusetts Legislature "to confer upon the subject of their public grievances." The delegates were from the New England States, whose chief industries being in ships and fac-

Grand Army of the Republic held a National Convention November 20th, 1866. It was organized to perpetuate the friendships of the war.

National Labor Convention met at Philadelphia August 16, 1869.

National Woman's Suffrage Convention, presided over by Henry Ward Beecher, was held at Cleveland, O., November 24, 1869.

National Colored Labor Convention was held in Washington, D. C., on December 10, 1869.

Woman's National Suffrage Association was organized in 1869.

Brewers' Congress was held in Boston on June 3, 1874, representing a capital of $89,910,823, beside $17,000,000

in malt houses. They employed 56,000 persons and made 9,000,000 barrels of beer in 1873.

Ex-Confederate and Union soldiers met at Cincinnati, Ohio, September 4th, 1877, to arrange for a reunion of both armies, to take place in 1878.

Knights Templars of the United States met in grand convention at Chicago, Ills., August 16, 1880. It was the largest gathering ever made of this character. The festivities lasted a week.

PUBLIC INSTITUTIONS.

Independence Hall in Philadelphia was begun in 1729, and was not completed till 1734.

ence. It was built after 7 years study by Herr Walcker, of Ludwigsburg.— It is 60 feet high, 48 feet wide and 24 feet deep. It has nearly 6,000 pipes and cost $60,000.

Ford's Theater in Washington, D. C., where President Lincoln was murdered, was opened as an Army Medical Museum April 13, 1867.

American Museum of Natural History, incorporated in New York in 1869, for which a building five times greater than the national capitol is proposed to contain the collections for this great enterprise.

Albany, N. Y.—Corner stone of the capitol laid June 24, 1871.

Astor Library in New York City was opened January 9, 1854.

Mount Vernon, the home of George Washington, was purchased by the "Ladies' Mt. Vernon Association" in 1858 for $200,000. Their design is to make it a place of national resort.

Army Medical Museum, May 21, 1862.—The valuable collection in Ford's Theater, Washington, D C., originated in a request to army surgeons to preserve and forward for a museum all specimens of morbid anatomy that would be valuable; also everything relating to death or injury by war, and disease in camp.

Boston Music Hall Organ, November 2, 1863.—This great organ was inaugurated at this date before a vast audi-

Mercantile Library of New York was opened for the first time on Sunday, May 12, 1872.

Corner Stone of American Museum of Natural History, corner Eighth avenue and Seventy-seventh street, New York, laid June 2d, 1874, by President Grant.

SECRET SOCIETIES.

Masonic Lodge.— Albion Lodge, formerly No. 17 E. R., of Quebec, is the oldest lodge of Free Masons in America. It was instituted in 1721.

Masonic Grand Lodge was constituted at Boston July 30, 1733, for New England, named St. John's Grand Lodge.

Society of Cincinnati was organized at Newburg, N. Y., June 19, 1783, by army officers, to commemorate their experiences in the war, and to promote brotherhood between the States. It still exists.

Odd Fellows' · Lodge was established in New York City in 1806. It was named "Shakespeare Lodge." Another was instituted there in 1816 named the Prince Regent Lodge. It was short lived.

Painters' Society was organized in 1850 by water color artists.

Baltimore, Md. — Odd Fellows' Lodge was organized at Baltimore, Md., April 26, 1819. It was called Washington Lodge No. 1, and was the first permanent one in America.

1872, the Geneva Commission awarded $15,500,000 in gold to the United States, for damages to American commerce by the Confederate privateers Alabama, Florida and ·Shenandoah, which were fitted out in English ports in violation of neutrality laws.

Washington Commission appointed to arbitrate respective claims of American and Englishmen, for losses occasioned during the civil war, awarded the sum of $1,929,819 to England, September 25, 1873.

SCIENTIFIC DISCOVERIES.

Inoculation for Small-Pox was first tried in America in 1721 by Dr. Zabdiel Boylston, of Boston, at the suggestion

Knights of Pythias.—Washington Lodge No. 1, of this order was organized in Washington, D. C., February 19th, 1864.

INTERNATIONAL AWARDS.

Treaty of Washington.—February 27, 1871, a joint high commission composed of five British and five American statesmen, met at the capitol, by which it was agreed to submit the Alabama claims of the United States to a tribunal to sit at Geneva, Switzerland, the coast fishing question to one at Halifax, and the San Juan boundary question to the German Emperor.

Alabama Award.—September 14,

of Cotton Mather. The plague was raging with great virulence. Boylston encountered fierce opposition from doctors and others. Cotton Mather defended him against their abuse, and, beginning in his own family, he inoculated 286 persons, of whom only 6 died. Of 5,759 others attacked by the disease 844 died. This success soon silenced all opposition.'

Vaccination was first performed in America in 1799 by Dr. Benjamin Waterhouse, of Boston, upon his own children.

Chloroform as an anæsthetic was discovered by Dr. Samuel Guthrie, of Sackett's Harbor, N. Y., in 1832.

Ether was first used in performing a

surgical operation March 30, 1842, by Dr. C. W. Long, of Jefferson, Ga.

Water-Cure Establishment, the first in America, was opened in 1844 in New York City.

Laughing Gas was first used in dentistry by Dr. Horace Wells, of Hartford, Conn., in 1844.

Ether as an Anæsthetic was first publicly used in surgical operations at the Massachusetts General Hospital on October 16th, 1846.

Blue Glass excitement arose in January, 1877, resulting from experiments by General Pleasanton, whose theory was that sunlight passing through it would heal many diseases. Some singular cures were reported.

England Demanded the release of Alexander McLeod, a Canadian, who, in 1841, was arrested and tried for participating in the destruction of the Caroline at Navy Island. The demand was refused, but the charge against him was not proven.

Spanish Authorities at Havana, refused, in November, 1852, to receive mails and passengers from the American steamship "Crescent City," plying between New York and New Orleans.

American Steamer "Black Warrior" was seized by the Cuban authorities in the harbor of Havana, February 28, 1854.

FOREIGN TROUBLES.

French Indignities.—C. C. Pinckney, of South Carolina, our minister to France, was refused recognition and ordered to leave France, in February, 1797, the French government having taken offence at Jay's treaty.

French Hostility to Mr. Adams' election was such that in May, 1797, the capture of American vessels and hanging of American seamen found in foreign ships was decreed.

British Minister at Washington, also consuls at New York and Cincinnati, were sent home by the United States in 1855, for encouraging the enlistment on our soil of soldiers for the Crimean war.

Spanish Man-of-War Vasco de Nunez overhauled the American steamer Florida, December 14, 1871, and examined her papers, which, being correct, she was allowed to proceed on her voyage.

Russian Minister Catacazy was recalled by his government, December 16, 1871, at the request of the United States for discourtesy to the authorities.

Fictitious Names of States, Cities and Noted Persons.

Albany Regency.—A name popularly given in the United States to a junto of astute Democratic politicians, having their headquarters at Albany, N. Y., who controlled the action of the Democratic party for many years, and who had great weight in national politics. The effort to elect William H. Crawford President, instead of John Q. Adams, was their first great struggle.

Badger State.—A name given to Wisconsin.

Bay State.—A popular name of Massachusetts, which, previous to the adoption of the Federal Constitution, was called the Colony of Massachusetts.

ping, and discharged their small arms and cannon at everything they saw floating on the river during the ebb tide.

Blue Hen, The.—A cant or popular name for the State of Delaware. The sobriquet is said to have its origin in a certain Captain Caldwell's fondness for the amusement of cock-fighting. Caldwell was an officer in the First Delaware Regiment in the war of the Revolution, and was greatly distinguished for his daring and bravery. He was exceedingly popular in the regiment, and its high state of discipline was generally conceded to be due to his exertions; so that when officers were sent on recruiting ser-

Bayou State.—A name sometimes given to the State of Mississippi, which abounds in bayous or creeks

Bear State.—A name by which the State of Arkansas is sometimes designated on account of the number of bears that infest its forests.

Battle of the Kegs.—The subject and title of a mock heroic poem, by Francis Hopkinson. This ballad, very famous in Revolutionary times, was occasioned by the following incident: Certain machines in the form of kegs, charged with gun powder were sent down the river to annoy the British shipping, then at Philadelphia. The danger of these machines being discovered, the British manned the wharves and ship-

vice to fill vacancies occasioned by death or otherwise, it was a saying that they had gone home for more of Caldwell's game cocks; but as Caldwell insisted that no cock could be truly game unless the mother was a Blue hen, the expression Blue Hen's chickens was substituted for game cocks.

Bluff City.—A descriptive name applied to the city of Hannibal, Mo.

Boston Massacre.—A name popularly given to a disturbance which occurred in the streets of Boston on the evening of March 5th, 1770, when a sergeant's guard belonging to the British garrison fired upon a crowd of people (who were surrounding them and pelting them with snow-balls), and killed three men, besides wounding several others. The leader of the town people was a black man named Crispus Attucks.

Boston Tea Party.—A name given to the famous assemblage of citizens in Boston, December 16, 1773, who met to carry out the non-importation resolves of the colony, and who, disguised as Indians, went on board three ships, which just arrived in the harbor, and destroyed several hundred chests of tea. The British Parliament retaliated by closing the port of Boston.

Brother Jonathan.—A sportive collective name for the people of the United States, originating as follows:—When General Washington, after being appointed commander of the army, went

the subject." He did so, and the Governor was successful in supplying many of the wants of the army. The origin of the expression being soon lost sight of, the name Brother Jonathan came to be regarded as the national sobriquet.

Buckeye State.—The State of Ohio, so called from the Buckeye tree, which abounds there.

City of Brotherly Love.—Philadelphia is sometimes so called, this being the literal signification of the name.

City of Churches.—A name popularly given to the city of Brooklyn, N. Y., from the unusually large number of churches which it contains.

City of Elms.—A familiar denomination of New Haven, Connecticut,

to Massachusetts to organize it, and make preparations for the defense of the country, he found a great want of ammunition and other means necessary to meet the powerful foe he had to contend with, and great difficulty in obtaining them. If attacked in such conditions, the cause at once might be hopeless. On one occasion at that anxious period, a consultation of the officers and others was had, when it seemed that no way could be devised to make such preparations as were necessary. His Excellency Jonathan Trumbull, the elder, was then Governor of Connecticut, and, as Washington placed the greatest reliance on his judgment and aid, he remarked:—We must consult Brother Jonathan on

many of the streets of which are thickly shaded with lofty elms.

City of Magnificent Distances.—A popular designation given to the city of Washington, the capitol of the United States, which is laid out on a very large scale, being extended to cover a place of four miles and a half long, and two miles and a half broad, or eleven square miles. The entire sight is traversed by two sets of streets from seventy to one hundred feet wide, at right angles to one another, the whole again intersected obliquely by fifteen avenues from one hundred and thirty to one hundred and sixty feed wide

City of Rocks.—A descriptive name

popularly given in the United States to the city of Nashville, Tenn.

City of Spindles.—A name popularly given to the city of Lowell, Mass., the largest cotton manufacturing town in the United States.

City of the Straits.—A name given to Detroit, which is situated on the west bank of the river or strait connecting Lake St. Clair with Lake Erie. Detroit is a French word meaning "strait."

Corn-Cracker. — A popular nickname or designation for the State of Kentucky. The inhabitants of the State are often called Corncrackers.

Cow-Boys.—A band of marauders in the time of the American Revolution,

Crescent City.—A popular name for the City of New Orleans, the older portion of which is built around the convex side of a bend of the Mississippi river. In the progress of its growth up stream, however, the city has so extended itself as to fill the hollow of a curve in the opposite direction, so that the river front presents an outline resembling the character S.

Empire City.—The city of New York, the chief city of the Western world, and the metropolis of the Empire State.

Empire State, The. — A popular name of the State of New York, the most populous and the wealthiest State in the Union.

consisting mostly of refugees who adhered to the British side, and who infested the so-called "neutral grounds," lying between the American and British lines, plundering all those who had taken the oath of allegiance to the Continental Congress. (See Skinners).

Cradle of Liberty. — A popular name given to Faneuil Hall, a large public edifice in Boston, Mass., celebrated as being the place where the orators of the Revolution roused the people to resistance to British oppression.

Creole State.—A name sometimes given to the State of Louisiana, in which the descendants of the original French and Spanish settlers constitute a large proportion of the population.

Excelsior State.—The State of New York, sometimes so called for the motto "Excelsior" upon its coat of arms.

Falls City. — Louisville, Kentucky, popularly so called from the falls which, at this place, impede the navigation of the Ohio river.

Father of Waters. — A popular name given to the Mississippi river on account of its great length (3,160 miles), and the very large number of its tributaries, of which the Red, the Arkansas, the Ohio, the Missouri, the Illinois, the Des Moines, the Wisconsin, and the St. Peter's or Minnesota, are the most important. The literal signification of the name, which is of Indian origin, is said to be Great River.

Fern, Fanny.—A pseudonym adopted by Mrs. Sarah P. Parton (born 1811), a popular American authoress.

Flour City.—A popular designation in the United States of the city of Rochester, N. Y., a place remarkable for its extensive manufactories of flour.

Flower City.—Springfield, Ill., the capital of the State, which is distinguished for the beauty of its surroundings.

Forest City.—1. Cleveland, Ohio, so called from the many ornamental trees with which the streets are bordered. 2. A name given to Portland, Maine, a city distinguished for its many elms and other beautiful shade trees.

Garden of the West.—A name usually given to Kansas, but sometimes applied to Illinois and others of the Western States, which are all noted for their productiveness.

Garden of the World.—A name frequently given to the vast country comprising more than 1,200,000 square miles, which is drained by the Mississippi river and its tributaries—a region of almost unexampled fertility.

Gate City.—Keokuk, Iowa, popularly so called. It is situated at the foot of the lower rapids of the Mississippi river (which extends twelve miles, with a fall of twenty-four feet), and is the natural head of navigation. A portion of

Freestone State. — The State of Connecticut, sometimes so called from the quarries of freestone which it contains.

Funk, Peter.—A person employed at petty auctions to bid on articles put up for sale, in order to raise their prices; probably so called from such a name having frequently been given when articles were bought in. To *funk*, or *funk out*, is a vulgar expression, meaning to *slink away; to take one's self off.* In some localities it conveys the added notion of great fear.

Garden City.—A popular name for Chicago, a city which is remarkable for the number and beauty of its private gardens.

the city is built on a bluff one hundred and fifty feet high.

Gotham.—A popular name of the City of New York, first given to it in "Salmagundi" (a humorous work by Washington Irving, and William Irving and James K. Paulding), because the inhabitants were such wiseacres.

Granite State.—A popular name for the State of New Hampshire, the mountainous portions of which are largely composed of granite.

Green Mountain State.—A popular name for the State of Vermont, the Green Mountains being the principal mountain range in the State.

Grundy, Mrs.—A person frequently referred to in Morton's comedy "Speed the plow," but not introduced as one of the *dramatis personæ*. The solicitude of Dame Ashfield in this play, as to *what will Mrs. Grundy say?* has given the latter great celebrity, the interrogatory having acquired a proverbial currency.

Hamilton, Gail. — A pseudonym adopted by Miss Mary Abigail Dodge, of Hamilton, Mass., a popular American writer of the present day.

Hawkeye State.--The State of Iowa, said to be so named after an Indian chief, who was once a terror to voyagers to its borders.

Hoosier State.--The State of Indiana, the inhabitants of which are often called Hoosiers. This word is a corruption of

famous Jeffreys during the "Bloody Assizes." The name is thought by some to be derived from Richard Jacquett, who held the manor of Tyburn, near London, where criminals were formerly executed.

Keystone State. — The State of Pennsylvania, so called from its having been the central State of the Union at the time of the formation of the Constitution. If the names of the thirteen original States are arranged in the form of an arch, Pennsylvania will occupy the place of the keystone.

King Cotton.—A popular personification of the great staple production of the Southern States of America. The

husher, formerly a common term for a bully throughout the West.

Hub of the Universe.—A burlesque and popular designation of Boston, Massachusetts, originating with the American humorist, O. W. Holmes.

Iron City.—A name popularly given in the United States to Pittsburg, Pa., a city distinguished for its numerous and immense iron manufactures.

Ketch, Jack.—A hangman or executioner; so called in England from one John Ketch, a wretch who lived in the time of James II., and made himself universally odious by the butchery of many brave and noble victims, particularly those sentenced to death by the in-

supremacy of cotton seems to have been first asserted by the Hon. James H. Hammond, of South Carolina, in a speech delivered by him in the Senate of the United States on the 4th of March, 1858.

Kitchen Cabinet.—A name sportively given, in the United States, to the Hon. Francis P. Blair and the Hon. Amos Kendall, by the opponents of President Jackson's administration. Mr. Blair was the editor of *The Globe*, the organ of the President, and Kendall was one of the principal contribtors to the paper. As it was necessary for Jackson to consult frequently with these gentlemen, and as, to avoid observation, they were accustomed, when they called upon him, to go in by a back door, the Whig party styled them, in derision, the "Kitchen Cabinet," alleging that it was by their advice. that the President removed so many Whigs from office and put Democrats in their place.

Lake State.—A name populary given to the State of Michigan, which borders upon the four lakes—Superior, Michigan, Huron and Erie.

Land of Steady Habits.—A name by which the State of Connecticut is sometimes designated, in allusion to the moral character of its inhabitants.

Learned Blacksmith.—An epithet sometimes applied to Elihu Burritt, born in 1811, who began life as a blacksmith,

Lumber State.—The State of Maine, the inhabitants of which are largely engaged in the business of cutting and rafting lumber, or of converting it into boards, shingles, scantling and the like.

Mad Anthony. — A sobriquet of Major General Anthony Wayne, distinguished for his military skill and impetnous bravery in the war of the revolution.

Mason and Dixon's Line.—A name given to the southern boundary of the free State of Pennsylvania, which formerly separated it from the slave States of Maryland and Virginia. It lies in latitude 49° 43ˈ 26.3ˈˈ, and was run, with the exception of about 22 miles,

and afterward distinguished himself as a linguist.

Lion of the Sea.—A name formerly given to the Cape of Good Hope.

Little Giant.—A popular sobriquet conferred upon the Hon. Stephen A. Douglass, a distinguished American statesman (born in 1813, died 1861), in allusion to the disparity between his physical and intellectual proportions.

Little Magician.—A sobriquet conferred upon the Hon. Martin Van Buren, President of the United States from 1837 to 1841, in allusion to his supposed political sagacity and talent.

Lone Star State. — The State of Texas, so called from the device on its coat of arms.

by Charles Mason and Jeremiah Dixon, two English mathematicians and surveyors, between November 15, 1763, and December 26, 1767. During the exciting debates in Congress in 1820, on the question of excluding slavery from the State of Missouri, the eccentric John Randolph, of Roanoke, made great use of the phrase, which was caught up and re-echoed by every newspaper in the land, and thus gained a celebrity which it still retains.

Mill Boy of the Slashes.—A sobriquet conferred upon Henry Clay (1777-1852), a distinguished American orator and statesman, who was born in the neighborhood of a place in Hanover county, Virginia known as the *slashes*, (a local term for a low, swampy country), where there was a mill, to which he was often sent when a boy.

Monumental City. — The city of Baltimore, so called from the monuments it contains.

Mormons.—The last of a pretended line of Hebrew prophets, existing among a race of Israelites, principally the descendants of Joseph, who are fabled to have emigrated from Jerusalem to America about six hundred years before Christ. This imaginary prophet is said to have written the book called "The Book of Mormon," which contains doctrines upon which the " Mormons," as "Latter Day Saints," found their faith, but the real author was one Solomon Spalding (born 1761 and died 1816), an inveterate scribler, who had in early life been a clergyman The work fell into the hands of Joseph Smith, who claimed it as a direct revelation to himself from heaven, and, taking it as his text and authority, began to preach the new gospel of "Mormonism."

Mother of Presidents.—A name frequently given to the State of Virginia, which has furnished six Presidents to the Union.

Mother of States.—A name sometimes given to Virginia, the first settled of the thirteen States which united in the Declaration of Independence.

Mound City.—A name given to St. Louis on account of the numerous artificial mounds that occupied the site on which the city is built.

Nutmeg State.—A popular name for the State of Connecticut, the inhabitants of which have such a reputation for shrewdness that they have been jocosely accused of palming off wooden nutmegs on unsuspecting purchasers, instead of the genuine article.

Old Bullion.—A sobriquet conferred on Col. Thomas H. Benton (1782-1852), a distinguished American statesman, on account of his advocacy of a gold and silver currency as the true remedy for the financial embarrassments in which the United States were involved after the expiration of the charter of the national bank, and as the only proper medium for government disbursements and receipts.

Old Colony.—A name given to that portion of Massachusetts included within the original limits of the Plymouth colony, which was formed at an earlier date than the colony of Massachusetts Bay. In 1692 the two colonies were united in one province, bearing the name of the latter, and at the formation of the Federal Union became the State of Massachusetts.

Old Dominion.—A name given to the State of Virginia.

Old Hickory.—General Jackson was known among the soldiers who served under him as "Old Hickory," a sobriquet given him during the Creek war.—

His brigade was making a forced march, without baggage or tents, to surprise the Indians in one of their villages, and were for several days and nights exposed to the peltings of a March storm, the rain freezing as it fell. General Jackson got a severe cold, but did not complain as he tried to sleep in a muddy bottom among his half frozen soldiers. Captain Allen and his brother John cut down a stout hickory, peeled off the bark and made a covering for the General, who was with difficulty persuaded to crawl into it. The next morning a drunken citizen entered the camp, and seeing the tent kicked it over. As Jackson crawled from the ruins the toper cried: "Hello, Old Hickory; come out of your bark and jine us in a drink!" Thenceforth the General was known in camp as "Old Hickory," and when he was talked of as a Presidential candidate the nickname was adopted by his supporters. The "liberty tree" of the Revolution was revived in the "hickory tree" planted at every country cross-roads and village by the enthusiastic Democrats, while they sang:—

"Freemen, cheer the hickory tree,
Long its boughs have sheltered thee."

Old Hunkers.—A nick-name applied to the ultra-conservative portion of the Democratic party in the United States, and especially in the State of New York.

Old Ironsides.—A title popularly conferred upon the United States frigate Constitution, which was launched at Boston, September 20th, 1797 She became greatly celebrated on account of the prominent part she took in the bombardment of Tripoli, in 1804, and for the gallantry she displayed during the war of 1812.

Old North State.—A name by which the State of North Carolina is sometimes known.

Old Public Functionary.—A name given to James Buchanan, fifteenth President of the United States. He first applied the expression to himself in his annual message to Congress, in the year 1859. Sometimes humorously abbreviated O. P. F.

Old Wagon.— A sobriquet given to the frigate United States, which was launched at Philadelphia in 1798, and was afterward rebuilt on the original model. She got her nick-name previous to the war of 1812, from her dull sailing qualities, which were subsequently very much improved.

Old-style Jonathan.—A nom de plume of Washington Irving, under which he contributed in 1842 to the *Morning Chronicle*, a Democratic journal of New York City.

Palmetto State. — The State of South Carolina, so called from the arms of the State, which contain a palmetto.

Panhandle, The.—A fanciful and cant name given to the most northerly portion of the State of West Virginia, a long, narrow projection between the Ohio river and the Western boundary of Pennsylvania.

Partington, Mrs.— An imaginary old lady whose laughable sayings have been recorded by the American humorist, B. P. Shillaber. She is distinguished, like Smollett's "Tabitha Bramble," and Sheridan's "Mrs. Malaprop," for her amusing affectation and misuse of learned words.

Pathfinder of the Rocky Mountains. A title applied to Major-General John C. Fremont, who conducted four exploring expeditions across the Rocky Mountains.

Pennsylvania Farmer. — A surname given to John Dickinson (1732–

and distinguished for their circulation of the prudential virtues, as temperance, frugality, order, justice, cleanliness, charity, and the like, by means of maxims or precepts, which, it has been said, "are as valuable as anything that has descended from Pythagoras." — See *Saunders, Richard.*

Prairie State.—A name given to Illinois in allusion to the wide-spread and beautiful prairies, which form a striking feature of the scenery of the State.

Puritan City.—A name sometimes given to the city of Boston, Massachusetts, in allusion to the character of its founders and early inhabitants.

Quaker City.—A popular name of

1808) an American statesman and author, and a citizen of Pennsylvania. In the year 1768 he published his "Letters from a Pennsylvania Farmer to the Inhabitants of the British Colonies."— These were republished in London, with a preface by Dr. Franklin, and were subsequently translated into French and published in Paris.

Pine Tree State.—A popular name of the State of Maine, the central and northern portion of which are covered with extensive pine forests.

Poor Richard.—The feigned author of a series of almanacs (commenced in 1732 and continued for twenty-five years) really written by Benjamin Franklin,

Philadelphia, which was planned and settled by William Penn, accompanied by a colony of English Friends

Queen City.—A popular name of Cincinnati, so called when it was the undisputed commercial metropolis of the West.

Queen City of the Lakes.—A name sometimes given to the city of Buffalo, N.Y., from its position and importance.

Railroad City.—Indianapolis, the capitol of the State of Indiana, is sometimes called by this name, as being the terminus of various railroads.

Rail-splitter.—A cant designation of Abraham Lincoln, the sixteenth President of the United States, who is said to have supported himself for one winter, in early life, by splitting rails for a farmer.

Red-Coats.—The name given by the Americans in the Revolutionary War to the British soldiery, in allusion to their scarlet uniform.

Regulators.—The popular name of a party in North Carolina, which arose in 1768, and had for its object the forcible redress of public grievances.

Rhody, Little.—A popular designation of Rhode Island, the smallest State in the Union.

Rough and Ready.—A sobriquet given to General Zachary Taylor (born 1790—died 1850), twelfth President of

Sambo.—A cant designation of the negro race. No race has ever shown such capabilities .of adaptation to varying soil and circumstances as the negro. Alike to them the snows of Canada, the hard, rocky land of New England, or the gorgeous profusion of the Southern States. *Sambo* and Cuffy expand under them all.

Saunders, Richard.—A feigned name under which Dr. Franklin, in 1732, commenced the publication of an Almanac—commonly called "Poor Richard's Almanac," of which the distinguished feature was a series of maxims of prudence and industry in the form of proverbs.

the United States, as expressive of prominent traits in his character.

St. Nicholas.—The patron saint of boys. He is said to have been Bishop of Myra, and to have died in the year 326 The young were universally taught to revere him, and the popular fictions which represent him as the bearer of presents to children on Christmas Eve is well known. He is the Santa Claus (or Klaus) of the Dutch.

Sam.—A popular synonym in the United States for the Know-Nothings, or Native American party. The name involves an allusion to *Uncle Sam*, the common personification of the United States Government

Scarlet Woman, The.—In the controversial writings of the Protestants, a common designation of the Church of Rome, intended to symbolize its vices and corruptions. The allusion is to the description contained in Revelation, chapter xvi : 1-6.

Seven Sleepers.—According to a very widely diffused legend of early Christianity, seven noble youths of Ephesus, in the time of the Decian persecution, who, having fled to a certain cavern for refuge, and having been pursued, discovered and walled in for a cruel death, were made to fall asleep, and in that state were miraculously kept for almost two centuries. Their names are traditionally said to have been Maximican, Malchus, Martinian, Denis, John, Scrapton and Constantine. The church has consecrated the 27th of June to their memory. The Koran relates the tale of the seven sleepers, deriving it probably from the same source as the Christian legend, and declares that out of respect to them the sun altered his course twice a day that he might shine into the cavern.

Seven Wonders of the World.—A name given to seven very remarkable objects of the ancient world, which have been variously enumerated. The following classification is one of the most generally received: 1. The Pyramids of Egypt; 2. The Pharos of Alexander; 3. The walls and hanging gardens of Babylon; 4. The Temple of Diana at Ephesus; 5. The Statue of the Olympian Jupiter; 6. The Mausoleum of Artemisia; 7 The Colossus of Rhodes.

Skinners.—A name assumed by a predatory band in the Revolutionary War, who, professing allegiance to the American cause, but influenced by a desire to plunder, roamed over the "neutral ground" lying between the hostile armies, robbing those who refused to take the oath of fidelity.

Slick, Sam.—The title and hero of various humorous narratives, illustrating and exaggerating the peculiarities of the Yankee character and dialect, written by Judge Thomas C. Haliburton, of Nova Scotia. Sam Slick is represented as a Yankee clockmaker and peddler, full of quaint drollery, unsophisticated wit, knowledge of human nature, and aptitude in the use of what he calls "soft sawder."

Smoky City.—A name sometimes given to Pittsburg, Pa., an important manufacturing city. The use of bituminous coal occasions dense volumes of smoke to fill the air in and around the place, soiling the garments of passengers and giving the buildings a dark and sooty appearance.

Stonewall Jackson.—A sobriquet given during the American civil war to Thomas Jonathan Jackson (born 1824, died 1863), a General in the service of the Confederate States. This famous appellation had its origin in an expression used by the Confederate General Bee, on trying to rally his men at the battle of Bull Run, July 21, 1862, "There is Jackson standing like a stone wall." From that day he was known as "Stonewall" Jackson, and his command as the Stonewall Brigade.

Sucker State.—A cant name given in America to the State of Illinois, the inhabitants of which are very generally called Suckers throughout the West.— The origin of this term is said to be as follows: The western prairies are in many places full of the holes made by the crawfish (a fresh-water shell-fish, similar in form to the lobster), which descend to the water beneath. In early times, when travelers wended their way over these immense plains, they very prudently provided themselves with a long hollow reed, and when thirsty thrust it into these natural artesians, and thus easily supplied their longings. The crawfish well generally contains pure water, and the manner in which the traveler drew forth the refreshing element gave him the name of Sucker.

Swedish Nightingale. — A name popularly given to Jenny Lind (Madame Goldschmidt, born 1821), a native of Stockholm, and the most celebrated of female vocalists.

Tammany, St.—The name of an Indian Chief who, in the United States, has been popularly canonized as a saint, and adopted as the tutelary genius of one branch of the Democratic party.— Tammany was of the Delaware nation, and lived probably in the middle of the seventeenth century. He resided in the country which is now Delaware until he was of age, when he moved beyond the Alleghanies, and settled on the banks of the Ohio. He became chief sachem of his tribe, and being always a friend of the whites, often restrained his warriors from deeds of violence. His rule was always discreet, and he endeavored to induce his followers to cultivate agriculture and the arts of peace rather than those of war. When he became old he called a council to have a successor appointed, after which the residue of his life was spent in retirement, and tradition relates that "young and old repaired to his wigwam to hear him discourse wisdom." His great motto was, "Unite in peace for happiness, in war for defense." When and by whom he was first styled *saint,* or by what whim he was chosen the patron of Democracy, does not appear.

Tippecanoe. — A sobriquet conferred upon General William H. Harrison, afterward President of the United States, during the political canvass which preceded his election, on account of the victory gained by him over the Indians in the battle which took place on the 6th of November, 1811, at the junction of the Tippecanoe and Wabash Rivers.

Topsy.—A young slave girl in Mrs. Stowe's novel, "Uncle Tom's Cabin," who is made to illustrate the ignorance, low moral development and wild humor of the African character, as well as its capacity for education.

Turpentine State.—A popular name for the State of North Carolina, which produces and exports large quantities of turpentine.

mediately after the last declaration of war with England, Elbert Anderson, of New York, then a contractor, visited Troy, on the Hudson, where was concentrated and where he purchased a large contract of provisions, beef, pork, etc. The inspectors of these articles, at the place, were Messrs. Ebenezer and Samuel Wilson. The latter gentleman, invariably known as "Uncle Sam," generally superintended in person a large number of workmen, who, on this occasion, were employed in overhauling the possessions. Many of these workmen, being of a character denominated "fond of powder," were found, shortly after, following the recruiting drum and pushing toward the frontier lines, for the double purpose of meeting the enemy and of eating the provisions they had lately labored to put in good order.— Their old jokes accompanied them, and before the first campaign ended, this identical one first appeared in print; it gained favor rapidly till it penetrated, and was recognized in every part of the country, and will, no doubt, con-

provisions purchased by the contractors of the army. The casks were marked E. A.—U. S. This work fell to the lot of a facetious fellow in the employ of the Messrs. Wilson, who, on being asked by some of his fellow-workmen the meaning of the mark (for the letters U. S. for United States were then almost entirely new to them), said he did not know, unless it meant Elbert Anderson and "Uncle Sam," alluding exclusively to the said "Uncle Sam" Wilson. The joke took among the workmen, and passed currently; and "Uncle Sam" himself being present, was occasionally rallied

tinue so while the United States remain a nation.

Underground Railroad, The.— A popular embodiment of the various ways in which fugitive slaves from the Southern States were assisted in escaping to the North, or to Canada; often humorously abbreviated U. G. R. R.

Wagon Boy, Ohio's.—A sobriquet of the Hon. Thomas Corwin (born 1794), a distinguished American statesman.— While yet a lad Harrison and his army were on the Northern frontier, almost destitute of provisions, and a demand was made on the patriotism of the people to furnish the necessary subsistence. The elder Corwin loaded a wagon with supplies, which was delivered by his son, who remained with the army during the rest of the campaign, and who is said to have proved himself "a good whip and an excellent reinsman."

Western Reserve, The.—A name popularly given to a region of country reserved by the State of Connecticut at the time of the cession of the Northwest Territory to the United States. Disputes arose, after the war of the Revolution, between several of the States respecting the right of soil in their territory, which were only.allayed by the cession of the whole to the United States, Connecticut reserving a tract of 3,666,921 acres near Lake Erie. In 1800 jurisdiction over this tract was relinquished to the Federal Government, the State reserving the right of the soil to settlers, while the Indian titles to the rest of the soil were bought up by the general government. In 1799, the Northwestern Territory, over which Congress had exercised jurisdiction since 1787, was admitted to a second grade of territorial government. Shortly after, Ohio was detached from it and erected into an independent territory,. and in 1803 it was received as a State into the Union.

White House, The.—In the United States a name properly given to the executive or presidential mansion at Washington, which is a large building of freestone painted white.

Wicked Bible.—A name given to an edition of the Bible published in 1632 by Baker & Lucas,. because the word *not* was omitted in the seventh commandment. The printers were called before the High Commission, fined heavily, and the whole impression destroyed.

Wolverine State.—The State of Michigan, popularly so called for its abounding with wolverines.

Yellow Jack.—Among sailors a common personification of the yellow fever. Although used as a proper name, it is probable that the original meaning of the appellation was nothing more than *yellow flag*, a flag being termed *jack* by seamen, and *yellow* being the color of that customarily displayed from lazarettos, or naval hospitals, or from vessels in quarantine.

Young America.—A popular collective name for American youth, or a personification of their supposed characteristics.

BIOGRAPHY OF DISTINGUISHED PERSONS.
(Alphabetically Arranged).

Adams, John.—Was born in Braintree, Mass., October 19, 1735, and died July 4, 1826. He graduated at Harvard College in 1755, and was admitted to the bar in 1758. He served as President of the United States from 1707 to 1801. He was a member of the first and second Congresses, and nominated Washington as Commander-in-Chief. Thomas Jefferson wrote the Declaration of Independence, but Adams secured its adoption in a three days' debate. In his position as President he lost the reputation he had gained as Congressman.— His enemies accused him of being a bad judge of men, of clinging to old unpopular notions, and of having little control over his temper. They also ridiculed his egotism, which they declared to be inordinate. He lived, however, to see the prejudice against his administration give place to a more just estimate of his great worth and exalted integrity. As a Delegate to the Constitutional Convention he was honored as one of the fathers of the Republic Adams and Jefferson were firm friends during the Revolution, but political strife alienated them. On their return to private life they became reconciled. They died on the same day, the fiftieth anniversary of American independence. Adams' last words were: "Thomas Jefferson still survives." Jefferson was, however, already dead in his Virginia home.— Thus, by the passing away of these two remarkable men was made memorable the 4th of July, 1826.

Adams, John Quincy.—Died in Washington, D. C., February 23, 1848. He was born at Quincy, Mass., July 11, 1767. When 11 years old his father, John Adams, Minister to France, took him to Paris. When 14 years old he went to Russia as private secretary to Francis Dana. In 1794 President Washington appointed him Minister to the Netherlands. He was next made Minister to Berlin. President Madison appointed him Minister to Russia. In 1815 he was transferred to the English court. In 1817 he was Secretary of State under Monroe. He was elected President in 1825. He was stricken by paralysis in his seat in the House of Representatives, to which he was elected in 1831, and died in an adjoining room. His last whisper was: "This is the last of earth; I am content."

Adams, Samuel.—Died October 2, 1803. He was born in Boston September 27, 1722. He graduated at Harvard in 1740, and at once took an active interest in politics, becoming prominent and influential. He served ten years in the Assembly, and was a strong advocate of the Continental Congress, of which he was for years a member. He signed the

Declaration of Independence and filled the offices of Lieutenant Governor and Governor of Massachusetts.

Allan, Ethan.—The Green "Mountain Champion of Liberty," died February 13th, 1789, sixty years old. He was was born in Connecticut, but removed to the present State of Vermont when a child. He was one of the first to respond to the call of war. His fame rests chiefly on his successes at Ticonderoga and Crown Point. He was captured at Montreal and taken to England. He was there offered a tract of land in America if he would become a British officer.— Said he. "That reminds me of Satan's offer to Jesus Christ, of all the kingdoms

raids at the head of British and Tory forces upon unprotected colonists, rendered his name infamous. In England the "treason was accepted but the traitor despised."

Atkinson, Henry.—Was a native of South Carolina, and entered the army as a Captain in 1808. He was retained in the army after the war of 1812, was made Adjutant General, and was finally appointed to the command of the Western army. He died in Jefferson Barracks in June, 1842.

Ashe, John.—Was born in England in 1721, and came to America when a child. He was engaged in the Regulator war in North Carolina in 1771, and

in the world if he would fall down and worship him, when at the same time the poor devil had not a foot of land on the earth." He suffered a prolonged imprisonment, but was exchanged in 1778 and made a Brigadier General.

Arnold, Benedict.—Died June 14, 1801, in obscurity, in London, England. He was born in Norwich, Conn., Jan. 3, 1740. He was a cruel, tyrannical and reckless boy, and a rash and fearless man. He was with Ethan Allan at Ticonderoga, with Washington at Cambridge, and made a celebrated march into Canada, which resulted in disaster. His attempted treason at West Point, and his subsequent fierce and brutal

was a general in the Continental army. He died of small-pox in 1781.

Andrew, John Albion. — Widely known as the war governor of Massachusetts, died at Boston, October 30th, 1867, aged 49 years.

Balboa Beheaded by Davila, Governor of Darien, in 1517, who had grown jealous of his fame. He was born in Spain, and being oppressed with debt went to Hayti. His discovery of the Pacific ocean worked a change in the feelings and bearing of the man, and he rose to rank among the great explorers of his time. His record was free from stain. He perished in his 42d year, a victim to despicable jealousy and enmity.

Bainbridge, William (Commodore), was born in New Jersey in 1774.— He was the Captain of a merchant vessel at the age of 19. He entered the naval service in 1798. He was distinguished during the war of 1812, and died in 1833.

Barney, Commodore was born in Baltimore in 1759. He entered the naval service of the Revolution in 1775, and was active during the whole war. He bore the American flag to the French National Convention in 1796, and entered the French service. He returned to America in 1800, and took part in the war of 1812, and died at Pittsburg in the year 1818.

Black Hawk, a celebrated Indian chief of the Sacs and Foxes, died October 3, 1838, in Iowa, aged 71 years.— Their home was on Rock river, Illinois. Black Hawk fought on the British side in 1812. By a treaty made with Keokuk, one of their chiefs, July 15th, 1832, the Sacs and Foxes relinquished their lands east of the Mississippi to the United States, but Black Hawk and part of the tribe refused their assent, and would not leave. The "Black Hawk War" ensued, the Indians were defeated and Black Hawk captured. He was taken to St. Louis and afterward to Washington, where he excited great curiosity. Lands in Iowa were subsequently assigned to

Bell, Hon. John of Tennessee, died September 10, 1869.

Bennett, James Gordon, Sr. — Founded the New York *Herald* in May, 1835, with a capital of $500, in a cellar on Wall street, New York. He encountered severe trials in his enterprise, having suffered once from robbery and twice from fire during the first fifteen months of his business experience, but being possessed of an indomitable will, he overcame all obstacles. He was born in Scotland in 1795, and came to America with $25, and found his first steady employment as a proof reader in Boston, and in 1822 emigrated to New York City. He died June 1, 1872.

him, upon which he spent the remainder of his days.

Boehm, Rev. Henry an eminent Methodist Minister, died on Staten Island, New York, January 1, 1876, aged 101 years.

Boliver, Simon the South American patriot, died at San Pedro, December 18, 1830. He was born at Caraccas July 24, 1783. He spent his life and fortune in the effort to make his country free.

Bonaparte, Jerome Napoleon died at Baltimore, Md., June 17, 1870.— He was the son of Jerome Napoleon, brother of the Emperor.

Boone, Daniel died at Charlotte, Mo., September 26, 1820. He was born in Bucks county, Pa., February 11, 1735. He was famous as a pioneer, hunter and explorer. In 1769 he penetrated into Kentucky from North Carolina, where he had been living. He was several times captured by Indians. In 1775 he founded Boonesborough. Twenty years afterward Kentucky was admitted as a State into the Union. He then went to Missouri and afterward explored Arkansas, and in 1814 trapped beavers on the Great Osage, being then 80 years old.— His remains now lie at Frankfort, Ky., where they were buried at public expense.

Botts, Hon. John Minor of Virginia, died September 16, 1869.

the Pilgrims who came over in the Mayflower, died April 16, 1644. He was born at Scrooby, England, in 1560. He was imprisoned for his religious views and went to Holland, and from there came to America with the Colony, the religious care of which devolved upon him in the absence of the pastor, John Robinson. He continued in pastoral charge until 1629, but declined to administer the sacraments. He was greatly venerated. He left a library of 275 volumes, 64 of which were 'in the learned languages.

Brown, Ossawattomie. — In the terrible civil war which raged in Kansas in 1856, between slave and free State set-

Bradford, William one of the Pilgrims who came over in the Mayflower, died at Plymouth, Mass., May 9th, 1657. He was born in Yorkshire, England, in 1588. He was elected successor to Gov. Carver in 1621, and held the office for 31 years. He was a man of ability, and Plymouth Colony owed its success largely to his wise administration. He wrote a history of the Colony from 1602 to 1647.

Bragg, Braxton F. an ex Confederate General, died at Galveston, Texas, September 27, 1876, aged 61 years.

Breckenridge, John C. Vice-President of the United States under Buchanan, died May 18, 1875. He was born near Lexington, Ky., January 21, 1821.

Brewster, Elder William one of

tlers, John Brown, with small bands of men, often held large numbers at bay.— With thirty men he made a successful attack upon 500 at Ossawattomie, from which he gained this sobriquet.

Brown, Jacob was born in Pennsylvania in 1775. He engaged in his country's service in 1813, and soon became distinguished. He was made a Major-General in 1814. He was Commander-in-Chief of the United States army in 1821, and held that rank and office when he died, in 1838.

Brown, Major was born in Massachusetts in 1788; was in the war of 1812, and was promoted to Major in 1843. He was wounded in the Mexican war by the bursting of a bomb-shell, and died on the ninth of May, 1846. He was fifty-eight years of age.

Buchanan, James was born in Franklin county, Pennsylvania, April 13, 1791, and died at Wheatland, June 1st, 1868. He was a graduate of Dickinson College, and was admitted to the bar in 1812. He was President from 1857 to 1861, and was so constantly in office from 1820 up to that time that he was known by the sobriquet of "Public Functionary." The "bachelor-President," as Mr. Buchanan was sometimes called, was 66 years old when he was called to the executive chair. He had just returned to his native country, after an absence of four years as Minister to England. Pre-

sey in 1756. In his twentieth year he joined the Continental army, and accompanied Arnold in his expedition against Quebec. Ill health compelled him to leave the army in 1779, and he became a distinguished lawyer and an active public man. He died on Staten Island, N. Y., in 1836.

Burlingame, Hon. Anson United States Minister to China, died at St. Petersburg, Russia, February 23d, 1870, aged 48 years.

Butler, Zebulon was born in Connecticut in 1731. He served in the Revolution as a Colonel, and died in Wyoming in 1795.

Calhoun, John C. died March 31,

viously to that he had been well known in public life as Congressman, Senator, and as Secretary of State under President Polk. Much was hoped from his election, as he avowed the object of his administration to be "to destroy any sectional party, whether North or South, and to restore, if possible, that national fraternal feeling between the different States that had existed during the early days of the Republic." But popular passion and sectional jealousy were too strong to yield to pleasant persuasion.— When Mr. Buchanan's administration closed the fearful conflict was near at hand. He retired to his estate in Pennsylvania, where he died.

Burr, Aaron was born in New Jer-

1850, at Washington, D. C. He was born March 18th, 1782, in Abbeyville county, South Carolina, of Irish-Presbyterian parentage, He graduated in Yale College in 1804, studied law at Litchfield, Conn., and was admitted to the bar in South Carolina; was elected to the State Legislature, and in 1811 to Congress. Was Secretary of War under Monroe, Vice-President of the United States from 1824 to 1832. He was the champion of Nullification, and but for President Jackson's decision and energy would have led South Carolina out of the Union in 1832. He was a man of distinguished ability, of honor, and a Christian gentleman.

Carroll, Charles of Carrollton, Md.,

the last surviving signer of the Declaration of Independence, died November 14th, 1832. He was born at Annapolis, Md., September 30, 1737. He was worth $2,000,000 at the outbreak of the Revolution. He was a member of the Colonial Congress when he signed the Declaration of Independence. Some one jocosely said: "There were so many Carrolls that the British would not know which one it was," whereupon he promptly added "of Carrollton."·

Carson, "Kit" the famous frontier leader and scout, died May 23d, 1868, at Fort Lyon, Colorado. He was born in Kentucky, December 24, 1809. He was Fremont's guide, Indian agent in New

water. William Bradford was chosen his successor.

Channing, William E., D. D., an eminent Unitarian minister, died at Bennington, Vermont, October 2, 1842, aged 62 years.

Chandler, John was a native of Massachusetts and served as a general in the war of 1812. Some years after the war he was a United States Senator from Maine. He died at Augusta, in that State, in 1844.

Clark, George Rogers was a native of Virginia, and was born in 1752. He was one of the most accomplished and useful officers of the Western pioneers

Mexico, and Brevet Brigadier General in the civil war. His first name was Christopher.

Cartwright, Peter a famous backwoods Methodist preacher, died at Pleasant Plains, Ills., September 25, 1872.— He was born in Virginia September 1st, 1785.

Carver, Governor died April 6th, 1621, less than four months after the landing of the Pilgrims. He was a serious loss to the Colony. He was possessed of skill and prudence, and was helpful and unselfish, spending his property freely, and laboring with his own hands for the good of his fellow members. It was largely owing to him that the Pilgrims were enabled to cross the

during the Revolution. He died near Louisville, Ky., in 1848.

Clay, Henry died June 29th, 1852, aged 75 years. He was born in Hanover county, Virginia. His father was a Baptist preacher. He studied law and was admitted to the bar at 21. He emigrated to Lexington, Ky., in 1799, was elected to the Legislature in 1804 and to the United States Senate in 1806. He was chosen Speaker of the House of Representatives in 1811, which position he occupied until 1825, except for one term. He was one of the United States Commissioners at the treaty of Ghent. He received 37 electoral votes for President in 1824. He was Secretary of State under John Q. Adams. In 1832 he received the electoral votes of six States. In 1844 he was the Whig candidate for President, but was defeated by Mr. Polk. He was in the United States Senate when he died. He was opposed to slavery, but favored gradual emancipation. He was a strong advocate for a protective tariff. He was an able and eloquent statesman.

Clay, Green was born in Virginia in 1756 and was made a brigadier of Kentucky volunteers early in 1813. He commanded at Fort Meigs in 1813. He died in 1826.

Clinton, George of New York, Vice-President of the United States, died on the 20th of April, 1812, at Washington, D. C. He was born July 26, 1739.

voyages in the Mediterranean, to the Azores, the Canaries, and the coast of Guinea. He first conceived the idea that land existed to the westward while constructing maps and charts at Lisbon, which was then the headquarters of geographical discovery. He first laid his theory and project before John I., of Portugal, then before the Republic of Genoa and before other courts, all of whom treated his schemes as visionary. Finally, Ferdinand and Isabella of Spain, furnished him with three small vessels and 120 men, agreeing to reward him by making him High-Admiral Governor and Viceroy over all lands he might discover, and a tenth of all the produce of

Columbus returned to Palos, March 15, 1493, and received a joyous welcome. The Pinta arrived the evening of the same day. Her commander, Martin Alonzo Pinzon, had forwarded a letter to Ferdinand and Isabella from Bayonne, hoping to receive for himself the honor due to Columbus. Receiving instead a reprimand, his proud spirit was broken, and he shortly after died of chagrin.— Columbus died May 20, 1506, at Valladolid, aged seventy years. His body was laid in the Convent at St. Thomas. He ranks among the great navigators of the world. He was the son of a wool comber and was born at Genoa; was educated at Pavia, evincing early a taste for astronomy and cosmography. He made repeated

of the countries. The little fleet sailed from Palos, August 3, 1492, and America was discovered October 12th. Notwithstanding the vast territory and wealth he had added to Spain, he was treated with jealousy and ingratitude, and died in poverty and neglect.

Cortez, Hernando was born in Spain in 1485. He came to Hayti when Ovando was Governor, and participated in the conquest of Cuba under Velasquez, and began to exhibit the popular characteristics which afterward gave him such a strong hold upon his soldiers. When the Governor had fitted out his expedition for the conquest of Mexico, he appointed Cortez Captain-General, who immediately devoted himself and his fortune to the project. After conquering Mexico he died, December 2, 1547, near Seville, Spain, aged 63 years. He was pre-eminently a representative soldier among the explorers of his time. He was really a great general, and his victories were gained, not by dash and superior force, but by good judgment and military perception.

Crockett, David with five companions, were murdered at Fort Alamo, after they had surrendered, March 6th, 1836. He was born at Limestone, Tenn., August 17, 1786. He was a noted hunter and backwoodsman. Was in the Creek war with General Jackson in 1813. Was elected to the State Legislature several

the Revolution, and, in the war of 1812, was appointed Major-General and Commander-in-Chief of the armies. He was born in New Hampshire. He returned to private life in 1815, and died at Roxbury, near Boston, in 1829, at the age of 78 years.

DeKalb, Baron was a native of Alsace, a German province ceded to France. He had been in America as a secret French agent about fifteen years before. He came to America with Lafayette in 1777, and Congress commissioned him a Major-General. He died of wounds received at the battle of Camden in 1780.

Decatur, Stephen was born in 1779,

times, and in 1827 to Congress, to which he was re-elected twice. He participated in the war for Texan independence. He was a man of great native force of character and originated the popular saying: "First, be sure you're right, then go ahead."

Cushman, Charlotte the famous actress, died in Boston, Mass , February 18, 1876, aged 59 years.

Dahlgreen, Admiral died in Washington, D. C., July 12th, 1870. He was born in Philadelphia in 1810, and was appointed midshipman from the State of Pennsylvania, February 1st, 1826, and served with distinction in the United States navy until the time of his death.

Dearborn, Henry was an officer of

in Maryland. He entered the navy at the age of 19. After his last cruise in the Mediterranean he superintended the building of gunboats. He rose to the rank of Commodore, and during the war of 1812 he was distinguished for his skill and bravery. He afterward humbled the Barbary powers, and after returning home he was killed in a duel with Commodore Barron, in March, 1820.

DeSoto.—Hernando de Soto was born about the year 1496, in Estremaduro, Spain. He came to America in the year 1519, and after having traveled through the region of the Arkansas river and selected a site on the Mississippi for a colony, died May 21, 1542, and was buried by his followers in the Mississippi, the river he had discovered.

Douglass, Fred escaped from his master in Baltimore September 3, 1838. He has since become a famous negro orator and journalist.

Douglas, Stephen A. died at Chicago, Ill., June 3, 1861. He was born at Brandon, Vt., April 23, 1813. He was a prominent American statesman.

Drake, Sir Francis who was one of the first adventurers, with Sir John Hawkins, to introduce slaves into this country, was born in the south of England in the year 1545. After experiencing many misfortunes in battles on the Mexican coast he returned home a poor man, and died in 1595.

bile, he rendered himself famous, where his deeds excited the astonishment of all who knew the fortifications, as they were believed to be impregnable until captured by him. His services were so important that Congress, in 1866, created the office of Admiral and appointed him to fill the position.

Forrest, Edwin.—He was born in Philadelphia in 1806, and died of apoplexy, December 12, 1872, at the age of sixty-six years. He was an eminent actor and developed a dramatic taste when a mere boy, and appeared on the regular stage when but thirteen years old. In 1858 he retired to private life, and at his death provided a fund for aged and destitute actors.

Endicott, John died in Boston, March 15, 1665, at the age of 76 years.— He was born in Dorchester, England, and he, with others, settled in Salem, Mass., in 1628, and was chosen first Governor of Massachusetts. He was subsequently re-elected to that office several times, which he filled with great satisfaction to the people.

Farragut, Admiral was born near Knoxville, Tenn., July 5, 1801, and died at Portsmouth, N. H., August 14, 1870, at the age of 69 years. He entered the United States navy at eleven years of age, and made a brilliant career up to the time of his death. In 1862, during the civil war, at New Orleans and Mo-

Fessenden, Hon. William Pitt of Maine, died September 8, 1869.

Fillmore, Millard being elected Vice-President to President Taylor, became his constitutional successor, and served the unexpired term from 1850 to 1853. He was born in Cayuga county, N. Y., January 7, 1800, and died March 8, 1874. He had not a very liberal education, and, when young, served as an apprentice to the fuller's trade. In the year 1821 he was admitted to the bar, and practiced law with success. From 1832 to 1840 he was a member of Congress; in 1842 he was nominated by the Whigs of New York for Governor, and was defeated, and in 1856 the Native

American party run him for President, and he received only the electoral vote of Maryland. Upon the death of President Taylor the entire cabinet resigned.

Franklin, Benjamin died April 17, 1790. He was born in Boston, Jan. 17, 1706. His father designed him for the ministry, but after a little schooling, at 12 years of age, he was bound apprentice to his brother James, a printer, who published the New England *Courant* — When 14 years old he wrote a number of articles and slipped them under the office door at night. They were published and met with great favor. When his brother learned the author he gave him no encouragement. Franklin left him secretly and went to Philadelphia, where he ob-

Fulton, Robert the inventor and discoverer of steam navigation, was born in Pennsylvania, and was a student of West, the great painter, for several years. He had more genius for mechanics than for the fine arts, and he turned his efforts in that direction. He died in 1815, soon after launching a steamship-of-war, at the age of 50 years.

Gaines, Edmund P. was born in Virginia in 1777. He entered the army in 1799, and rose gradually until he was made Major-General for his gallantry at Fort Erie in 1814. He remained in the army until his death in 1849.

Gates, Gen. Horatio died at New York, April 10th, 1806. He was born in England in 1728. He was wounded

tained employment from Mr. Skinner.— He soon attracted the attention of Gov. Keith and other prominent men. He went into business for himself, publishing "Poor Richard's Almanac," and subsequently "The Pennsylvania Gazette." He started the Philadelphia Library Company, invented the Franklin Stove, organized a fire company in 1737, a militia company in 1743, and in 1749 was the chief founder of the Academy of Science, now the University of Philadelphia. He assisted in establishing newspapers in other colonies, and made famous electrical experiments. He held various offices of public trust and was of great service to his country in her hour of peril.

at Braddock's defeat. Congress made him Brigadier-General at the beginning of the Revolution, and gave him command of the Northern army in 1776. He gained great reputation by the surrender of Burgoyne, but it is questionable whether he is entitled to the credit. His already excessive pride was inflated, and he aspired to be Commander-in-Chief.— A conspiracy was formed, known as "Conway's Cabal," to place him in Washington's stead. It failed, and he was ordered South, and by his mismanagement of the army nearly ruined his previous reputation. He was utterly defeated at Camden, which about ended his military life. He retired to New

York and served one term in the Legislature in 1792.

Grant, Ulysess S. was born at Point Pleasant, Clermont county, Ohio, April 27, 1822. He was very unwilling to follow his father's trade, which was that of a tanner, and at seventeen an appointment was secured for him at West Point. His name having been wrongly registered, Grant vainly endeavored to set the matter right, but finally accepted his "manifest destiny," assumed the change thus forced upon him, and thenceforth signed himself "Ulysses Simpson," the latter being his mother's family name.— Two years after completing his four years' course as cadet, the Mexican war broke out, in which Grant conducted himself with great gallantry, receiving especial mention and promotion. In 1847 he was made first lieutenant, captain in 1853, and in 1854 he resigned his commission and entered the leather and saddlery business at Galena, Illinois, in 1859, where he remained until the opening of the war in 1861, when he immediately offered his services in behalf of the Union. His modesty and diffidence delayed their acceptance, and Governor Yates, of Illinois, was the first to avail himself of them. Grant finally took the field as Colonel of the Twenty-first Regiment Illinois Volunteers. In Feb., 1862, he was made a Major-General and commanded the armies of the Southwest. On the 12th of March, 1864, he was made Lieutenant-General and put in command of all the armies, and took personal direction of the military operations in Virginia, and on the 9th of April, 1865, General Lee surrendered the Confederate armies to him, at Appomattox Court-House, and hostilities were ended. He was nominated and elected by the Republicans President of the United States in 1868, and re-elected by the the same party in 1872. His term expired in 1877.

Green, General Nathaniel died of sunstroke at Mulberry Grove, Ga., June 19, 1786. He was born at Warwick, R. I., May 27th, 1742, of Quaker parents.— Was elected to the General Assembly in 1770. After the battle of Lexington he entered the army and was made Brigadier-General. At Brandywine and Germantown his skill prevented final disaster. He succeeded Gates in command of the Southern army, which was in chaotic condition, but by skillful generalship he thwarted Cornwallis and forced him out of the South. He was a patriot, a hero and an honest man.

Greeley, Horace.—He started the first penny paper ever published in New York in 1833, known as the "Morning Post." It was not a success, and after being the author of several other publications he founded the "New York Tribune," April 10, 1841. The first issue was 5,000 copies, and Mr. Greeley said he "experienced considerable difficulty in giving them away." He was born in Amherst, N. H., February 3, 1811, and died at Pleasantville, N. Y., November 29th, 1872, sixty-one years of age. He learned the printer's trade, and after working in Jamestown and Lodi, N. Y., and Erie, Pa., he went to New York City in 1831, with a cash capital of $10, and his clothes done up in a bundle. He secured employment there, and by working on a difficult job, which no other printer could or would do, he managed to earn $5 00 or $6.00 per week. In May, 1872, he was the Liberal Republican candidate for President of the United States. He was the author of numerous standard works.

Hall, Charles Francis.—He was

tinguished himself by a wonderful speech. He was Washington's confidential Secretary and aid-de-camp during the Revolution. He served in the Continental Congress, and after the war studied and practiced law in New York. He was a member of the convention that framed the Federal Constitution, and was one of the authors of the "Federalist." Was the first Secretary of the Treasury. In 1798 he was appointed under Washington to command the Uninited States army. Of him Daniel Webster said: "He smote the rock of public resources and abundant streams of revenue burst forth. He touched the dead corpse of public credit, and it sprang upon its feet."

an Arctic explorer, and died suddenly in Greenland, November 8, 1871, at the age of fifty years. The first of his life was spent in blacksmithing, and a later period in journalism. In some way he became interested in the efforts to find Sir John Franklin, and by his first experiences in the Arctic regions became fully acquainted with northern life. It was supposed by some that he was poisoned, but it is judged by the best authorities that he died of appopletic troubles.

Hamilton, Alexander died July 12, 1804. He was born January 11, 1757, in the West Indies. At sixteen he came to New York and entered King's, now Columbia College. At the "great meeting in the fields," July 6, 1774, he dis-

Hancock, John died October 8th, 1793. He was born at Quincy, Mass., Jan. 12, 1737, and graduated at Harvard in 1754. He was a successful merchant, and represented Boston in the State Assembly in 1766. Was President of the Provincial Congress in 1774, also a delegate to and President of the Continental Congress. He was Governor of Massachusetts when he died. He was the first signer of the Declaration of Independence, and, with Samuel Adams, denounced by the British Government as "Arch Rebels," and a price was set upon their heads.

Harrison, William Henry was born in Charles City county, Virginia, February 9, 1773. He entered the army

in 1791, after graduating from Hampden-Sydney College. After reaching the grade of Captain he resigned in 1797, and was appointed Governor of Indiana in 1801, and continued to act in that capacity until 1813. He was elected President of the United States in 1840, and had scarcely entered upon the duties of his office when he died at Washington, April 4, 1841. In 1812 he distinguished himself during the war, especially in the battle of the Thames. His military reputation made him available as a Presidential candidate. His character was unimpeachable, and the chief slur cast upon him by his opponents was that he had lived in a "log cabin," with nothing to drink but "hard cider." His

"The principles of the government, I wish them carried out; I ask nothing more."

Hayes, Rutherford B. was born at Delaware, Ohio, October 4, 1822. He graduated at Kenyon College, Ohio. At the commencement of the civil war he enlisted in the Twenty-third Ohio volunteers, and served with the regiment till he received the command of a brigade in 1864. During the battles of the Army of the Potomac Colonel Hayes received a severe wound in the arm, but remained with his regiment to the last, and was the first officer whose command established a position at South Mountain.— Two years later he had become Brigadier-General Hayes, and was elected to

friends turned this to good account.— The campaign was noted for immense mass-meetings, long processions, song-singing and general enthusiasm. "Hard cider" became a party watch-word, and "log cabins" a regular feature in the popular parades. He was elected by a very large majority, and great hopes were entertained of his administration. Though advanced in years, he gave promise of endurance. But "he was beset by office-seekers; he was anxious to gratify the numerous friends and supporters who flocked about him; he gave himself incessantly to public business, and at the close of the month he was on a sick bed." His illness was of eight days' duration. His last words were,

Congress from the Second Ohio District by the Republicans. During his political career he was three times elected Governor of Ohio and twice a member of Congress. In 1876 he was elected President of the United States, and took the oath of office March 3d, and was inaugurated March 5th. Pending the time of the election, and before the meeting of the electoral commission, the country was greatly agitated and seemed threatened with civil war, but immediately after his inauguration quiet and confidence was restored, and peace reigned throughout the United States.

Harper, John the great New York publisher, died April 22d, 1875, aged 78.

Henry, Patrick died June 6th, 1799,

at Red Hill, Charlotte county, Virginia. He was born May 29, 1736. His youth and early manhood gave no indication of his wonderful ability. He was regarded as a "lazy pettifogger" until 1763, when, in a case involving the right of the State to tax the parson's tobacco, his matchless eloquence burst forth and he became famous. In 1765 he was elected to the House of Burgesses, where his speeches gave a tremendous impetus to the patriot cause. He was twice elected Governor of Virginia, and was appointed Secretary of State by Washington, but declined. Adams also appointed him Envoy to France, but his health preventing his acceptance.

Hiacoomes, an Indian preacher, died in New England, aged 80 years, in 1690. He was the first Indian converted in New England.

Howe, Elias the inventor of the first successful sewing machine, died October 3, 1867, in Brooklyn, N. Y., aged 48.

Howard, John Eager of the Maryland line, was born in Baltimore county in 1752. He went into military service at the commencement of the war. He was a colonel, and was in all the principal battles of the Revolution; was chosen Governor of Maryland in 1778, and was afterward a United States Senator. He died in 1827.

Howe, Dr. Samuel Gridley the inventor of printing raised letters for the blind, died in Boston, January 8th, 1876, aged 74 years.

Hudson, Sir Henry his son and seven men, were turned adrift in an open boat in Hudson's bay, by his mutinous crew, June 21, 1611. A gun, some ammunition and a bag of meal were tossed to them. Six of them were invalids.— Green, the leader, and some of the other mutineers, were soon killed by the Esquimaux. The survivers reached England, but Hudson was never again seen.

Hull, William was born in Connecticut in 1753. He rose to the rank of Major in the Continental army. Though severely censured for his surrender of Detroit in 1812, he was a good man and distinguished for his bravery. He was appointed Governor of the Michigan Territory in 1805. After the close of his unfortunate campaign he never appeared in public life. He died near Boston in 1825.

Hull, Isaac was made a lieutenant in the navy in 1798, and in 1812 was made commodore, in command of the United States frigate Constitution. He died in Philadelphia, Pa., in February, 1843.

Hunt, Harriet K., M. D., was the first female physician in the United States to open a medical office. It was in 1835 in Boston. She had studied with Dr. Mott, and received her diploma from the Woman's Medical College of Philadelphia.

Izard, George was born in South Carolina in 1777. He was a general, and made military life his profession. After the war he left the army. He was Governor of Arkansas Territory in 1825, and died at Little Rock, Ark., in 1828.

Hood, General John B. died of yellow fever at New Orleans, August 31, 1879. He was born in Bath county, Ky., in the year 1830. He graduated from West Point in 1853, and on April 15th, 1861, he resigned his commission in the Federal army to join the Confederates, where he soon rose to the rank of Major General. At the battle of Chickamauga he lost a leg and was made Lieutenant-General. He was a brave officer, but

functions of the old Congressional Caucus, met at Baltimore on the 22d of May, 1832, and nominated Jackson and Van Buren as the Democratic candidates for President and Vice-President. The Whig candidates, less "regularly" nominated, were Henry Clay of Kentucky, and John Sergeant, of Pennsylvania, who were the anti-Masonic candidates. The leading issue of the campaign grew out of the question of the re-charter of the United States Bank, the Whigs favoring and the Democrats opposing it. Jackson was of Scotch-Irish descent. His father died before he was born, and his mother was very poor. As a boy, Andrew was brave and impetuous, passionately fond of athletic sports, but not at all addicted to

toward the end of the civil war met with frequent defeats.

Jackson, Andrew was born in Waxhaw settlement, North or South Carolina, March 15th, 1767, and died at the "Hermitage," near Nashville, June 8th, 1845. He served as President of the United States from 1829 to 1837. The nomination of Presidential candidates by "Convention," as the term is now understood and applied, dates from the year 1832. At the first election Jackson was nominated by the Legislature of Tennessee and other States, as well as by several bodies of citizens and Conventions, but the first regularly constituted Convention of a party as an organized body, and fulfilling all the assumed

books. His life was crowded with excitement and adventure. At fourteen, being captured by the British, he was ordered to clean the commander's boots. Showing the true American spirit in his refusal, he was sent to prison with a wound on head and arm. Here he had the small-pox, which kept him ill for several months. Soon after his mother had affected his exchange, she died of ship fever while caring for the imprisoned Americans at Charleston. Left entirely destitute, young Jackson tried various employments, but finally settled down to the law, and in 1796 was elected to Congress. His imperious temper and inflexible will supplied him with constant quarrels. Often they were passionate word contests, sometimes they became hand-to-hand encounters, and on one occasion a formal duel was fought, in which he killed his adversary, himself being severely wounded. The scars he bore upon his person were of wounds received in private battles, some of which left a mark for life. Jackson first distinguished himself as a military officer in the war against the Creek Indians, which he made a signal victory. His dashing successes in the war of 1812 completed his military reputation, and ultimately won him the Presidency. His nomination was at first received in many States with ridicule, as, whatever might be his military prowess, neither his temper nor ability seemed to recommend

place in the nation. Adams, the first time barely successful, was unfortunate in his administration; Jackson, triumphing the second, was brilliant in his Presidential career.

Jackson, "Stonewall," (General Thos. J.) died at Guiney's Station, near Richmond, Va., May 10th, 1863, from wounds received at Chancellorsville and Pneumonia. He was born at Clarksburg, Va., January 21, 1824; educated at West Point, and served in the Mexican war. He was Lee's most efficient General, and commanded the respect of his antagonists.

Jasper, Sergeant William during the attack upon Fort Moultrie by the British fleet, June 28, 1776, leaped over

him as a statesman. However, his re-election proved his popular success as a President. His chief intellectual gifts were energy and intuitive judgment. He was thoroughly honest, intensely warm-hearted, and had an instinctive horror of debt. His moral courage was as great as his physical, and his patriotism was undoubted. He died at the Hermitage, his home near Nashville, Tennessee.— Jackson and Adams were born the same year, yet how different was their childhood! One born to luxury and travel, a student from his earliest years, and brilliantly educated, the other poor, hating books, and seeking any kind of work to escape from want   Yet they were destined twice to compete for the highest

the wall in the midst of the falling shot, and seized the American flag, which had been shot down, and replaced it. He modestly declined a lieutenant's commission the next day.

Jay, John L.L. D., died May 17th, 1829, at Bedford, Westchester county, N. Y. He was born in New York, Dec. 12, 1745, graduated at Columbia College, 1764, and afterward practiced law as partner of Robert R. Livingstone. He was the author of the address to the people of Great Britain, adopted by the Continental Congress, of which he was President, in 1778, and Minister to Spain in 1780. With Franklin and Adams he negotiated peace with Great Britain in 1782, and was made Chief Justice of the

United States from 1789 to 1795. In 1794 he negotiated a treaty with Great Britain determining the eastern boundary of Maine, and by which $10,000,000 were paid to American citizens because of illegal captures by British cruisers. He was Governor of New York for six years, and was deeply interested in all philanthropic projects, including the abolition of slavery. He was a constant Bible student.

Jefferson, Thomas was born at Shadwell, Virginia, April 2d, 1743, and died July 4, 1826. After graduating from William and Mary College he adopted the profession of the law. Jefferson served two terms as President of the United States, from 1800 to 1808. He was a

courtly ceremonies as in the days of Washington and Adams. On his inauguration day he rode down to Congress unattended, and, leaping from his horse, hitched it, and went into the chamber dressed in plain clothes, to read his fifteen-minutes' inaugural. Some of the sentences of that short but memorable address have passed into proverbs. The unostentatious example thus set by the nation's President was wise in its effects. Soon the public debt was diminished, the army and navy reduced, and the Treasury replenished. A man of such marked character necessarily made bitter enemies, but Jefferson commanded the respect of even his opponents, while the admiration of his friends was un-

bold horseman, a skillful hunter, an elegant penman, a fine violinist, a brilliant talker, a superior classical scholar and a proficient in modern languages. The immortal document, the Declaration of Independence, was, with the exception of a few words, entirely his work. Like Washington, he was of aristocratic birth, but his principles were intensely democratic. He hated ceremonies and titles; even "Mr." was distasteful to him. These traits were the more remarkable to one of his superior birth and education, and peculiarly endeared him to the common people. Coming into power on a wave of popularity, he studiously sought to retain this favor. There were no more brilliant levees or

bounded. The last seventeen years of his life was spent at Monticello, near the place of his birth. By his profuse hospitality, he had, before his death, spent his vast estates. He died poor in money, but rich in honor. His last words were: "This is the fourth day of July."

Jesup, Thomas S. was born in Virginia in 1778. He was a brave and useful officer during the war of 1812, and was retained in the army. He was breveted Major-General in 1828, and was succeeded in command in Florida by Colonel Zachary Taylor in 1838. He died in Washington City.

' *Johnson, Hon. Reverdy* a distinguished jurist, died February 10, 1876, at Annapolis, Md., 80 years old.

Johnson, Andrew was born near Raleigh, N. C., December 29, 1808. He was Vice-President when Abraham Lincoln was assassinated, and by his death Mr. Johnson became the constitutional President of the United States. He died July 31st, 1875, while serving as United States Senator from Tennessee. When only ten years of age Mr. Johnson was bound apprentice to a tailor of Raleigh. Never having been a day at school in his life, he yet determined to secure an education. From a fellow-workman he learned the alphabet, and from a friend something of spelling. Thenceforth, after spending ten or twelve hours a day at his trade, he spent two or three every night in study. In 1826 he went West to seek his fortune, with true filial affection carrying with him his mother, who was dependent on his labor for support. After his marriage at Greenville, Tenn., he continued his studies under the instruction of his wife, pursuing his trade as before by day. His political life commenced with his election as Alderman. He was successively chosen Mayor, member of the Legislature, Presidential Elector, State Senator, twice Governor, and for fifteen years United States Senator. Remaining true to the Union when his State seceded, his loyalty attracted general attention. A life-time Democrat, he was elected on the Republican ticket as Vice-President, in reward for his faithfulness. Coming into office with a Republican Congress, it is not strange that his way was hedged with difficulties, and his Presidential career a most unhappy one.

Jones, John Paul died in Paris on July 18, 1792. He was born in Scotland in 1747, and at 12 years old shipped on the Friendship for Virginia. In 1775 Congress appointed him first lieutenant of the "Alfred." He received from France the first salute from a foreign nation to our "Stars and Stripes.". He was transferred to the Providence, and on his first cruise took 100 cannon from 16 prizes. In the Ranger he entered the British port of Whitehaven, where were 300 ships guarded by a strong battery.— In a row boat, with only one man, he pulled under the guns of the battery, entered it alone, killed the sentinel and spiked the guns. He then kindled a fire in the steerage of a large ship and leisurely returned to his vessel. Had his orders been executed all the shipping had been fired. His popular fame rests on his great fight in the Bon Homme Richard and the Serapis, in which he was beaten two or three times, but continued the fight until the British gave up. The King of France gave him a gold mounted sword and Congress a gold medal.

Kane, Dr. E. K. arrived at New York October 11, 1855. He had achieved fame as an Arctic explorer, and was enthusiastically received wherever he went. The hardships he had undergone wrecked his constitution, and he died February 16, 1857, aged 36 years.

Kearney, Stephen W. was a native of New Jersey. He was a gallant soldier in the war of 1812. He was breveted a Brigadier in 1846, and Major-General in December the same year, for gallant conduct in the Mexican war. He died at Vera Cruz, in October, 1848, at the age of 54 years.

Kenton, Simon died in Logan Co., Ohio, April 29th, 1836. He was born in Fauquier county, Va., April 3, 1755. He went West in his teens and joined Boone. He became noted as a pioneer and Indian hunter, yet he never treated an Indian unkindly out of battle. He

Kossuth, Louis the Hungarian Governor and patriot, arrived December 5, 1851, upon the United States war steamer Mississippi, as a guest of the government. His eloquent speeches in behalf of European liberty created great enthusiasm, and his sojourn here for 8 months' was one continuous ovation. He left the United States July 16th, 1852, under the name of Alexander Smith, and resumed his efforts for Hungarian freedom, but unsuccessfully.

Lafayette arrived in New York August 15, 1824, as the guest of Congress. He was born in France in 1757. He was an active patriot during the Revolution, and contributed men and money to the patriot cause. He was commissioned

was at one time captured by them and lashed to a horse bare-backed, and left to plunge through the forests for several days behind his captors. At the end of the journey his flesh was torn and limbs broken, yet he recovered. Congress confirmed his title to Kentucky lands and granted him an annuity of $240 a year.

Knox, General Henry died at Thomaston, Me., October 25, 1806. He was born in Boston, July 25, 1750. During the Revolution he was intimate with General Washington and was relied upon by him in all matters connected with artillery. He was the first Secretary of War, and prominent in establishing the United States navy.

Major-General by the Continental Congress July 31, 1777. He died in France in 1834, at the age of 77.

Laselle was murdered by two of his mutinous companions March 19th, 1687, who themselves were murdered. He was 43 years old. His great ambition was to colonize the banks of the Mississippi, but his premature death defeated the project. Some of his followers finally reached France and told the story of their wanderings.

Lawrence, James was a native of New Jersey, and received a midshipman's warrant at the age of 16. He is remembered by every American as the author of those brave words: "Don't give up the ship." On this occasion he was wounded while commanding the United States frigate Chesapeake, and the engagement took place in 1814. He died four days after receiving the wound at the age of 31 years.

Lee, Major-General Charles died October 2d, 1782, at Philadelphia. He was born in England in 1731. He was well educated, and developing a strong military taste, was commissioned an officer in the British army when 11 years old. He was in the French and Indian war, and was adopted by the Mohawks, who named him "Boiling Water." He was wounded at Ticonderoga and was under Burgoyne in Portugal. Accepted a Major-General's commission in the American army, thereby forfeiting his English estates, from which his income was $7,000 per year, for which Congress agreed to remunerate him. He worked zealously for the American cause, but became lukewarm just prior to the battle of Monmouth, and was suspected of traitorous designs. He died in poverty.

"Light Horse Harry" was the sobriquet of Captain Henry Lee, whose capture was attempted January 20, 1778, at his post near Valley Forge, by 200 British cavalrymen. Lee, with seven men, defended the house, also the adjacent barn containing their horses, and drove off the enemy with a loss of four killed and three wounded. He was made Major, and authorized to raise a corps of his own. It was called "Lee's Legion." He was father of General R. E. Lee, of late Confederate fame. He was born in Virginia in 1756, and died there in 1818.

Lee, Richard Henry died June 19, 1794, at Chantilly, Westmoreland Co., Va. He was born at Stratford, Va., January 30, 1732. He was one of the signers of the Declaration of Independence, and one of the illustrious statesmen, orators and patriots of the Revolution. He originated the idea of a general convention, which resulted in the Continental Congress, of which he was a member, chairman of its most important committees, and president in 1783. He offered the resolution in June, 1776, upon which was based the Declaration of Independence. He was the first United States Senator from Virginia.

Lee, General Robert E.—Was born at Stafford, Westmoreland county, Va., January 19, 1807, and died from the effects of a stroke of paralysis October 12, 1870. He graduated at West Point in 1829, and was appointed lieutenant in the corps of engineers, and, at a later date served as chief engineer in General Scott's army in Mexico. When Virginia seceded from the Union he resigned his commission from the regular army, and cast his influence and strength with the Southern Confederacy. June 3, 1862, he was placed in command of the Confederate army of Northern Virginia, and soon organized an effective force that finally raised the siege of Richmond, and drove the Federal troops under McClellan beyond Malvern Hill. At his surrender at Appomattox he commanded about 60,000 troops while General Grant had about 140,000. In 1865 General Lee was chosen president of Washington College, Lexington, Va., and it was here, in discharge of his duty, that he died.

Lincoln, Abraham was born in Hardin county, Kentucky, on the 12th of February, 1809. He was elected President in 1860, and was re-elected in 1864, and had entered upon the duties of his office for the second time when he was assassinated by John Wilkes Booth, April 14th, 1865, and died the following day. His father was unable to read or write. Abraham's education consisted in very little schooling. When he was eight years old his father moved to Indiana, the family floating down the Ohio on a raft. When nineteen years of age the future President hired out as a hand on a flat-boat at $10 a month, and made a trip to New Orleans. On his return he accompanied the family to Illinois, driving the cattle on the journey, and on reaching their destination helped them to build a cabin and split rails to enclose the farm. He was now in succession a flat-boat hand, clerk, captain of a company of volunteers in the Black Hawk War, country store-keeper, postmaster, and surveyor, yet he managed to get a knowledge of law by borrowing books at an office, before it closed at night, and returning them at its opening in the morning. On being admitted to the bar he rapidly rose to distinction. At twenty-five he was sent to the Legislature, and was thrice re-elected. Turning his attention to politics he soon became a leader. He was sent to Congress; he canvassed the State, haranguing the people daily on great national questions, and, in 1858, he was a candidate for Senator, a second time, against Stephen A. Douglass. The two rivals stumped the State together. The debate, unrivalled for its statesmanship, logic and wit, won for Lincoln a national reputation. He lost the election in the Legislature, as his party was in the minority. After his election to the Presidency, his history, like Washington's, is identified with that of his country. He was a tall, ungainly man, little versed in the refinements of society, but gifted by nature with great common sense, and everywhere known as "Honest Abe." Kind, earnest, sympathetic, faithful, democratic, he was only anxious to serve his country. His wan, fatigued face, and his bent form, told of the cares he bore and the grief he felt.

Lincoln, Benjamin was born in Massachusetts in 1733. He was a farmer. He joined the Continental army in 1777, and rose rapidly to the position of Major General. He died in 1810.

Lind, Jenny arrived in the United

States in September, 1850, having been engaged by P. T. Barnum to give 150 concerts. The seats for her first concert were sold at auction, and Gennire, a New York hatter, paid $500 premium for the first choice. She received $10,000 for this concert, which she donated to benevolent objects.

Livingstone, David W. the African traveller and missionary, died May 1st, 1873, in Africa. The intelligence reached the United States January 26, 1874.

Logan, the Mingo Chief, of the Iroquois nation, was a son of Shikallimus, a Cayuga chief. He went to Ohio and became influential and eminent for his peaceable disposition and friendship for the whites. Enraged at last by the unprovoked murder of his family in 1774, he took the war path against them, but manifested his humanity by saving captives from torture. The Indians were defeated in a great battle at the mouth of the Great Kanawha river. At the subsequent treaty of peace Logan eloquently expressed himself as follows: "I appeal to any white man to say if ever he entered Logan's cabin hungry and he gave him not meat; if ever he came cold and naked and he clothed· him not. During the course of the last long and bloody war Logan remained idle in his cabin, an advocate for peace. Such was my love for the whites that my countrymen pointed as they passed and said, 'Logan is the friend of the white man.' I had even thought to have lived with you, but for the injuries of one man. Colonel Cressap, the last spring, in cold blood and unprovoked, murdered all the relatives of Logan, not even sparing my women and children. There runs not a drop of my blood in the veins of any living creature. This called on me for revenge. I have sought it; I have killed many; I have fully glutted my vengeance. For my country I rejoice at the beams of peace. But do not harbor a thought that mine is the joy of fear; Logan never felt fear. He will not turn on his heel to save his life. Who is there to mourn for Logan? Not one." He became intemperate, and was killed by Indians in self-defence at Detroit in 1780.

Madison, James died at Montpelier, Va., June 28, 1836. He was born at King George, Orange county, Va., March 16, 1757.[1] He graduated from Princeton College, New Jersey, in 1771. He was elected to the Virginia Convention in 1776. He lost his election next year for refusing to *treat the voters*. In 1780 he was chosen a member of the Contineutal Congress. In 1784 he was elected to the Virginia Assembly. His views were the basis of the Constitution of the United States adopted in 1787. He was a member of Congress from 1789 to 1797, and became the head of the ·Democratic-Republican party. He was Jefferson's

Secretary of State, and was elected President in 1809. His last appearance in public life was in 1829, as a member of the Virginia Convention to revise the State Constitution.

Marion, General Francis died near Eutaw, S. C., February 28th, 1795. He was born near Georgetown, S. C., in 1732. He was a noted partisan leader in the South. His famous brigade was armed with swords made from saw blades. By a succession of rapid and unexpected assaults he caused the British and their tory allies to dread his name. Cornwallis ordered Tarleton to "destroy Mr. Marion's band at all hazards," but after chasing them unsuccessfully, and receiving several severe

McDougal, General was born in Scotland, and came to America in early childhood. He rose to the rank of major-general, was a New York Senator and died in 1786.

Meade, General G. G. died in Philadelphia, November 6, 1872, at the age of fifty-six years. He was born at Cadiz, Spain, December 30th, 1815, when his father was United States Consul there.— He was a graduate of West Point, and served with distinction during the Florida and Mexican wars. He commanded the Army of the Potomac at the battle of Gettysburg, during the civil war.

Mercer, Hugh a general in the Continental army, was killed at the battle of Princeton. He was a native of Scotland,

blows in retaliation, Tarleton abandoned the chase, saying that "the devil himself could not catch that 'swamp-fox.'"

Macomb, Alexander was born in Detroit in 1782, and entered the army at the age of seventeen years. He was made a brigadier in 1814. In 1835 he was commander-in-chief of the armies of the United States, and died in 1841.

McDonough, Thomas was a native of Delaware, and a commodore in the navy. He was twenty-eight years of age at the time of the engagement at Plattsburg. The State of New York gave him one thousand acres of land on Plattsburg Bay for his services. He died in 1822 at the age of thirty-nine years.

and was practicing medicine in Fredericksburg, Va., when the Revolution broke out. He was 56 years of age when he died.

Mifflin, Thomas was born in Philadelphia in 1744. He was a Quaker, but joined the patriot army in 1775, and rapidly rose to the rank of major-general. He was a member of Congress after the war, and also Governor of Pennsylvania. He died in January, 1800.

Monroe, James was born in Westmoreland county, Va, April 28th, 1758, and died in the city of New York, July 4, 1831. He filled the office of President of the United States from the year 1817 to 1825. As a soldier under General Washington he bore a brave record, and especially distinguished himself in the battles of Brandywine, Germantown and Monmouth. Afterward he studied law and entered political life. Having been sent by Washington as Minister to France, he showed such marked sympathy with that country as to displease the President and his cabinet, who were just concluding a treaty with England, and wished to preserve a strictly neutral policy. He was, therefore, recalled. Under Jefferson, who was his warm friend, he was again sent to France in 1803, when he secured the purchase of Louisiana.— He is said to have always taken particular pride in this transaction, regarding his part in it as among the most important of his public services. Soon after his inauguration as President he visited the military posts in the north and east, with a view to thorough acquaintance with the capabilities of the country in the event of future hostilities. This tour was a great success. He wore a blue military coat of home-spun, light-colored breeches and a cocked hat, being the undress uniform of a Revolutionary officer. Thus was the nation reminded of his former military services. This, with his plain, unassuming manners, completely won the hearts of the people, and brought an overwhelming majority to the support of the administration. Monroe was a man more prudent than brilliant, who acted with a single eye to the welfare of the country. Jefferson said of him: "If his soul were turned inside out not a spot could be found on it."— Like that beloved friend, he died "poor in money, but rich in honor," and like him also, he passed away on the anniversary of the independence of the country he served so faithfully.

Montgomery, General Richard was born December 2, 1736, at Raphoe, Ireland. He was made brigadier-general by Congress and commanded the force that invaded Canada via Lake Champlain, and captured all opposing forces until he reached Quebec. His death there, December 31, 1775, caused the assault to fail. His remains rest beneath a monument erected by Congress in front of St. Paul's Church, New York.

Morgan, General Daniel was born in New Jersey in 1736, and died at Winchester, Va., July 6, 1802, at the age of 66 years. He was a teamster with Braddock's expedition, and received 500 lashes for an alleged insult to a British officer. At the outbreak of the Revolution he raised a company of riflemen and marched 600 miles in three weeks to join the camp in Boston. He was captured by the British at the assault at Quebec, was released, and did good service at New York, also in the South against Cornwallis. He served in the National Congress four years.

Moultrie, General William died

at Charleston, S. C., September 27, 1805. He was born in South Carolina in 1731. He was distinguished for his defense of Fort Moultrie, with but 31 guns, manned partly by raw recruits, against a British force with 200 guns. While a prisoner he was offered the command of a Jamaica regiment and money if he would serve them. "Not the fee simple of all Jamaica should induce me to part with my integrity," said the patriot.

Oglethorpe, James returned to England in 1743. He had given ten years of his life to the Colony of Georgia without compensation. Benevolence, integrity and honor were his crowning virtues. He lived to be 90 years old.

Opechaucanaugh, King of the Pamunkeys, was brother and successor to Powhattan. He was nearly 100 years old when he died, in 1644. In the winter of 1608 the settlers were in a starving condition. Captain Smith proceeded to Pamunkey determined to procure corn, but the Indians refused to trade. Suddenly he seized Opechancanaugh by the hair of the head, and, with a pistol at his breast, dragged the frightened chief out among the whites, nor would he release him until the Indians had filled his boats with provisions. He was always the enemy of the whites, and lead in the massacres of 1622 and 1644. In the latter he was carried upon a litter.— After his death his tribe was without a leader, and the tribe gradually migrated and dwindled away.

Osceola, the half-breed chief and leader in the second Seminole war, died on January 30th, 1838, at Fort Moultrie, aged thirty-four. He was a bold warrior, and did the whites great injury until he was captured by strategy in 1837.

Otis, James was born at Barnstable, Mass., in 1725. He was the leader of the Revolutionary party in Massachusetts at the beginning. He was wounded by a British official in 1769, and never entirely recovered. He was killed by lightning in 1772.

Pickens, Andrew was born in Pennsylvania in 1739, and served as a general in the Revolution. In childhood he went to South Carolina, and was one of the first in the field for liberty. He died in 1817.

Pierce, Franklin was born at Hillsborough, New Hampshire, on the 23d of November, 1804, and died October 8th, 1869. He graduated at Bowdoin College, Maine, in 1824; studied law and was admitted to the bar in 1827. He was President from 1853 to 1857. When the Mexican war broke out he enlisted as a volunteer, but soon rose to the office of brigadier-general. He distinguished himself under General Scott, against whom he afterwards successfully ran for the Presidency, and upon whom, during his administration, he conferred the title of lieutenant-general. On the question of slavery Mr Pierce always sided with the South, and opposed anti-slavery measures in every shape. In a message to Congress in 1856, he characterized the formation of a free State government in Kansas as an act of rebellion, and justified the principles of the Kansas and Nebraska Act. He, however, espoused the national cause at the opening of the civil war, and urged a cordial support of the administration at Washington.

Peabody, George died November 4, 1869, in London, England. He was born in Danvers, Mass., February 18th, 1795. He accumulated great wealth as a banker in London. His benificence was remarkable. He gave in 1852 to Kane's

Arctic Expedition	$ 10,000
Peabody Institute in Mass.	200,000
Peabody Institute in Danvers.	50,000
Peabody Institute, Baltimore.	1,000,000
Dwellings for London poor	2,500,000
Harvard College	150,000
Yale College	150,000
Education in the South	3,500,000
Peabody Institute at Salem	150,000
Public Library at Newburyport	20,000
Phillips' Academy, Andover	30,000
Maryland Historical Society	20,000
Public Library at Thetford, Vermont	10,000
Kenyon College, Ohio	25,000
Washington College, Virginia	60,000
Property left at his death was	5,000,000

Penn, William died July 30th, 1718, at Ruscombe, Eng., aged 74 years. He founded the State of Pennsylvania, which was originally called Sylvania, but afterwards the prefix "Penn" was added in honor of its founder. Penn was expelled from Christ College, Oxford University, for embracing Quakerism. His father opposed and frequently quarreled with him, but left him his estates. On a visit to Ireland he attended a Quaker meeting, for which he was thrown into prison. For preaching and writing Quaker doctrines he was imprisoned in the Tower. He was freed through the influence of the Duke of York. He was imprisoned in Newgate in 1671 for refusing to take an oath. The English government owed his father £16,000, for which Penn received a large tract of land in America and freedom to make laws for the government of the colonists who might settle thereon. He spent several years in America and gained the confidence of his settlers, also of the Indians. He was just and tolerant in his views, and left the impresss of his character upon his colony and their descendants.

Pike, Zebulon M. was born in 1779. While pressing toward the capture of York (Toronto), in 1813, the powder magazine of the fort blew up and Gen. Pike was mortally wounded. He was carried on board the flag-ship of Commodore Chauncey, where he died, with the captured British flag under his head, at the age of 34.

Phipps, Governor of Massachusetts, died February 18, 1695, in London, Eng. He was born at Woolwich, Maine, in 1650. He tended sheep until he was 18. He afterward built a vessel and sought for sunken treasure in the West Indies. He was successful, became rich and was knighted by the King. His expedition against Quebec was a failure, but he made a good Governor of Massachusetts.

Pochahontas was married, April 13, 1613, to a young Englishman named John Rolfe. She had been baptized by the name of Rebecca. Pochahontas and her husband visited England in 1616, and were received at court with great favor.

was educated by his uncle in London. The Randolphs claim descent from Pochahontas.

Polk, James Knox died at Nashville, Tenn., June 15, 1849. He was born in Mecklenburg county, North Carolina, November 2, 1795. He was a member of Congress from 1825 to 1839, Governor of Tennessee in 1839, and President of the United States in 1844. The annexation of Texas and war with Mexico occurred during his administration.

Pontiac was chief of the Ottowa tribe of Indians. He was a power among other tribes who had confederated with the Ottowas for the overthrow of the English. In September, 1765, he held a grand council with George Crog-

She died in England in June 1617, aged 22 years. She was the daughter of Powhattan, the powerful chief of a tribe of Indians in Virginia. Her successful intervention saved Capt. John Smith from death while her father's captive, and afterward, by revealing to him a plot to destroy himself and his men, she saved other white setttlers. She was enticed on board a vessel by Captain Argall, taken to Jamestown and held as a hostage for certain prisoners taken by her father. She became acquainted with John Rolfe, a mutual attachment sprung up, and they were married with her father's approval, who ever after was a firm friend of the whites. She left an infant son, named Thomas Rolfe, who

han, at Detroit, at which a treaty of peace was made. After that he lived in peace on the banks of the Maumee, until April, 1769, when he paid a visit to St. Louis, Mo. He was dressed in full French uniform, which had been presented to him by the Marquis de Montcalm. He crossed the river at a place where some Illinois Indians were holding a council. Here he was killed unawares by an Indian who had been bribed with a barrel of whiskey to commit the deed. His body was buried with the honors of war by St. Ange, the commander at St. Louis.

Porter, Commodore David was among the most distinguished of the American naval commanders. He was a resident Minister of the United States in Turkey, and died near Constantinople in March, 1843.

Prescott, William was born at Groton, Mass.; was a colonel at the battle of Bunker Hill, and served under Gates until the surrender of Burgoyne, when he left the army. He died in 1795.

Powhattan, the father of Pochahontas, died April, 1618. He was one of the most powerful sachems of his time, and ruled over Virginia and Maryland. He was friendly to the English until they provoked him by their injustice. He plotted their destruction two or three times, but did not accomplish it. He died at an advanced age.

Putnam, General Israel died at

1618. He was a scholar and a broadminded man. The English court banished him several times, and imprisoned him in the Tower for 12 years, during which he wrote his history of the world. He visited South America twice and was the founder of the Roanoke Colony.

Raymond, Hon. Henry J. the founder of the New York *Times,* died June 18, 1869.

Richardson, Albert D. a brilliant author, and war correspondent of the New York *Tribune,* was shot by one McFarland, November 26, 1869, for paying attention to his divorced wife. He died within a week, but was married to Mrs. McFarland on his death bed by Rev. Henry Ward Beecher. McFarland was

Brooklyn, Conn., May 19th, 1790. Was born in Salem, Mass., January 7, 1718.— He commanded a company of rangers in the French and Indian war, and was one of the four major generals made by Congress at the beginning of the Revolution. He was a man of great courage. When 25 years old he crawled into the den of a she wolf and killed her. At Fort Edward, during a fire, he stood between 300 barrels of powder and the flames, pouring on water until it was saved, although he was severely burned. He did such effective service during the war that the British vainly endeavored to bribe him to their side.

Raleigh, Sir Walter was beheaded by the English government October 29,

tried for murder, but was acquitted, being adjudged insane.

Scott, General Winfield died at West Point, New York, May 29, 1866.— He was born at Petersburg, Va., June 13, 1786. He was educated for the law. In 1808 he was made captain of light artillery, and lieutenant-colonel in July, 1812, in which war he took a prominent part, and at the close of which the President offered to make him Secretary of War, but he declined. Congress voted him thanks and a gold medal for his services. He was made commander-in-chief of the United States army in 1841. In the Mexican war he achieved renown. In 1852 he was nominated for President by the Whigs. His age prevented his

active service during the rebellion, but he was devoted to the Union.

Schuyler, Richard was born in Albany, New York, in 1733, and died in 1804. He was a captain under Sir William Johnson, and was in active public service until the Revolution. He was a general in the patriot army, and was a legislator after the war.

Shelby, Isaac was born in Maryland in 1750. He entered military life in 1774, and went to Kentucky as a land surveyor in 1775. He engaged in the war of the Revolution, and was distinguished in the battle on King's Mountain, in October, 1780. He was made Governor of Kentucky in 1792 and soon afterward retired

He was one of the signers of the Declaration of Independence.

Siamese Twins, Chang and Eng, died January 17th, 1874, at their home in North Carolina. Chang died suddenly, and the shock caused the death of Eng a few hours later.

Smith, Samuel the commander of Fort Mifflin in 1777, was born in Pennsylvania in 1752. He entered the Revolutionary army in 1776; served as a general in command when Ross attacked Baltimore in 1814; afterward represented Baltimore in Congress, and died in April, 1839.

Singer, Isaac Merritt the inventor of the Singer Sewing Machine, died in London, Eng., July 23, 1875, aged 64.

to private life, from which he was drawn in 1813. He died in 1826.

Sherman, Roger died at New Haven, Conn., July 23, 1793. He was born in Newton, Mass., April 19th, 1721, and was a shoemaker until 22 years old. By using his leisure moments for study he became a fine mathematician. He also read law and was admitted to the bar in 1754. He filled the offices of Assistant Governor of Connecticut 19 years, Judge of Common Pleas and Superior Courts 23 years, treasurer of Yale College 10 years, member of Continental Congress from 1774 to 1789, and of the United Congress from 1789 till he died. He was also Mayor of New Haven nine years.—

Standish, Miles died at Duxburg, Mass., October 3, 1656, at the age of 72 years. He came over with the Pilgrims on the Mayflower, and was elected military captain of Plymouth colony. He was always the leader of the colony in their military affairs, and was the originator of what was known as the pine-tree shilling, from a pine tree stamped upon one side. The whole issue became known as the pine-tree money. This mint operated for thirty years, in spite of the fact that in England it was regarded as an insult to royal power. The master of the mint was allowed fifteen pence out of every twenty shillings. The mint largely increased the circulation of coin in place of wampum, bullets and articles of barter. The only other colony which issued silver coins before the Revolution was Maryland. Several others, however, minted copper coins. The dies for the Boston mint were made by Joseph Jenks at the iron-works at Lynn.

Stanton, Hon. E. M. of Ohio, died December 24, 1869.

Stark, John "the hero of Bennington," died May 8th, 1822, at Manchester, N. H. He was born at Londonderry, N. H., August 28th, 1728. He had great physical strength and endurance, and would walk 120 miles at a time. His youth was spent in hunting and Indian warfare. He started for Boston ten minutes after hearing of the battle of Lexington. In 1776 and 1777 he did excellent

he wrote a book on military science, which was the text book of our officers during the Revolution. He was made a major-general by Congress, and in 1790 was voted an annuity of $2,500 per annum life.

Stewart, A. T. the great dry goods millionaire, died in New York, April 10, 1876, aged 73 years.

Stewart, Admiral Charles of the United States navy, died November 6th, 1869.

Stirling, William Alexander was a descendent of the Scotch Earl of Stirling. He was born in the city of New York in 1726. He became atttached to the patriot cause and served as a faithful officer during the war. He was made

service in New York and New Jersey. He sent all his sons to battle. He was made commander of the Northern Department. He was a brave man and a patriot.

Steuben, Baron.—Baron Frederick William Augustus Steuben died near Utica, N. Y., November 28, 1794. He was born at Magdeburg, Prussia, Nov. 15, 1730. He gained great celebrity in the 7-years war, in the service of Frederick the Great. He voluntarily left home, wealth and honor to aid the American cause. He introduced the Prussian drill into the army at Valley Forge, which materially contributed to its success in the following campaigns. At the solicitation of Washington and Congress

prisoner at the battle of Long Island.— He died in 1783.

Stringham, Silas H.—Rear Admiral Silas H. Stringham, United States navy, died in Brooklyn, N. Y., February, 1876, aged 78 years.

Stuyvesant, Peter died in August, 1682. He was born in Friesland in 1602, and, although educated for the ministry, entered the army. He served in the West Indies, where he lost a leg. In 1647 he was appointed Governor of New Amsterdam by the Dutch. He conciliated the Indians and adjusted the boundaries between his own and the English province. He ruled absolutely for 20 years, and refused to surrender to the fleet sent by James, Duke of York, which came to take possession of the grant given him by Charles II., but as his people would not fight he retired to his East River farm for the remainder of his life. He and his wife were buried in St. Mark's Church, on Tenth street, New York.

Sullivan, John was born in Maine in 1740. He was a delegate to the first Continental Congress in 1774, and was one of the first eight brigadiers in the Continental army. He resigned his commission of general in 1779; was afterward member of Congress and Governor of New Hampshire, and died in 1795.

Sumner, Charles was born in Boston, Mass., January 6, 1811, and died in

field. Ill health compelled him to leave the army just before the close of the war in 1781. He was afterward Congressman, and died on the high hills of Santee, S. C., in 1832, at 98 years of age.

Taylor, Zachary was born in Orange county, Virginia, November 24, 1784. He entered upon the duties of President in 1849, and died at the Presidential Mansion July 9th, 1850, after an illness of five days. Soon after his birth his parents removed to Kentucky. His means of education were of the scantiest kind, and until he was twenty-four years of age he worked on his father's plantation. Madison, who was a relative, and at that time Secretary of State, then secured for him an appointment in the

Washington, D. C., March 11, 1874. His parents belonged to the New England aristocracy, and the name of the Sumner family appears prominently in Massachusetts politics and society from an early date. In politics Mr. Sumner was a Whig, and earnestly opposed slavery on the grounds of justice and humanity. He opposed the Mexican war on the ground that it would increase the slave territory, and cause useless blood-shed. He succeeded Daniel Webster as United States Senator from Massachusetts in 1851, and held that position when he died. He was a great jurist, and the author of many standard publications.

Sumpter, Thomas was a native of South Carolina, and was early in the

army as lieutenant. From this he rose by regular and rapid degrees to a major generalship. His triumphant battles at Palo Alto, Resaca de la Palma, Monterey, and Buena Vista won for him great applause. He was the popular hero of a successful war. The soldiers admiringly called him "Old Rough and Ready."— Having been offered the nomination for President, he published several letters defining his position as "a Whig, but not an ultra-Whig," and declaring that he would not be a party candidate or the exponent of party doctrines. Many of the Whig leaders violently opposed his nomination. Daniel Webster called him "an ignorant frontier colonel." The fact that he was a slave-holder was warmly urged against him. He knew nothing of civil affairs, and had taken so little interest in politics that he had not voted in forty years. But he was nominated and elected. His nomination caused a secession from the Whigs, resulting in the formation of the Free-Soil party. He felt his want of qualifications for the position, and sometimes expressed his regret that he had accepted it; yet he maintained as President the popularity which had led to his election, and was personally one of the most esteemed who have filled that office.

Tecumseh, the Shawnee Chief, killed in the battle of the Thames, October 5, 1813, was born near Springfield, Ohio, in 1768. He was one of the greatest of In-

Plymouth, Mass., and was one of the first eight brigadiers appointed by Congress in 1775. He died with the small-pox in 1776, at Chambly, in Canada.

Thomson, Charles was born in Ireland in 1730, and came to America when he was only eleven years of age. He settled in Pennsylvania, and was Secretary of Congress perpetually from 1774 until the adoption of the Federal Constitution, and the organization of the new government in 1789. He died in 1824 at the age of 94.

Trumbull, Jonathan L.L. D., died at Lebanon, Conn., August 17, 1785. He was born there June 10, 1710. He was in public life fifty years, as member of the Colonies' Assembly and Governor.—

dian leaders, but was not bloodthirsty. With his brother Elskwatawa, "The Prophet," he labored incessantly to unite the Western tribes against the whites, but General Harrison checkmated their plans. Deeming the war of 1812 his opportunity, he joined the British, who made him a brigadier-general, and he was of great aid to Proctor. General William Tecumseh Sherman was named after this brave warrior.

Thomas, George H.—He was a major-general in the United States army, and died in San Francisco, Cala., March 28, 1870. He was born in Southampton county, Va., July 31, 1816, and served with great distinction in the civil war.

Thomas, General was a native of

Washington often consulted him for advice, and called him "Brother Jonathan," which term grew into use as a name for the United States Government.

Twiggs, David E. was born in Georgia in 1790. He was a major at the close of the war of 1812, and was retained in the army. He was breveted major-general after the battle of Monterey, and for his gallantry there he received a gift of a sword from Congress.

Tyler, John was born in Charles City county, Virginia, March 20, 1790, and died at Richmond, Virginia, January 17, 1862. He studied law, and was elected to Congress in 1816, and served some five years; was elected United

States Senator in 1827; re-elected in 1833, and was president of the Peace Convention at Washington in 1861. Mr. Tyler became President upon the death of Mr. Harrison as his constitutional successor as Vice-President of the United States. His administration was not successful.— He opposed the measures of his party and made free use of the veto power.— His former political friends denounced him as a renegade, to which he replied that he had never professed to endorse the measures which he opposed. The feeling increased in bitterness. All his cabinet except Webster resigned. He was, however, nominated by a convention composed chiefly of office-holders, for the next Presidency; he accepted, but

started a new organization of the Democratic party in New York, his native State, which had the power for over twenty years. In 1831 he was appointed Minister to England, whither he went in Sept., but when the nomination came before the Senate in December it was rejected on the ground that he had sided with England against the United States in certain matters, and had carried party contests and their results into foreign negotiations. His party regarded this as an extreme political persecution, and the next year elected him to the Vice-Presidency. He thus became head of the Senate which a few months before had condemned him, and where he now performed his duties with "dignity, cour-

finding no popular support soon withdrew from the canvass. In 1861 he became presiding officer of the peace convention in Washington. All efforts at reconciliation proving futile, he renounced his allegiance to the United States and followed the Confederate fortunes. He died in Richmond, where he was in attendance as a member of the Confederate Congress.

Van Buren, Martin was born at Kinderhook, New York, December 5, 1782, and died at the same place, July 24th, 1862. He studied law and was admitted to practice in 1803; was elected President of the United States and served four years, from 1837 to 1841. He early took an interest in politics, and in 1818

tesy and impartiality." As a President, Van Buren was the subject of much partisan censure. The country was passing through a peculiar crisis, and his was a difficult position to fill with satisfaction to all. That he pleased his own party is proved from the fact of his renomination in 1840 against Harrison. In 1844 he was once more urged by his friends, but failed to get a two-thirds vote in the convention on account of his opposition to the annexation of Texas. In 1848 he became a candidate of the "Free Democracy," a new party advocating antislavery principles. After this he retired to his estate in Kinderhook, N. Y., where he died.

Vanderbilt, Cornelius died Jan.

4, 1877. He was born on Staten Island, N. Y., May 27, 1794. He began with a small ferryboat between Staten Island and New York, became the owner of 66 steamers, and then, turning his attention to railroads, became chief owner of 2,128 miles of railroad, earned the name of "Railroad King," and died worth $80,000,000.

Van Dorn, a Confederate General, was killed May 8, 1863, by Dr. Peters, in Tennesseee.

Van Ness, Mrs. Maria died Sept. 9, 1832, aged 50 years. She was daughter of David Burns, who owned most of the land upon which Washington now stands, who became a millionaire from its sale. She married D. P. Van Ness, afterward Mayor of the city. She was noted for benevolence, and founded the City Orphan Asylum. She was buried with public honors.

Vassar, Mathew the founder of Vassar College, died suddenly while addressing the trustees of that institution, June 23, 1868. He was born in England in 1792.

Williams, Roger.—He was born in Wales, England, in 1599, and came to America in 1630. He laid the foundation for the settlement of Rhode Island, and died in Providence in April, 1683, at the age of eighty-four years. He encountered many hardships, for opinion's sake, in the settlement of that State.

Warren, Dr. Joseph killed June 17, 1775, during the retreat from Breed's Hill. He had been elected major-general, but refused to command and fought as a private. He was born at Roxbury, Mass,, June 11th, 1741, and graduated at Harvard in 1759. Samuel Adams was his intimate friend. He was President of the Massachusetts Provincial Congress, and Chairman of the "Committee of Safety" in 1774. He was an ardent patriot and his loss was severely felt.— Edward Everett eulogized him. Daniel Webster embalmed his memory in his immortal oration at Bunker Hill monument. Mrs. Adams wrote: "Not all the havoc and desolation they have made has moved me like the death of Warren. We mourn for the citizen, the physician, the Senator, the warrior."

Washington George died at Mount Vernon, Va., December 14, 1799. He was born at Bridges Creek, in Westmoreland county, Va., February 22d, 1732. His father died when he was 11 years old.— When 14 he received an appointment in the navy, which he declined to please his mother. He was appointed Public Surveyor. During the French and Indian war he was Braddock's aid-de-camp, and after his defeat commanded the forces on the frontier. He married Mrs. Martha Custis, January 6, 1759. He was in the Virginia House of Burgesses for fifteen years. He was active in calling the first General Congress, and contributed his greatest efforts in making its proceedings successful. He was appointed commander-in-chief of the army at the breaking out of hostilities, and his conduct of the war demonstrated the wisdom of the selection. He was elected the first President of the Republic, was his own successor, and could have been elected a third time but for his positive declination. His wisdom and prudence kept the government from sinking in its infancy, and contributed largely to placing it upon a firm foundation. In deference to the wishes of his countrymen he accepted the command of the United States army, upon the prospect of a war with France, but in the midst of preparations for it he was suddenly cut off. His death

wounded his antagonist in the hand.—Some months afterward Tarleton said, sneeringly, to Mrs. Willie Jones, a witty American lady, "that Colonel Washington, I am told, is illiterate, and can not write his own name." "Ah! Colonel," said Mrs. Jones, "you ought to know better, for you bear evidence that he can *make his mark.*" At another time he expressed a desire to see Colonel Washington. Mrs. Jones' sister immediately replied: "Had you looked behind at the Cowpens you might have had that pleasure."

Wayne, General Anthony died December 14, 1796, at Presque Isle, now Erie, Penna. He was born in Chester county, Penna., Jan. 1, 1745. He was

was a national calamity. Congress adjourned, and the sorrow occasioned was not confined to this country. Both in France and Great Britain high tribute was paid to his character. He was "first in war, first in peace, and first in the hearts of his countrymen."

Washington, William a relative of the General, was born in Stafford county, Va. He entered the army under Mercer, and greatly distinguished himself at the South as a commander of a corps of cavalry. Taken prisoner at the battle of Eutaw Springs, he remained a captive until the close of the war, and died in Charleston in 1810. In a personal combat with the British Colonel Tarleton, at the battle of the Cowpens, Washington

elected to the Assembly in 1773. At the outbreak of the Revolution he was made Colonel and sent to Canada, and was with the army at Three Rivers and Ticonderoga. He was appointed to Washington's army as brigadier. He showed great bravery and presence of mind at Germantown, Brandywine, Monmouth, and especially at Stony Point. He subdued the Northwestern Indians and earned from them the title of the "White Leader who never sleeps." He was generally known as "Mad Anthony," from his readiness to undertake apparently impossible projects.

Webster, Daniel died October 24th, 1852, at Marshfield, Mass. He was born at Salisbury, N. H., January 18th, 1782.

He graduated from Dartmouth College in 1801. He was admitted to the bar in Boston in 1805. In 1812 he was elected to Congress. His first speech, June 10, 1813, awakened the admiration and astonishment of the House. He practiced law from 1816 to 1822, and conducted several very important cases, exhibiting legal abilities of amazing breadth and resource. In 1822 he was re-elected to Congress; in 1827 to the United States Senate until 1841. In 1830 he delivered his immortal reply to Hayne, of South Carolina. He was Secretary of State under President Harrison. He also was Secretary under President Fillmore. His advocacy of the fugitive slave law at this time alienated many of his friends.

brigadier in 1812; resigned his commission in 1815, and died in Tennessee in 1826.

Wool, General John Ellis was a native of New York. He entered the army in 1812, and soon rose to the rank of lieutenant-colonel, for gallant conduct on Queenstown Heights, in 1812. He was breveted brigadier in 1825, and for gallant conduct at Buena Vista, in 1847, was breveted major-general.

Worth, General William J. was born in Columbia county, New York, in 1794; was a gallant soldier during the war of 1812; was retained in the army, and for his gallanty at Monterey, during the Mexican war, he was made a major-general, by brevet, and received the gift

Mr. Webster's two Bunker Hill orations added to his fame as an orator. He was known as the greatest of American statesmen and constitutional lawyers.

Whitefield, George, the famous preacher, arrived at Savannah, Ga., on May 7th, 1838.

Williams, Roger and John Eliot, two young ministers, and John Winthrop, Jr., son of the Governor, arrived at Massachusetts Bay in 1631.

Wilson, Henry ex-Vice-President of the United States, died in Washington, D. C., November 22d, 1884, aged sixty-four years.

Winchester, James was born in Maryland in 1756. He was made a

of a sword from Congress. He was of great service during the whole war with Mexico. He died in Texas in May of the year 1849.

Young, Brigham the Mormon ruler, died at Salt Lake City, Utah, August 29, 1877. He was born in Wittingham, Vt., June 1, 1801. He was one of the "twelve apostles," and rose to great power. He introduced the infamous doctrine of polygamy, and conducted the "Saints" across the mountains to Salt Lake, July 24, 1847. He was a scoundrel of considerable executive ability and great cunning. He managed to defy and outwit the Federal authorities while he lived, and at death had twenty wives and a fortune of $6,000,000.

DECLARATION OF INDEPENDENCE.

July 4, 1776.—The Declaration of Independence, which had been presented by the committee appointed to draft it, was adopted by Congress. It was written by Thomas Jefferson, and chiefly defended at its presentation by John Adams. The old bell-ringer in the belfry of the State House waited anxiously to hear the announcement of the passage of the declaration. At last his little boy standing below shouted up to him,— "Ring! Ring!" Then he rang with all his might, and soon Philadelphia was alive with joy, which continued to overflow during the whole night which followed.

these are life, liberty, and the pursuit of happiness; that, to secure these rights, governments are instituted among men, deriving their just powers from the consent of the governed; that, whenever any form of government becomes destructive of these ends, it is the right of the people to alter or abolish it, and to institute a new government, laying its foundation on such principles, and organizing its powers in such form, as to them shall seem most likely to effect their safety and happiness. Prudence, indeed, will dictate that governments long established should not be changed for light and transient causes, and ac-

A Declaration by the Representatives of the United States of America, in Congress assembled:—

When, in the course of human events, it becomes necessary for one people to dissolve the political bands which have connected them with another, and to assume among the powers of the earth the separate and equal station to which the laws of nature and of nature's God entitle them, a decent respect to the opinions of mankind requires that they should declare the causes which impel them to the separation.

We hold these truths to be self-evident: That all men are created equal; that they are endowed by their Creator with certain unalienable rights; that among

cordingly, all experience hath shown that mankind are more disposed to suffer, while evils are sufferable, than to right themselves by abolishing the forms to which they are accustomed. But when a long train of abuses and usurpations, pursuing invariably the same object, evinces a design to reduce them under absolute despotism, it is their right, it is their duty, to throw off such goverment, and to provide new guards for their future security. Such has been the patient sufferance of the colonies; and such is now the necessity which constrains them to alter their former systems of government. The history of the present King of Great Britain is a history of repeated injuries and usurpations, all having in direct object the establishment of an absolute tyranny over these States. To prove this, let facts be submitted to a candid world:—

He has refused his assent to laws the most wholesome and necessary for the public good.

He has forbidden his governors to pass laws of immediate and pressing importance, unless suspended in their operation till his assent should be obtained; and, when so suspended, he has utterly neglected to attend to them.

He has refused to pass other laws for the accommodation of large districts of people, unless those people would relinquish the right of representation in the legislature: a right inestimable to them, and formidable to tyrants only.

He has called together legislative bodies at places unusual, uncomfortable, and distant from the repository of their public records, for the sole purpose of fatiguing them into compliance with his measures

He has dissolved representative houses repeatedly, for opposing, with manly firmness, his invasions on the rights of the people.

He has refused, for a long time after such dissolutions, to cause others to be elected; whereby the legislative powers, incapable of annihilation, have returned to the people at large, for their exercise; the State remaining, in the meantime,

exposed to all the danger of invasions without, and convulsions within.

He has endeavored to prevent the population of these States; for that purpose obstructing the laws for the naturalization of foreigners; refusing to pass others to encourage their migration hither, and raising the conditions of new appropriations of lands.

He has obstructed the administration of justice, by refusing his assent to laws for establishing judiciary powers.

He has made judges dependent on his will alone, for the tenure of their offices, and the amount and payment of their salaries

He has erected a multitude of new offices, and sent hither swarms of officers to harass our people, and eat out their substance.

He has kept among us, in times of peace, standing armies, without the consent of our legislature.

He has affected to render the military independent of, and superior to, the civil power.

He has combined with others to subject us to a jurisdiction foreign to our constitution, and unacknowledged by our laws; giving his assent to their acts of pretended legislation:—

For quartering large bodies of armed troops among us:

For protecting them, by a mock trial, from punishment for any murders which they should commit on the inhabitants of these States;

For cutting off our trade with all parts of the world;

For imposing taxes upon us without our consent;

For depriving us, in many cases, of the benefits of trial by jury;

For transporting us beyond seas to be tried for pretended offences;

For abolishing the free system of English laws in a neighboring province, establishing therein an arbitrary government, and enlarging its boundaries, so as render it at once an example and fit instrument for introducing the same absolute rule into the colonies;

For taking away our charters, abolishing our most valuable laws, and altering, fundamentally, the powers of our governments;

For suspending our own legislatures, and declaring themselves invested with power to legislate for us in all cases whatsoever;

He has abdicated government here, by declaring us out of his protection and waging war against us.

He has plundered our seas, ravaged our coasts, burned our towns, and destroyed the lives of our people.

He is at this time transporting large armies of foreign mercenaries to complete the works of death, desolation and tyranny, already begun with circumstances of cruelty and perfidy scarcely paralleled in the most barbarous ages, and totally unworthy the head of a civilized nation

He has constrained our fellow-citizens taken captive on the high seas, to bear arms against their country, to become the executioners of their friends and brethren, or to fall themselves by their hands.

He has excited domestic insurrections amongst us, and has endeavored to bring on the inhabitants of our frontiers, the merciless Indian savages, whose known rule of warfare is an undistinguished destruction of all ages, sexes and conditions.

In every stage of these oppressions, we have petitioned for redress in the most humble terms; our repeated petitions have been answered only by repeated injury. A prince whose character is thus marked by every act which may define a tyrant, is unfit to be the ruler of a free people.

Nor have we been wanting in attention to our British brethren. We have warned them, from time to time, of attempts made by their legislature to extend an unwarrantable jurisdiction over us. We have reminded them of the circumstances of our emigration and settlement here. We have appealed to their native justice and magnanimity, and we have conjured them, by the ties of our common kindred, to disavow these usurpations, which would inevitably interrupt our connections and correspondence. They, too, have been deaf to the voice of justice and consanguinity. We must, therefore, acquiesce in the necessity which denounces our separation, and hold them, as we hold the rest of mankind, enemies in war; in peace, friends.

We, therefore, the representatives of the United State of America, in general congress assembled, appealing to the Supreme Judge of the world for the rectitude of our intentions, do, in the name and by the authority of the good people of these colonies, solemnly publish and declare: That these United colonies are, and of right ought to be, *Free and Independent States;* that they are absolved from all allegiance to theEnglish crown,

John Adams, Robert Treat Paine, Elbridge Gerry.

Rhode Island, Etc.—Stephen Hopkins, William Ellery.

Connecticut.—Roger Sherman, Samuel Huntington, William Williams, Oliver Wolcott

New York.—William Floyd, Philip Livingston, Francis Lewis, Lewis Morris.

New Jersey.—Richard Stockton, John Witherspoon, Francis Hopkinson, John Hart, Abraham Clark.

Pennsylvania.—Robert Morris, Benjamin Rush, Benjamin Franklin, John Morton, George Clymer, James Smith, George Taylor, James Wilson, George Ross.

and that all political connection between them and the State of Great Britain is, and ought to be, totally dissolved; and that, as *Free and Independent States,* they have full power to levy war, conclude peace, contract alliances, establish commerce, and to do all other acts and things which Independent States may of right do. And for the support of this Declaration, with a firm reliance on the protection of Divine Providence, we mutually pledge to each other our lives, our fortunes, and our sacred honor.

JOHN HANCOCK.

New Hampshire. — Josiah Bartlett, William Whipple, Matthew Thornton.

Massachusetts Bay.—Samuel Adams,

Delaware.—Cæsar Rodney, George Read, Thomas M'Kean.

Maryland. — Samuel Chase, William Paca, Thomas Stone, Charles Carroll of Carrollton.

Virginia.—George Wythe, Richard Henry Lee, Thomas Jefferson, Benjamin Harrison, Thomas Nelson, Jr., Francis Lightfoot Lee, Carter Braxton.

North Carolina. — William Hooper, Joseph Hewes, John Penn.

South Carolina.—Edward Rutledge, Thomas Hayward, Jr., Thomas Lynch, Jr., Arthur Middleton.

Georgia.—Button Gwinnett, Lyman Hall, George Walton.

Noted Events Commencing with the Christian Era.

[From the Year 4 to 1600.]

4. Leap year corrected, having formerly been every third year.

19. The Jews banished from Rome.

40. The name of Christians first given at Antioch to the followers of Christ.

49. London founded by the Romans.

60. Chistianity about this time first preached in Great Britain.

64. Nero sets fire to the city of Rome, and throws the blame on the Christians.

68. Nero, the Roman emperor, commits suicide.

70. Vespasian, who was appointed by Nero, in the year 66, to wage war against

179. Reign of Lucius, the first Christian king of Britain and in the world.

189. The capitol of Rome destroyed by lightning.

191. Rome nearly destroyed by fire.

193. The Roman empire is bought at auction by Eidius Julianus, who is put to death by order of the Senate.

251. Monastic life begins about this time.

274. France, Spain and Britain reduced to obedience to Rome. Silk first brought from India. The manufacture of it first introduced into Europe by some

the Jews, was now declared emperor by the army, and was acknowledged all over the East; in the beginning of whose reign Jerusalem is taken by the Romans under Titus, and all the awful predictions of our Lord, as well as those of the ancient prophets, are exactly accomplished. The city is desolated; the temple destroyed, so that not one stone was left above another; 1,100,000 persons perished miserably in the siege, and the remnant of the Jews are scattered to all nations.

107. The first creditable historian among the Chinese.

167. A plague prevails all over the known world.

Monks, in 551; first worn by the clergymen in England in 1534.

330. Fearful persecution of Christians in Persia, lasting forty years.

340. One hundred and fifty Greek and Asiatic cities destroyed by an earthquake.

373. The Bible translated into the Gothic language.

394. Complete downfall of paganism.

419. Many cities in Palestine destroyed by an earthquake.

432. St. Patrick preaches the gospel in Ireland.

433. Part of Constantinople destroyed by fire.

447. Atilla, "The scourge of God," with his Huns, ravages the Roman empire and attempts to form an immense empire from China to the Atlantic. He died suddenly on the first night of his nuptials, in 453.

468. The principle established that every accused person shall be tried by his peers or equals.

476. Rome taken by Odoacer, King of the Heruli. This terminates the existence of the Roman empire, and is the commencement of the Kingdom of Italy under Odoacer. Odoacer's sack of Rome was the great event which preceded the middle or "dark ages." The form of the old Roman government remained—the

tian era introduced by Dionysius, the monk.

526. Two hundred and fifty thousand persons destroyed by an earthquake at Antioch.

531. Chess introduced into Persia from India.

541. The reign of Totila, who twice pillages Rome, and reduces the inhabitants to such distress that the ladies and people of quality are obliged to beg for bread at the doors of the Goths. This continues till 542.

542. Plague at Constantinople. During three months 5,000 to 10,000 die daily.

Senate, the Consuls, etc.; but Italy, ravaged by a succession of wars, plagues, famines, and every form of public tyranny and domestic slavery, was nearly a desert.

480. An earthquake lasting forty days, destroys the greater part of Constantinople.

493. Theodoric introduces the architecture of Greece to improve the buildings of Italy.

508. Prince Arthur begins his reign over the Britains.

511. A great insurrection in Constantinople; 10,000 killed.

516. Computation of time by the Chris-

551. The manufacture of silk brought from Europe into India by monks.

557. A terrible plague all over Europe, Asia and Africa, which lasted nearly fifty years.

569. The Turks first mentioned in history.

581. The city of Paris destroyed by fire.

605. Use of bells introduced into churches.

607. The burning of candles by day.

609. The Jews of Antioch massacre the Christians.

612. Mohammed publishes his Koran.

617. First code of laws published in England.

632. Death of Mohammed, aged 63 years.

632. Africa and Asia, with the churches of Jerusalem, Alexandria and Antioch, lost to the Christian world by the progress of Mohammedanism.

636. Christianity introduced into the Chinese empire.

640. The library of Alexandria is burnt by the Saracens.

643. The temple of Jerusalem converted into a Mohammedan mosque.

644. Pope Martin I. ordains celibacy of the Roman Catholic clergy.

660. Organs first used in churches.

664. Glass brought into England by Benalt, a monk.

ers, commence their work of destruction.

746. A dreadful pestilence over Europe and Asia prevails for three years.

748. The computation of time from the birth of Christ first used in historical writings.

780. Leo IV., Emperor of Rome, is succeeded by his wife Irene and his son Constantine VI.

781. Irene, queen mother, restores image worship.

786. Constantine imprisons his mother for her cruelty.

788. Pleadings in the courts of justice first practiced.

794. Masses first said for money.

685. The Britons, after a struggle of nearly one hundred and fifty years, are totally defeated by the Saxons, and driven into Wales and Cornwall.

711. The custom of kissing the Pope's foot first introduced.

716. The art of making paper brought from Samarcand by the Arabs.

726. Image worship being forbidden by the Emperor Leo, causes great excitement and many disturbances. The Greek possessions in Italy were lost on this account.

727. In Britain the King of Wessex begins the tax called "Peter's pence," to support a college at Rome.

730. The Iconoclasts, or image break-

797. Irene murders her son and reigns alone in Rome.

813. Insurrection at Rome against the Pope.

814. Germany separated from France.

826. The Danish prince, Harold, is dethroned by his subjects for being a Christian.

843. The Danes ravage Great Britain and burn the city of London.

844. Persecution of Christians in Spain.

846. An earthquake prevails over the greater part of the known world.

863. The certain history of Denmark now commences with the reign of Gormo the Old, who subdued Gutland and united all the small Danish States under his scepter till 920.

872. Clocks first brought to Constantinople from Venice.

879. Carles III., of Germany, was the first sovereign who added "in the year of our Lord" to his reign.

890. Alfred the Great, establishes a regular militia and navy, and the mode of trial by jury. He also institutes fairs and markets.

900. England divided into counties, hundreds and tithings.

912. The patronage of the papal chair is now in the hands of harlots.

931. Mere children elevated to the highest offices in the church.

941. Arithmetic brought into Europe by the Saracens. Manufactories of lin-

England, on St. Brice's day, upon which Sweyn, king of Denmark, lands a large armament and brings war and all its miseries upon the country.

1004. All old churches rebuilt, about this time, in the Gothic style.

1005. A pestilence raged all over Europe and lasted three years.

1010. St. Adalbert arrives in Prussia to preach Christianity, but is murdered by the Pagans. His death is afterward revenged by Boleslaus, a Poland, with fearful ravages.

1013. The Danes, under Sweyn, become masters of England.

1015. A law is passed in England forbidding parents to sell their children.

ens and woolens in Flanders, which becomes the seat of Western commerce.

955. Hungarians driven out of Germany.

959. Wolves expelled from England and Wales, in consequence of a reward being offered for the purpose by the king. Violent disputes between the Monks and clergy; St. Dusten, Archbishop of Canterbury, attempts to reform the church by enforcing clerical celibacy.

981. Greenland discovered by the Norwegians.

986. Louis V., the Indolent of France, poisoned by his wife, Blanche, and in him ended the race of Charlemagne.

1002. Massacre of all the Danes in

1017. Rain of the color of blood fell for three days in Aquitaine.

1024. Musical scale, consisting of six notes, invented by Guido Aretino.

1028. Romanus III., of Rome, a patrician, becomes emperor of the East by marrying Zoe, the daughter of the late monarch.

1034. Zoe, after prostituting herself to a Paphlagonian money-lender, causes her husband, Romanus, to be poisoned, and afterward marries her favorite, who ascends the throne under the title of Micheal IV.

1038. The Pope, for his scandalous conduct, driven from Rome, but re-established by the emperor, Conrad.—

Earthquakes and famine at Constantinople.

1039. Hardicanute, the third Anglo-Danish monarch of England, taxed England like a conquered country, was a glutton and drunkard, and died of apoplexy.

1042. Zoe and her sister Theodora are made sole empresses of Rome by the populace, but after two months Zoe, though sixty years old, takes her third husband, Constantine X., who succeeds. The Danes expelled from England.

1053. The Welsh and Irish several times invade England, but are repulsed.

1062. Seventy thousand Europeans are killed or made prisoners by the Turks in Palestine.

gives rise to the Crusades. Great struggle between Christianity and Mohammedans.

1091. The Saracens, of Spain, beset on all sides by the Christians, call in the aid of the Moors, from Africa, who seize the territory they came to protect and subdue the Saracens.

1095. Peter, the Hermit, preaches against the Turks in all the countries of Christendom.

1096. The first Crusade; Peter, the Hermit, and Walter, the Penniless, set out with a rabble, 300,000 of whom perish before the warriors are ready to start. There were 600,000 warriors and 100,000 cavalry.

1099. Jerusalem taken by the Crusa-

1065. Jerusalem taken by the Turks.

1070. Popery at the height of its power, claiming supreme dominion, temporal and spiritual, over all the States of Christendom.

1072. Surnames first used among the English nobility.

1073. Booksellers first heard of.

1076. Justices of Peace first appointed in England.

1080. Doomsday book began to be compiled from a general survey of the estates of England, and finished in six years.

1087. After the capture of Jerusalem by the Turks the Christian pilgrims are insulted, robbed and oppressed, which

ders on July 15th, when 70,000 infidels were put to the sword.

1110. Writing on paper made of cotton rags commences about this time.

1137. A pretended Messiah in France.

1138. A pretended Messiah in Persia.

1147. Alphonsus of Spain, assisted by a fleet of Crusaders on their way to the Holy land, takes Lisbon from the Moors.

1163. London bridge, consisting of nineteen small arches, first built of stone.

1167. English commerce confined to the exportation of wool.

1172. Henry II. King of England takes possession of Ireland, which from that period is governed by an English Viceroy or Lord-Lieutenant.

1176. Dispensing of justice by circuits first established in England.

1178. Pope Alexander, by a special act, relieves the clery of Berkshire from keeping the archdeacon's dogs and hawks during his visits.

1179. The Waldenses spread over the valley of Piedmont. They circulated the Scriptures; they were the forerunners of Protestantism; were condemned by the eleventh general council and severely persecuted.

1180. Glass windows begin to be used in private houses in England. Bills of exchange used in commerce.

1181. Digest of the laws of England made about this time by Glanville.

pretense of establishing the worship of one God. He died in 1227.

1208. London incorporated and obtained its first charter from King John.

1210. Ireland completely subdued, and English laws and customs introduced by King John.

1213. The Pope declares King John, of England, a usurper, and John submits to hold his crown as a vassal of the Pope.

1214. Period of the Troubadors in France, the Minstrels in England, and the Minnesengers in Germany.

1217. Jerusalem taken by the Turks, who drove away the Saracens.

1229. The Scriptures forbidden to all laymen.

1189. Great massacre of the Jews at the coronation of Richard 1.

1196. The Jews become the principal bankers in the world.

1199. The power of the Pope supreme. Rome mistress of the world and kings her vassals.

1204. Jews of both sexes imprisoned; their eyes or teeth plucked out and numbers inhumanly butchered, by King John, of England. The Inquisition established by Pope Innocent III.

1206. Reign of Genghis Kahn, first emperor of the Moguls and Tartars, one of the most bloody conquerors of the world. Fourteen millions of the human race perished by his sword, under the

1233. The houses of London and other cities in England, France and Germany still thatched with straw.

1234. They circumcise and attempt to crucify a child at Norwich; the offenders are condemned in a fine of 20,000 marks.

1247. The first concordance of the Bible was made under the direction of Hugo de St. Charo, who employed as many as 500 monks upon it.

1254. The Jews persecuted everywhere.

1257. Certain record of the first gold coin in England.

1260. Kublia Khan builds Pekin, China, and makes it his capital.

1264. The Commons of England first summoned to Parliament.

1268. No Pope for about three years.

1269. Statute passed in England that no Jew should be allowed to enjoy a freehold.

ˈ1274ˈ Every Jew lending money on interest compelled to wear a plate on his breast signifying that he was a usurer, or to quit the realm of England.

1277. First Nepotism. Pope Nicholas III. enriching his family at the expense of the church, introduces Nepotism.—Two hundred and sixty-seven Jews hanged and quartered for clipping coin, or cutting pieces from silver and gold.

1279. The Tartars subdue China.

1282. The Sicilians massacre the French throughout the whole island of Sicily, without respect to sex or age, to

1298. Silver-hafted knives, spoons and cups a great luxury at this time. Tallow candles so great a luxury that splinters of wood were used for lights.

1300. University of Lyons founded.—Rapid advance in civilization. Revival of ancient learning; improvements in the arts and sciences, and progress of liberty.

1303. Vacancy in the Papal chair nearly eleven months, with the papal power on the decline.

1305. Sir William Wallace of Elderslie, the Scottish hero of the 13th century, is betrayed to the English King by Sir John Monteith, and at London put to death in this year, aged about 30.

1306. In Scotland Robert Bruce is de-

the number of 8,000, on Easter day, the first bell for vespers being the signal,—This horrid affair is known in history by the name of "Sicilian Vespers."

1287. Fifteen thousand six hundred and sixty Jews are apprehended in one day and banished from England.

1289. England pays her last tribute to the Pope.

1291. End of the Crusade to recover Jerusalem. It cost the lives of 2,000,000 men.

1293. From this year there is a regular succession of English Parliaments.

1297. Sir William Wallace, Sir William Douglas, Robert Bruce and other chiefs head a rebellion against the English.

clared King and is obliged to flee, but on the death of Edward, of England, resumes his position. Edward II., of England, a weak King, was murdered in Berkeley Castle by order of the Queen's paramour. Isabella, daughter of the King of France, married Edward II.—Her favorite, Mortimer, died by the gibbet, and she was confined for the rest of her life in her own house at Risings, near London.

1310. Chimneys first used in domestic architecture.

1312. Knight Templars wholly suppressed by the Pope and the King of France.

1314. Battle of Bannockburn, between Edward II. and Robert Bruce, which

establishes the latter on the throne of Scotland, July 25.

1314. The Cardinals meet in Italy, and not agreeing in the election of a Pope, they set fire to the conclave and separate, by which the Papal chair is left vacant for two years.

1315. A famine prevails in England so dreadful that the people devoured the flesh of horses, dogs, cats and vermin.

1316. Pope John XXII. imposes taxes upon all countries of Europe to enrich the treasury of the church.

1317. Massacre of the Jews at Verdun by the peasantry; five hundred defend themselves in a castle, where, for want of weapons, they throw their children at their enemies, then destroy one another.

1344. The first creation to titles by patents used by Edward III.

1348. One million five hundred thousand Jews are massacred in Europe, on suspicion of having poisoned the springs during a fatal distemper.

1349. The order of the Garter first instituted in England by Edward III.

1352. The Turks first enter Europe.

1357. Coal first brought to London.

1362. Law pleadings made in English by favor of Edward III., instead of French, which had continued from the time of the Conqueror.

1365. Collection of Peter's pence forbidden by the English government.

1368. A striking clock in Westminster.

1369. John Wickliffe, the English re-

1319. Dublin University established.

1324. John Wickliffe, the first English reformer is born. He studied at Oxford, and is justly called "The Morning Star of the Reformation," as he led to the truth under Luther and the other reformers of the 16th century. He died in 1384.

1336. Giotto, a celebrated Florentine painter, who studied with Ceniabue, was only a shepherd's lad. He was a friend of Dante and Petrarch, and is said to be the first who produced life-like portraits. He died at this time, aged 60.

1337. First comet observed whose course is described with exactness.

1340. Gunpowder invented by Swartz, a Monk of Cologne.

former, begins to be publicly known by his disputes with the Friars.

1370. A perfect clock made at Paris by Vick.

1378. Louis, of Hungary, dies, and the history of Hungary now presents a frightful catalogue of crimes. Charles Duras is murdered; Elizabeth, Queen of Louis, is drowned, and King (Hungarian Queens reign with the title of King) Mary, their daughter, marries Sigismond, Marquis of Brandenburg, and causes the rivers of Hungary to flow with blood.

1381. Bills of exchange first used in England.

1384. Cannon first used by the English in the defense of Calais.

1384. Persia invaded by Tamerlane, a

Tartar, who made pyramids of the heads of the slain.

1385. Linen weavers from Netherlands first establish business in London.

1391. Playing cards were first invented in France to amuse the king. The English forbidden to cross the sea for benefices.

1393. Charles, of France, seized with madness.

1394. The Jews banished from France by Charles VI.

1399. Tamerlane, in command of the Mogul Tartars, takes the city of Delhi, defeats the Indian army, conquers Hindoostan, and butchers 100,000 of its people.

France. She was sold to the English, and after the formality of a trial, was burnt alive as a witch in 1431.

1415. John Huss and Jerome Prague, Bohemians, two of the first reformers, are burnt for heresy at Constance, which occasions an insurrection, when Sigismund, who betrayed them, is deposed, and the Imperialists are driven from the Kingdom.

1420. Paris taken by the English, who held it fifteen years.

1428. Joan of Arc, the Maid of Orleans, compels the English to raise the siege of that town. Wickliffe's remains burnt and his ashes thrown into the swift waters. Giovanni de Medici, one

1400. A wonderful canal completed in China about this time.

1402. Battle of Angora, in which Bajazet I, King of the Turks, is taken prisoner by Tamerlane Bajazet was exposed in a large iron cage, which he had destined for his adversary, and dashed his head against the bars and killed himself. At this defeat the Persian empire fell under the control of Tamerlane.

1409. At the council of Pisa for the election of a Pope, Gregory and Benedict were disposed of, and Alexander V. elected. Neither of them would yield, so there were three Popes at once.

1410. Joan of Arc born, sometimes called Maid of Orleans, a peasant girl of

of the greatest merchant princes of Florence, died, and his son, Casmo de Medici, carried on the work his father begun. He induced artists and scholars to take up their abode in Florence. He died in 1461.

1429. Joan of Arc raised the siege and entered Orleans with supplies April 29, and the English, who were before the place from October 12 preceding, abandoned the enterprise the following May. She captured several towns in possession of the English, whom she defeated in a battle near Patay, June 10.

1431. Joan of Arc was taken at the siege of Compeigne, and, to the great disgrace of the English, was burnt for a witch five days after at Rouen, in the 22d (some say 29th) year of her age.

1438. Fifty thousand persons died of famine and plague in Paris during this year, when the hungry wolves entered the city and committed great desolation.

1440. The great invention of printing is due to Guttenberg, who was assisted in improving it by Schæffer and Faust.

1442. The beginning of the negro slave trade.

1444. The earliest edition of the Bible was commenced this year by Guttenberg and finished in 1460.

1446. The sea broke in at Dort, Holland, and over 100,000 people were overwhelmed and perished, 300 villages were

Roxburgh. He was succeeded by his son James III. Engraving and etching on copper invented. An almanac in Lambeth palace was written at this time.

1461. Edward IV., succeeded Henry VI.. having waged against him a civil war for six years. This was the war of the Roses, as the struggles between the houses of York and Lancaster were called.

1462. Mentz taken and plundered and the art of printing in the general ruin is spread to other towns. Ivan the Great, of Russia, throws off the Mogul yoke, and takes the title of Czar.

1466. Faust dies at Paris, whither he journeys twice to sell his Latin Bible.

overflowed, and the tops of their towers and steeples were for ages after to be seen rising out of the water. The inundation arose in the breaking down of the dykes.

1450. Insurrection in England by Jack Cade, calling himself Mortimer.

1453. "Civil wars of the Roses" occur in England about this time, when the house of York began to aspire to the crown, and by their ambitious views to deluge the whole kingdom in blood.

1457. Glass first manufactured in England.

1460. James II. of Scotland was killed by the bursting of one of the badly made guns as he was besieging the English in

1468. John Guttenberg died, aged 68. He was the inventor of movable types in printing, and was the partner of the famous Faust at Mentz.

1471. Warwick, Richard Nevil, the "King Maker," was the most distinguished actor in the wars of the Roses. He was slain at the battle of Barnet, Easter day, over whom Edward IV. gained a decisive victory. Richard III., married Anne, daughter of Warwick, and widow of Edward, Prince of Wales, whom Richard had murdered. King Henry, of England, is murdered in the Tower, aged 50 years.

1474. The foundation of the present monarchy of Russia commenced.

1476. Certain persons obtain license from Edward IV. to make gold and silver from mercury.

1477. Watches are said to have been first invented at Nuremburg.

1483. The Severn overflowed during ten days, and carried away men, women and children in their beds, and covered the tops of many mountains. The waters settled upon the lands, and were called the Great Waters for 100 years.

1484. Æsop's Fables, printed by Caxton, is supposed to be the first book with its leaves numbered.

1485. Richard III., King of England, and last of the Plantagenets, defeated and killed at the battle of Bosworth, on August 22d, by Henry VII , which puts an end to the civil wars between the houses of York and Lancaster. The crown of Richard was found in a hawthorn bush on the plain where the battle was fought, and Henry was so impatient to be crowned that he had the ceremony performed on the spot with that very crown.

1488 James IV. of Scotland succeeded James III., who fell in a brawl with some of the Barons.

1492. Five hundred thousand Jews are banished from Spain and one hundred and fifty thousand from Portugal.

1505. Shillings first coined in England.

1508. Negro slaves imported into Hespanolia.

1511. Cuba conquered by three hundred Spaniards.

1514. Cannon bullets of stone still in use.

1517. Europeans first arrive in Canton, China. First patent for importing negroes to America granted by Spain.

1524. Some of the states of Europe were alarmed by the prediction that another general deluge would occur, and arks were everywhere built to guard against the calamity, but the season happened to be a very dry one.

1529. The name of Protestant given to those who protested against the Church of Rome at the diet of Spires, in Germany.

1537. Papal bull declares the American natives to be rational beings.

1539. Cannon first used in ships.

1543. Silk stockings first worn by the French king.

1547. First law in England establishing the interest of money at ten per cent

1548. Formal establishment of Protestantism in England.

1552. Books of geography and astronomy destroyed in England as being infested with magic.

1553 Lady Jane Gray, daughter of the Duke of Suffolk, and wife of Lord Guilford Dudley, was proclaimed Queen of England on the death of Edward VI.— Ten days afterwards returned to private life; was tried November 13th, and beheaded February 12th, 1554, when but seventeen years of age, with her husband and his father.

1553. Elizabeth Croft, a girl eighteen years of age, was secreted in a wall and with a whistle made for the purpose uttered many seditious speeches against the Queen and Prince of England, and also against the mass and confession, for which she was sentenced to stand upon a scaffold at St. Paul's Cross during sermon time and make public confession of her imposture. She was called the Spirit of the Wall. While Servetus, the

gleemen or harpers of the Saxons.— Queen Elizabeth, of England, was presented with a pair of black silk stockings by her silk woman, and she never wore cloth ones any more.

1561. Philip II. commences his bloody persecution of the Protestants.

1563. Captain, afterwards Sir John Hawkins, was the first Englishman, after the discovery of America, who made traffic of the human species.

1564. William Shakespeare, the great poet and dramatist, was born at Stratford-on-Avon, to which place he returned from London and lived till 1616.

1568. Battle of Langside, between the forces of the Regent of Scotland, the Earl of Murray, and the army of Mary,

founder of the Unitarian sect, was proceeding to Naples, through Geneva, Calvin induced the magistrates to arrest him on charge of blasphemy and heresy, and, refusing to retract his opinions, he was condemned to the flames, which sentence was carried into execution October 27.

1554. The wearing of silk forbidden to the common people of England. The Company of Stationers of London is of great antiquity, and existed long before printing was invented; yet it was not incorporated until the second year of Philip and Mary.

1560. Minstrels continued until this time. They owed their origin to the

Queen of Scots, in which the latter suffered a complete defeat, on May 15.— Immediately after this fatal battle the unfortunate Mary fled to England, and landed at Workington, in Cumberland, May 16, and was soon after imprisoned by Elizabeth.

1571. Battle of Lepanto. The great naval engagement between the combined fleets of Spain, Venice and Pius V., and the whole maritime force of the Turks. The Christian fleet for a time prostrated the whole naval power of Turkey.

1572. Massacre of St. Bartholomew.— Seventy thousand Hugenots, or French Protestants, throughout the kingdom of

France were murdered under circumstances of the most horrid treachery and cruelty. It began at Paris in the night of the festival of St. Bartholomew, Aug. 14, by secret orders from Charles IX., King of France, at the instigation of the queen dowager, his mother.

1585. Sextus V. rose from a shepherd boy to be Pope, is active and energetic, corrects abuses in the church and restores the Vatican Library.

1587. Mary, Queen of Scots, during the reign of Elizabeth, was beheaded in Fotheringay Castle, in which she had been long previously confined, February 8, after an unjust and cruel captivity of almost nineteen years in England.

and is that now in general use in England and the United States.

1605. The memorable conspiracy in England, known by the name of the Gunpowder Plot, for springing a mine under the House of Parliament, and destroying the three estates of the realm, king, lords and commons, was discovered November 5. This diabolical scheme was projected by Robert Catesby, and many high persons were leagued in the enterprise. Guy Faux was detected in the vaults under the House of Lords, preparing the train for being fired the next day! Hugh Calverly, having murdered two of his children and stabbed his wife in a fit of jealousy, being arranged for his crime at York

1589. Coaches first introduced into England.

1592. Massacre of the Christians at Crotia by the Turks, when 65,000 were slain.

1603. Thirty thousand five hundred and seventy-eight persons perished of the plague in London alone in this and the following year. It was also fatal in Ireland.

1604. The celebrated religious conference held at Hampton Court Palace, in order to effect a general union between the prelates of the Church of England and the dissenting ministers. This conference led to a new translation of the Bible, which was executed in 1607-1611,

assizes, stood mute, and was therefore pressed to death in the castle, a large iron weight being placed upon his breast.

1606. Demetrius Griska Eutropeia, a friar, pretended to be the son of Basilowitz, czar of Muscovy, whom the usurper Boris had put to death, but he claimed another child had been substituted in his place. He was supported by the armies of Poland. His success astonished the Russians, who invited him to the throne and delivered into his hands Fedor, the reigning czar, and all his family, whom he cruelly put to death. His imposition being discovered he was assassinated in his palace.

1611. Two hundred thousand persons

perished of a pestilence at Constantinople.

1619. Harvey discovers or confirms the circulation of the blood.

1620. Battle of Prague between the Imperialists and Bohemians of Germany. The latter, who had chosen Frederick V., of the Palatine, for their king, were totally defeated. The unfortunate king was forced to flee with his family into Holland, leaving all his baggage and money behind him. He was deprived of the hereditary dominions, and the Protestant interest ruined in Bohémia.

1620. Pilgrims landed at Plymouth, Mass., December 21st (commonly called December 22d), of the year.

Called also the battle of Lippstadt. In this battle Gustavus Adolphus, king of Sweden, the most illustrious hero of his time, and the chief support of the Protestant religion in Germany, and in alliance with Charles I. of England, was foully killed in the moment of victory.

1633. The art of preserving flowers in sand discovered.

1641. The first attempt at reporting for newspapers commenced in reporting the proceedings of the English Parliament.

1647. The tyranny of the Spaniards leads to an insurrection at Naples, excited by Maraniello, a fisherman, who in fifteen days raises an army of 200,000

1622. The first newspaper ever printed in England was issued, called "The Weekley Newes."

1624 George Fox born, the founder of the society of Friends or Quakers. He was clad in a perennial suit of leather, and wandered in solitude, seeking some light to guide him, studying the Bible and himself. He died in 1690.

1628. The discovery of the circulation of the blood by Dr. Harvey furnished an entirely new system of physiological and pathological speculation.

1629. St. Peter's Church at Rome completed, having been commenced about the middle of the 15th century.

1632. Battle of Lutzengen, or Lutze.

men. The insurrection subsides and Maraniello is murdered.

1648. Eighty-one Presbyterians expelled from the English Parliament, which received the name of the 'Rump.'

1648. Advertisements were first inserted in newspapers about this time.

1650. Quakers or Friends. Originally called Seekers, from their seeking the truth. Justice Bennett, of Derby, gave the society the name of Quakers at this time, because Fox (the founder) admonished him and those present with him to tremble at the word of the Lord.

1652. First war between the English and the Dutch.

1656. James Naylor personated our Savior; he was convicted of blasphemy, scourged, and his tongue bored with a hot iron on the pillory, by sentence of the House of Commons under Cromwell's administration.

1656. The plague brought from Sardinia to Naples, being introduced by a transport with soldiers on board, raged with such violence as to carry off four hundred thousand of the inhabitants in six months.

1662. Charles II. is said to have first encouraged the appearance of women on the stage of England, but the queen of James I. had previously performed in a theater at court. An earthquake

destroy the rigging of an enemy's ships, invented by the Dutch Admiral De Witt.

1667. The method of preparing phosphorus from bones discovered by Chas William Scheele, an eminent Swedish Chemist.

1690. The first newspaper issued in America, named "Public Occurrences, Foreign and Domestic," was published at Boston, September 25th.

1669. Candia or Crete obtained from the Venetians by the Turks after a siege of twenty-four years, during which over 200,000 people perished.

1672. White slaves were sold in England to be transported to Virginia; av-

throughout China buries 300,000 persons in Pekin alone.

1663. The first idea of a steam engine was suggested by the Marquis of Worcester in his "Century of Inventions" as "a way to drive up water by fire."

1665. Memorable plague in London which carried off 68,596 persons.

1666. Great fire in London, September 2, destroying eighty-nine churches, including the Royal Exchange, the Custom House, Sion College, and many other public buildings, besides 13,200 houses, laying waste 400 streets. This conflagration continued three days and nights, and was at last only extinguished by the blowing up of houses. Chain-shot, to

erage price for five year's service, $25, while a negro was worth $125.

1674. John Milton, one of the chief poets and greatest men of England died, aged 66 years. His task of writing two "Defences of the people of England" totally destroyed his already impaired vision. He afterwards fulfilled the prediction uttered in one of his former books by bringing out the great English epic " Paradise Lost." In his domestic life Milton endured much trouble. Deserted for a while by his first wife he saw no relief but in divorce. As he was blind, his daughter, as an amanuensis, assisted him in producing "Paradise Lost."

COMMANDERS-IN-CHIEF of the U. S. ARMY AND NAVY.

UNITED STATES ARMY.

The following is a list of the officers who have acted as commanders-in-chief of the army of the United States, by seniority of rank, or by special assignment of the President:—

1. George Washington, from June, 1775, to December, 1783.

2. Henry Knox, from December, 1783, to June, 1784.

3. Major Doughty, from June, 1784, to September, 1789. [There was no United States army during this period, except two companies of artillery commanded by a major. The continental line had been disbanded, and a new army had not been formed.]

"major-general commanding" settled the dispute.]

10. James Wilkinson, from June, 1800, to January, 1812.

11. Henry Dearborn, from January, 1812, to June, 1815, the period of the war of 1812.

12. Jacob Brown, from June, 1815, to February, 1828.

13. Alexander McComb, from May, 1828, to June, 1841.

14. Winfield Scott, from June, 1841, to November, 1861, the longest term of all. Scott was the first officer after Washington, who held the rank of lieutenant general. This was conferred upon him by Congress after the outbreak of the

4. Josiah Harmar, from September, 1789, to March, 1791.

5. Arthur St. Clair, from March, 1791, to March, 1792.

6. Anthony Wayne, from March, 1792, to December, 1796.

7. James Wilkinson, from December, 1796, to July, 1798.

8. George Washington, who was created a lieutenant-general, resumed the command of the army, from July, 1798, to December, 1799.

9. Alexander Hamilton, from December, 1799, to June, 1800. [It used to be a mooted question in the War Department whether Hamilton had ever commanded the army; but the recent discovery of an order bearing his signature as

civil war, but did not pass to his successor in command.

15. George B. McClellan, from November, 1861, to March, 1862.

16. Henry W. Halleck, from July, 1862, to March, 1864.

17. Ulysses S. Grant, from March, 1864, to March, 1869.

18. William T. Sherman, from March, 1869, to November, 1883, when he retired.

19. Phillip H. Sheridan, from November, 1883. The title of general did not pass from Sherman to Sheridan. Sheridan remains lieutenant general. The grade of both continues only while they live, and there is no further promotion beyond the grade of major-general.

Since the foundation of the government there have been but three commanders of the army with the full title of general. The first was Washington, upon whom the rank was conferred by Congress a few weeks before his death, and a few months after he had been made lieutenant-general, in anticipation of a war with France. The second was Grant, to honor whom Congress revived the grade in 1866. The third was Sherman, who was promoted to Grant's place in 1869.

———o———

UNITED STATES NAVY.

The War Department had charge of naval affairs until April, 1798. Benjamin Stoddard, of Maryland, was the first

its renewal on paper, in 1794, Captain John Barry was named his senior officer, in which position he died.

After the reorganization of the navy, under the Constitution, all ranks above captain were abolished. Captains were the highest rank of American naval officers, "though a practice had grown up, without legal authorities, of bestowing the title of commodore on a captain commanding a squadron." Capt. Shubrick and Captain French Favert, each when in command of squadrons, took the title of admiral, and hoisted the "wide flag at the fore," but were rebuked by the Navy Department. In 1856 Congress bestowed the rank of "flag officer" on captains in command of

Secretary of the Navy, and was appointed May 21, 1798, George Cabot, of Massachusetts, appointed May 3, the same year, having declined.

The Continental Congress, on Nov. 15, 1776, provided for the following grades above the rank of captain: Admiral, to rank as general; vice-admiral, to rank as lieutenant general; rear admiral, to rank as major general; commodore, as brigadier general. Eseek Hopkins, who had, on Dec. 27, 1775, been appointed Commander-in-Chief of the Navy, was its first commodore. In Jan., 1777, Commodore James Nicholson, of Maryland, succeeded Eseek Hopkins as Commander-in-Chief of the United States Navy, and held that place until its dissolution. On

squadrons. July 16, 1862, Congress created the grades of rear-admiral and commodore, and on the same day D. G. Farragut became rear admiral. On Dec. 21, 1864, Congress created the office of vice-admiral, and provided that the vice-admiral should be the ranking officer in the navy. Dec. 31, 1864, Rear Admiral Farragut was commissioned vice-admiral.— July 25, 1866, the office of admiral being created, he was promoted to that rank. Upon his death, Aug. 14, 1870, Vice-Admiral D. D. Porter succeeded. In 1873 Congress provided that whenever a vacancy should occur in the office of admiral or vice-admiral, the office itself should cease to exist. Stephen C. Rowan is the vice-admiral.

BUSINESS FORMS.

Commercial Terms.—The following is the definition of terms used in commercial reports and transactions between buyer and seller of stock and grain:

If wheat is selling at $1.10@1.15 in June, and the seller agrees to deliver it to the buyer in July, it is understood that the person who sells the wheat can deliver it to the purchaser at any time during the month of July.

To sell *short*, is contracting to deliver a certain amount of grain or stock at a fixed price, within a certain length of time, when the seller has not the stock on hand. The person who sells "short" finds it to his interest to depress the market, in order that he may buy and fill his contract at a profit. The "shorts" are termed "bears."

Buying *long*, is contracting to purchase grain or shares of stock at a fixed price, deliverable within a time named, expecting to make a profit by the rise of prices. The "longs" are termed "bulls."

Promissory Notes.—A promissory note is an agreement in writing to pay a certain sum of money at a time therein named, or on demand, or at sight, to the person therein designated, or his order or assigns, or to the bearer. The person making the note is called the drawer or maker.

A note is void when founded upon fraud. Thus, a note obtained from a person when intoxicated, or obtained for any reason which is not legal, cannot be collected.*

*If, however, the note is transferred to an innocent holder, the claim of fraud or no value received will not avail. The party holding the note can collect it if the maker is able to pay it.

A note given upon Sunday is also void in some States.

No notes bear interest unless it is so specified on the note; but after they are due they are entitled to the legal rate allowed by the State. If it is intended that the note should draw more than the legal rate, it should be so specified on the note as follows: "with interest at the rate of — per cent. until paid."

Notes payable on demand or at sight, draw no interest until after presentation or demand of the same has been made; after that they draw the legal rate of interest of the State.

If "with interest" is included in the note, it draws the legal rate allowed by the State where it is given, from the time it was made.

If the note is made payable to a person or order, to a person or bearer, to a person or his assigns, or to the cashier of an incorporated company or order, such notes are negotiable.

When transferring the note, the endorser frees himself from responsibility, so far as the payment is concerned, by writing on the back, above his name, "Without recourse to me in any event."

When a note is made payable at a definite period, three days beyond the time expressed on the face of the note are allowed to the person who is to pay the same. These three days are called days of grace. *Notes payable on demand are not entitled to days of grace.*

A note made payable at a bank, and not taken up when it is due, and a demand has been made for payment, when the three days of grace have expired and payment refused, the endorser of the note is then responsible for the amount without any further notice. Any demand before the three days of grace have expired does not affect the endorser.

The days of grace, which must be computed according to the laws of the State where the note is payable, are to be reckoned exclusive of the day when the note

(Business Forms—Promissory Notes, continued.)

would otherwise become due, and without deduction for Sundays or holidays; in which latter case, by special enactments in most of the States, notes are deemed to become due upon the secular day next preceding such days. Thus, a note due upon the twenty-fifth day of December, is payable on the twenty-fourth, as the day when due is Christmas day; if the twenty-fourth chance to be Sunday, it is due upon the twenty-third.

In order to charge an indorser, the note, if payable at a particular place, must be presented for payment at the place upon the very day it becomes due; if no place of payment be named, it must be presented, either to the maker personally, or at his place of business, during business hours, or at his dwelling house, within reasonable hours; if payable by a firm, a presentment may be made to either of the partners, or at the firm's place of business; if given by several persons jointly, not partners, the demand must be made upon all. If the note has been lost, mislaid, or destroyed, the holder must still make a regular and formal demand, offering the party, at the same time, a sufficient indemnity in the event of his paying the same.

NOTE ON DEMAND.

$50.00.   PHILADELPHIA, PA., June 1, 18—.
On demand I promise to pay to Simon Miller, or order, Fifty Dollars, value received, with interest.
                                                          HAMILTON GRIFFIN.

NEGOTIABLE NOTE.

With interest at legal rate per cent. from date.
$300.   HARRISBURG, PA., June 1, 18—.
Three months after date, for valued received. I promise to pay George Menzel, or order, Three Hundred Dollars, with interest.   JAMES SPENCE

NEGOTIABLE NOTE.

With interest at ten per cent. after maturity, until paid.
$200.   ROCHESTER, N. Y., May 1, 18—.
For value received, ninety days after date, I promise to pay Philip Jones, or order, Two Hundred Dollars, with interest at ten per cent, after maturity, until paid.   AMOS GILBERT.

NOTE NOT NEGOTIABLE.

$700.   ALBANY, N. Y., March 6, 18—.
Six months after date, for value received, I promise to pay Joseph Hollingsworth, Seven Hundred Dollars.   PETER HERSCH.

NOTE FOR TWO OR MORE PERSONS.

$2,000.   CLINTON, IA., April 4. 18—.
We, or either of us, promise to pay to the order of John Scott, Two Thousand Dollars, for value received.   GEORGE HARRIS.
                                                          ENIS FLETCHER.

FORM FOR PENNSYLVANIA.

$300.   READING, PA., Feb. 6, 18—.
For value received, I promise to pay to the order of Jasper Williams, Three Hundred Dollars, sixty days after date, without defalcaltion.   THOMAS DAYWALT.

MARRIED WOMAN'S NOTE IN NEW YORK.

$100.   SYRACUSE, N. Y., June 10, 18—.
For value received, I promise to pay to W. L. Brown, or order, One Hundred Dollars, one year from date, with interest. And I hereby charge my individual property and estate with the payment of this note.   EMILY CUMMINGS.

NOTE PAYABLE BY INSTALLMENTS.

$900.   LANCASTER, PA., June 5, 18—.
For value received, I promise to pay to Philip Jones, or order, Nine Hundred Dollars in the following manner, to-wit: One Hundred Dollars in one month from date; Two Hundred Dollars in two months; Three Hundred Dollars in three months, and Two Hundred Dollars in nine months from date, with interest on the several sums as they become due.   PETER HERSCH

(Business Forms—continued.)

NOTE PAYABLE IN MERCHANDISE.

$900.   HAVERHILL, MASS., February 2, 18—.

For value received, on or before the tenth day of June next, we promise to pay W. Stoneham & Co., or order, Nine Hundred Dollars, in good merchantable Lumber, at our yard in this city, at the market value on the maturity of this note.   HARRIS & BENDER.

JOINT NOTE.

$500.   ROCHESTER, N. Y., June 11, 18—.

Six months after date, we jointly and severally promise to pay to William Schofield, or order, Five Hundred Dollars, for value received, with interest at ten per cent.   JOHN HELM.
                                                                 SIMON LEVY.

FORM OF A NOTE FOR INDIANA.

$300.   FORT WAYNE, IND., September 12, 18—

On demand, for value received, I promise to pay John Duncan, or order, Three Hundred Dollars, with interest; payable without any relief whatever from valuation or appraisement.
                                                                 PHILIP MAYO.

FORM OF GUARANTEE.

For and in consideration of One Dollar, to me in hand paid by John Wannamaker & Co., of Philadelphia, who, at my request propose opening a credit with John W. Martin, of Hagerstown, Md., I do hereby guarantee the payment to John Wannamaker & Co., their successors and assigns, of all indebtedness which said John W. Martin has incurred or may incur for goods and merchandise sold to him, or delivered at his request by said John Wannamaker & Co., their successors and assigns, upon credit or for cash, or on note, or otherwise, without requiring any notice in respect thereto.

This guarantee to be open and continuing, covering all interest on any such indebtedness, and also any costs and expenses which may be incurred by John Wannamaker & Co., their successors and assigns, in collecting.

Further, it shall remain in full force until revoked by a written notice from me, provided, however, that my liability hereunder for purchases made shall not at any time exceed $3,000.

Witness my hand and seal,   }
    Philadelphia, May 10, 1880. }   C. M. RAINS

———o———

DUE-BILLS.

FORM OF DUE-BILL PAYABLE IN MONEY.

$100.   ROCHESTER, N. Y., October 2, 18—.

Due Thomas A. Sutton, or order, on demand, One Hundred Dollars, value received.
                                                                 JAMES T. PALMER.

PAYABLE IN FLOUR.

$100.   MINNEAPOLIS, MINN., January 5, 18—.

Due on demand, to George Stover, One Hundred Dollars in Flour, at the market value when delivered. Value received.   JEFFERSON MILL.

PAYABLE IN MONEY AND MERCHANDISE.

$300.   BLOOMINGTON ILL., March 2, 18—.

Due on the 15th of May next, to Henry G. Funk, or order, Two Hundred Dollars in cash, and One Hundred Dollars in merchandise from our store.   ANDERSON, BENEDICK & CO.

PAYABLE IN MERCHANDISE.

$60.   CHAMBERSBURG, PA, October 4, 18—.

Due John Long, Sixty Dollars in merchandise from our store.   SMITH & BROWN

BILLS OF EXCHANGE.

A Bill of Exchange is an order from an American Bank or Broker, directing some foreign Bank or Broker to pay a certain sum of money to the person named in the bill. This bill of exchange is then sent to the person named in it, who draws the amount specified in the bill. For instance, a merchant in New York owed a merchant in London five hundred dollars. Instead of remitting the money to the merchant in London, he would buy a Bill of Exchange from a Bank or Broker in New York for the amount, and transmit it to his creditor in London, and thus liquidate the debt. Bankers and Brokers charge a commission for issuing bills of exchange.

Drafts.--Drafts are similar to bills of exchange, only that they are local in their application, instead of being an order on a foreign Bank or Broker. They are confined to Banks and Brokers in this country. For instance, a person in Cincinnati owed a gentleman in Philadelphia two hundred dollars ; he could buy a draft for that amount in Cincinnati, from some Bank or Broker there, ordering some Philadelphia Bank or Broker to pay the two hundred dollars to the party named in the draft. The draft is sent by mail to the party in whose favor the draft is drawn. A commission is also charged for issuing drafts. Drafts can be sent through banks for collection.

FORM OF A BANK DRAFT.

$200.   SECOND NATIONAL BANK,   No. 63.

CINCINNATI, Ohio, April 2, 18—.
DUPLICATE UNPAID

Pay to the order of William Blakely Two Hundred Dollars.

BARTON DAVIS, Cashier.

To Marine National Bank of Baltimore.

Sight Draft.--Sight drafts are only drawn when it is expected the debt will be paid immediately on the presentation of the draft. The following is the form of f

SIGHT DRAFT.

BALTIMORE, Md., Jan. 6, 1882.

$500. At sight, pay to the order of Lett & Allen, Five Hundred Dollars, value received, and charge the same to our account.

HAYES & KELLER.

To John Duncan, Wilmington, Del.

TIME DRAFT.

CHICAGO, Ill., Feb. 2, 188-.

$100. Sixty days after date, pay to the order of Simon Miller, One Hundred Dollars, value received, and charge to our account.

JOHN PHILLIPS & CO.

To W. P. Harris & Co., Indianapolis, Ind.

Acceptance.--If the person upon whom the draft is drawn consents to its payment, he writes across the face of the draft as follows : "Accepted, September 9, 1881. Byron Alger."

Sight drafts and time drafts can be collected through Banks.

Laws of Grace on Sight Drafts.--Grace on Sight Drafts is ALLOWED in the following States :

Alabama, Arkansas, Dakota, Indiana, Iowa, Kentucky, Maine, Massachusetts, Michigan, Minnesota, Mississippi, Montana, Nebraska, New Hampshire, New Jersey, North Carolina, Oregon, Rhode Island, South Carolina, Utah, Wisconsin, Wyoming, Canada.

Grace on Sight Drafts is NOT ALLOWED in the following States :

California, Colorado, Connecticut, Delaware, District of Columbia, Florida, Georgia, Idaho, Illinois, Kansas, Louisiana, Maryland, Missouri, Nevada, New York, Ohio, Pennsylvania, Tennessee, Texas, Vermont, Virginia, West Virginia.

LEGAL FORMS.

Articles of Agreement.--An agreement is simply a contract between centain parties therein named, binding them to perform certain duties, enumerated in the agreement, within a specified time.

Everything relating to an agreement should be reduced to writing. Let nothing be "taken for granted." By doing this there can be no misunderstanding, and the terms of the agreement will be faithfully executed without recourse to law. No particular form is necessary, but make the specifications explicit.

All agreements, to be legal. should specify some consideration—otherwise they are void.

The time for filling the provisions of an agreement should be specified.

If fraud or misrepresentation is made by one party to the agreement, or the date is changed, the contract becomes void.

Each of the contracting parties should have a copy of the agreement, signed by all the parties interested in the agreement.

GENERAL FORM OF AGREEMENT.

THIS AGREEMENT, made the tenth day of May, A. D. 18—, between Simon Lechrone, of Chambersburg, County of Franklin, State of Pennsylvania, of the first part, and George Balsley, of the same place, of the second part :—

WITNESSETH. that the said Simon Lechrone, in consideration of the agreement of the party of the second part, hereinafter contained, contracts and agrees to and with the said George Balsley, that he will deliver, in good and marketable condition, at the town of Chambersburg, Pa., during the months of August and September, of this year, five hundred bushels of wheat, in the following lots and at the following specified times, namely: two hundred bushels by the tenth of August, one hundred bushels additional by the twentieth of August, one hundred bushels more by the first of September, and the entire five hundred bushels to be delivered by the twenty-fifth of September.

And the said George Balsley, in consideration of the prompt fulfillment of this contract, on the part of the party of the first part, contracts to and agrees with the said Simon Lechrone to pay for said wheat one dollar per bushel, for each bushel, as soon as delivered.

In case of failure of agreement by either of the parties hereto, it is hereby stipulated and agreed that the party so failing shall pay to the other one hundred dollars as fixed and settled damages.

In witness whereof, we have hereunto set our hands the day and year first above written.

SIMON LECHRONE,
GEORGE BALSLEY.

ARTICLES OF AGREEMENT FOR WARRANTY DEED.

ARTICLES OF AGREEMENT, made this tenth day of August, in the year of our Lord one thousand eight hundred and eighty, between Alexander Hamilton, of Waynesboro, Franklin County, State of Pennsylvania, party of the first part. and Hiram A. Stover, of Hagerstown, Washington County, State of Maryland, party of the second part.

WITNESSETH, that said party of the first part hereby covenants and agrees, that if the party of the second part shall first make the payment and perform the covenants hereinafter mentioned on his part to be made and performed, the said party of the first part will convey and assure to the party of the second part, in fee simple, clear of all incumbrances whatever, by a good and sufficient Warranty Deed, the following lot, piece, or parcel of ground, viz : The east sixty (60) feet of the west half of lot number ten (10), in block number five (5), Brown's Addition to Cincinnati, as recorded at Cincinnati, Hamilton County, Ohio.

And the said party of the second part hereby covenants and agrees to pay to said party of the first part the sum of Two Thousand Dollars, in the manner following: Six Hundred Dollars, cash in hand paid, the receipt whereof is hereby acknowledged, and the balance in three annual payments as follows, viz: Four Hundred Dollars, August, 10, 1881, Four Hundred Dollars, August 10, 1882; and Six Hundred Dollars, August 10, 1883 ; with interest at the rate of ten per centum, per annum, payable on the dates above specified, annually, on the whole sum remaining from time to time unpaid, and to pay all taxes, assessments, or impositions, that may be legally levied or imposed upon said land. subsequent to the year 1880 . And in case of the failure of the said party of the second part to make either of the payments, or perform any of the covenants on his part hereby made and entered into, this contract shall, at the option of the party of the first part, be forfeited and determined, and the party of the second part shall forfeit all payments made by him on this contract, and such payments shall be retained by the said party of the first part. in full satisfaction and in liquidation of all damages by him sustained. and he shall have the right to re-enter and take pos-

(*Legal Forms—continued.*)
session of the premises aforesaid, with all the improvements and appurtenances thereon, paying said Hiram A. Stover the appraised value of said improvements and appurtenances ; said appraisement to be made by three arbitrators, one being chosen by each of the said parties, the other being chosen by the first two.

It is mutually agreed that all the covenants and agreements herein contained shall extend to and be obligatory upon the heirs, executors, administrators, and assigns of the respective parties.

In witness whereof, the parties to these presents have hereunto set their hands and seals, the day and year first above written.

Signed, sealed, and delivered in presence of } ALEXANDER HAMILTON, [SEAL.]
PETER DALE.   } HIRAM A. STOVER.   [SEAL.]

AGREEMENT FOR BUILDING A HOUSE.

This agreement, made the fifth day of May, one thousand eight hundred and seventy-nine, between James Downey, of Louisville, county of Jefferson, State of Kentucky, of the first part, and Alexander Marshall, of the same place, county and State, of the second part—

Witnesseth, that the said James Downey, party of the first part, for consideration hereinafter named, contracts and agrees with the said Alexander Marshall, party of the second part, his heirs, assigns and administrators, that he, the said Downey, will, within one hundred and ten days, next following this date, in a good and workmanlike manner, and according to his best skill, well and substantially erect and finish a dwelling house on lot number nine, in block number eight, in Grove's addition to Louisville, facing on Market street, which said house is to be of the following dimensions, with brick, stone, lumber, and other materials, as are described in the plans and specifications hereto annexed.

[*Here describe the house, material for construction, and plans in full.*]

In consideration of which the said Alexander Marshall does, for himself and legal representatives, promise to the said James Downey, his heirs, executors and assigns, to pay, or cause to be paid, to the said Downy, or his legal representatives, the sum of Ten Thousand Dollars, in the manner as follows, to-wit: Fifteen Hundred Dollars at the beginning of said work, Fifteen Hundred Dollars on the fifth day of June next, Fifteen Hundred Dollars on the second day of July next, Twenty-five Hundred Dollars on the first day of August next, and the remaining Three Thousand Dollars when the work shall be fully completed

It is also agreed that the said James Downey, or his legal representatives, shall furnish, at his or their own expense, all doors, blinds, glazed sash, and window frames, according to the said plan that may be necessary for the building of said house.

It is further agreed that in order to be entitled to said payments (the first one excepted, which is otherwise secured), the said James Downey, or his legal representatives, shall, according to the architect's appraisement, have expended, in labor and material, the value of said payments, on the house, at time of payment.

For failure to accomplish the faithful performance of the agreements aforesaid, the party so failing, his heirs, executors, or assigns, agrees to forfeit and pay to the other party, or his legal representatives, the penal sum of Fifteen Hundred Dollars, as fixed and settled damages, within one month from the time of so failing.

In witness whereof, we have hereunto set our hands, the year and day first above written.
JAMES DOWNEY.
ALEXANDER MARSHALL.

AGREEMENT FOR SALE AND DELIVERY OF PERSONAL PROPERTY.

Articles of agreement, made this ninth day of May, in the year of our Lord one thousand eight hundred and seventy-nine, between William Heering, of Millersburg, Holmes county, Ohio, party of the first part, and George Sale, of Wooster, Wayne county, Ohio, party of the second part—

Witnesseth, That the said party of the first part hereby covenants and agrees, that if the party of the second part shall first make the payments and perform the covenants hereinafter mentioned on his part to be made and performed, the said party of the second part will, on or before the first day of June next, deliver, in a clean and marketable condition, one thousand bushels of wheat, of his own production, at the warehouse of Carpenter & Smith, Cleveland, Ohio. And the said party of the second part hereby covenants and agrees to pay to said party of the first part the sum of one dollar and twenty cents per bushel, in the manner following: Six hundred dollars cash in hand paid, the receipt whereof is hereby acknowledged, and the balance at the time of delivery of said wheat. And in case of the failure of the said party of the second part to make either of the payments, or perform any of the covenants on his part hereby made and entered into, this contract shall, at the option of the party of the first part, be forfeited and determined, and the party of the second part shall forfeit all payments made by him on this contract, and such payments shall be retained by the said party of the first part in full satisfaction and in liquidation of all damages by him sustained, and he shall have the right to take possession of said wheat, remove, and sell the same elsewhere as he may deem for his interest.

It is mutually agreed that all the covenants and agreements herein contained, shall extend to and be obligatory upon the heirs, executors, administrators, and assigns of the respective parties.

In witness whereof, the parties to these presents have hereunto set their hands, the day and year first above written.
WILLIAM HEERING.
GEORGE SALE.

(Legal Forms—continued.)

Bills of Sale.—A written agreement by which a party transfers to another all his right, title and interest in personal property, for a consideration, is termed a bill of sale.

According to law, the ownership of personal property is not changed until the delivery of such property, and the purchaser is in actual possession of the same ; in some States, however, a bill of sale is *prima facia* evidence of ownership, even against all creditors, providing the sale was not made for the purpose of defrauding creditors.

The fairness or unfairness of such a sale is determined by a jury, and where it is proven that fraud existed in the transaction, such bill of sale will be ignored and declared void.

COMMON FORM OF BILL OF SALE.

Know all men by this instrument, that I, George Mason, of Sag Harbor, Suffolk county, New York, of the first part, for and in consideration of Five Hundred Dollars, to me paid by James Dougherty, of the same place, of the second part, the receipt whereof if hereby acknowledged, have sold, and by this instrument do convey unto the said Dougherty, party of the second part, his executors, administrators, and assigns, my undivided half of fifty acres of corn, now growing on the farm of Jacob Lescher, in the town above mentioned; four cows, two horses, and nine sheep, belonging to me and in my possession at the farm aforesaid ; to have and to hold the same unto the party of the second part, his executors and assigns forever. And I do, for myself and legal representatives, agree with the said party of the second part, and his legal representatives, to warrant and defend the sale of the afore-mentioned property and chattels unto the said party of the second part. and his legal representatives, against all and every person whatsoever.

In witness whereof, I have hereunto affixed my hand, this tenth day of June, one thousand eight hundred and seventy.   GEORGE MASON.

BILL OF SALE OF PERSONAL PROPERTY.

Know all Men by these Presents, That I, Peter J. Hirsch, of Lebanon, Lebanon county, Pennsylvania, farmer, in consideration of Nine Hundred Dollars ($900), to me in hand paid by Louis Fisher, of the same place. the receipt whereof is hereby acknowledged, do hereby bargain, sell and deliver unto the said Louis Fisher the following property, to-wit:

Five horses at $120	$600
Two sets of Harness at $25	50
One Farm Wagon at $40	40
One Spring Wagon at $35	35
Ten Hogs at $10	100
One Mule at $75	75
Total	$900

To have and to hold the said goods and chattels unto the said Louis Fisher, his executors, administrators, and assigns, to his own proper use and benefit forever. And I, the said Peter J. Hirsch, do avow myself to be the true and lawful owner of said goods and chattels ; that I have full power, good right, and lawful authority to dispose of said goods and chattels in manner as aforesaid ; and that I will, and my heirs, executors, and administraters shall warrant and defend the said bargained goods and chattels unto the said Louis Fisher, his executors, administrators, and assigns, from and against the lawful claims and demands of all persons.

In witness wereof, I, the said Peter J. Hirsch, have hereto set my hand this fifth day of June, in the year of our Lord, Eighteen Hundred and Eighty.   PETER J. HIRSCH.

Bonds.—A bond is a written acknowledgment of an obligation, whereby the maker binds himself to pay a certain sum of money to another person or persons, at a time therein named, for some *bona fide* consideration.

The person giving the bond is termed the *obligor;* the person receiving the bond is called the *obligee.*

Bonds are generally given under certain conditions, binding the person giving the same to perform some specific duties. For the violation of a bond there is usually some penalty attached, of sufficient amount to cover double the amount involved, to be forfeited in case the *obligor* fails to perform the duties named in the bond.

(Legal Forms—continued.)

A bond **may be drawn** so as to render either the *obligor* or *obligee* liable to the penalty attached.

In case of providential interference, whereby the conditions of a bond are rendered impossible, the party obligated is released from the responsibility of the penalty.

A suit on a bond must be brought within twenty years after right of action is allowed, or within such time as provided by the laws of the different States.

COMMON FORM OF BOND.

Know all Men by this instrument, That I, James Mayo, of Richmond, Henrico county, State of Virginia, am firmly bound unto William Byrd, of the place aforesaid, in the sum of one thousand dollars, to be paid to said Wm. Byrd, or his legal representatives; to which payment to be made, I bind myself, or my legal representatives, by this instrument.

Sealed with my seal, and dated this second day of May, one thousand eight hundred and seventy-nine.

. The condition of this bond is such that, if I, James Mayo, my heirs, administrators, or executors, shall promptly pay the sum of five hundred dollars in three equal annual payments from the date hereof, with annual interest, then the above obligation to be of no effect; otherwise to be in full force and valid.   JAMES MAYO. [SEAL.]

Sealed and delivered in presence of }
     JOHN CLARKE.   }

BOND TO A CORPORATION.

Know all Men by these presents, That I, Charles Burton, of Harrisburg, Dauphin county, State of Pennsylvania, am firmly bound unto the Harrisburg Plow Manufacturing Company, in the sum of twenty thousand dollars, to be paid to the said company, or their assigns, for which payment to be made I bind myself and representatives firmly by these presents.

Sealed with my seal, and dated this September first, eighteen hundred and seventy-nine.

The condition of the above bond is such that, if I, the said Charles Burton, my heirs, administrators, or assigns, shall pay unto the said Harrisburg Plow Manufacturing Company, or assigns, ten thousand dollars, in two equal payments, viz: Five thousand dollars January 1, 1880, and five thousand dollars July 1st next following, with accrued interest, then the above to be void, otherwise to remain in full force and effect.   CHARLES BURTON. [SEAL.]

Sealed and delivered in presence of }
     SAMUEL ROYER.   }

Chattel Mortgages.—A mortgage on personal property is called a Chattel Mortgage, and is given by a debtor to a creditor to secure the payment of a certain sum of money that may be due.

The property so mortgaged may remain in the possession of either the debtor or creditor while the mortgage is in force. To secure the property against other creditors the persons holding the mortgage must have a correct copy of the mortgage filed in the Clerk's or Recorder's office of the town, city or county where the person giving the mortgage resides, and where the property is, when mortgaged.

It is necessary in some States for a justice of the peace, where the property mortgaged is located, to acknowledge and sign the mortgage, making a transcript of the same upon his court docket, while the mortgage at the same time should be recorded the same as transfers of real estate.

CHATTEL MORTGAGE.

This Indenture, made and entered into this fifth day of April, in the year of our Lord one thousand eight hundred and seventy-nine, between Philip Marsh, of the town of Madison, the county of Dane, and State of Wisconsin, party of the first part, and Giles Williams, of the same town, county and State, party of the second part.

Witnesseth, that the said party of the first part, for and in consideration of the sum of nine hundred dollars, in hand paid, the receipt whereof is hereby acknowledged, does hereby grant, sell, convey and confirm unto the said party of the second part, his heirs and assigns forever, all and singular, the following described goods and chattels, to-wit:

Two four-year old cream-colored horses, one Chickering piano, No. 6,132; one tapestry carpet, 16x18 feet in size; one marble-top centre table, one Stewart cooking stove, No. 4½; one black walnut bureau with mirror attached, one set of parlor chairs (six in number), upholstered in green rep, with lounge corresponding with same in style and color of upholstery, now in possession of said Marsh, at No. 45 Hill street, Madison, Wis.

Together with all and singular, the appurtenances thereunto belonging, or in any wise appertaining; to have and to hold the above described goods and chattels, unto the said party of the second part, his heirs and assigns, forever.

(Legal Forms—continued.)

Provided, always, and these presents are upon this express condition, that if the said Philip Marsh, his heirs, executors, administrators, or assigns, shall, on or before the fifth day of April, A. D., one thousand eight hundred and eighty-nine, pay, or cause to be paid, to the said Giles Williams, or his lawful attorney or attorneys, heirs, executors, administrators, or assigns, the sum of nine hundred dollars, together with the interest that may accrue thereon, at the rate of ten per cent. per annum, from the fifth day of April, A. D., one thousand eight hundred and seventy-nine, until paid, according to the tenor of one promissory note bearing even date herewith for the payment of said sum of money, that then and from thenceforth these presents, and everything herein contained, shall cease, and be null and void, anything herein contained to the contrary notwithstanding.

Provided, also, that the said Philip Marsh may retain the possession of and have the use of said goods and chattels until the day of payment aforesaid; and also, at his own expense, shall keep said goods and chattels; and also, at the expiration of said time of payment, if said sum of money, together with the interest as aforesaid, shall not be paid, shall deliver up said goods and chattels, in good condition, to said Giles Williams, or his heirs, executors, administrators or assigns.

And provided, also, that if default in payment as aforesaid, by said pa y of the first part, shall be made, or if said party of the second part shall at any time before said promissory note becomes due, feel himself unsafe or insecure, that then the said party of the second part, or his attorney, agent, assigns, or heirs, executors, or administrators, shall have the right to take possession of said goods and chattels, wherever they may or can be found, and sell the same at public or private sale, to the highest bidder for cash in hand, after giving ten days' notice of the time and place of said sale, together with a description of the goods and chattels to be sold, by at least four advertisements, posted up in public places in the vicinity where the said sale is to take place, and proceed to make the sum of money and interest promised as aforesaid, together with all reasonable cost, charges and expenses in so doing; and if there shall be any overplus, shall pay the same without delay to the said party of the first part, or his legal representatives.

In testimony whereof, the said party of the first part has hereunto set his hand and affixed his seal, the day and year first above written. PHILIP MARSH. [SEAL.]

Signed, sealed and delivered in presence of }
  GEORGE SNYDER. {

Remarks.—It is a rule when a person gives a mortgage, and retains the possession of the property, to invest the holder of the mortgage with power to take possession of the goods and chattels mortgaged, at any time he may consider the same not sufficient security for his claims, ; or, if he deems that that he has satisfactory evidence that such property is about to be removed, whereby he would be defrauded of his claim, or for any other reason whatsoever, he can take possession of such property, if he considers that procedure necessary to secure his claim. Then, according to the law of the State governing such procedures, after having given legal notice of sale, he is allowed to sell such property, at public sale, to the highest bidder. From the proceeds of the money realized from such sale, he can retain a sufficient amount to cover his demand, and enough to pay all the expenses, returning the surplus to the mortgagor.

REAL ESTATE MORTGAGE TO SECURE PAYMENT OF MONEY.

This Indenture, made this tenth day of September, in the year of our Lord one thousand eight hundred and seventy-six, between George Cole, of Shippensburg, county of Cumberland, and State of Pennsylvania, and Mary, his wife, party of the first part, and Jacob Wagner, party of the second part.

Whereas, the said party of the first part is justly indebted to the said party of the second part in the sum of four thousand dollars, secured to be paid by two certain promissory notes bearing even date herewith, the one due and payable at the First National Bank in Shippensburg, Pa., with interest, on the tenth day of September, in the year one thousand eight hundred and seventy-seven; the other due and payable at the First National Bank at Shippensburg, Pa., with interest, on the tenth day of September, in the year one thousand eight hundred and seventy-eight.

Now, therefore, this indenture witnesseth that the said party of the first part, for the better securing the payment of the money aforesaid, with interest thereon, according to the tenor and effect of the said two promissory notes above mentioned; and, also, in consideration of the sum of one dollar to them in hand paid by the said party of the second part, at the delivery of these presents, the receipt whereof is hereby acknowledged, have granted, bargained, sold, and conveyed and by these presents do grant, bargain, sell, and convey unto the said party of the second part, his heirs and assigns, forever, all that certain parcel of land, situate, etc.

[Describing the premises.]

(Legal Forms—continued.)

To have and to hold the same, together with all and singular the tenements, hereditaments, privileges and appurtenances thereunto belonging or in any wise appeartaining. And also, all the estate, interest, and claim whatsoever, in law as well as in equity, which the party of the first part have in and to the premises hereby conveyed unto the said party of the second part, his heirs and assigns, and to their only proper use, benefit and behoof. And the said George Cole, and Mary, his wife, party of the first part, hereby expressly waive, relinquish, release and convey unto the said party of the second part, his heirs, executors, administrators and assigns, all right, title, claim, interest, and benefit whatever, in and to the above described premises, and each and every part thereof, which is given by or results from all laws of this State pertaining to the exemption of homesteads.

Provided, always, and these presents are upon this express condition, that if the said party of the first part, their heirs, executors, or administrators, shall well and truly pay, or cause to be paid, to the said party of the second part, his heirs, executors, administrators, or assigns, the aforesaid sums of money, with such interest thereon, at the time and in the manner specified, in the above-mentioned promissory notes, according to the true intent and meaning thereof, then, in that case, these presents and everything herein expressed, shall be absolutely null and void.

In witness whereof, the said party of the first part hereunto set their hands and seals the day and year first above written.   GEORGE COLE.   [SEAL.]
Signed, sealed and delivered in presence of   MARY COLE.   [SEAL.]
  JOHN ALTIC.
  EDWARD ARTZ,

PROXY.

Know all Men by these Presents. That I, Joseph Rankin, do hereby constitute and appoint Simon D. Peck attorney and agent for me, and in my name, place and stead, to vote as proxy at the annual election for directors of the Chicago, Burlington & Quincy railroad, at Chicago, Illinois, according to the number of votes I should be entitled to if taen personally present, with power of substitution.

In witness whereof, I have hereunto set my hand and seal this eighth day of June, one thousand eight hundred and seventy-one.   WINFIELD BENNETT.   [SEAL.]
  Witness,
  BARTON COOK.

Deeds.—A deed is a written or printed instrument by which lands and improvements thereon are conveyed from one person to another, signed, sealed and properly subscribed to.

The person who makes a deed is called the grantor, and the person or party to whom the deed is given is called the grantee. The wife of the grantor must acknowledge the deed, in case there is no law providing for the same, or else she will be entitled to a one-third interest in the property, as dower, during her life, after the death of her husband. The acknowledgment of the deed must be made of her own free will and accord, and the commissioner, or officer before whom the acknowledgment is made must sign his name as a witness to the fact that her consent was given free and without compulsion.

The law provides that an acknowledgment of a deed can only be made before certain persons authorized to take the same; these including in different States, Justices of the Peace, Notaries, Masters in Chancery, Judges and Clerks of Courts, Mayors of Cities, Commissioners of Deeds, etc. In certain States one witness is required to the deed besides the person taking the acknowledgment. In others two witnesses are necessary. In some States none are required.

To render a deed valid, there must be a realty to grant, and a sufficient consideration.

To enable a person legally to convey property to another, the following requisites are necessary: 1st, He or she must be of sane mind; 2d, of age; and 3d, he or she must be the rightful owner of the property.

Special care should be taken to have the deed properly acknowledged and witnessed, and the proper seal attached.

The deed takes effect upon its delivery to the person authorized to receive it.

(Legal Forms—continued.)

Any alterations or interlineations in the deed should be noted at the bottom of the instrument, and properly witnessed. After the acknowledgment of a deed, the parties have no right to make the slightest alteration. An alteration after the acknowledgment, in favor of the grantee, vitiates the deed.

By a general Warranty Deed, the grantor agrees to warrant and defend the property conveyed against all persons whatsoever. A Quit Claim Deed releases what interest the grantor may have in the land, but does not warrant and defend against others.

Deeds, upon their delivery, should be recorded in the Recorder's office without delay.

WARRANTY DEED WITH COVENANTS.

This indenture, made this sixteenth day of June, in the year of our Lord one thousand eight hundred and seventy-five, between Nathaniel Myers, of Newark, county of Licking, State of Ohio, and Sarah, his wife, of the first part, and Isaiah Long, of the same place, of the second part.

Witnesseth, that the said party of the first part, for and in consideration of the sum of Two Thousand Dollars in hand, paid by the said party of the second part, the receipt whereof is hereby acknowledged, have granted, bargained and sold, and by these presents do grant, bargain and sell unto the said party of the second part, his heirs, and assigns, all the following described lot, piece or parcel of land, situated in the town of Newark, in the county of Licking, and State of Ohio, to-wit:

[Here describe the property.]

Together with all and singular the hereditaments and appurtenances thereunto belonging or in any wise appertaining, and the reversion and reversions, remainder and remainders, rents, issues, and profits thereof; and all the estate, right, title, interest, claim, and demand whatsoever, of the said party of the first part, either in law or in equity, of, in, and to the above bargained premises, with the hereditaments and appurtenances: To have and to hold the said premises above bargained and described, with the appurtenances, unto the said party of the second part, his heirs and assigns forever. And the said Nathaniel Myers, and Sarah, his wife, parties of the first part, hereby expressly waive, release, and relinquish unto the said party of the second part, his heirs, executors, administrators, and assigns, all right, title, claim, interest, and benefit whatever, in and to the above described premises, and each and every part thereof, which is given by or results from all laws of this State pertaining to the exemption of homesteads.

And the said Nathaniel Meyers, and Sarah Meyers, his wife, party of the first part, for themselves and their heirs, executors, and administrators, do covenant, grant, bargain, and agree, to and with the said party of the second part, his heirs and assigns, that at the time of the ensealing and delivery of these presents they were well seized of the premises above conveyed, as of a good, sure, perfect, absolute, and indefeasable estate of inheritance in law, and in fee simple, and have good right, full power, and lawful authority to grant, bargain, sell, and convey the same in manner and form aforesaid, and that the same are free and clear from all former and other grants, bargains, sales, liens, taxes, assessments, and encumbrances of what kind or nature soever; and the above bargained premises in the quiet and peaceable possession of the said party of the second part, his heirs and assigns, against all and every person or persons lawfully claiming or to claim the whole or any part thereof, the said party of the first part shall and will warrant and forever defend.

In testimony whereof, the said parties of the first part have hereunto set their hands and seals the day and year first above written. NATHANIEL MEYERS. [SEAL.]

Signed, sealed and delivered in presence of }   SARAH MEYERS. [SEAL.]
    ABRAM STONER. }

QUIT-CLAIM DEED.

This indenture made the sixth day of May, in the year of our Lord one thousand eight hundred and seventy-eight, between John Kepler, of Reading, county of Berks, and State of Pennsylvania, party of the first part, and Daniel Dechert, of the same place, party of the second part.

Witnesseth, that the said party of the first part, for and in consideration of Eight Hundred Dollars in hand, paid by the said party of the second part, the receipt whereof is hereby acknowledged, and the said party of the second part forever released and discharged therefrom, has remised, released, sold, conveyed, and quit-claimed, and by these presents does remise, release, sell, convey, and quit-claim unto the said party of the second part, his heirs and assigns forever, all the right, title, interest, claim and demand, which the said party of the first part has in and to the following described lot, piece, or parcel of land, to wit:

[Here describe the land.]

To have and to hold the same, together with all and singular the appurtenances and privileges thereunto belonging, or in anywise thereunto appertaining, and all the estate, right, title, interest, and claim whatever, of the said party of the first part, either in law or in equity, to the only proper use, benefit and behoof of the said party of the second part, his heirs and assigns forever.

In witness whereof, the said party of the first part hereunto set his hand and seal, the day and year above written. JOHN KEPLER. [SEAL.]

Signed, sealed and delivered in presence of }
    SAMUEL HUBER. }

(Legal Forms--continued.)

LONG FORM QUIT-CLAIM DEED—HOMESTEAD WAIVER.

This indenture, made the first day of October, in the year of our Lord one thousand eight hundred and seventy-six. between John Fisher, of Janesville, county of Rock, State of Wisconsin, party of the first part, and Henry Stevens, of the same place, party of the second part.

Witnesseth, that the said party of the first part, for and in consideration of Six Thousand Dollars in hand, paid by the said party of the second part, the receipt whereof is hereby acknowledged, and the said party of the second part forever released and discharged therefrom, has remised, released, sold, conveyed, and quit-claimed, and by these presents does remise, release, sell, convey, and quit-claim, unto the said party of the second part, his heirs and assigns forever, all the right, title, interest, claim, and demand which the said party of the first part has in and to the following described lot, piece, or parcel of land. to-wit:

Here describe the land.]

To have and to hold the same, together with all and singular the appurtenances and privileges thereunto belonging, or in anywise thereunto appertaining; and all the estate, right, title, interest, and claim whatever, of the said party of the first part, either in law or equity, to the only proper use, benefit, and behoof of the said party of the second part, his heirs and assigns forever.

And the said John Fisher, party of the first part, hereby expressly waives, releases, and relinquishes unto the said party of the second part, his heirs, executors, administrators, and assigns, all right, title, claim, interest, and benefit whatever, in and to the above described premises, and each and every part thereof, which is given by or results from all laws of this State pertaining to the exemption of homesteads.

And the said party of the first part, for himself and heirs, executors, and administrators, does covenant, promise, and agree, to and with the said party of the second part, his heirs, executors, administrators, and assigns, that he hath not made, done, committed, executed, or suffered, any act or acts, thing or things, whatsoever, whereby, or by means whereof, the above mentioned and described premises, or any part or parcel thereof, now are, or any time hereafter, shall or may be impeached, charged, or incumbered, in any way or manner whatsoever.

In witness whereof, the said party of the first part hereunto sets his hand and seal the day and year first above written.   JOHN FISHER. [SEAL.]

Signed, sealed and delivered in presence of⎰
    JACOB FORNEY.   ⎱

STATE OF WISCONSIN,⎰ ss.
    Rock County.   ⎱

I, James Sullivan, a Justice of the Peace in and for the said county, in the State aforesaid, do hereby certify that John Fisher, who is personally known to me as the same person whose name is subscribed to the foregoing instrument, appeared before me this day in person, and acknowledged that he signed, sealed and delivered the said instrument as his free and voluntary act, for the uses and purposes therein set forth, including the release and waiver of the right of homestead.

Given under my hand and seal, this first day of October, A. D., 1876.
                                        JAMES SULLIVAN,
                                        Justice of the Peace. [SEAL.]

RELEASE.

Know all men by these presents that I, John Brookins, of Eaton, of the county of Preble, and State of Ohio, for and in consideration of One Dollar, to me in hand paid, and for other good and valuable considerations, the receipt whereof is hereby confessed, do hereby grant, bargain, remise, convey, release, and quit-claim unto Simon Foote, of Eaton, of the county of Preble, and State of Ohio, all the right, title, interest, claim, or demand whatsoever, I may have acquired in, through, or by a certain Indenture or Mortgage Deed, bearing date the tenth day of September, A. D., 1876, and recorded in the Recorder's office of said county, in book A of Deeds, page 45, to the premises therein described, and which said deed was made to secure one certain promissory note, bearing even date with said Deed, for the sum of Six Hundred Dollars.

Witness my hand and seal this sixth day of August, A. D., 1878.

                                        JOHN BROOKINS. [SEAL.]

STATE OF OHIO,⎰ ss.
    Preble County.⎱

I, Edward Carroll, a Notary Public in and for said County, in the State aforesaid, do hereby certify that John Brookins, personally known to me as the same person whose name is subscribed to the foregoing Release, appeared before me this day in person, and acknowledged that he signed, sealed, and delivered the said instrument of writing as his free and voluntary act, for the uses and purposes therein set forth.

Given under my hand and seal, this sixth day of August, A. D., 1878.
                                        EDWARD CARROLL, N. P.

⎰ NOTARIAL ⎱
⎱   SEAL.   ⎰

(Legal Forms—continued.)

Landlord and Tenant.--A person leasing real estate to another is termed a land-lord ; the person occupying such real estate is known as a tenant. The person making the lease is known in law as the lessor ; the person to whom the lease is made, as the lessee. No particular form of wording a lease is necessary. It is important, how-ever, that the lease state, in a plain, straightforward manner, the terms and condi-tions of the agreement, so that there may be no misunderstanding between the land-lord and tenant.

It is essential that the lease state all the conditions, as additional verbal promises avail nothing in law. It is held, generally, that a written instrument contains the de-tails, and states the bargain entire, as the contracting parties intended.

The tenant can sub-let a part, or all, of his premises, unless prohibited by the terms of his lease.

A lease by a married woman, even if it be upon her own property, at common law, is not valid ; but, by recent statutes, she, in many States, may lease her own property and have full control of the same ; neither can the husband effect a lease that will bind her after his death. His control over her property continues only so long as he lives.

Neither a guardian nor a minor can give a lease, extending beyond the ward's ma-jority, which can be enforced by the lessee ; yet the latter is bound unless the lease is annulled.

If no time is specified in a lease, it is generally held that the lessee can retain pos-session of the real estate for one year. A tenancy at will, however, may be termin-ated in the Eastern States by giving three months' notice in writing ; in the Middle and Southern States, six months ; and in the Western States, one month ; though re-cent statutes, in some States, have somewhat modified the above.

The lease that specifies a term of years without giving the definite number is with-out effect at the expiration of two years. A lease for three or more years, being signed by the Commissioner of Deeds, and recorded in the Recorder's office, is an effectual bar to the secret or fraudulent conveyance of such leased property ; and it further obviates the necessity of procuring witnesses to authenticate the validity of the lease.

Duplicate copies of a lease should always be made, and each party should retain a copy of the same.

A new lease invalidates an old one.

A landlord misrepresenting property that is leased, thereby subjecting the tenant to inconvenience and loss, such damages can be recovered from the landlord by de-duction from the rent.

A lease on property that is mortgaged ceases to exist when the person holding such mortgage forecloses the same.

A landlord, consenting to take a substitute, releases the first tenant.

Where there is nothing but a verbal agreemew the tenancy is understood to com-mence at time of taking possession. When there is no time specified in the lease, tenancy is regarded at commencing at the time of delivering the writings.

If it is understood that the tenant is to pay the taxes on the property he occupies, such fact must be distinctly stated in the lease, as a verbal promise is of no effect.

SHORT FORM FOR LEASE FOR A HOUSE.

This instrument, made the first day of May, 1878, witnesseth that Louis Ripple, of Springfield county of Sangamon, State of Illinois, hath rented from Samuel French, of Springfield aforesaid, the dwelling and lot No. 10 Broadway, situated in said town of Springfield, for five years from the above date, at the yearly rental of Two Hundred and Forty Dollars, payable monthly, on the first day of each month, in advance, at the residence of said Samuel French.

At the expiration of said above mentioned term, the said Ripple agrees to give the said French peaceable possession of the said dwelling, in as good condition as when taken, ordinary wear and casualties excepted.

In witness whereof, we place our hands and seals the day and year aforesaid.

Signed, sealed and delivered in presence of }   LOUIS RIPPLE. [SEAL.]
GEORGE BESORE, Notary Public.   SAMUEL FRENCH. [SEAL.]

(Legal Forms--continued.)

LEASE OF DWELLING HOUSE FOR A TERM OF YEARS, WITH A COVENANT NOT TO SUB-LET.

This indenture, made this first day of May, 1878, between Wilson Hayes, of Chambersburg, county of Franklin, State of Pennsylvania, party of the first part, and John Miller, of the same town, county and State, party of the second part.

Witnesseth, that the said party of the first part, in consideration of the covenants of the said party of the second part, hereinafter set forth, does by these presents lease to the said party of the second part the following described property, to-wit: The dwelling house and certain parcel of land, situated on the south side of Main street, between Queen and King streets, known as No. 105 Main street.

To have and to hold the same to the said party of the second part, from the first day of May, 1878, to the thirtieth day of April, 1880. And the said party of the second part, in consideration of the leasing the premises as above set forth, covenants and agrees with the party of the first part to pay the said party of the first part, as rent for the same, the sum of One Hundred and Eighty Dollars per annum, payable quarterly in advance, at the residence of the said party of the first part, or at his place of business.

The said party of the second part further covenants with the party of the first part, that at the expiration of the time mentioned in this lease, peaceable possession of the said premises shall be given to said party of the second part, in as good condition as they now are, the usual wear, inevitable accidents, and loss by fire, excepted; and that upon the non-payment of the whole or any portion of the said rent at the time when the same is above promised to be paid, the said party of the first part may, at his election, either distrain for said rent due, or declare this lease at an end, and recover possession as if the same were held by forcible detainer; the said party of the second part hereby waiving any notice of such election, or any demand for the possession of said premises.

And it is further covenanted and agreed between the parties aforesaid, that said John Miller shall use the above mentioned dwelling for residence purposes only, and shall not sub-let any portion of the same to others, without permission from said Wilson Hayes.

The covenants herein shall extend to and be binding upon the heirs, executors, and administrators of the parties to this lease.

Witness the hands and seals of the parties aforesaid.

WILSON HAYES.   [SEAL.]
JOHN MILLER.   [SEAL.]

———————o——————

LEASE OF FARM AND BUILDINGS THEREON.

This indenture, made this fifth day of May, 1877, between George Dalby, of the town of Mattoon, State of Illinois, of the first part, and Thomas Quarles, of the same place, of the second part.

Witnesseth, that the said George Dalby, for and in consideration of the covenants hereinafter mentioned and reserved, on the part of the said Thomas Quarles, his executors, administrators, and assigns, to be paid, kept, and performed, hath let, and by these presents doth grant, demise, and let, unto the said Thomas Quarles, his executors, administrators, and assigns, all that parcel of land situate in Mattoon aforesaid, bounded and described as follows, to-wit:

[*Here describe the land.*]

Together with all the appurtenances appertaining thereto. To have and to hold the said premises, with appurtenances thereto belonging, unto the said Quarles, his executors, administrators, and assigns, for the term of five years from the fifth day of June next following, at a yearly rent of Eight Hundred Dollars, to be paid in equal payments, semi-annually, as long as said buildings are in good tenantable condition.

And the said Quarles, by these presents, covenants and agrees to pay all taxes and assessments, and keep in repair all hedges, ditches, rail, and other fences; (the said George Dalby, his heirs, assigns, and administrators, to furnish all timber, brick, tile, and other materials necessary for such repairs.)

Said Quarles further covenants and agrees to apply to said land, in a farmer-like manner, all manure and compost accumulating upon said farm, and cultivate all the arable land in a husband-like manner, according to the usual custom among farmers in the neighborhood; he also agrees to trim the hedges at a seasonable time, preventing injury from cattle to such hedges, and to all fruit and other trees on the said premises. That he will seed down with clover and timothy seed twenty acres yearly of arable land, plowing the same number of acres each spring of land now in grass, and hitherto unbroken.

It is further agreed that if the said Quarles shall fail to perform the whole or any one of the above mentioned covenants, then and in that case the said George Dalby may declare this lease terminated, by giving three month's notice of the same, prior to the first of April of any year, and may distrain any part of the stock, goods, or chattels, or other property in possession of said Quarles, for sufficient to compensate for the non-performance of the above written covenants, the same to be determined, and amounts so to be paid to be determined by three arbitrators, chosen as follows: Each of the parties to this instrument to choose one, and the two so chosen to select a third; the decision of said arbitrators to be final.

In witness whereof, we have hereunto set our hands and seals.

Signed, sealed and delivered in presence of }
     RICHARD MOORE.   {

GEORGE DALBY.   [SEAL.]
THOMAS QUARLES.   [SEAL.]

(Legal Forms—continued.)

LANDLORD'S AGREEMENT.

This certifies that I have let and rented, this first day of April, 1877, unto John Pittman, my house and lot, No. 27 Mulberry street, in the city of Baltimore, State of Maryland, and its appurtenances; he to have the free and uninterrupted occupation thereof for one year from this date, at the yearly rental of Twelve Hundred Dollars, to be paid monthly in advance; rent to cease if destroyed by fire, or otherwise made untenantable.   JOSHUA GIDDINGS.

TENANT'S AGREEMENT.

This certifies that I have hired and taken from Joshua Giddings, his house and lot No. 27 Mulberry street, in the city of Baltimore, State of Maryland, with appurtenances thereto belonging, for one year, to commence this day, at a yearly rental of Twelve Hundred Dollars, to be paid monthly in advance; unless said house becomes untenantable from fire or other causes, in which case rent ceases; and I further agree to give and yield said premises one year from this first day of April, 1877, in as good condition as now, ordinary wear and damage by the elements excepted.
Given under my hand this day.   JOHN PITTMAN.

NOTICE TO QUIT.

To Byron Conoly:
SIR—Please observe that the term of one year, for which the house and land, situated at No. 21 State street, and now occupied by you, were rented to you, expired on the first day of April, 1877, and as I desire to repossess said premises, you are hereby requested and required to vacate the same.
Respectfully yours,   WILLIAM CROUCH.
READING. PA., April 2, 1877.

TENANT'S NOTICE OF LEAVING.

DEAR SIR—The premises I now occupy as your tenant, at No. 21 State street, I shall vacate on first day of April, 1877. You will please take notice accordingly.
Dated this first day of March, 1887.   BYRON CONOLY
To William Crouch, Esq.

——o——

Partnership.—A partnership is an agreement between two or more persons to unite their labor, time and means together in business, to share alike in the profit or loss that may arise from such investment.

A partnership may consist of extra skill and labor, or superior knowledge of the business, on the part of one partner, while the other, or others, contribute money, each sharing alike in the profits in proportion to the amount of money invested by each partner, and the time devoted to the business, as may be specified in the articles of agreement between the person or persons composing the partnership. The responsibility of each partner is in proportion to the amount he invests, and the profit he realizes.

A partnership formed without limitation is termed a general partnership. An agreement entered into for the performance of only a particular work, is termed a special partnership; while the partner putting in a limited amount of capital, upon which he receives a corresponding amount of profit, and is held correspondingly responsible for the contracts of the firm, is termed a limited partnership, the conditions of which are regulated by statute in different States.

A partner signing his individual name to negotiable paper, which is for the use of the partnership firm, binds all the partners thereby. Negotiable paper of the firm, even though given on private account by one of the partners, will hold all the partners of the firm when it passes into the hands of holders who were ignorant of the facts attending its creation.

Partnership effects may be bought and sold by a partner; he may make contracts; may receive money; endorse, draw, and accept bills and notes; and while this may be for his own private account, if it apparently be for the use of the firm, his partners will be bound by his action, provided the parties dealing with him were ignorant of the transaction being on his private account; and thus representation or misrepresentation of a partner having relation to business of the firm, will bind the members in the partnership.

(Legal Forms—continued.,

An individual lending his name to a firm, or allowing the same to be used after he has withdrawn from the same, is still responsible to third persons as a partner

A partnership is presumed to commence at the time articles of copartnership are drawn, if no stipulation is made to the contrary and the same can be discontinued at any time, unless a specified period of partnership is designated in the agreement; and even then he may withdraw by giving previous notice of such withdrawal from the same, being liable, however, in damages, if such are caused by his withdrawal.

Should it be desired that the executors and representatives of the partner continue the business in the event of his death, it should be so specified in the articles, otherwise the partnership ceases at death. Should administrators and executors continue the business under such circumstances, they are personally responsible for the debts contracted by the firm.

If it is desired that a majority of the partners in a firm have the privilege of closing the affairs of the company, or in any way regulating the same, such fact should be designated in the agreement; otherwise such right will not be presumed.

Partners may mutually agree to dissolve a partnership, or a dissolution may be effected by a decree of a Court of Equity. Dissolute conduct, dishonesty, habits calculated to imperil the business of a firm, incapacity, or the necessity of partnership no longer continuing, shall be deemed sufficient causes to invoke the law in securing a dissolution of partnership, in case the same cannot be effected by mutual agreement.

After dissolution of partnership, immediate notice of the same should be given in the most public newspapers, and a notice likewise should be sent to every person having special dealings with the firm. These precautions not being taken, each partner continues liable for the acts of the others to all persons who have no knowledge of the dissolution.

It is advisable, in entering into an agreement of partnership, to provide conditions of dissolution, such as how the stock on hand is to be disposed of, the value of good will, &c.

PARTNERSHIP AGREEMENT.

This agreement made this fifteenth day of December, 1881, between Hiram Blodgett, of Cincinnati, Hamilton county, Ohio, of the first part, and James Black, of the same place, of the second part, witnesseth:

The said parties agree to associate themselves as copartners, for a period of three years from this date, in the business of buying and selling groceries and such other goods and commodities as belong in that line of trade; the name and style of the firm to be "Blodgett & Black."

For the purpose of conducting the business of the above named partnership, Hiram Blodgett has, at the date of this writing, invested Two Thousand Dollars as capital stock, and the said James Black, has paid in the like sum of Two Thousand Dollars, both of which amounts are to be expended and used in common, for the mutual advantage of the parties hereto, in the management of their business.

It is hereby also agreed by both parties hereto, that they will not, while associated as copartners, follow any avocation or trade to their own private advantage; but will, throughout the entire period of copartnership, put forth their utmost and best efforts for their mutual advantage, and the increase of the capital stock.

That the details of the business may be thoroughly understood by each, it is agreed that during the aforesaid period, accurate and full book accounts shall be kept, wherein each partner shall record, or cause to be entered and recorded, full mention of all moneys received and expended, as well as every article purchased and sold belonging to or in anywise appertaining to such partnership; the gains, profits, expenditures and losses being equally divided between them.

It is further agreed that once every year, or oftener, should either party desire, a full, just and accurate exhibit shall be made to each other, or to their executors, administrators, or representatives, of the losses, receipts, profits and increase made by reason of or arising from such copartnership. And after such exhibit is made. the surplus profit, if such there be resulting from the business, shall be divided between the subscribing partners, share and share alike.

Either party hereto shall be allowed to draw a sum, the first year not exceeding six hundred dollars per annum, from the capital stock of the firm, in monthly installments of fifty dollars each; which amount may be increased by subsequent agreement.

And further, should either partner desire, or should death of either of the parties, or other reasons, make it necessary, they, the said copartners, will each to the other, or, in case of death of either, the surviving party to the executors or administrators of the party deceased, make a full, accurate and final account of the condition of the partnership as aforesaid, and will, fairly and accurately adjust the same. And also, upon taking an inventory of said capital stock, with increase and profit thereon, which shall appear or is found to be remaining, all such remainder shall be equally apportioned and divided between them, the said copartners, their executors or administrators, share and share alike.

It is also agreed that in case of a misunderstanding arising with the partners hereto, which cannot be settled between themselves, such difference of opinion shall be settled by arbitration, upon the following conditions, to-wit: Each party to choose one arbitrator, which two thus elected shall choose a third; the three thus chosen to determine the merits of the case, and arrange the basis of a settlement.

In witness whereof, the undersigned hereto set their hands the day and year first above written

HIRAM BLODGETT.
JAMES BLACK.

Signed in presence of,
PETER WAGONER.
WILLIAM DAILY

EXEMPTION LAWS.

AN ABSTRACT FROM THE LAWS OF THE DIFFERENT STATES, SHOWING THE AMOUNT OF PROPERTY EXEMPT FROM FORCED SALE, FROM ATTACHMENT OR LEVY AND SALE ON EXECUTION.

Alabama.—*Home worth $2,000, and Personal Property.*—The personal property of any resident of this State, to the value of $1,000, to be selected by such resident, shall be exempt from sale on execution, or other final process of any court, issued for the collection of any debt contracted since adoption of the present constitution (1868). Every homestead not exceeding eighty acres of land, the dwelling and appurtenances thereon to be selected by the owner, not in village, town or city, or in lieu thereof, at the option of the owner, any lot in a city, town, or village, with the dwelling and appurtenances thereon, owned and occupied by any resident of the State, and not exceeding $2,000 in value, shall be exempted from sale on execution, or any other final process from court, since the adoption of the present constitution.

Arkansas.—*Homestead worth $2,500, and Personal Property* to head of a family in addition to wearing apparel, $500—To any party who is not married, in addition to wearing apparel $200, except for purchase money. 160 acres of land, or one town or city lot, being the residence of a householder or the head of a family, the appurtenances and improvements thereto belonging, to the value of $2,500, and personal property as above stated.

Colorado.—*Home worth $2,000 and Personal Property.*—There is exempted a homestead worth not to exceed $2,000, and to the head of a family owning and occupying the same, there are exempted various articles of personal property, according to the size of the family, such as is usually determined by the statutes. The tools, working animals, books and stock in trade, not exceeding $300 in value, is exempted to any person not the head of a family, when used and kept for the purpose of carrying on a business or trade.

Connecticut.—*No Home exempted. Personal Property of the following value :* Necessary apparel and bedding, household furniture necessary for supporting life, arms, military equipments, implements of the debtor's trade, one cow, ten sheep (not exceeding in value $150), are protected, and certain specified amounts of family stores, one stove, the horse, saddle and bridle, buggy and harness (not exceeding in value $200) of any practicing physician or surgeon ; one sewing machine in use, one pew in church in use, and a library (not exceeding in value $500); one boat used in fishing, not exceeding $200 in value.

Delaware.—*No Home exempted. Personal Property* $150 *and* $200.—Family bible, school books, and family library, family pictures, seat or pew in church, lot in burial ground, all wearing apparel of debtor and family, and, in addition to above, tools, implements, and fixtures necessary to carry on a trade or business, not exceeding seventy-five dollars in New Castle and Sussex counties, and fifty dollars in Kent County. There is exempted to the head of a family, in addition to above, other personal property not exceeding two hundred dollars in New Castle County, and not exceeding one hundred and fifty dollars in Kent County, consisting of household goods only; but their is no such additional exemption in Sussex County. Sewing-machines owned and used by seamstresses or private families,are exempt from execution on attachment process, and also from distress for rent. In New Castle County all wages are exempt from execution attachment. Widows in all cases shall have the benefit of the same exemption out of the husband's goods that the husband would have had if living. Funeral expenses, reasonable bills for medicine and medical attendance, nursing, and necessaries of last sickness, are paid out of personalty of a deceased person before there is any application to the execution.

District of Columbia.—*No home exempted. Personal Property of the following value :* The following property of a householder is exempt from distraint, attachment, or sale on execution, except for servants' or laborers' wages due: wearing apparel, household furniture to the amount of $300 ; provisions and fuel for three months ; mechanics' tools or implements of any trade, to the value of $200, with stock to the same amount ; the library and implements of a professional man or artist, to the value of $300 ; a farmer's team and other utensils, to the value of $100 ; family pictures and library, in value $400.

Florida.—*Farm, or House and Lot, and Personal Property.*—Homestead of one hun-dred and sixty acres of land and improvements, if in the country ; a residence and one-half acre of ground, if in a village or city ; together with $1,000 worth of per-sonal property. An additional sum of $1,000 worth of property is exempt from all debts incurred prior to May 10, 1865.

Georgia.—*Home worth $2,000, and Personal Property.*—Each head of a family, or guardian, or trustee, of a family of minor children is entitled to a homestead of realty to the value of $2,000 in specie, and personal property to the value of $1,000 in specie, to be valued at the time they are set apart.

Idaho.—*Home worth $5,000, and Personal Property.*—The head of a family, being a householder, either husband or wife, may select a homestead not exceeding in value $5,000 ; while furniture, teams, tools, stock, and other personal property enumerated by statute, to the value of $300 or more, according to valuation, shall be exempt from execution, except for a judgment recovered for its price, or upon a mortgage thereon.

Illinois.—*Home worth $1,000, and Personal Property.*—Lot of ground and buildings thereon, occupied as a residence by the debtor, being a householder and having a fam-ily, to the value of $1,000. Exemption continues after the death of the householder for the benefit of widow and family, some one of them occupying the homestead until youngest child shall become twenty-one years of age, and until death of widow. There is no exemption from sale for taxes, assessments, debt or liability incurred for the purchase or improvement of such homestead. No release or waiver of exemption is valid, unless in writing, and subscribed by such householder and wife (if he have one), and acknowledged as conveyances of real estate, are required to be acknowl-edged. The following articles of personal property owned by the debtor are exempt from execution, writ of attachment, and distress for rent: *First.*—Necessary wearing apparel, Bibles, school books, and family pictures of every person. *Second.*—Other property worth $100 to be selected by the debtor. When the debtor is the head of a family, and resides with the same, in addition, other property worth $300 may be se-lected ; though such exemption shall not be allowed from any money due such debtor. A debtor taking the benefit of this act shall make a schedule, subscribed and sworn to, of all his or her personal property, including moneys on hand and due the debtor ;

and any property owned by the debtor, and not included in said schedule, shall not be exempt as aforesaid. And thereupon the officer having an execution against the same, shall summon three householders who, upon oath, will appraise and fix a fair value upon each article in said schedule, and the debtor shall then select from such schedule such articles as he or she may desire to retain, the aggregate value of which shall not exceed the amount exempted, to which he or she may be entitled, and deliver the remainder to the officer having the writ. The officer having the writ is authorized to administer the oath to the debtor and appraisers. To head of family $50 exempt from garnishment for wages.

Indiana.—*Home, and Personal Property of the following value :* Any resident householder has an exemption from levy and sale under execution, of real or personal property, or both, as he may select, to the value of $600. The law further provides that no property shall be sold by virtue of an execution for less than *two-thirds* of its appraised cash value. The provisions of this law can be waived in contracts. To do this, the note or contract should read : *" Payable without any relief whatever from valuation or appraisement laws."*

Iowa.—*Farm of 40 Acres, or House and Lot in City and Personal Property.*—The homestead must embrace the house used as a home by the owner thereof, and if he has two or more houses thus used by him, at different times and places, he may select which he will retain as a homestead. If within a town plat it must not exceed one-half acre in extent, and if not in a town plat it must not embrace in the aggregate more than forty acres. But if when thus limited, in either case its value is less than $500, it may be enlarged till its value reaches that amount. All wearing apparel kept for actual use, and suitable to the condition of the party. and trunks to contain the same, one shot-gun, or rifle, the proper tools, instruments, or books of any farmer, mechanic, surveyor, clergyman, lawyer, physician, teacher or professor ; the horse or team consisting of not more than two horses or mules, or two yoke of cattle and wagon with harness, by use of which any physician, public officer, farmer, teamster, or other laborer, habitually earns his living. All private libraries, family Bibles, portraits, pictures, musical instruments, and paintings not kept for sale. If the debtor is the head of a family there is further exempt, two cows, one calf, one horse, fifty sheep, their wool and goods manufactured therefrom, six stands of bees, five hogs, and all pigs under six months ; the necessary food for all animals exempt for six months ; all flax raised by the defendant, on not exceeding one acre ; one bedstead and necessary bedding for every two in the family ; all cloth manufactured by the defendant, not exceeding 100 yards in quantity ; household and kitchen furniture not exceeding $200 in value ; all spinning-wheels, one sewing-machine, looms, and other instruments of domestic labor kept for actual use ; the necessary provisions and fuel for the use of the family for six months ; a pew in church, and a lot in burying ground not exceeding one acre. The printer has exempted the necessary type, presses, etc., for his office to the value of $1,200. The earnings of a debtor for personal services, or those of his family, at any time within ninety days next preceding the levy are also exempt from attachment and execution. None of the foregoing exemptions are for the benefit of a singleman not the head of the family, nor of non-residents, nor of those who have started to leave the State, but their property is liable to execution, with the exception of ordinary wearing apparel and trunks to contain the same ; and, in the latter case, of such wearing apparel and such property as the defendant may select, not to exceed $75, to be selected by the debtor and appraised. But no exemptions shall extend to property against an execution issued for the purchase money thereof.

California.—*Home worth $5,000, and Personal Property.*—The homestead not exceeding $5,000 in value, if declaration of homestead is properly filed in the recorder's office of the county where situate, by a husband or wife, or other head of a family, is exempt from execution, except in the following cases: 1st, where the judgment was obtained before the declaration of homestead; 2d, on debts secured by mechanic's, laborer's or vendor's liens upon the premises; 3d, on debts secured by mortgage upon the premises, executed by husband and wife, or an unmarried claimant; 4th, on debts secured by mortgage on the premises before the declaration of the homestead. The other exemptions are chairs, tables, desks and books, to the value of $200; necessary household, table and kitchen furniture, including one sewing machine, stoves, stove pipe and stove furniture, wearing apparel, beds, bedding and bedsteads, hanging pictures, oil paintings and drawings, drawn or painted by a member of the family; family portraits in their frames; provisions sufficient for three months; farming utensils or implements of husbandry; also two oxen, or two horses, or two mules, and their harness, one cart or wagon, and food for such oxen, etc., for one month; all seed, grain or vegetables, actually provided for planting or sowing within the ensuing six months, not exceeding $200 in value; 75 bee hives; one horse and vehicle of a maimed or crippled person when necessary in his business; tools of a mechanic or artisan necessary to his trade; notarial seal, records and office furniture of a notary; instruments and chest of a surgeon, physician, surveyor, dentist, necessary to their profession, with their scientific and professional libraries and office furniture; the law professional libraries and office furniture of attorneys and judges, and libraries of ministers of the gospel; the cabin or dwelling of a miner not exceeding $500 in value; also his sluices, pipes, hose, windlass, derricks, cars, pumps, tools, implements, and appliances necessary for mining operations, not exceeding $500 in value; and two horses, oxen or mules, and harness, and food of horses, etc., for one month, when necessary to be used in any windlass, derrick, car, pump or hoisting gear; two oxen, horses, or mules, with harness, and hack, carriage, cart, etc., by which a cartman, drayman, peddler, teamster, etc., earns his living, and the horse, vehicle and harness of a physician or minister of the gospel, with food for one month; three cows with their sucking calves, and four hogs with their sucking pigs; poultry, not exceeding $25 in value; earnings of debtor for services rendered within thirty days before levy, necessary for the use of his family residing in the State, supported by his labor; shares in a homestead corporation not exceeding $1,000 in value, when the holder does not own a homestead; all benefits of life insurance whose annual premiums do not exceed $500; fire engines, etc, of fire companies; arms and accoutrements required to be kept by law; court houses, jails, and buildings and lots, cemeteries, and certain other public property.

Kansas.—*Home of 160 Acres of Farm Land, or House and One Acre in a Village or City, and Personal Property.*—A homestead to the extent of one hundred and sixty acres of farming land, or of one acre within the limits of an incorporated town or city, occupied as a residence by the family of the owner, together with all the improvements on the same, shall be exempt from forced sale under any process of law, and shall not be alienated except by joint consent of husband and wife, when that relation exists. No value is affixed to the homestead. It may be worth a million of dollars. No personal property is exempt for the *wages of a servant, mechanic, laborer, or clerk.* Every person residing in this State, and being the head of a family, shall have exempt from seizure upon attachment or execution, or other process issued from any court in this State: Family Bibles, school books, and family library; family pictures and musical instruments used by the family; all wearing apparel of the family; all beds, bedsteads and bedding used by the debtor and his family; one cooking stove and appendages, and all other cooking utensils, and all other stoves and appendages, necessary for the use of the debtor and his family; one sewing machine, one spinning wheel, and all other implements, and all other household furniture not herein enumerated, not exceeding $500; two cows, ten hogs, one yoke of oxen, and one horse or mule, and in lieu of one yoke of oxen and one horse or mule, a span of horses or mules, and twenty sheep and their wool; necessary food for the support of the stock for one year; one wagon, two plows, drag, and other farming utensils not exceeding $300; grain, meat, vegetables, groceries, etc., for the family for one year; the tools and implements of any mechanic, miner or other person, kept for the purpose of carrying on his business, and in addition thereto stock in trade not exceeding $400 in value; library, implements, and office furniture of any professional man.

Kentucky.—*Home worth $1,000, and Personal Property.*—On all debts or liabilities created after the first day of June, 1866, so much land, including the dwelling house and appurtenances, as shall not exceed in value $1,000; one work beast or yoke of oxen, two cows and calves, five sheep; wearing apparel, and the usual household and kitchen furniture, of about the value of $100; also one sewing machine.

Louisiana.—*Home of 160 Acres of Land, and Personal Property, in all worth $2,000.*—One hundred and sixty acres of land, with buildings and improvements thereon, occupied as a residence, and *bona fide* owned by the debtor, having a family, a person or persons dependent upon him for support; together with personal property, making in all a value not exceeding $2,000.

Maine.—*Home worth $500, and Personal Property.*—There is exempted a lot of land, dwelling house, etc., not exceeding $500 in value; necessary apparel; a bed, bedstead and bedding for every two members of the family; one cooking stove, all stoves used for warming buildings, and other necessary furniture to the value of $50; one sewing machine for use, not exceeding $100 in value; all tools necessary for the debtor's occupation; all Bibles and school books for the use of the family; one copy of the Statutes of the State, and a library not exceeding $150 in value; one cow and one heifer, two swine, ten sheep, and the wool and lambs from them; one pair of working cattle, or instead thereof, one pair of mules, or two horses not exceeding $300 in value; all produce of farms until harvested; corn and grain for use of debtor and family, not exceeding thirty bushels; all potatoes raised or purchased for use in family; one barrel of flour; a sufficient quantity of hay to winter all exempted stock; all flax raised for use, on one-half acre of land; lumber to the amount of $10, twelve cords of fire-wood, five tons of anthracite coal, fifty bushels of bituminous coal, and all charcoal for use in the family; one pew in church; domestic fowls to value of $50; one horse-sled or ox-sled, $20 in value; one harness worth $20 for each horse or mule; one cart or truck wagon, one harrow, one plow, one yoke, two chains, and one mowing machine; for fishermen, one boat not exceeding two tons burthen.

West Virginia.—*Home worth $1,000, and Personal Property.*—Homestead to the of $1,000 is exempt, where the property of that value is devised or granted to debtor, being a husband or parent, and resident in the State, as a homestead; and where he, previously to contracting the debt or liability, has placed a declaration of his intention to keep the property as a homestead on the land records of the county in which the real estate is situated. Personal property to the value of $300 is also exempted, provided debtor is a resident and a parent.

Washington Territory.—*Home worth $1,000, and Personal Property.*—To each householder, being the head of a family, a homestead worth $1,000, while occupied by such family. All wearing apparel, private libraries, family pictures and keepsakes; to each householder, one bed and bedding, and one additional bed and bedding for every two additional members of the family, and other household goods of the coin value of $150; two cows and their calves, five swine, two stands of bees, twenty-five domestic fowls, and provisions and fuel for six months. To a farmer, one span of horses and harness, or two yoke of oxen, and one wagon, with farming utensils not exceeding $200 coin value. To attorneys, physicians and clergymen, their libraries valued at not to exceed $500, with office furniture and fuel. Small boats and firearms kept for use, not exceeding $50 in coin value; parties engaged in lightering, two lighters and a small boat valued at $250; the team of a drayman. To a mechanic, the tools and implements of his trade and materials not exceeding in value $500. To a person engaged in logging, three yoke of cattle and yokes, chains and tools to the value of $300.

Mississippi.—*Home worth $2,000, and Personal Property.*—On debts contracted after September 1, 1870, only eighty acres of land to the head of every family, being a housekeeper, to a resident of any incorporated town, being the head of a family, and a housekeeper, $2,000 worth of real property, comprising the proper homestead. It is understood that on debts contracted before September, 1870, the exemptions of the code of 1857 are applicable, viz: One hundred and sixty acres of land, homestead $1,500; tools of a mechanic, agricultural implements of a farmer, implements of a laborer; wearing apparel; books of a student, libraries, books and maps; two horses or mules (the new exemption gives an additional mule or horse, making two exemptions), one hundred and fifty bushels of corn, four cows and calves, eight hundred pounds of pork, twenty bushels of wheat; one yoke of oxen, one wagon; furniture, $250.

Missouri.—*Home worth $1,500 to $3,000 and Personal Property.*—Married men are allowed a homestead of one hundred and sixty acres of land to the value of $1,500. In cities of forty thousand inhabitants or over, homesteads shall not include more than eighteen square rods of ground, nor exceed in value $3,000. In cities of less size, homesteads shall not include over thirty square rods, nor exceed $1,500 in value. Personal property to the value of *not less* than $300 to the heads of families. Before 1865, certain property of husband, but *not* that acquired by *purchase* after marriage, was exempt from liabilities of wife incurred before marriage. Since statute of 1865, husband is so liable.

Michigan.—*Home worth $1,500, and Personal Property.*—Any quantity of land, not exceeding forty acres, and the dwelling house thereon, with its appurtenances, to be selected by the owner thereof, and not included in any recorded town plat, city or village, or, instead thereof, at the option of the owner, a quantity of land not exceeding in amount one lot, being within a recorded town plat, or city, or village, and the dwelling house thereon, and its appurtenances, owned and occupied by any resident of the State, not exceeding in value $1,500. Household furniture to amount of $250, stock in trade, a team or other things which may be necessary to carry on the pursuit of particular business, up to $250; library and school books not exceeding $150; to a householder, ten sheep, two cows, five swine, and some minor things. There are some other exemptions beside a homestead, but they are trivial.

Minnesota.—*Home of Eighty Acres in Farm Lands, or House and Lot in Village or City, and Personal Property.*—Eighty acres of land selected as a homestead, or a lot and dwelling house thereon, in any incorporated town-plat, city, or village, being a homestead; the family Bible, family pictures, school books, or library, and musical instruments; all wearing apparel of the debtor and his family, all beds, bedsteads, and bedding kept and used by the debtor and his family; all stoves and appendages put up or kept for the use of the debtor and his family; all cooking utensils, and all other household furniture not herein enumerated, not exceeding $500 in value; three cows, two swine, one yoke of oxen and a horse, or in lieu, of one yoke of oxen and a horse, a span of horses or mules, twenty sheep and the wool from the same, either in the raw material or manufactured into cloth or yarn; the necessary food for all the stock mentioned in this section, for one year's support, either provided or growing, or both, as the debtor may choose; also, one wagon, cart, or dray, one sleigh, two plows, one drag, and other farming utensils, including tackle for teams, not exceeding $300 in value; the provisions for the debtor and his family necessary for one year's support, either provided or growing, or both, and fuel necessary for one year; the tools and instruments of any mechanic, miner or other person, used and kept for the purpose of carrying on his trade, and in addition thereto, stock in trade not exceeding $400 in value. Also the library and implements of any professional man. All of which articles hereinbefore intended to be exempt shall be chosen by the debtor, his agent, clerk, or legal representative, as the case may be; one sewing machine; the earnings of minor children. None of these articles of personal property are exempt from exe. cution or attachment for the purchase money thereof.

Montana.—*Home worth $2,500, and Personal Property.*—A homestead not exceeding in value $2,500; in a city or village not to exceed one quarter of an acre, or farm land not exceeding eighty acres, the debtor taking his choice selecting either, with all improvements thereon included in the valuation. The lien of a mechanic, laborer, or mortgage lawfully obtained upon the same, is not affected by such exemption. In addition to the homestead, personal property to the value of $1,400, and more, according to the value of articles enumerated by statute, is allowed to the householder occupying the same.

Nebraska.—*Home worth $2,000, and Personal Property $500.*—A homestead not exceeding in value $2,000, consisting of the dwelling house in which the claimant resides and its appurtenances; and the land on which the same is situated, not exceeding 160 acres, to be selected by the owner thereof, not in any city or incorporated village; or instead thereof at the option of the claimant, contiguous land, not exceeding two lots in such city or village, owned and occupied by the head of a family. All heads of families who have no lands, town lots or houses, have exempt from forced sale the sum of $500 in personal property. Other personal property is exempted, which is enumerated by statute.

Nevada.—*Home worth $5,000, and Personal Property.*—The husband, wife, or other head of the family, is entitled to a homestead not exceeding in value $5,000, and a debtor has exempted from attachment personal property not exceeding in value $1,500. enumerated in the statute.

New Hampshire.—*Home worth $500, and Personal Property.*—Homestead to the value of $500; necessary apparel and bedding, and household furniture to the value of $100; Bibles and school books in use in the family; library to the value of $200; one cow, one hog and one pig, and pork of same when slaughtered; tools of occupation to the value of $100; six sheep and their fleeces; one cooking stove and its furniture; provisions and fuel to the value of $50, and one sewing machine; beasts of the plow, not exceeding one yoke of oxen, or a horse, and hay not exceeding four tons.

New Jersey.—*Home worth $1,000, and Personal Property $200.*—Personal property (exclusive of wearing apparel) to the amount of $200, owned by a resident head of a family, appraised by three persons appointed by the sheriff; the widow or administrator of a decease person may claim the same exemption by conforming to the provisions of the statute; the lot and building thereon occupied as a residence, being a householder and having a family, to the value of $1,000, is exempt from execution.

New York.—*Home worth $1,000, and Personal Property.*—Homestead to the value of $1,000, owned and occupied by debtor, being a householder and having a family. In addition to the household articles usually enumerated as exempt from the sale under execution, and the tools of any mechanic, not exceeding $25 in value, there are exempted necessary household furniture and working tools; team and food for said team for a period not exceeding ninety days; professional instruments, furniture and library owned by any person being a householder, or having a family for which he provides, to the value of not exceeding $250, and a sewing machine. Such exemption does not apply to any execution issued on a demand for purchase money of such furniture, tools or team, or the food of said team, or professional instruments, furniture or library, sewing machine or the articles now enumerated by law; nor to any judgment rendered for a claim accruing for work and labor performed in a family as a domestic; nor to any judgment obtained in any court in the City of New York, for work, labor or services done or performed by any female employee, when such amount does not exceed the sum of $15 exclusive of costs.

New Mexico.—*Home worth $1,000; Provisions, $25; Furniture, $10; Tools, $20.*— Real estate to the value of $1,000 is exempt in farm if the heads of families reside on the same; also the clothing, beds and bed clothing necessary for the use of the family, and firewood sufficient for thirty days, when actually provided and intended therefor; all Bibles, hymn books, Testaments, and school books used by the family, and family and religious pictures; provisions actually provided to the amount of $25, and kitchen furniture to the amount of $10, both to be selected by the debtor; also tools and instruments belonging to the debtor that may be necessary to enable him to carry on his trade or business, whether agricultural or mechanical, to be selected by him, and not to exceed $20 in value. Real estate when sold must be first appraised by two freeholders of the vicinity, and must bring two-thirds of the appraised value.

North Carolina.—*Home worth $1,000, and Personal Property $500.*—Every homestead, and dwelling and buildings used therewith, not exceeding in value $1,000, to be selected by the owner thereof; or, in lieu thereof, at the option of the owner, any lot in a city, town or village, with the dwellings used thereon, owned and occupied by any resident of the State, and not exceeding the value of $1,000. Personal property to the value of $500.

Ohio.—*Home worth $1,000, and Personal Property.*—There is exempted by law the family homestead, not exceeding in value $1,000; the wearing apparel of such family; beds, bedsteads, bedding necessary for the use of the family; one stove and pipe, fuel necessary for sixty days. In case the debtor is not the owner of the homestead, he is entitled to hold, exempt from levy and sale, personal property not exceeding $500, in addition to the chattel property as aforesaid.

Ontario, Canada.—*Grants that are Free. and Homesteads in the Possession of Actual Settlers*, in the Algoma and Nippissing Districts, and certain lands between the River Ottawa and Georgian Bay, are exempt from siezure, while their personal property, beds, bedding, and wearing apparel of the debtor and his family, household furniture, provisions, farm stock, tools and implements, to the value of $60, are exempt from siezure.

Oregon.—*Personal Property.*—Books, pictures and musical instruments to the value of $75; wearing apparel to the value of $100, and if a householder to the value of $50 for each member of the family; tools, implements, apparatus, team, vehicle, harness, or library, when necessary in the occupation or profession of a judgment debtor, to the amount of $400; if the judgment debtor be a householder, ten sheep with one year's fleece, two cows, five swine, household goods, furniture, and utensils to the value of $300. No article of property is exempt from execution issued upon a judgment for the purchase price.

Pennsylvania.—*Real or Personal. $300.*—Property, either real or personal, to the value of $300. The exemption may be waived in note or contract.

Quebec, Canada.—*Personal Property enumerated as follows* is exempt from forced sale, being used and owned by debtor: Bed, bedding, and bedstead; necessary apparel for himself and family; set of table and stove furniture; all spinning wheels and weavers' looms in use in the family; one axe, one gun, one saw, six traps, fish-nets in common use; and ten volumes of books; fuel and food for thirty days, worth $20; one cow, four sheep, two hogs, with necessary food for thirty days; tools and instruments used in his trade to the value of $20; fifteen hives of bees, and wages and salaries not yet due; besides certain other properties granted by the courts.

Rhode Island.—*No Home Exempted, but Personal Property.*—The law exempts from sale on execution the household furniture and family stores of a housekeeper, provided the same do not exceed in value $300; all the necessary wearing apparel of a debtor and his family; one cow, one hog, the tools or implements of a debtor's profession to the value of $200. There is no homestead exemption.

South Carolina.—*Home worth $1,000; Personal Property, $500.*—There is exempt from sale and execution in the State a homestead not exceeding in value $1,000. Household furniture, beds, and bedding, family library, arms, carts, wagons, farming implements, tools, cattle, work animals, swine, goats and sheep, not to exceed in value in the aggregate the sum of $500; in addition thereto all necessary wearing apparel.

Tennessee.—*Home worth $1,000, and Personal Property.*—The homestead, consisting of the dwelling house, outbuildings, and land appurtenant, to the value of $1,000; also personal property to the value of $500.

Texas.—*Home worth $5,000, and Personal Property.*—To every citizen, householder, or head of a family, two hundred acres of real estate, including homestead, in the country, or any lot or lots in a town or city, used as a homestead, not to exceed $5,000 in value at the time of their designation as a homestead (subsequent increase in value by improvement or otherwise does not subject it to forced sale); household or kitchen furniture, $500. To every citizen not the head of a family, one horse, saddle and bridle; all wearing apparel, and tools, books, and apparatus of his trade or profession; also five cows, twenty hogs; one year's provisions, and in case of death of husband, the court will set aside to the widow and children other property or money to the value of the foregoing exemptions, if the estate has not got the specific articles exempted.

Utah.—*Home worth $1,000, and Personal Property. To each member of the family, $250.*—To the head of a family is allowed a homestead not exceeding in value $1,000, to be selected by the debtor, and personal property to the value of $700 or more, according to the value of articles exempt by statute; aside from the homestead each member of the family is allowed $250. No property shall be exempt from sale on a judgment received for its price, on a mechanic's lien, or a mortgage thereon.

Vermont.—*Home worth $500, and Personal Property.*—Homestead to the value of $500, and products; suitable apparel, bedding, tools, and articles of furniture as may be necessary for upholding life; one sewing machine kept for use; one cow, the best swine, or the meat of one swine; ten sheep, one year's product of said sheep in wool, yarn or cloth; forage sufficient for keeping ten sheep and one cow through one winter; ten cords of firewood, or five tons of coal, twenty bushels of potatoes; such military arms and accoutrements as the debtor is required by law to furnish; all growing crops, ten bushels of grain, one barrel of flour, three swarms of bees and hives, together with their produce in honey; two hundred pounds of sugar, and all lettered gravestones; the Bibles, and all other books used in a family; one pew in church; live poultry not exceeding in value $10; the professional books and instruments of physicians; professional books of clergymen and attorneys, to the value of $200; one yoke of oxen or steers, or two horses, used for work, as the debtor may select, in lieu of oxen or steers, but not exceeding in value the sum of $200, with sufficient forage for the keeping of the same through the winter; "also one two-horse wagon with whiffletrees and neckyoke, or one ox cart, as the debtor may choose; one sled, or one set of traverse sleds, either for oxen or horses, as the debtor may select; two harnesses, two halters, two chains, one plow and one ox yoke, which with the oxen, or steers, or horses which the debtor may select for team work shall not exceed in value two hundred and fifty dollars. Provided that the exemptions hereby made are not to extend to or effect any attachment in any suit founded on any contract made on or before the first day of December, 1879, or to any execution issued on a judgment founded on any such contract."

Virginia—*Home and Personal Property,* $2,000.—Every householder or head of a family shall be entitled to hold exempt from levy his real and personal property, or either, including money or debts due him, to a value not exceeding $2,000, to be selected by him. The personal property exempted is defined by the statue of the State. The homestead exemption may be waived by express stipulation in the body of the bond, note, or other evidence of the contract, but there can be no waiver of the poor law exemption; and a deed of trust upon such articles as are exempted by the poor law exemption is void. The exemption may be claimed on legal or equitable estate of any kind. It is provided that a deed of the property claimed under this exemption shall be recorded, but the exemption may be claimed after suit and judgment as well as before. The property set apart as homestead exemption may be mortgaged or sold by the joint act of husband and wife, or, if the householder be unmarried, by his act alone. If the householder die without claiming the exemption, the right survives to the widow and the infant children. It is provided that the homestead exemption shall not extend to any execution, order, or other process issued on any demand, in the following cases: 1st. For the purchase price of said property, or any part thereof. 2d. For services rendered by a laboring person or a mechanic. 3d. For liabilities incurred by any public officer, or officer of a court, or any fiduciary, or any attorney at law, for money collected 4th. For a lawful claim for taxes, levies, or assessments, accruing after the first day of June, 1866 5th. For rent hereafter accruing. 6th. For the legal or taxable fees of any public officer, or officers of a court, hereafter accruing.

Wisconsin.—*Farm of Forty Acres, or House and Lot in Village or City, and Personal Property.*—A homestead, consisting of any quantity of land not exceeding forty acres, used for agricultural purposes, and the dwelling house thereon and its appurtenances, to be selected by the owner thereof, and not included in any town plat, or city, or village, or instead thereof, at the option of the owner, a quantity of land not exceeding in amount one-fourth of an acre, being within a recorded town plat, or city, or village, and the dwelling house thereon, and its appurtenances, owned and occupied by any resident of the State, shall not be subject to forced sale on execution, or any other final process from a court, for any debt or liability contracted after January 1, 1849. Family Bible, family pictures, or school books; library of debtor; but not circulating libraries; wearing apparel of debtor and family; all stoves put up and kept for use, all cooking utensils, and all other household furniture not herein enumerated, not exceeding $200 in value; two cows, ten swine, one yoke of oxen and one horse, or a span of horses or mules; ten sheep and the wool from same, either raw or manufactured; the necessary food for above stock for a year's support; one wagon, cart, or dray, one sleigh, one plow, one drag, and other farming utensils, including tackle for teams, not exceeding $50 in value; provisions and fuel for one year; tools and implements or stock in trade of a mechanic or miner, or other person, not exceeding $200 in value; library or implements of any professional man, not exceeding $200 in value; all moneys from insurance of exempt property; earnings of all persons for sixty days next preceding the issuing of any process; all sewing machines kept for use; any swords, plate, books, or other articles, presented by Congress or the members thereof.

Wyoming.—*Home worth $1,500, and Personal Property.*—A homestead consisting of a house and lot in a village or city. or land not exceeding one hundred and sixty acres, the value not in either case exceeding $1,500, is allowed to a householder occupying the same. Also the following property of a householder being the head of a family, is exempt: Wearing apparel, family Bibles, pictures, school books, cemetery lots, bedding, furniture, provisions, and such other articles as the debtor may select, not exceeding in value $500. Tools, team, or stock in trade of a mechanic, miner, or other person. kept and used for the purpose of carrying on his business or trade, not exceeding $300, are exempt. Library, instruments and implements of any professional man, worth not more than $300. The person claiming exemption must be a *bona fide* resident of the territory.

———o———

LETTERS.—Penalty for Opening.

Section 3892 of the Revised Statutes of the United States contains the law on this subject. which is as follows : " Any person who shall take any letter, postal card or packet, although it does not contain any article of value or evidence thereof, out of a post-office or branch post-office, or from a letter or mail-carrier, or which has been in any post-office or branch post-office, or in the custody of any letter or mail-carrier, before it has been delivered to the person to whom it was directed, with the design to obstruct the correspondence or to pry into the business or secrets of another, or shall secrete, embezzle or destroy the same, shall, for every such offence, be punishable by a fine of not more than five hundred dollars or by imprisonment at hard labor for not more than one year or by both."

Commercial Travelers' License Laws.

No law exists in the following States, requiring Commercial Travelers to take out a license, viz: Colorado, Connecticut, Illinois, Indiana, Iowa, Kentucky, Massachusetts, Minnesota, Mississippi, Missouri, Nebraska, New Hampshire, New Jersey, New York, Ohio, Pennsylvania, Rhode Island, Tennessee, Utah, Vermont, West Virginia, Wisconsin and Wyoming.

Alabama.—There is no State Law, but in the city of Mobile an ordinance fixes the license fee at $3.00 per day, or $7.50 per week.

California.—In San Francisco, every person, who, within the limits of the City and County, engages in the business or occupation, or calling, or what is commonly known as a commercial traveler or drummer, or commercial agent or traveling agent, and sells or offers to sell, or solicits for the sale or purchase of any goods, or wares, or merchandise, shall pay a license as hereinafter specified. Those doing a business to the amount $90,000 and over per quarter, shall pay a license of $100 per quarter. Those doing a business to the amount of $50,000 per quarter, and less than $90,000 per quarter, shall pay a license of $60 per quarter. Those doing a business to the amount of $20,000 per quarter, and less than $50,000 per quarter, shall pay a license of $40 per quarter. Those doing a business of less amount than $20,000 per quarter, shall pay a license of $25 per quarter. In all cases where the "Collector of Licenses" believes, or it is charged by a citizen of this City and County, that any particular person is liable to the license provided for in this section, such person may be required by said Collector of Licenses, to subscribe to a sworn statement that he has truly and correctly answered all questions touching his liability to said license and amount of the same. In case of refusal of said person to answer truly and correctly the questions put to him, he shall be guilty of a misdemeanor and punished accordingly.

Florida.—There is no State Law, but in the City of Pensacola a license is required, for which the charge is $100 per annum, or $50 semi-annually ; no license is issued for less than $50.

Delaware.—A vendor of goods by samples must pay a license fee of $25. Penalty, imprisonment not exceeding two years, or a fine not exceeding $500, or both.

District of Columbia.—The law imposes a license fee of $200 per annum, commencing April 1, 1880. No license will be issued for a fraction of a year, except the last two or three months. The penalty for imprisonment is from $5 to $50, in addition to the license fee, half of which goes to the informer. In 1881 the law was interpreted to permit manufacturers themselves to sell their own goods without payment. An agent cannot do so, however, without a license.

Georgia.—There is no State Law on the subject, except the act of September 29, 1881, which imposed a tax of $200 yearly upon manufacturers and dealers in iron safes. Atlanta, Augusta and Savannah, have ordinances imposing license fees as follows : In Augusta, $25 per annum ; the Mayor is authorized to issue licenses for a less period. He usually fixes the rate for less periods at $3 for one day, $5 for two days, and $10 for one week. In Savannah, commercial travellers are required to "pay the same tax required of resident dealers in the same articles, without reference to the time of the year when the business is commenced." In Atlanta, no tax is imposed if the travellers sells to none, but "Registered Merchants" of the city. If he sells to others, the tax is $25 per annum and Clerk's fees, or $5 per month and Clerk's fees.

Maine.—The Revised Statutes of 1871, Chapter 44, impose a license fee of $25 yearly, but the law is seldom or never enforced.

Louisiana.—The Constitution of 1879, prohibits any political corporation from imposing any greater license tax than is imposed by the General Assembly for State purposes. The New Orleans ordinance of December 24, 1879, imposed a license tax on commercial travelers of $10 per week, but the General Assembly, by Act of April 10, 1880, fixed the State tax at $25 per month.

Maryland.—Section 41 of article 56 of Code Public General Laws, forbids all persons, whether resident or non-resident, to barter or sell any goods, chattels, wares or merchandise within the State, without first obtaining a license ; subsequent sections regulate the license fees by sliding scale ranging from $12 to $150, according as the stock in trade, generally kept on hand by the concern in which the applicant is engaged, varies from $1000 to more than $40,000, at the principal season of trade.

Michigan.—Act No. 226, of 1875, provides that the agents of business houses without the State, soliciting orders within the State, for spirtous and intoxicating, or brewed malt, or fermented liquors, at wholesale (5 gals. or over, or 1 doz. quart bottles or more) shall pay a tax of $300 for spirtous and intoxicating liquors and $100 for malt, brewed, or fermented liquors, to the Auditor General, on or before the fourth (4) Friday of June, in each year.

New Mexico.—A license costing $250 per annum is necessary. Quarterly licenses, at proportionate rates, are granted.

North Carolina.—By the laws of 1879, the yearly tax on commercial travelers, who sell spirtous, vinous or malt liquors, is fixed at $200, and on other commercial travelers at $100 to be paid to the State Treasurer. Selling without a license is punishable by a fine of $50, or imprisonment for 30 days and an additional forfeit of $200, to be collected by distress or otherwise, one-half of which, $200 goes to the informer and the sheriff.

South Carolina.—There is no State Law, but the Charleston ordinance imposes a license tax of $10 per week.

Texas.—By the laws of 1881, an annual State occupation tax of $50, is required to be paid by every commercial traveler, drummer, solicitor of trade, by sample or otherwise, to the Comptroller, who gives a receipt for the same. No city, town or county, can levy any occupation tax upon drummers, etc. Every drummer, etc., shall first file the Comptroller's receipt for registration with the County Clerk of any county, where he makes any sales or solicits orders. The registration fee is twenty-five cents. Solicitors for maps, religious, historical, or literary works, or for nurseries, are not included within the provisions of the act. A penalty of not not less than $25 nor more than $100 is prescribed for soliciting orders, or making sales without having the Comptroller's receipt duly recorded.

Virginia.—In this State the law provides, that "the specific tax for the privilege of selling by sample, card, description or other representation, shall be $100 ; and any sample merchant, who shall permit any person except a duly authorized agent or salesman to sell under his license, otherwise than for his exclusive use and benefit, shall pay a fine of $50 for each offense." Agents or salesmen must have, in addition to the license, power of attorney from the person to whom the license is granted, "which said license and power of attorney shall be exhibited whenever required by any officer of the law." Each additional agent or salesman, employed to sell as aforesaid, shall pay an additional tax of $50. This does not include liquor merchants, who are required to pay $350, together with an additional tax of one-quarter of one per cent. on the gross sales, for the privilege of selling by wholesale. In the city of Norfolk, a tax of $100 is imposed upon persons soliciting order for printing to be done out of the city.

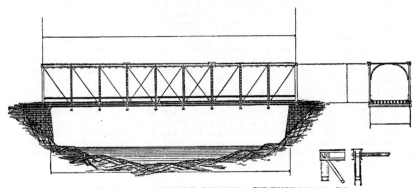